Inflation in open economies

Studies in inflation

This is the fifth volume in a series of studies in inflation under the general editorship of D. E. W. Laidler and J. M. Parkin

The first four volumes are

Incomes policy and inflation
edited by Michael Parkin and Michael T. Sumner

Inflation and labour markets
edited by D. Laidler and D. L. Purdy

Essays on money and inflation
by D. E. W. Laidler

Inflation in the world economy
edited by Michael Parkin and George Zis

Edited by Michael Parkin
and George Zis

Inflation in
open economies

Manchester University Press

University of Toronto Press

Published by
Manchester University Press
Oxford Road
Manchester M13 9PL

ISBN 0 7190 0648 1

Published in Canada and the United States 1976 by
University of Toronto Press
Toronto and Buffalo

ISBN 0 8020 2248 0

PRINTED BY Unwin Brothers Limited
THE GRESHAM PRESS OLD WOKING SURREY ENGLAND

Produced by 'Uneoprint'
A member of the Staples Printing Group

Contents

Foreword to the series

In July 1971 a group of some twenty economists, econometricians and accountants, financed by the Social Science Research Council began work at the University of Manchester on a five-year research programme on the problem of inflation. The research consists largely of a series of self-contained investigations of various aspects of the inflationary process. In order to ensure that our own work does not develop in isolation from that being carried out elsewhere, it is the policy of the Manchester-SSRC Inflation Programme regularly to invite scholars from other Universities in the United Kingdom and elsewhere to present papers at Manchester. Though our own work and that of our colleagues at other institutions, consists of self-contained projects, certain common themes continue to emerge as research progresses.

The purpose of this series of volumes is to bring together in a convenient form papers on related aspects of inflation so that other research workers and students will have easy access to a relatively integrated body of material. Though each volume will contain a large proportion of previously unpublished work, previous publication in a learned journal will not disqualify an otherwise relevant paper from being included in this series.

In promoting a wider understanding of the inflationary process original research is vital, but the dissemination of the results of that research is just as vital. It is our hope that this series of volumes will enable the results of our own work at Manchester, and that of our colleagues elsewhere, to reach a wide audience.

David Laidler
Michael Parkin

Introduction

The international monetary system established at Bretton Woods
in 1944, which became more and more precarious towards the end
of the 1960s, finally collapsed on 15 August 1971 when the United
States abandoned convertibility. Attempts to patch up the system
at the Smithsonian meetings in December 1971 produced exchange-
rate realignments which were recognised as representing a
temporary measure; and the Committee of Twenty was established
in June 1972, to work out a permanent and durable solution to the
world's international monetary problems. However, the oil price
increases towards the end of 1973 put a halt to the progress towards that goal. Countries both advanced and developing exhibited
nationalistic tendencies in their search for ways and means to
minimise the impact of the oil price increases on their economies.
The recycling of oil funds assumed prime importance, while problems relating to the creation of a durable international monetary
system were set aside as being less urgent. However, the 'oil
crisis' proved to be less grave than originally feared. By mid-
1975 the exchange reserves of most industrialised countries had
begun to rise and rates of inflation had been substantially reduced
from the peak reached during 1974. The economically predictable
response to the increase in the relative price of oil, i.e. a reduction in the quantity demanded, has exposed the wide divergence of
views among the OPEC countries, their monopoly power having
been seriously undermined. Consequently on these developments,
the search for a new set of international monetary arrangements
has been renewed, with countries seeking to build on the broad
agreements reflected in the deliberations and the proposals advanced by the Committee of Twenty. The Outline of Reform (1974)
rejects flexible exchange rates as a permanent basis for international monetary relations, developing countries being particularly
opposed to such a system. Countries agree that a system of predominantly fixed exchange rates, which, however, incorporates well-
defined rules under which countries can resort to exchange-rate
changes or to the temporary adoption of flexible exchange rates, is
likely to provide the required monetary foundation for the expan-

sion of world trade and the achievement of the benefits of international specialisation. In the suggestion that Special Drawing
Rights become the principal international asset there is implicit
a recognition that no international monetary system can survive
if its main feature, as in the Bretton Woods system, involves the
use of a national currency as international money.

The acceleration of inflation throughout the world in the
second half of the 1960s was associated with increasing and
increasingly divergent rates of domestic credit expansion which
had the consequence of generating recurring international monetary crises and ultimately the collapse of the IMF system. Thus
a study of the determinants of inflation rates during the era of the
IMF system is likely to provide us with insights relevant for the
reform of the international monetary system. The papers in this
volume relate to the experiences of individual countries and of the
world economy during the period of the Bretton Woods system.

The debate on the causes of rising prices has assumed special
significance as policy-makers in country after country have had to
face the social consequences of accelerating inflation. A variety
of diagnoses have been advanced. However, if one were to abstract
from the details of some of these diagnoses, essentially the debate
has been between those who regard inflation as a monetary problem and those who view it as a socio-political wage-push phenomenon. This particular division, when applied to the IMF period,
provides the basis for the contrasting diagnoses of inflation. To
the monetarist inflation was an international monetary problem,
while to those subscribing to the wage-push view rising prices
were the outcome of forces peculiar to each country and variable
over time. Control of the money supply is the policy prescription
of the monetarist, and the policy of wage and price controls—with
or without the objective of altering the income distribution—is the
recommendation of the alternative view. The essays in this volume
attempt to shed light on some of the various issues that have
emerged in the course of the debate on the causes of inflation. In
Chapter 1 a selective survey of the literature is presented.

Monetary theory suggests that under a system of flexible
exchange rates the inflation rate in each country will be determined largely by the rate of growth of the money supply in the particular economy. Thus, inflation rates across countries will reflect national rates of monetary expansion. Under fixed exchange
rates, however, individual economies are linked to each other, so
that national rates of inflation cannot diverge from each other,
except in the very short run and then only marginally. A further
implication of fixed exchange rates is that national monetary
authorities lose control over the rate of growth of the nominal
supply of their currency, though they retain control over the composition of the backing of their money supply between exchange

reserves and domestic assets. Thus, an attempt by any country to pursue a monetary rule while maintaining a fixed exchange rate is unlikely to be successful. Analyses of a country's rates of monetary expansion would be of limited value in explaining the rate of inflation in the particular economy. The rate of growth of a country's money supply will only determine its balance of payments position: an excessive rate of monetary expansion, relatively to the rest of the world, leading to a deficit while a balance of payments surplus emerges in response to monetary stringency.

The era of the IMF system provides a framework in which the predictions of monetary theory regarding the determinants of inflation can be tested. Whatever the intentions of the Bretton Woods participants may have been, the set of arrangements decided upon in 1944 came to mean a system of fixed exchange rates, particularly in the case of the industrialised countries. Studies therefore, that attempted to isolate the determinants of inflation in particular economies for the period up to 1971 by concentrating on purely national variables, whether in support of the monetary or the cost-push interpretation, could not but reach misleading conclusions. These same studies, by ignoring the international character of inflation, provided the basis for policy prescriptions that could hardly be expected to succeed, unless by some sheer accident they accorded with the policies that would have followed from a recognition of the interdependence of economies under a regime of fixed exchange rates. In recent years, however, under the influence of work carried out primarily by Mundell (1968, 1971) and Johnson (1972), economists have been rediscovering the predictions of Hume's theories of balance of payments and inflation. All the papers in Parkin and Zis (1976), for example, analysed inflation either at the world level or, when the experience of a particular country was considered, on the basis of the linkages of the economy under investigation to the world economy in aggregate. The same theoretical framework is broadly applied in the essays in the present volume.

The studies of Horsman, Jonson, Hall and Spinelli consider the inflationary experiences of the UK, Australia, New Zealand and Italy respectively, emphasis being placed on the interaction of these economies with the rest of the world. All four countries have characteristics that are of special interest for analyses of the inflationary processes. Australia and New Zealand have attained a level of development which differentiates them from both the advanced industrialised and the third world countries. Furthermore, New Zealand has operated an extensive network of controls over its external transactions, and a study of its inflation record is of special interest in determining whether such controls can insulate a country from external influences. On the other hand Australia, with its long established Commonwealth and State Wages

Boards which determine 'award wages', provides a test case of
how far extra-market forces can influence wage and price inflation
and the extent to which they can offset international impulses.
Jonson advances an empirically supported explanation of the
Australian experience which, though it takes into account the
country's institutional peculiarities, is similar to that put forward
for other countries on fixed exchange rates.

The influence of trade union militancy in generating inflationary pressures has long attracted the attention of economists, particularly in the Anglo-Saxon countries. The trade union movements of the UK and the USA, though they have concentrated on
economic issues rather than on the pursuit of socialist transformation of society, have sought to achieve their objectives by consensus rather than confrontation. In contrast to the reformist
character of these movements which have, on the whole, rejected
Marxist theories, there does exist in Italy a revolutionary trade
union movement closely allied to the Communist Party, the second
largest political party in the country. True, the Italian trade union
movement is fragmented. However, such is the dominance of the
Communist section and such is the degree of co-ordination that
has been achieved among the different sections, that the unity of
Italian trade unionists is, at least, comparable to that in the USA
and the UK. Furthermore, Italy has experienced a number of
industrial confrontations of explosive dimensions, while successful
short general strikes have been a common occurrence. It may,
therefore, be argued that Italy is one of the best countries in providing information relevant for the trade union militancy hypothesis.
Indeed, Italian economists have argued that cost-push forces have
been a major determinant of wage inflation, while empirical work
by Ward and Zis (1974) is consistent with the hypothesis that trade
union militancy has been a significant factor, both statistically and
economically, in determining the rate of change of money wage
rates for the whole period 1956-71. This literature is reviewed by
Spinelli, who disputes the reliability of these empirical results and
argues that there is no foundation for the conclusion that trade
unions have had an independent influence on Italian wage inflation.
Instead, he successfully explains wage and price inflation in terms
of an excess demand-inflation expectations model.

The remaining country study relates to the UK economy. Much
has been written on the British experience which seems to have
provided the basis for a number of rather eccentric diagnoses.
Horsman adapts Mortensen's model in such a way as to take into
account the openness of the UK economy and presents empirical
results which demonstrate the importance of external influences in
the determination of wage inflation.

A common feature of the country studies is the suggestion that
there does not exist a long-run trade-off between excess demand

and inflation. Whether such a trade-off exists or not has long been
a source of contention among researchers into the causes of inflation. The empirical results in this volume, by supporting the
extreme expectations hypothesis, further suggest that the evidence
in favour of a long-run trade-off may well have been founded on a
mis-specification error. Indeed, the essay by Parkin and Smith
argues that to ignore the implications of openness of an economy
on fixed exchange rates when fitting wage equations amounts to the
exclusion of a variable, with the consequent result that the coefficient on the expected rate of inflation is biased, the estimated
value being below unity. They show that the results obtained by a
number of economists are what the extreme expectations hypothesis
would predict if it were assumed that wage inflation is determined
by purely national variables.

Inflation is transmitted to countries on fixed exchange rates
through a variety of channels. The country studies investigate a
number of these channels, while the transmission of inflation is the
main theme of the essay by Beenstock and Minford.

Balance of payments considerations have been a major determinant of economic policies in the advanced economies throughout
the post-war period. These considerations have been even more
pressing for the third world countries which have found their
attempts to accelerate their rates of growth often frustrated by
forces external to them. Kirkpatrick and Nixson provide a comprehensive survey of the issues and problems confronting developing countries in an interdependent world economy.

The essays in this volume, in conjunction with those in Parkin
and Zis (1976), provide an impressive body of empirical evidence
in support of the diagnosis that inflation during the era of the IMF
system was an international monetary phenomenon. If this diagnosis is accepted, then the policy prescription that follows is that
the rate of growth of the world money supply must be controlled
for price stability to be achieved. Parkin *et al* investigate the factors that determined the growth of the world money supply during
the period 1961-71 and conclude that its rate of expansion was
influenced in an important and predictable way by the growth of
world high-powered money. Responsibility is, therefore, placed
upon the individual countries on fixed exchange rates to pursue
domestic credit policies such that the world aggregate of high-
powered money grows at a rate consistent with world price stability. This conclusion rests on their observation that a well defined relationship did not exist between the aggregate of domestic
credit policies and the growth of foreign exchange reserves. That
the control of the growth of international liquidity would not have
been sufficient to ensure the control of the rate of expansion of
the world money supply during the 1960s is the conclusion reached
by Parkin in his essay investigating the hypothesis that world price

stability could be promoted by operating a rule on international liquidity expansion that determines the rate of growth of the world money supply.

Any set of international monetary arrangements involves commitments by individual countries that are essentially political in character. Fixity of exchange rates amounts to a surrender of monetary independence by national monetary authorities, though, of course, this is not the case for reserve currency countries. However, each government will accept the economic implication of any particular system of fixed exchange rates only so long as the political benefits outweigh the costs of surrendering its monetary independence. The international monetary system at any period is, therefore, likely to reflect the balance of political forces prevailing in the world. The international political relationships and their development, which were reflected in the evolution and the ultimate collapse of the IMF system, are the theme of Chapter 4.

The questions raised in this volume are numerous but not comprehensive; the answers offered are interesting and important but not definitive; the policy prescriptions advanced are feasible but controversial. If these studies stimulate further research on the determinants of inflation in open economies the endeavours embodied in this volume will have more than served their purpose.

These papers, unlike those in the companion volume (Parkin and Zis (1976)), were not presented at a conference. They have all been given at the Manchester University Inflation Workshop, to the members of which we wish to express our appreciation for their valuable comments. We would like further, to record our and the authors' debt to Mrs E. Newman who patiently and cheerfully coped with all the irritations involved in the preparation of this volume.

Michael Parkin
George Zis

REFERENCES

Johnson, H. G. (1972), *Inflation and the Monetarist Controversy* (De Vries Lectures, Amsterdam, North Holland).

Mundell, R. (1968), *International Economics* (London, Macmillan).

—— (1971), *Monetary Theory: Inflation, Interest and Growth in the World Economy* (California, Goodyear).

Parkin, M. and G. Zis (eds.) (1976), *Inflation in the World Economy* (Manchester University Press).

Ward, R. and G. Zis (1974), 'Trade union militancy as an explanation of inflation: an international comparison', *The Manchester School*, vol. XLII.

1 Inflation: an international monetary problem or a national social phenomenon?

George Zis*

To reduce, and ultimately stabilise, at lower levels the rate of price inflation is rapidly becoming the main economic objective of all industrialised countries. For policy-makers inflation is currently a problem as serious as was the problem of unemployment during the inter-war years. Yet, governments' attempts to control inflation have not on the whole been successful. This relative failure may well be attributed to a wrong diagnosis of the nature of the problem, leading to the application of inappropriate cures. Economists have advanced a variety of diagnoses of the causes of inflation which have provided the bases for various policy prescriptions. Essentially, however, there are two schools of thought. First there are those economists who regard inflation as an international monetary phenomenon, the causes of which are to be found at the world rather than at the individual economy level. Second, there are those economists who view world inflation as the aggregate of national problems, the causes of which should be sought within the particular structure of each individual economy. Depending on which view is adopted, alternative policy prescriptions follow. If inflation is a world problem, then its solution requires international policies. If, however, world inflation is a series of national problems, then each country should adopt such policies as are appropriate to contain its own special inflationary pressures. The need to discriminate between these alternative diagnoses, therefore, derives from the associated differences in policy recommendations.

This paper provides a selective survey of the literature on competing explanations of inflation, discusses the ability of such explanations to explain post-war developments, considers their policy implications, and evaluates the success of alternative anti-

* *Reprinted from the British Journal of International Studies.* I am indebted to D. Laidler and M. Sumner for many helpful comments on an earlier draft, and to R. Ward for assistance. I am also grateful to a referee for helpful suggestions. Of course responsibility for errors, and for the views expressed, is my own.

inflation policies that have been adopted by the major industrial countries.[1]

During the 1950s and early 1960s the distinction between cost-push and demand-pull inflation dominated the debate on the causes of rising prices. Johnson (1969) traced the origins of both strands of thought to features present in Keynes's *General Theory*. Under conditions of unemployment, an increase in aggregate expenditure leads to a rise in real output. If, however, full employment prevails, the money price level of full employment output is the variable that rises in response to an increase in aggregate expenditure. Thus, excess aggregate demand leads to inflation.

In the *General Theory* money wages are taken to be exogenously determined, and this treatment of money wages permits the adoption of any assumption about the way that money wages are determined. This feature of Keynes's analysis, combined with the influence of the theory of monopoly, provided the rationale for the cost-push explanation of inflation which treats trade unions as analogous to monopoly firms marketing a commodity.

Under the cost-push explanation, trade unions are alleged to be able to push wages up independently of the state of demand in the labour market. Then employers are assumed to raise their product prices in order to maintain their profit margins. Thus, trade union pushfulness is diagnosed as the source of inflationary pressures in the economy. The policy implication of this diagnosis is that trade union power should be curbed or, at least, that policies should be instituted with the aim of setting some well-defined limits to the extent that trade unions are allowed to push wages up. Incomes policies provide such a set of arrangements.

There are in the cost-push explanation a number of propositions worth noting. Firstly, it is assumed that employers can and do put prices up once the trade unions have pushed wages up, so that incomes policies, by operating on wage settlements, lead to price inflation being reduced. This sequence of adjustments may be questioned on the grounds that in an open economy employers cannot determine their prices independently of the rest of the world. Further, if employers can simply raise their prices in response to wage increases so that profit margins are maintained we should not observe strike activity, employers would agree to whatever wage demands were made and then raise their prices. Secondly, a particular conception of the role of trade unions is implicit in the cost-push view. Unions are not seen as defensive organisations aiming at maintaining their members' living standards, usually reacting to developments in the economy. Instead, they are seen as aggressive monopolies which can substantially affect their members' pay and conditions. What is involved here is a view of the role of unions in an advanced capitalist society, and of their ability to effect changes. Neither mainstream economists nor Marxists have advanced a coherent, well-articulated theory of the role of trade unions.

With the demand-pull explanation the policy implications were that fiscal and monetary policies were sufficient to bring inflation under control. Demand management policies would affect aggregate demand for goods and, through their impact on prices and profits, the demand for labour. Therefore wage inflation would also be controlled.

Schultz (1969) presented a theory of inflation which attempted to combine elements from both the demand-pull and cost-push explanations of inflation. According to the 'sectoral demand-shift' theory of inflation, neither monopoly power nor excess demand is the prime cause of inflation. Rising prices are the outcome of the combination of both these factors. Schultz argued that in a growing economy demand shifts from sector to sector. Prices rise in the sectors where demand has increased but do not fall in the declining sectors. Thus, although there is no general excess demand in the economy, inflation emerges as a result of this escalation in the prices of the expanding sectors and the rigidities in the declining sectors.

While this debate over cost-push and demand-pull inflation was taking place, Phillips (1958) presented statistical evidence to support the existence of an inverse relationship between unemployment, taken as a proxy for excess demand in the labour market, and the rate of change in money wage rates. The Phillips curve approach to the problem of inflation became rapidly accepted and provided the basis for highlighting the conflict in the policy objectives of full employment and price stability. Policy-makers were provided with a simple choice in the formulation of anti-inflation measures.

Doubts regarding the validity of the Phillips curve approach to inflation as a basis for formulating policy emerged during the end of the 1960s when accelerating rates of inflation coincided with higher levels of unemployment. This phenomenon, combined with the increased industrial unrest in some advanced economies during the recent past, led to a revival of the view that trade union militancy is the source of inflationary pressures. Further, accelerating inflation coupled with higher unemployment and increased industrial unrest provided the basis for an argument that the recent inflation is not an economic problem but a sociological phenomenon. Certain economists now argue that the study of past inflationary periods is unlikely to shed any light on the causes of price rises since the mid-1960s, as this recent inflation is 'new', stemming primarily from social conflicts absent in the past: Bach (1973), Jones (1973). Harrod (1972), for example, has argued that the causes of inflation are closely related to the causes of students' unrest, both phenomena reflecting a new environment of permissiveness; employers are not tough with unions while consumers accept prices charged without arguing. Marris (1972), who also subscribes to the sociological explanation of inflation, argues that trade unions have become more militant because they are not any more afraid of unemployment, while the commitment to the objective of full employment has led employers to be more willing to grant wage increases since they now operate in an environment in which uncertainty has been reduced. Further, he argues that slow rates of growth in real income result in workers' frustration leading to wage explosions. The UK, Italy, and France are quoted as countries in which the frustration hypothesis is alleged to have been relevant, although he does admit that there are problems with this explanation in the case of the latter two countries, since rates of growth of real income were substantial during the period that inflation rates accelerated. Finally, 'anger' over the existing distribution of income, rather than 'frustration' arising from slow rates of growth, is advanced as an explanation of union militancy.

Views not dissimilar to those of Marris were expressed by Balogh (1970) who argued that income inequality and conspicuous consumption result in high wage demands which employers willingly concede because they can then raise their prices. Balogh argues that union militancy, however, cannot change the distribution of income and goes on to advocate incomes policies as the means of establishing a 'just' distribution of income in an economy free from the consequences of inflation. If inflation is a sociological phenomenon, policy measures that attempt to influence economic variables are not likely to succeed in containing inflation. Thus, the NIESR has abandoned its attempt to forecast wages on the basis of indicators of pressure of demand, of past prices, or of previous rises in real income: Bispham (1972).

The policy implication which follows from the diagnosis that inflation is a sociological phenomenon rather than an economic one is that incomes policies are needed. However, the adoption of some well-defined limits beyond which money incomes cannot rise is not alone sufficient to ensure success. What is further required, according to the sociological diagnosis, is the introduction of rules aimed at the redistribution of income in directions which would blunt the inflationary pressures generated by social conflict stemming from dissatisfaction with the existing distribution and/or with the rate of growth of real income. Members of the sociological school are unequivocal advocates of incomes policies, unlike those who had adhered to the cost-push view of inflation and regarded rising prices as an economic phenomenon.[2] In the latter case the recommendation of incomes policies and rejection of demand management as the appropriate weapon relied on the empirical proposition that trade union militancy is not related to the state of economic activity. Only if union pushfulness was shown to be unrelated to excess demand did demand management become inappropriate. If, on the other hand, union aggressiveness depended on the state of economic activity, there was still a role to be played by monetary and/or fiscal policies. In such a situation, however, incomes policies would still be desirable, as they could ensure that the cost of reducing the rate of inflation would be less than if the authorities relied only on demand management policies.

Galbraith (1967) presents an analysis of inflation that has many similarities to that of Schultz (1969). It rejects the distinction between cost-push and demand-pull theories and treats inflation as the consequence of 'wages and prices pressing each other up in a continuing spiral' when aggregate demand is maintained at high levels. Galbraith's diagnosis of inflation derives from his analysis of the American economy which is seen to be divided between the technologically advanced sector of the large corporations and the sector of the small firms. Planning is seen as an essential characteristic of the large corporations which rely on the application of the latest technology as the main instrument for growth. Inflation is seen as, at least, an obstacle to planning. Thus the opposition to unpredictable changes in prices. The regulation of wage and price changes by the central government is viewed as a means of facilitating planning as well as preventing people employed outside the technologically advanced sector from sustaining a loss in their real incomes. Galbraith accepts that wage and price restraints are unlikely to have a significant impact on inflation if aggregate demand exceeds that level which is consistent with full employment. If excess aggregate demand prevails, then, he argues, 'the proper remedy is higher taxes or reduced government spending to cut down on the demand'.

The emergence of the large multinational corporation provided the basis for Levinson's (1971) analysis of inflation. National boundaries are seen as becoming increasingly irrelevant, multinational firms determining their pricing policies on an international rather than a national basis. Prices are set so as to maximise global profits. Inflation is, therefore, diagnosed to be the consequence of profits push. As the state has suffered a relative decline with the rapid growth of the multinational corporations, Levinson advocates trade union collaboration on an international scale as the policy most likely to succeed in defending the incomes of working people.

Hines (1964) was the first to present evidence in support of the hypothesis that unions push wages up independently of the state of demand in the labour market. The rate of change in the level of unionisation, ΔT, was used as an index of trade union militancy, and this was shown to be positively related to changes in money wage rates while bearing no relationship to the level of unemployment which was used as a proxy for excess demand. Godfrey (1971) and

Taylor (1972) used strike activity as a proxy for trade union aggressiveness, but Pencavel (1970) has shown that strike activity is related to the level of excess demand. Ashenfelter, Johnson, and Pencavel (1972) entered both ΔT and strike activity as independent variables in the wage equation they estimated for the USA, while Ashenfelter and Johnson (1969) presented evidence that US strike activity is related to the level of excess demand in the economy. No firm conclusions can, therefore, be reached on whether or not incomes policy is the *only* appropriate anti-inflation policy. If strike activity is the relevant union militancy index, then demand management policies are a potent tool. If, on the other hand, ΔT is chosen as a better indicator of union aggressiveness, then incomes policies become all important according to the evidence presented by Hines.

The above findings, however, are of doubtful usefulness as a basis for policy prescriptions. First, Johnston and Timbrell (1973) have presented evidence which contradicts that of Godfrey (1971) and Taylor (1972) regarding the presence of a relationship between wage inflation and strike activity in the UK. Results presented by Ward and Zis (1974) accord with those of Johnston and Timbrell with respect to the UK; contradict the cost-push hypothesis in the cases of Germany, Belgium and the Netherlands; are ambiguous in isolating the impact of trade union militancy on wage inflation in France, but do suggest that trade union pushfulness was a significant, independent force in the determination of money wage increases in Italy during the period 1956-71. Secondly, Purdy and Zis (1974a) have shown that, even if Hines's particular arguments were to be accepted uncritically, the relative contribution of 'militancy' to post-war inflation in the UK was not sufficiently large for the relationship to be used as a basis for policy recommendations.

Both indices of trade union militancy used in studies relating to the experiences of the UK and the US have been criticised. It has been argued by Purdy and Zis (1974b) that neither the change in density of unionisation nor strike activity can be accepted as a satisfactory indicator of union aggressiveness. They have offered some rationalisations which would lead to the change in density of unionisation being interpreted as an indicator of employers' militancy, while they have argued that there is no reason why strike activity should be regarded as a better indicator of union militancy than of employers' intransigence during wage negotiations.

The fundamental weakness of the studies which sought to isolate the independent impact of union pushfulness in wage negotiations stems from their lack of an underlying theoretical framework. Unions are conceived to be monopolies analogous to any monopoly firm marketing a commodity. This conception of the union is unsatisfactory as it ignores the fact that the union and the union members have separate identities. Thus Purdy and Zis

(1974b) were able to offer an explanation of the relationships between the change in density of unionisation and wage rate inflation
in which the members rather than the unions were assumed to be
the active agents, and to reject Hines's arguments that his evidence
confirms the cost-push hypothesis. Furthermore, though the
analysis is usually set within a framework where unions negotiate
with employers, the impact of the latter's attitudes on the wage
settlement has been completely ignored. The employers are
assumed to be passive, granting wage demands and maintaining
their profit margins by simply raising their prices. This assumption is hardly acceptable when all industrial countries are open
economies linked with each other through a system of essentially
fixed exchange rates such as that in operation until August 1971.
Finally, Purdy and Zis (1974b) have drawn attention to the distinction between power and militancy, a distinction that has been
ignored in all the studies seeking to isolate the impact of trade
union pushfulness.

The emphasis on statistically identifying the determinants of
money wage changes, though price inflation was the problem for
which a solution was sought, largely reflects the view that prices
automatically adjust to costs. Thus, if the influences determining
changes in wage costs could be isolated, then policies aimed at controlling price inflation could be devised. The main aspect of this
approach to the determination of price inflation is that it rested on
the proposition that there exist some statistically identifiable and
stable relationships between wage inflation and a few independent
variables as well as between price inflation and costs. In contrast
to this approach, the economists who argue that the recent inflation
is 'new' and of a sociological nature deny the existence of such
relationships. They doubt the usefulness of model-building and the
relevance of hypothesis-testing as a means of discriminating
among competing diagnoses of the causes of inflation. Furthermore, they would argue that the focus on trade union militancy was
too narrow a framework and that for the explanation of recent
inflation a broader conception of social conflict is required. To the
criticism that they have not advanced well defined hypothesis about
the way inflation is generated, their implied response is that precisely because inflation is a 'new' sociological problem its nature
cannot be specified with any rigour. The implication then is that
the acceptance or rejection of the diagnoses articulated by eminent
economists such as Hicks (1974), Phelps Brown (1971), Wiles (1973),
Balogh (1970) and Harrod (1972) becomes a matter of faith. Be
that as it may, one could still argue that the exercise of confronting
the cost-push and sociological explanations of inflation with the
experiences of the major industrial countries is of some interest.

What are then the facts that an adequate theory of inflation
would have to explain ? Fig. 1. 1 presents the annual rates of infla-

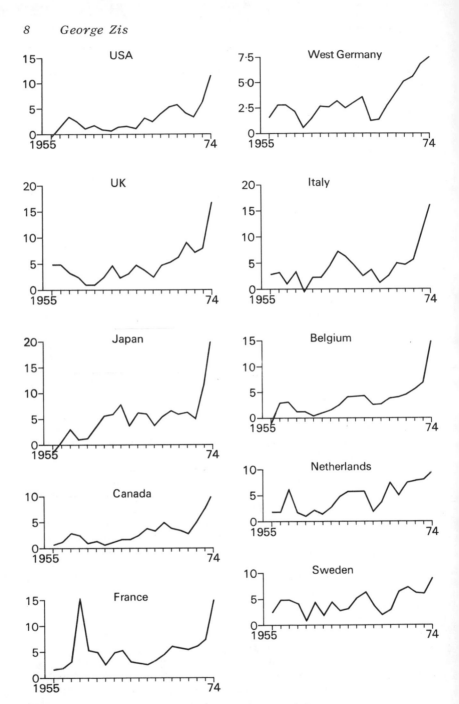

Figure 1.1 Annual rates of price inflation (%)

tion for the Group of Ten countries during the period 1955-74. One aspect common to all countries is the chronic nature of inflation, rates of price increases being positive in all economies since 1956, the US, Japan, and Belgium having experienced small declines in their price levels in 1955. Though inflation rates fluctuated between 1955 and 1964, the average rate for the next decade is substantially greater than that for the first half of the period under consideration. For all countries with the possible exception of Japan, an upward trend in their rate of inflation can be identified for the period after 1966. Since 1972 the rate of price increases has accelerated even further. Another aspect of the 1960s that did attract the attention of researchers was the relative magnitude of inflation rates in the major countries. Thus the OECD (1970) presented evidence suggesting that inflation rates were converging, while Genberg (1976) has shown that the rates of inflation in sixteen OECD countries during the period 1959-70 differed less than the rates of price increase in fifteen large cities in the USA. However, during the period 1972-74 inflation rates in the Group of Ten countries have steadily diverged, with the Japanese price level registering an increase of 22·63 per cent in contrast to the German rate of inflation 7·38 per cent in 1974.

In brief then, the phenomena that an adequate theory of inflation needs to explain are:

1   the chronic nature of inflation;
2   the simultaneous acceleration of rates of price increases since the mid-1960s;
3   the broad similarity of inflation rates in the different economies during the 1960s and their divergence since 1972;
4   the coexistence of higher levels of unemployment with rising rates of price increase in recent years.

Fig. 1. 2 presents the strike activity record, as measured by working days lost, of the Group of Ten countries. Strike activity is here used as a broad indicator of social conflict and *not* as an index of trade union militancy. To the numerous and valid objections that can be raised against this interpretation of strike activity, the response would be that a better indicator of social conflict allowing international comparisons does not exist nor has been suggested. The choice of this particular measure of strike activity rather than the number of workers involved in disputes or the number of strikes would appear to be justified on the grounds that variations in the number of strikes, in their duration and in the number of workers involved would be reflected in the number of working days lost through industrial disputes.

We may now turn to consider the broad developments in strike activity as portrayed by Fig. 1. 2. In the cases of Germany, Belgium, the Netherlands, Sweden, France,[3] and Japan, no rising

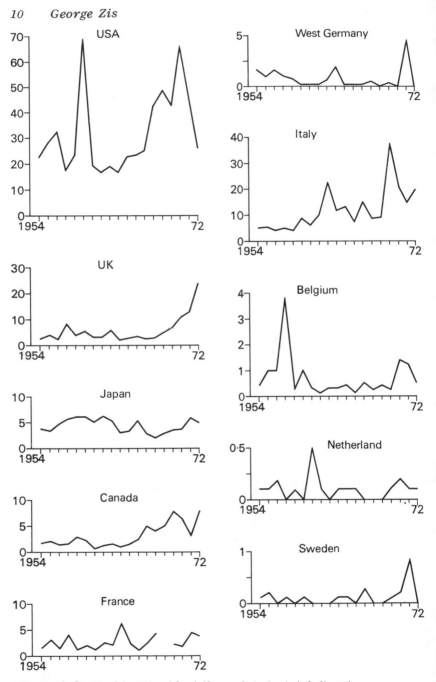

Figure 1.2 Working time lost through industrial disputes (thousand days per year)

trend in strike activity can be discerned during the period 1954-72.
In the cases of Canada and especially Italy there is a clear suggestion of a rising trend. For the UK no trend can be identified for the
period 1954-65, but between 1966 and 1972 there was a distinct upward trend in strike activity. A similar upward trend which, however, was sharply reversed in the subsequent two years, is present
for the USA for the years 1963-70.

To the extent that our indicator of social conflict is adequate,
a closer examination of Fig. 1.2 would suggest that the USA, the UK,
Japan, West Germany, Belgium, and Sweden were subjected to
stronger inflationary pressures, as reflected by the average number of working days lost through industrial disputes per year,
during the period 1954-9 than during the 1960s. In all these countries, however, the average rate of price inflation was higher for
the decade 1960-9 than for the period 1955-9. For the remaining
four countries, and especially in the case of Italy, the average
level of social conflict as measured by our indicator was higher
in the 1960s than in the 1950s, thus broadly corresponding to
movements in their inflation rates.

It may be objected that these observations are irrelevant in
evaluating the sociological explanation of inflation since the
adherents to this school of thought place emphasis on developments
since the mid-1960s. If, then, we compare the average level of
strike activity during the second half of the 1960s with that for the
period 1960-4, social conflict appears to have risen in the former
period in the cases of the USA, the UK, Canada, Italy, and Sweden.
To this group of countries France should be added, since any
reasonable figure for 1968 would cause the level of strike activity
in the second half to be higher than the average for the first half
of the 1960s. Of these six countries, however, the level of social
conflict as measured by our indicator was lower for the period
1965-9 than for the years 1954-9 for the UK, and the same for
Sweden. If we now turn to the three year period 1970-2, the average
level of strike activity is higher than for the 1960s for all
countries. The same is true if the comparison is with the period
1954-9, Belgium being the only exception.

The implied rise in social conflict as reflected by the average
level of strike activity for the period 1970-2 casts doubt on rather
than supports the sociological explanation of inflation. By 1970
inflation rates had begun to accelerate in all countries under
consideration, and the question arises as to whether rising inflation led to social conflict and not *vice versa*. However, the
sociological thesis appears to be consistent with developments
in inflation rates in the cases of the USA, UK, Canada, France, Italy,
and Sweden—i.e. the countries which exhibit, in varying degrees, an
upward trend in their strike activity since the mid-1960s, the
clearest case being that of the UK. It is, therefore, not surprising

that the most eminent proponents of the sociological thesis are British. However, it may well be argued that only in the cases of the UK and the USA has there been an acceleration of strike activity similar to the acceleration of price inflation.

A feature of the major economies, and particularly of the UK, since the mid-1960s has been that rises in unemployment were associated with high rates of price inflation. Indeed, on certain occasions rising unemployment coincided with accelerating rates of inflation. This phenomenon contradicted the generally accepted Phillips curve inverse relationship between excess demand, as proxied by unemployment, and the rate of wage inflation. For the sociological school there is no puzzle. Inflation is a sociological problem the existence of which is independent of and cannot be affected by changes in economic variables. Only the removal or amelioration of the causes of social conflict that have emerged since the mid-1960s will have an impact on the inflation rate, demand management policies being of little or no relevance as a means of moderating inflation. The causes of social conflict that generate inflation are not necessarily the same across countries nor within a country through time. Thus, anti-inflation policies must focus on the social peculiarities of each economy and must be flexible, adjusting to changing social conditions.

The international character of inflation is of course not denied by the sociological school. Events such as that of May 1968 in France, the industrial unrest in 1969 in Italy, students' unrest in the UK and West Germany, social tensions connected with the intensification in the USA of war in Vietnam are advanced as expressions of social conflict in the major economies generating inflationary pressures. However, in contrast to the differences in strike-activity trends across countries, the major economies followed similar paths in their inflation rates until 1972. One particular aspect of this similarity that an adequate theory of inflation ought to explain is the simultaneous acceleration of inflation rates throughout the major economies since the mid-1960s. If we were to adopt the sociological view of inflation—that each country's experience is to be explained by developments peculiar to itself—then we might be forced to attribute the simultaneous acceleration of inflation in all countries to coincidence. Such an explanation would be less than satisfactory.

Alternatively, one could argue that the international character of inflation can be explained in terms of trade union militancy which is transmitted internationally through a demonstration effect and which does not necessarily reflect itself in increased industrial unrest. However, it is difficult to conceive of a situation in which trade unions become more militant independently of developments within the country in which they are operating and simply in response to the results of trade union power in other countries. If such an explanation of the international character of inflation is to be sustained, the conditions under which trade union militancy is transmitted from country to country need to be specified. Unless this is done, it is not clear why trade union militancy is transmitted to some countries and not to others and why the transmission mechanism operates in some periods and not in others. Further, what presumably leads trade unions to look to trade unions' attitudes in other countries is the results of the latter's behaviour. Now if militant strike activity leads to some 'gain' which is judged to be desirable in some countries, the implication must be that the trade unions in other countries will pursue similar policies to the unions which achieved that particular gain. However, the variety of trade union policies in the West would cast doubts on the ability of the 'demonstration effect' argument to explain the international character of inflation in general, and the simultaneous acceleration of inflation across countries in particular.

However, if the sociological view of inflation is not too convincing in explaining the direction of changes in rates of inflation across countries and the timing of these changes by appealing to the existence of demonstration effects, its failure is complete in accounting for the similarity of *levels* of inflation across the major economies during the 1960s. Indeed, such are the implications of the view that the world-wide inflation is simply the aggregate of a series of national problems that no attempt has been made by adherents to the sociological view to explain the similarity in rates of price rises across countries during the 1960s.

The policy implications of the diagnosis that inflation is a sociological phenomenon capable of being transmitted internationally through a 'demonstration effect' is that an international incomes policy be adopted. Unlikely as this may sound, this is not far from what the OECD (1970) recommends when countries are advised to adopt incomes policies as well as to co-ordinate their anti-inflation policies and, more recently, to institute internationally co-ordinated price freezes: OECD (1973). Such a recommendation in favour of the adoption of price and incomes policies must rest on the hope that such policies are likely to be more successful in the future, because in addition to setting limits to income increases it is now suggested that they should also affect the distribution of income and thus ease the inflationary pressures stemming from socio-political sources. Cagan *et al.* (1972), Parkin, Sumner, and Jones (1972) and Ulman and Flanagan (1971) have concluded that past experiments with incomes policies were either a failure or, at best, their impact was uncertain in the countries that made use of them.

In summary, then, the sociological explanation of inflation is not persuasive when used as a basis for analysing the experience of each of the Group of Ten countries—the UK and, perhaps, the

USA being the only exceptions. In the case of Italy, the view that inflation is 'new' cannot be sustained since an upward trend in strike activity is present for the whole period since 1954, and not since the mid-1960s as would be required by the diagnosis of inflation as a sociological phenomenon. This is consistent with the findings of Ward and Zis (1974) that trade union militancy was a significant influence in the determination of changes in money wage rates in Italy during the period 1956-71. The above conclusions are crucially dependent on the adequacy of strike activity, as measured by working days lost through industrial disputes, as an indicator of social conflict. However, independently of whether or not our indicator is satisfactory, the sociological view of inflation is hardly acceptable as an explanation of the international aspects of inflation.

The alternative to the hypothesis that world inflation is simply the aggregate of independent national problems is the view that inflation is an international phenomenon to be explained by developments at the world rather than the country level: Johnson (1972a), (1972b), and Mundel (1971). Since such an analysis derives from the view that inflation is a monetary phenomenon, it is perhaps worth while stating some of the key propositions of the monetarists' position. Friedman's (1970) restatement of the quantity theory is not a theory of either prices or output. The redefined quantity theory is a theory of the demand for money, the essence of which is that there is a stable functional relationship between the quantity of real money balances demanded and a few independent variables. The restated quantity theory, then, suggests that the price of money in terms of all goods is determined through the interaction of the demand for and the supply of it, i.e. just as the market price for any category of goods is reached. Now if the prices of all goods and services are persistently rising—that is, inflation prevails—the implication is that the price of money, in terms of all goods and services, is persistently falling. For this to happen, assuming a stable demand for money function, the supply of money must rise at a rate substantially higher than the rate of increase in the supply of all other goods and services. Thus, the monetarists' policy prescription is that if price stability is to be maintained the rate of monetary expansion must equal the rate of growth of output, assuming that the ratio of income to real cash balances is constant over time.

It has often been alleged that monetarists are vague about the way a change in the rate of monetary growth leads to price inflation. The sequence of adjustments ensuing a change in the rate of growth of the money supply suggested by the monetarists is as follows. Assume that the economy under consideration is fully employed and that its government abstains from operations in the foreign exchange market, i.e. the country in question operates a system of flexible exchange rates. Now suppose that the rate of monetary expansion increases. This leads to an increase in the amount of real cash balances that people and firms hold. They now hold a volume of real cash balances in excess of that which they desire. Their response is to attempt to eliminate their excess cash balances. They will, therefore, try to exchange their excess cash balances for other assets as well as for goods and services. Thus aggregate demand in the economy will increase. Producers cannot increase their output. Responding to the increase in the demand for their goods and services, they will attempt to hire additional labour to expand their production; but if the economy is already fully employed all they achieve is to raise wages. Thus the excess demand created by the expansion in the money supply leads to a rise of prices and wages. As prices rise the real value of cash balances held falls. Prices rise until the excess real cash balances are eliminated, people now holding the desired level of cash balances. If the rate of monetary expansion is maintained at its new higher level prices will continue to rise, i.e. inflation will emerge.

However, an increase in domestic price inflation will not be the only consequence of the rise in the rate of monetary expansion. When people and firms attempt to eliminate their excess money balances they will do so partly by offering, say, sterling in exchange for goods produced abroad and for foreign financial securities. This increase in the supply of sterling in the foreign exchange market will lead to a fall in the price of sterling in terms of all other currencies, assuming that the demand for the UK currency has not correspondingly increased; i.e., sterling will depreciate. If the higher rate of monetary expansion is maintained the international value of sterling will continuously fall. Thus, an increase in the rate of growth of the money supply will lead to inflation and a falling international value for the currency in a fully employed economy on flexible exchange rates.

The above analysis and the policy prescriptions that follow from it have to be substantially modified when we come to apply it in the post-1945 period. The need for modification arises from the fact that the major countries operated a system of essentially fixed exchange rates for the period up to August 1971. Fixed exchange rates lead to countries being linked with each other in a way similar to that in which regions within an economy are linked through the use of a common currency. The interdependence of economies that arises from fixed exchange rates was reinforced during the 1960s by the rapid abolition of tariffs and the emergence of an international capital market in the form of the Euro-dollar market. Further, at least within the Six, labour mobility increased following the formation of the EEC. The rapid growth of multinational corporations, which hold large amounts of short-term capital, is a

further factor contributing to the interdependence of economies.
These developments have led to a situation where economies are
linked with each other, forming a world market for manufactured
goods and a number of primary commodities. Given this degree of
integration among the advanced economies, prices are determined
on a world basis rather than on a national basis. Economies on
fixed exchange rates, therefore, become regions of a larger unit
that encompasses all these countries whose governments are com-
mitted to maintain some given fixed price for their currency in
terms of all other currencies. The monetary analysis of inflation
presented above for a country on flexible exchange rates then becomes relevant for this larger unit, the components of which are
the individual economies. It is, therefore, the rate of growth of the
world money supply that determines the world rate of inflation
which individual countries then have to accept. The policy prescription that follows is that, if inflation is to be eliminated and
fixed exchange rates are to be maintained, the world money supply
should grow at a rate similar to the rate of growth of world output.
The capacity of individual countries to influence the world rate of
inflation directly depends on their size, and more specifically on
the ratio of their money supply to the world money supply. The
higher the ratio, the greater will be the impact of a country's
monetary policy on the world rate of inflation.

If the rate of inflation is determined at the world level by the
rate of growth of the world money supply, what is the link between
the rate of price increase and domestic monetary policies ? Suppose
that the authorities in some country on fixed exchange rates increase the rate of monetary expansion. Assuming that the economy
is small and fully employed, individuals now find themselves with
excess money balances. They will attempt to exchange them for
goods and financial assets, i.e. aggregate demand will increase.
However, the country under consideration being only a 'region' of
the world economy, this increase in aggregate demand will not be
large enough to have a significant impact on world aggregate
demand, the increase in the world money supply not being sufficient
to affect the world rate of inflation. Individuals in the country which
has increased its rate of monetary expansion will eliminate their
excess money balances through the balance of payments, that is by
exchanging them for foreign goods and securities. Thus as a result
of the increase in its rate of monetary expansion the country will
develop a balance of payments deficit which in turn will lead to a
reduction in its foreign reserves, while its rate of price inflation
will remain unchanged, given that the ratio of its money to the
world money supply is too small.

In the opposite situation, when the money supply, or its rate of
growth, is reduced, individuals and firms will find that their real
balances are below the desired level. They will, therefore, attempt

to accumulate money balances. They can do so by exchanging goods for money balances from abroad, that is, the country will develop a balance of payments surplus, its prices not being affected by the monetary contraction. Thus, under a system of fixed exchange rates, national monetary authorities lose control over the rate of expansion of their nominal money supply. Their freedom is limited to the ability to choose the level of foreign exchange reserves they desire to hold. If they want to increase their holdings of reserves they will reduce the rate of monetary expansion, and *vice versa* if they find that their foreign exchange reserves are in excess of the desired level.

Now let us assume that the world rate of inflation rises. Can an individual country prevent its rate of inflation from rising? Suppose that with this objective in mind the monetary authorities attempt to maintain the rate of monetary expansion at the level prevailing prior to the increase in the world rate of inflation. If the rate of inflation in the country remains unchanged this will induce an increase in the foreign demand for the country's goods and services which in turn will result in an increase in the demand for the country's currency in the foreign exchange market. Since the country has not increased its demand for foreign currencies there will now emerge an excess demand for its currency in the foreign exchange market. If its price in terms of foreign currencies is to remain fixed, the country's monetary authorities will have to purchase the excess supply of foreign currencies with their own currency. Thus the rate of monetary expansion will increase, the country's rate of inflation rising to the world level. However, a country's rate of inflation may adjust to the world rate without it being preceded by an increase in the country's rate of monetary expansion induced by a balance of payments surplus, the case described above. This would happen if firms in the country under consideration automatically adjusted their prices to world prices; this would lead to a shortage of cash balances in the country. The rate of interest would, therefore, rise relative to the world rate of interest, which would induce a capital inflow. This in turn would lead, given the fixity of exchange rates, to an increase in the country's rate of monetary expansion. In this case the increase in the country's rate of inflation would precede the rise in the rate of growth of the country's money supply.

In summary, then, under a system of fixed exchange rates individual countries cannot pursue independent monetary policies. Surplus countries are importers while deficit countries are exporters of inflation. Domestic monetary policies determine a country's holdings of exchange reserves via their impact on its balance of payments.[4]

Can the analysis of inflation as an international monetary problem explain the experiences of the Group of Ten countries?

Before this question is answered, it must be pointed out that all the countries under consideration, with the exception of the USA, fit the description of 'small, open economy with fixed exchange rate'. Another major difference between the USA and the other countries is that the former's currency is an international money. That the dollar was a reserve currency implied that the USA was not put under pressure to correct balance of payments deficits; the other countries were first willingly and then reluctantly obliged to accumulate dollar balances as a result of their commitment to maintain fixed exchange rates. Non-reserve currency countries, of course, cannot sustain balance of payments deficits for any length of time.

All major economies have pursued demand management policies consistent with the promotion of the objective of full employment during the post-1945 period, and have largely been successful. The USA, in addition to the objective of full employment, attached high priority to the goal of price stability. In pursuit of this it adopted cautious monetary policies throughout the 1950s which ensured, because of its size relative to the world economy, that both the US and the world rates of inflation were moderate. Individual countries had the average world rate of inflation imposed on them, being able to deviate from it only marginally and in the short run. That they can do so stems from the fact that there exist some goods which do not enter into international trade so that their prices are determined at the national level. Thus movements in their prices partially absorb the effects of changes in domestic monetary policy; however this is only a transitory phenomenon. Results presented by Cross and Laidler (1976) suggest that the deviations of national rates of inflation from the world rate can be explained in terms of the level of excess demand in each individual economy.

Table 1.1 presents data relating to the average annual rates of growth of the money supply for the USA and for the Group of Ten countries as a whole. Over the period 1957-72 there has been a steady acceleration in the rate of growth of the aggregate money supply of the Group of Ten countries. This acceleration stemmed primarily from US monetary policies at least for the period until

Table 1.1 Average annual rates of growth of money supply (%)

	1957-64	1965-72	1957-60	1961-4	1965-8	1969-72
USA	4·9	8·9	3·2	6·6	8·3	9·4
Group of Ten	7·3	11·9	5·1	9·4	9·9	13·9

1968. Note that although the aggregate rate of growth of the money supply is consistently higher than that for the USA, implying that countries other than the USA in aggregate expanded their money supply at a faster rate, US monetary expansion was the source of inflationary pressures, given that its rate of growth of output was significantly less than that for all other countries in the Group of Ten, the UK being the only exception.

In the early 1960s the USA ceased to pursue cautious monetary policies, placing more reliance on fiscal policy in pursuing its objective of lowering its level of unemployment. The average annual rate of US monetary expansion for the years 1961-4 was more than twice that for the period 1957-60, which was the principal cause of an increase in the rate of growth of the world money supply from 5·1 per cent per annum to 9·4 per cent. US policies led to the emergence of world excess demand by 1964: Duck *et al.* (1976). The inflationary pressures thus generated received a further impetus when after 1965 the USA decided to finance the intensification of the Vietnam war and its domestic social programmes by expanding its money supply rather than by raising taxation. The US average rate of monetary expansion increased to 8·3 per cent for the period 1965-8, compared with an average rate of 6·6 per cent during the preceding four years. Cautious monetary policies in the rest of the world implied that the aggregate rate of growth for the Group of Ten countries rose only from 9·4 per cent to 9·9 per cent. However, as a consequence of US monetary policies, inflation rates began to rise throughout the world. Attempts by national governments to insulate themselves from the externally generated inflationary pressures, while maintaining their exchange rates, were on the whole unsuccessful.

Expansionary US monetary policies led to balance of payments deficits. The rest of the world became increasingly reluctant to accumulate dollar balances and thus indirectly make available resources for an unpopular war. Countries could only reduce their balance of payments surpluses by pursuing expansionary monetary policies. Indeed, during the period 1969-72 the average rate of growth of the money supply for the Group of Ten was 13·9 per cent in contrast to 9·9 per cent for the years 1965-8. This acceleration in monetary expansion stemmed primarily from policies pursued by countries other than the USA, the latter's average rate of growth of the money supply having increased only from 8·3 per cent to 9·4 per cent. That the USA was less responsible for the acceleration of the world money supply during the period 1969-72 is a conclusion that further rests on the fact that the US rate of growth of money supply for the years 1969 and 1970 was 5·1 per cent and 4·3 per cent respectively, the lowest annual rates for the decade of the 1960s. Thus the attempt by countries other than the USA to reduce their balance of payments surpluses and/or eliminate excess holdings of foreign exchange reserves led to an acceleration in the rate of growth of the world money supply which in turn resulted in the intensification of inflationary pressures. The end of the 1960s could, therefore, be characterised as the period of 'competitive inflation'.

The IMF system came to an end in August 1971. Since then, and particularly since March 1973, exchange rates have been allowed to be determined relatively freely, with governments abstaining from systematic interventions in the foreign exchange markets. The greater flexibility of exchange rates led to the weakening of the links among countries that prevailed up to 1971 through the commitment to fixed exchange rates, and which had resulted in countries experiencing similar rates of inflation. As a consequence of this weakening of links and of divergent monetary policies, the major industrial countries began to experience significantly different rates of inflation from 1972.[5]

In brief then, the similarity in rates of inflation, their simultaneous acceleration after the mid-1960s, and their divergence since 1972 are phenomena consistent with predictions that follow from the treatment of inflation as an international monetary problems.

How does the rise in social unrest in recent years fit the monetarists' diagnosis of inflation? For the monetarists, excess demand generated by expansive monetary policies is the main source of inflationary pressures. However, as inflation emerges, trade unions and firms will bargain and settle on money wage increases which will incorporate their expectations of price inflation during the period for which their agreement is to hold. In other words, though they bargain on money wages, what in effect they seek to agree upon is real wages. Unions, therefore, attempt to secure money wage increases that will ensure some given rise in real wages, while employers agree to money wage increases while holding some view on what future price rises will be. Thus the actual rate of inflation is determined by excess demand and the expected rate of inflation. Such a model of price determination is consistent with the co-existence of rising unemployment and accelerating inflation: Laidler (1971). If the actual rate of inflation was correctly anticipated then real incomes would rise in line with the expectations of the contracting groups. However, such an 'equilibrium rate of inflation' is not a feature of the world. Laidler (1974) argues that disequilibrium inflation, i.e. when the actual rate of inflation is higher than the expected rate, leads to the real value of money income increases being eroded by increasing prices at a rate faster than anticipated. People then attempt to realise the real income increases which they have been denied by unanticipated inflation. This attempt can take many forms, including industrial militancy. Thus, social unrest is viewed by monetarists as the consequence rather than the cause of inflation.

By 1970 all the countries in the Group of Ten had gone through a sustained period of inflation which had shown tendencies to accelerate from the mid-1960s onwards. By 1970 the redistributive effects of inflation had accumulated sufficiently for trade unions as well as other pressure groups to begin to exhibit increasing deter- mination to protect the real value of their members' money in- creases. The evidence, then, of rising social unrest, as measured by increasing strike activity, since 1970 throughout the Group of Ten countries is consistent with the hypothesis that unanticipated inflation leads to social tensions through its effects on the distri- bution of income and wealth.

It has been argued that inflation during the 1960s was an inter- national monetary problem, USA expansive monetary policies being largely responsible for the acceleration of price rises. Since the abandonment of fixed exchange rates, individual governments bear the major share of responsibility for the inflation experienced by their countries. There is a large measure of agreement among countries regarding the desirability of stable exchange rates, the promotion of which could be facilitated by fixity of exchange rates. One lesson that has been learnt is that in the reformed internation- al monetary system there should be international control of the growth of the world money supply. The emergence of a country as the *de facto* world banker, which is what the USA had come to be under the IMF system, is inimical to the objective of world price stability.

NOTES

[1]   The discussion will be confined to the Group of Ten countries, i.e. USA, UK, Canada, Sweden, Japan, West Germany, France, Italy, Belgium and the Netherlands.
[2]   Support for incomes policies has been voiced by economists who do not regard inflation as a cost-push or sociological phenomenon. Einzig (1970), for example, though he accepts the monetary nature of inflation nevertheless argues that incomes policies can usefully complement demand management policies, especially during periods when governments desire to reduce the rate of inflation.
[3]   No figures are available for France for 1968.
[4]   Divergent monetary policies give rise to balance of payments disequili- bria, which if not promptly eliminated undermine the stability of the inter- national monetary system. Triffin (1966) has on numerous occasions advocated the co-ordination of monetary policies among countries and suggested that the growth of international liquidity be brought under inter- national control. Such reforms would be conducive to world price stability as well as to promoting confidence in the durability of the international monetary system.
[5]   That is, since the spring 1973 domestic rates of inflation have largely

2 The determination and control of the world money supply under fixed exchange rates, 1961 – 71

Michael Parkin, Ian Richards and George Zis*

This paper analyses the factors which determine, and therefore could be used to control, the world money supply under a fixed exchange rate regime such as that which prevailed between 1945 and 1971. Our primary interest is to establish whether, for control of the world money supply, it is sufficient to control the stock of world foreign exchange reserves, or whether it is necessary to go further and have international control of domestic credit policies and even of domestic banking system regulations. The importance of these questions stems mainly from a concern with the determination of the world rate of inflation during the 1960s. Recent contributions in international monetary theory (Mundell (1971), Johnson (1972), Swoboda (1974)), reviving Hume's analysis of inflation and the balance of payments in a fixed exchange rate world, place the rate of growth of the *world* money supply at the centre of the determination of *world* inflation. National monetary policies are seen as major determinants of each country's balance of payments and only in the short run of deviations of that country's inflation rate from the world average.

Fig. 2. 1 sets out the annual rates of change of the world[1] money supply and world price level for the period 1956-71. The world rate of inflation was approximately 1·9 per cent in 1956, reached a peak of 3·2 per cent in 1958 and fell to just under 1·0 per cent in 1959. Through the 1960s the world rate of inflation increased, at first only slowly but since 1966 more rapidly, to a peak of 5·7 per cent in 1970. Turning to the behaviour of the world money supply, we observe that the rate of monetary expansion had

* This paper, which is part of the SSRC—University of Manchester Research Programme 'Inflation: its causes, consequences and cures', was prepared for presentation at the Money Study Group Conference in honour of James Meade, at Merton College, Oxford, September 1974. We are indebted to Malcolm Gray for his help and comments. Any remaining errors are our own responsibility. Reprinted from *The Manchester School* (September 1975).

militancy. Thus, social unrest is viewed by monetarists as the consequence rather than the cause of inflation.

By 1970 all the countries in the Group of Ten had gone through a sustained period of inflation which had shown tendencies to accelerate from the mid-1960s onwards. By 1970 the redistributive effects of inflation had accumulated sufficiently for trade unions as well as other pressure groups to begin to exhibit increasing determination to protect the real value of their members' money increases. The evidence, then, of rising social unrest, as measured by increasing strike activity, since 1970 throughout the Group of Ten countries is consistent with the hypothesis that unanticipated inflation leads to social tensions through its effects on the distribution of income and wealth.

It has been argued that inflation during the 1960s was an international monetary problem, USA expansive monetary policies being largely responsible for the acceleration of price rises. Since the abandonment of fixed exchange rates, individual governments bear the major share of responsibility for the inflation experienced by their countries. There is a large measure of agreement among countries regarding the desirability of stable exchange rates, the promotion of which could be facilitated by fixity of exchange rates. One lesson that has been learnt is that in the reformed international monetary system there should be international control of the growth of the world money supply. The emergence of a country as the *de facto* world banker, which is what the USA had come to be under the IMF system, is inimical to the objective of world price stability.

NOTES

[1]   The discussion will be confined to the Group of Ten countries, i.e. USA, UK, Canada, Sweden, Japan, West Germany, France, Italy, Belgium and the Netherlands.

[2]   Support for incomes policies has been voiced by economists who do not regard inflation as a cost-push or sociological phenomenon. Einzig (1970), for example, though he accepts the monetary nature of inflation nevertheless argues that incomes policies can usefully complement demand management policies, especially during periods when governments desire to reduce the rate of inflation.

[3]   No figures are available for France for 1968.

[4]   Divergent monetary policies give rise to balance of payments disequilibria, which if not promptly eliminated undermine the stability of the international monetary system. Triffin (1966) has on numerous occasions advocated the co-ordination of monetary policies among countries and suggested that the growth of international liquidity be brought under international control. Such reforms would be conducive to world price stability as well as to promoting confidence in the durability of the international monetary system.

[5]   That is, since the spring 1973 domestic rates of inflation have largely

been determined by the actions of national governments. The argument, which is popular particularly in the UK, that the increases in oil prices are responsible for the acceleration of inflation during 1974, apart from confusing relative and absolute prices, is unacceptable when we consider the relative experience of different countries. All that one needs to do is to compare West Germany, which is as dependent on oil imports as any country, and the UK. The former's rate of inflation in 1974 was less than half that of the UK. The difference between the two countries is to be found in the difference in the rates of growth of their money supply.

REFERENCES

Ashenfelter, O. C. and G. E Johnson (1969), 'Bargaining theory, trade unions and industrial strike activity', *American Economic Review*.

Ashenfelter, O. C., G. E. Johnson and J. H. Pencavel (1972), 'Trade unions and the rate of change of money wage rates in United States manufacturing industry', *Review of Economic Studies*.

Bach, G. L. (1973), *The New Inflation: Causes, Effects, Cures* (Prentice-Hall).

Balogh, T. (1970), *Labour and Inflation,* Fabian Tract 403 (London).

Bispham, G. A. (1972), 'The current inflation and short-term forecasting' in M. Parkin and M. Sumner (eds.), *Incomes Policies and Inflation* (Manchester University Press).

Cagan, P. *et al.* (1972), *Economic Policy and Inflation in the Sixties* (Washington, D.C. Domestic Affairs Studies).

Cross, R. and D. Laidler (1976), 'Inflation, excess demand and expectations in fixed exchange rate open economies—some preliminary empirical results', in M. Parkin and G. Zis (eds.), *Inflation in the World Economy* (Manchester University Press).

Duck, N., M. Parkin, D. Rose and G. Zis (1976), 'The determination of the rate of change of wages and prices in the fixed exchange rate world economy, 1956-71', in M. Parkin and G. Zis (eds.), *Inflation in the World Economy* (Manchester University Press).

Einzig, P. (1970), *Foreign Exchange Crises* (London, Macmillan).

Friedman, M. (1970), 'The counter-revolution in monetary theory', *I.E.A. Occasional Paper No. 33* (London).

Galbraith, J. K. (1967), *The New Industrial State* (Harmondsworth, Penguin Books).

Genberg, H. (1976), 'A note on inflation rates under fixed exchange rates', in M. Parkin and G. Zis (eds.), *Inflation in the World Economy* (Manchester University Press).

Godfrey, L. (1971), 'The Phillips curve: incomes policy and trade union effects', in H. G. Johnson and A. R. Nobay (eds.), *The Current Inflation* (London, Macmillan).

Harrod, R. (1972), 'The issues: five views', in R. Hinshaw (ed.), *Inflation as a Global Problem* (London, The John Hopkins University Press Ltd).

Hicks, J. (1974), *The Crisis in Keynesian Economics* (Oxford, Basil Blackwell).

Hines, A. G. (1964), 'Trade unions and wage inflation in the United Kingdom 1893-1961', *Review of Economic Studies*.

Johnson, H. G. (1969), 'A survey of theories of inflation', in *Essays in Monetary Economics* (London, Allen & Unwin).

―――― (1972a), *Inflation and the Monetarist Controversy* (Amsterdam, Dr F. De Vries Lectures, North-Holland).

—— (1972b), 'Inflation: a monetarist view', in *Further Essays in Monetary Economics* (London, Allen & Unwin).
Johnston, J. and M. Timbrell (1973), 'Empirical tests of a bargaining theory of wage rate determination', *The Manchester School*.
Jones, A. (1973), *The New Inflation: The Politics of Prices and Incomes* (Harmondsworth, Pengiun Books).
Laidler, D. (1971), 'The Phillips curve, expectations and incomes policy', in H. G. Johnson and A. R. Nobay (eds.), *The Current Inflation* (London, Macmillan).
—— (1974), 'Information, money and the macroeconomics of inflation', *Swedish Journal of Economics*, vol. 76.
Levinson, C. (1971), *Capital, Inflation and the Multinational* (London, Allen & Unwin).
Marris, S. (1972), 'World inflation: panel discussion', in E. Claassen and P. Salin (eds.), *Stabilisation Policies in Interdependent Economies* (Amsterdam, North-Holland).
Mundell, R. (1971), *Monetary Theory: Inflation, Interest and Growth in the World Economy* (California, Goodyear).
OECD (1970): *Inflation: The Present Problem*.
OECD (1973): *Economic Outlook* (July).
Parkin, M., M. Sumner and A. R. Jones (1972), 'A survey of the econometric evidence of the effects of incomes policy on the rate of inflation', in M. Parkin and M. Sumner (eds.), *Incomes Policy and Inflation* (Manchester University Press).
Pencavel, J. H. (1970), 'An investigation into industrial strike activity', *Economica*.
Phillips, A. W. (1958), 'The relationship between unemployment and the rate of change of money wage rates in the United Kingdom 1861-1957', *Economica*.
Phelps Brown, E. J. (1971), 'The analysis of wage movements under full employment', *Scottish Journal of Political Economy*.
Purdy, D. and G. Zis (1974a), 'Trade unions and wage inflation in the UK: a re-appraisal', in D. Laidler and D. Purdy (eds.), *Inflation and Labour Markets* (Manchester University Press).
—— (1974b), 'On the concept and measurement of trade union militancy', in D. Laidler and D. Purdy (eds.), *Inflation and Labour Markets* (Manchester University Press).
Schultz, C. L. (1969), 'Sectoral shifts and inflation', in R. J. Ball and P. Doyle (eds.), *Inflation* (Harmondsworth, Penguin Books).
Taylor, J. (1972), 'Incomes policy, the structure of unemployment and the Phillips curve: the United Kingdom experience 1953-70', in M. Parkin and M. Sumner (eds.), *Incomes Policy and Inflation* (Manchester University Press).
Triffin, R. (1966), 'The balance of payments seesaw', in W. Fellner *et al.* (eds.), *Maintaining and Restoring Balance in International Payments* (Princeton, N.J., Princeton University Press).
Ulman, L. and R. J. Flanagan (1971), *Wage Restraint: A Study of Incomes Policies in Western Europe*, (Berkeley, Cal., University of California Press).
Ward, R. and G. Zis (1974), 'Trade union militancy as an explanation of inflation: an international comparison', *The Manchester School*.
Wiles, P. (1973): 'Cost inflation and the state of economic theory', *Economic Journal*.

2 The determination and control of the world money supply under fixed exchange rates, 1961 – 71

Michael Parkin, Ian Richards and George Zis*

This paper analyses the factors which determine, and therefore could be used to control, the world money supply under a fixed exchange rate regime such as that which prevailed between 1945 and 1971. Our primary interest is to establish whether, for control of the world money supply, it is sufficient to control the stock of world foreign exchange reserves, or whether it is necessary to go further and have international control of domestic credit policies and even of domestic banking system regulations. The importance of these questions stems mainly from a concern with the determination of the world rate of inflation during the 1960s. Recent contributions in international monetary theory (Mundell (1971), Johnson (1972), Swoboda (1974)), reviving Hume's analysis of inflation and the balance of payments in a fixed exchange rate world, place the rate of growth of the *world* money supply at the centre of the determination of *world* inflation. National monetary policies are seen as major determinants of each country's balance of payments and only in the short run of deviations of that country's inflation rate from the world average.

Fig. 2.1 sets out the annual rates of change of the world[1] money supply and world price level for the period 1956-71. The world rate of inflation was approximately 1·9 per cent in 1956, reached a peak of 3·2 per cent in 1958 and fell to just under 1·0 per cent in 1959. Through the 1960s the world rate of inflation increased, at first only slowly but since 1966 more rapidly, to a peak of 5·7 per cent in 1970. Turning to the behaviour of the world money supply, we observe that the rate of monetary expansion had

* This paper, which is part of the SSRC—University of Manchester Research Programme 'Inflation: its causes, consequences and cures', was prepared for presentation at the Money Study Group Conference in honour of James Meade, at Merton College, Oxford, September 1974. We are indebted to Malcolm Gray for his help and comments. Any remaining errors are our own responsibility. Reprinted from *The Manchester School* (September 1975).

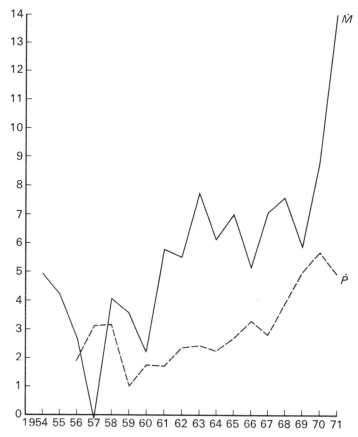

Figure 2.1 Annual rates of change of world money supply (solid line) and world price level (dotted line) (%)

a falling trend in the second half of the 1950s, the period when the world rate of inflation was moderate and falling. However, between 1961 and 1969, when inflation was on the increase, the average rate of growth of the world money supply sharply increased, varying between 5·12 per cent and 7·76 per cent. In 1970 and 1971 there was a further sharp increase in the rate of monetary expansion.

The data portrayed in Fig. 2.1, whilst not inconsistent with the hypothesis that world inflation is caused by world monetary expansion, do not indicate perfect correlation between those variables. The principal reason for this is probably that changes in the rate of monetary expansion first have effects on the level of real output and only after a lag affect prices. Pursuing this line of investigation, Duck *et al.* (1976) were able to provide a proximate explanation for the variations in the world rate of inflation in terms of an expectations-augmented excess demand model. They concluded that in the 1950s and early 1960s the world was in a state of excess supply, gradually moving into excess demand by 1964. The persistence of excess demand in the following years led to the acceleration of the world inflation rate. If it is the case that the developments of world excess demand are primarily generated by the behaviour of the world money supply, then it must be shown that there exists a stable world velocity or demand for money function. This was investigated by Gray, Ward, and Zis (1976), who showed that such a stable function does indeed exist.

The implication of these studies is that control of the world money supply is required if the problem of world inflation is to be solved. This paper, by focusing on the factors determining the rate of growth of the world money supply, seeks, therefore, to shed light on the means by which the world money expansion can be controlled.

The questions which we seek to answer, whilst clear, are not sufficiently well specified to enable us to proceed immediately to answer them. They require further refinement in order to break them down into a series of smaller questions each of which can be answered and which, when answered, provide conclusions relating to our primary questions. A useful starting point in this process is to note that, by definition, the world money supply is equal to the product of the world stock of high-powered money and the world money multiplier. We may then examine how these two variables have contributed to the behaviour of the world money supply, and also how each of them is determined and may be controlled. The money multiplier is determined by the demand function for high powered money in each country and may be taken *a priori* to depend on required reserve ratios and the opportunity cost of holding reserves. We examine empirically the nature of this dependence and are particularly interested in the interest elasticity of the demand for high-powered money by the banking system. The lower that elasticity is, the lower the interest elasticity of the money supply function will be, and hence the more precisely possible will it be to control the money supply. The world stock of high-powered money is simply the sum of the high-powered money stocks of the individual countries, which are in turn the sums of central bank holdings of foreign exchange reserves and domestic credit. It would be possible to treat all these variables as exogenous and subject to political control by each of the individual central banks. However, under the fixed exchange rate regime being analysed, it is interesting to treat the reserve issuing country as the world central bank issuing what we will call world 'super-high-powered money', and the other central banks using that as their reserve against which they issue high powered money to their domestic banking systems. We can define the high-powered money stock as the product of the stock of gold and foreign exchange reserves and a high-powered money multiplier, and ask questions about these two variables analogous to those posed above. These questions are: What have been the major sources of changes in the world high-powered money supply—changes in gold and foreign exchange reserves or changes in the high-powered money multiplier ? Is there a well-behaved multiplier relation between gold and foreign exchange reserves on the one hand and world high-powered money on the other ? The answers to these more detailed questions will enable us to answer the primary questions posed at the beginning. If the world money supply is capable of being controlled merely by controlling the quantity of foreign exchange reserves, then what we have called the 'high-powered money multiplier' and the money multiplier must be stable. Also, the reserve asset itself must be controllable. If the money multiplier is stable but the high-powered money multiplier is not, then control of central bank domestic credit in each and every country would be necessary for control of the world money supply. If the money multiplier is not well behaved, then detailed banking system regulations in national and/or Euro-currency markets becomes a necessary condition for control of the world money supply. To establish whether such controls need extending to Euro-currency markets, we investigate the determinants of definitions of the world money supply which include and exclude those deposits.

    The rest of the paper is organised in four main sections. In the next section (I) we examine the historical evolution of the world money supply, high-powered money, gold and foreign exchange reserves, and the money and high-powered money multipliers. Section II develops a simple model of the monetary system of a fixed exchange rate open economy, and shows that what is often called 'the money supply function' is really either a 'balance of payments function' or just one of several equations required to determine the stock of money and other variables of interest. Section III considers the world as a whole and develops world money supply and high-powered money functions. In Section IV world money supply functions are estimated and hypotheses about their parameters are tested.

    The major conclusions which we reach are the following. There appears to be a simple well-defined and interest-inelastic world money supply function. The growth of narrow money (notes and coin plus demand deposits) has been almost entirely due to the growth of high-powered money, whilst the growth of broader definitions of money has been contributed to by both high-powered money growth and a rising multiplier. The growth of high-powered money was, until 1968, mainly accounted for by domestic credit expansion,

whilst after that date increases in foreign exchange reserves arising mainly from US deficits were the dominant source of growth.
The broad money multipliers were increasing, apparently not as
equilibrium responses to changes in domestic banking system
regulations concerning required reserves or changes in interest
rates but rather as a gradual adjustment to a long-run equilibrium
stock of reserves. Thus, control of the world money supply apparently may be achieved by controlling the world stock of high-
powered money but would not require detailing regulation of
domestic private banking systems or Euro-currency markets.
However, the stock of high-powered money itself is almost totally
uncorrelated with world reserves. Hence, to achieve world monetary control in a fixed exchange rate system, arrangements not
present in the IMF system would be required to ensure a sufficient
degree of harmonisation of the domestic credit expansion policies
of the fixed exchange countries.

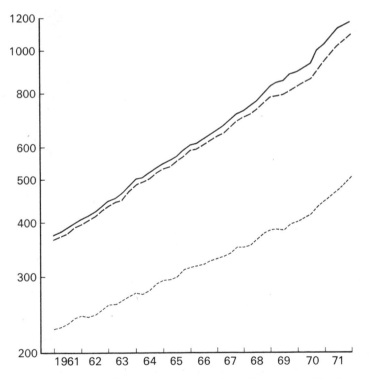

Figure 2.2 World money supply: broad money with Euro-
currencies (solid line); broad money without Euro-currencies
(broken line); narrow money (dotted line) (billion dollars)

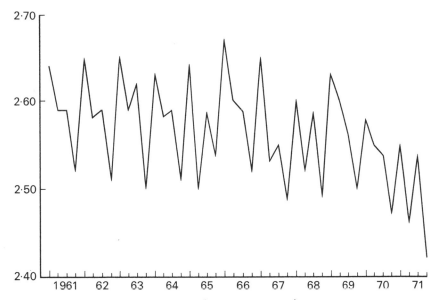

Figure 2.3 World multipliers (narrow money)

I A BRIEF HISTORICAL ACCOUNT OF MONEY SUPPLY GROWTH: 1961-1971

The course of the world money supply over the 1960s is dramatically set out in Fig. 2. 2. It is evident that the growth rate on all
definitions accelerated sharply after 1968 with the definition which
includes Euro-currencies pulling ahead of the others very sharply
at that time. We can define the world money supply M as

$$M \equiv mH$$

$$H \equiv R + C$$

where H is world high-powered money, R is the stock of foreign
exchange reserves held by central banks, C is central bank holdings
of domestic assets and m is the world money multiplier. How have
these components contributed to the behaviour of the world money
supply as depicted in Fig. 2. 2 ?

World m (shown in Fig. 2. 3), when calculated using narrow
money, has had a stable value during the period 1961-71. Though
seasonal movements are pronounced, there is hardly a trend
change, though towards the end of the period it may be argued that
a slight downward trend may be detected.

In contrast to world m for narrow money, when broad money
both with and without Euro-currencies is used, world m exhibits a

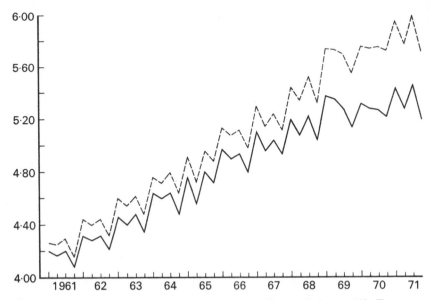

Figure 2.4 Broad money multiplier for all countries: with Euro-currencies (broken line); without Euro-currencies (solid line)

distinct upward trend during the period 1961-71 (see Fig. 2. 4). Naturally, the rise is greater for the definition of broad money which includes Euro-currencies. From the behaviour of the narrow money multiplier it is evident that the growth of world narrow money can only be explained in terms of the growth in world high-powered money. This is less apparent in the case of broad money where the multiplier does have an upward trend; however, that trend flattens after 1968 and therefore the behaviour of the broad money multiplier, although accounting for some of the increase in broad money, cannot account for the sharp acceleration that came in the late 1960s.

Consideration of the movements in world high-powered money (Fig. 2. 5) shows that indeed the growth rate of the base did accelerate sharply in 1968 and has maintained a higher growth rate than the average for the period before that date.

Let us now examine the rates of growth of the two components of the world high-powered money stock (also in Fig. 2. 5). We notice that the rate of growth of world reserves fluctuated but fell from 3·42 per cent in 1961 to 1·37 per cent in 1967. In 1968 it grew by 5·72 per cent but, as a result of US contractionary monetary policies, fell slightly in 1969. However, in the following year it registered a dramatic increase of 19 per cent, followed by an

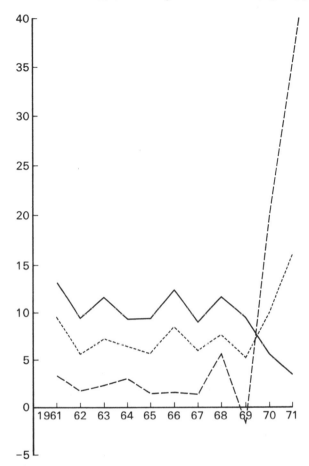

Figure 2.5 Annual rates of change of world domestic assets (solid line), world reserves (broken line), and aggregate world base money (dotted line) (%)

even more dramatic rise of 37.9 per cent in 1971. The activation of the Special Drawing Rights scheme obviously contributed to this acceleration. However, US deficits were primarily responsible for this acceleration in world reserves. In 1969 foreign exchange, i.e. mainly dollar balances, accounted for 39·3 per cent of world reserves.[2] This proportion was raised to 47·9 per cent in 1970 and to 60·2 per cent in 1971. If we now consider the rate of growth of world domestic assets we note that it has been steadily decreasing from 11.74 per cent in 1968 to 3·42 per cent in 1972, while in the period 1961-7 the rate of growth varied between 13·26 per cent and 8·95 per cent.

What emerges from this brief historical account of the growth of the world money supply in the 1960s is the clear and simple message that, although a trend increase in the broad money multiplier is apparent, the major source of monetary expansion, in proximate terms, is the US balance of payments. This dominant feature of the data does not require anything other than the simple visual display of the data contained in this section. However, if we are to account in detail not only for the dominant trend movements in the world money supply but also for the detailed cyclical and other developments, we need to specify a model of the determinants of the world money supply and estimate its parameters. We now turn to this.

II THE MONETARY SYSTEM OF A SINGLE FIXED EXCHANGE RATE OPEN ECONOMY

The conventional analysis of the determination of the money supply begins with the definition

$$M^S = H_p + D \tag{1}$$

where

M^S = nominal money supply

H_p − notes and coin held by the non-bank public

D = bank deposits (defined in various ways)

The non-bank holdings of H_p are conveniently specified as

$$H_p = \alpha D \tag{2}$$

where α is a function of the opportunity cost of holding H_p as compared with D. Combining (1) and (2) gives

$$M^S = (1 + \alpha) D \tag{3}$$

The balance sheet of the banks which issue D is

$$D = H_b + L \tag{4}$$

where

H_b = net deposits with the central bank plus till money,

and

L = loans of all types.

Banks may be postulated to make additional loans if they have excess reserves in accordance with

$$\Delta L = \gamma(H_b - H_b^*) \tag{5}$$

where

H_b^* are desired reserves given by

$$H_b^* = \beta D \tag{6}$$

and where β will depend positively on the required reserve ratio and negatively on the opportunity cost of holding reserves. The total stock of high powered money is simply

$$H = H_b + H_p \tag{7}$$

Using (3), (4), (5), (6) and (7), we may obtain

$$\Delta M^S = \Delta H + \gamma H - \gamma \left(\frac{\alpha + \beta}{1 + \alpha}\right) M \tag{8}$$

the stationary H^* and M^* form of which is

$$M^* = \left(\frac{1 + \alpha}{\alpha + \beta}\right) H^* \tag{9}$$

and which will be stable given the specified signs of the parameters.

Equations of the form of (8) and (9), usually with greater institutional detail and with a specific derivation and discussion of the arguments of α and β, are often presented as a 'money supply function'. However, they may only be interpreted as such if H is a variable which is subject to control by the central bank. Now in an open economy,

$$H \equiv ER + C \tag{10}$$

where

R = stock of foreign exchange reserves

E = exchange rate (units of domestic currency per unit of reserve 'currency')

C = domestic assets held by the central bank.

Clearly, in an open economy with a flexible exchange rate, H can be controlled by the central bank and (8) is interpretable as a money supply function.

If, on the other hand, we assume that exchange rates are fixed, that there exists a stable demand function of money

$$M^d = L(\quad)P \tag{11}$$

that the price level is determined by international arbitrage, and that the arguments of the demand for real balances function $L(\quad)$ are fixed (or, less strongly, that they are exogenous), then (8) with

(11) and the condition

$$M^d = M^s \tag{12}$$

serves to determine only the country's balance of payments as

$$\Delta R = \frac{1}{E} \{ \Delta M^d - \Delta C - \gamma(R + C) + \gamma \left[\frac{\alpha + \beta}{1 + \alpha} \right] \} \tag{13}$$

or, in its banking sector equilibrium form

$$\Delta R = \frac{1}{E} \{ \left[\frac{\alpha + \beta}{1 + \alpha} \right] \Delta M^d - \Delta C \} \tag{14}$$

Although unfamiliar in this form this is of course the familiar Johnson (1972) result. The virtue of (13) and (14) over the more familiar way of presenting the simplest monetary equilibrium theory of the balance of payments is that it makes it clear that it is the difference between changes in the demand for high-powered money and central bank domestic credit expansion which determines the balance of payments.

In most short-run situations, neither of the above interpretations of equations (8) or (13) will be appropriate, since domestic prices may temporarily differ from a fully arbitraged equilibrium with those of the rest of the world, and the arguments of the demand for money function, especially real output, may not be treated as being independent of domestic credit policy. In such a situation, (8) or (13) are only interpretable as just one (quasi-reduced form) of several equations required to determine the values and policy responses of the variables of interest.

Although the conventional analysis of the money supply does not yield a money supply function in an open economy except if that economy operates with a flexible exchange rate, it does yield such a function in a closed economy formed by aggregating all our fixed exchange rate open economies. We now turn to an examination of this.

III THE MONEY SUPPLY FUNCTION OF THE FIXED EXCHANGE RATE WORLD

The relation between M and H for a fixed exchange rate open economy (which we have suggested is *not* a money supply function) may be written as

$$\Delta M_i = \Delta H_i + \gamma_i H_i - \gamma_i \epsilon_i M_i \tag{15}$$

where

$$\epsilon_i \equiv \frac{\alpha_i + \beta_i}{1 + \alpha_i}$$

and the subscript i is introduced as the country index, $i = 1, \ldots n$.

Now

$$H_i \equiv R_i + C_i \tag{16}$$

where the exchange rate is normalised as unity, whence,

$$\Delta M_i = \Delta R_i + \Delta C_i + \gamma_i(R_i + C_i) - \gamma_i \epsilon_i M_i \tag{17}$$

Equation (17) is assumed to apply to every country in the fixed exchange rate system except the reserve currency country (the USA in terms of the world of the 1960s).

For the reserve currency country, equation (15) still describes the relation between M and H but high-powered money is given by

$$H_{00} = H_0 - \sum_{i=1}^{n} H_{0i} \tag{18}$$

where

H_0 = total liability of central bank

$H_{00} = H_{p0} + H_{b0}$

and

H_{0i} = foreign exchange reserve of country i

or

$$H_0 = G_0 + C_0 \tag{19}$$

where

G_0 = gold (primary reserve) of reserve issuer

and

C_0 = domestic credit of reserve issuing central bank.

Thus, for the reserve currency country,

$$\Delta M_i = \Delta G_0 + \Delta C_0 - \sum_{i=1}^{n} \Delta H_{0i} + \gamma_0(G_0 + C_0 - \sum_{i=1}^{n} H_{0i})$$
$$- \gamma_0 \epsilon_0 M_0 \tag{20}$$

and for each other country,

$$\Delta M_i = \Delta G_i + \Delta C_i + \Delta H_{0i} + \gamma_i(G_i + C_i + H_{0i}) - \gamma_i \epsilon_i M_i \tag{21}$$

where

$G_i + H_{0i} \equiv R_i$.

Approximating $\gamma_0 = \gamma_i = \gamma$ and $\epsilon_0 = \epsilon_i = \epsilon$ and aggregating over all countries gives

$$\Delta M = \Delta G + \Delta C + \gamma (G + C) - \gamma \epsilon M \tag{22}$$

with

$$M^* = \frac{1}{\epsilon}(G^* + C^*) = \left(\frac{1 + \alpha}{\alpha + \beta}\right)(G^* + C^*) \tag{23}$$

a full stock equilibrium for the banks.[3]

This is the world money supply function since, unlike the individual country equations (e.g. (15) or (17)) it determines the world money supply given the stock of gold (or other primary reserve) and the aggregate (net) stock of central bank domestic credit.

The world money multiplier (m) around which we organised our discussion of the proximate determinants of the world money supply can be obtained by noting that

$$m \equiv \frac{M}{G + C}$$

$$= \frac{1}{1 + \gamma \epsilon}\{\gamma + g_H + (1 - g_H)m_{-1}\} \tag{24}$$

where

$$g_H \equiv \Delta H / H \equiv \Delta (G + C)/(G + C)$$

and

$$m^* = \frac{1}{\epsilon} = (1 + \alpha)/(\alpha + \beta)$$

We now turn to a more detailed empirical study of the world money supply function.

IV ESTIMATION OF A WORLD MONEY SUPPLY FUNCTION

1 Data

The empirical aspects of our work define the world as the Group of Ten and use quarterly data from 1961(1) to 1970(4). The time period is restricted to the decade of the 1960s because they were the 'high years' of the IMF fixed exchange rate system. The Group of Ten is used because of the ready availability for those countries of reasonably reliable quarterly data on both the variables needed for this study and those needed for related studies of which the present one is a part. Throughout we work with three definitions of money:

M_1 = notes and coins in circulation *plus* demand deposits;

M_2 = M_1 *plus* time deposits and certificates of deposits.

M_3 = M_2 *plus* Euro-currency deposits.

Full details of all the data series used and the sources are presented in Appendix 2.1.

2 Formulation of the basic hypotheses for estimation and hypothesis testing

The basic money supply hypothesis in which we are interested is written in the preceding section as

$$\Delta M = (\Delta G + \Delta C) + \gamma(G + C) - \gamma \epsilon M \qquad (22)$$

where

$$\epsilon = (\alpha + \beta)/(1 + \alpha)$$

As it stands, (22) is most unsuitable for estimation of γ and ϵ for two reasons. First, M appears on both sides of equation (22). Second, ϵ is a function of the arguments of α and β. We can address the first problem easily simply by rearranging (22) to give

$$M = \frac{1}{1 + \gamma\epsilon}(M_{-1} + \Delta G + \Delta C) + \frac{\gamma}{1 + \gamma\epsilon}(G + C) \qquad (25)$$

The second problem is addressed by assuming that

$$\epsilon = \epsilon_0 + \epsilon_1 R^3 - \epsilon_2 r_L + \epsilon_3 r_B \qquad (26)$$

where

$$\epsilon_i \geq 0$$

R^3 = required reserve ratio(s)

r_L = interest rate(s) on banks earning assets

r_B = interest rate(s) on borrowed reserves.

However, in order to avoid tractable but difficult non-linear estimation problems we define

$$\lambda \equiv \frac{1}{1 + \gamma\epsilon}$$

and, using a Taylors series approximation, postulate

$$\lambda = \lambda_0 + \lambda_1 R^3 - \lambda_2 r_L + \lambda_3 r_B$$

so that

$$M = \lambda_0 z - \lambda_1 R^3 z + \lambda_2 r_L z - \lambda_3 r_B z + \gamma\lambda_0 H - \gamma\lambda_1 R^3 H$$
$$+ \gamma\lambda_2 r H - \gamma\lambda_3 r_B H \qquad (27)$$

where

$$z = M_{-1} + \Delta G + \Delta C \text{ and } H = G + C.$$

An interesting special case emerges if we assume $\gamma \to \infty$, i.e. that the banks eliminate their excess reserves so quickly that they are always in equilibrium. In this case, as is clear from (25),

$$M = \frac{1}{\epsilon} H \qquad (28)$$

which may be written as

$$M = \lambda_0 H - \lambda_1 R^3 H + \lambda_2 r_L H - \lambda_3 r_B H \qquad (29)$$

or more simply

$$m = \lambda_0 - \lambda_1 R^3 + \lambda_2 r_L - \lambda_3 r_B \qquad (30)$$

where
$$m \equiv M/H.$$

Table 2.1 Variance of three-month rates accounted for by each principal component[a]

| | Component | | | | | |
Rate	1	2	3	4	5	6
Euro-dollar	94·70	1·44	0·26	1·00	0·66	1·50
Belgium	78·39	12·92	0·05	4·33	0·51	3·81
West Germany	51·18	27·14	15·32	0·88	4·61	0·87
Netherlands	81·26	2·55	1·31	13·24	1·46	0·13
USA	88·55	6·46	1·12	0·00	0·05	0·03
UK	71·68	1·48	23·24	0·38	2·80	0·37
Canada	67·50	25·73	0·75	0·38	2·50	2·57
'Total'[b]	79·68	9·19	4·69	2·86	1·51	1·39

Source: Gray, Ward and Zis (1976).

Notes

[a] The numbers in this table may also be interpreted as the squares of the correlation coefficients between the components and the interest rates, that is as the R^2 that would be obtained from a regression of one on the other.
[b] This row gives the percentage of the generalised variance of the rates explained by each component. The generalised variance is the determinant of the covariance matrix of the seven series.

It is equations (27) and (30) which form the basis of our empirical work.

For the required reserve ratio (R^3) we use a weighted average of R^3 for each of the countries in the sample. For the interest rates r_L and r_B we use just one rate, namely that on Euro-dollars. Our justification for this last choice is that both short term lending rates and rediscount rates are highly colinear with the Euro-dollar rate. This is clear from a consideration of the principal components analysis presented in Tables 2.1 and 2.2. Using this simplification we drop the two separate interest rates from (27) and (30) and use just the Euro-dollar rate denoted r.

3 Results

We first estimated the equilibrium multiplier formulation of the money supply hypothesis, equation (30) with the addition of seasonal dummy variables, and the results are set out in Table 2.3. Superficially, these results might be taken to imply that the narrow

Table 2.2 Variance of each discount rate accounted for by each principal component[a]

Rate	Component					
	1	2	3	4	5	6
Euro-dollar	89·51	2·57	1·68	4·54	1·26	0·37
Belgium	79·82	9·54	0·18	3·26	0·15	2·61
Canada	52·96	12·53	29·20	0·09	1·98	2·73
France	80·30	7·66	1·32	5·63	4·40	0·12
West Germany	75·20	13·78	0·06	6·58	1·92	0
Italy	71·85	19·14	4·19	0·73	0	0·06
Japan	8·21	0·12	69·05	0·37	0·12	11·35
Holland	86·02	0·44	2·52	1·14	2·18	0·12
Sweden	67·23	0·82	7·80	18·02	0	1·27
UK	52·46	32·57	0·48	7·06	4·50	2·00
USA	85·38	5·30	1·90	0·22	0·93	2·54
'Total'[b]	74·94	9·43	5·63	4·85	1·85	1·19

Notes

[a],[b] As for Table 2.1.

Table 2.3

Dependent variable	Parameter							
	λ_0	λ_1	λ_2	d_1	d_2	d_3	s^2	DW
M1	2·402 (40·040)	0·063 (2·273)	−0·004 (0·125)	0·123 (8·563)	0·054 (3·766)	0·080 (5·660)	0·001	1·067
M2	5·881 (26·294)	−1·014 (9·853)	0·075 (6·142)	0·291 (5·457)	0·094 (1·782)	0·159 (3·001)	0·015	0·711
M3	6·189 (17·864)	−1·119 (7·522)	0·112 (5·98C)	0·313 (3·779)	0·087 (1·066)	0·165 (2·021)	0·037	0·471

Notes

M1 = Narrow money multiplier.
M2 = Broad money multiplier.
M3 = Broad money (with Euro—currencies) multiplier.
t-values in parentheses.

Table 2.4

Parameter	M_1 $\gamma = 1$	M_1 $\gamma = 1\cdot25$	M_1 $\gamma = 1\cdot5$	M_2 $\gamma = 1$	M_2 $\gamma = 1\cdot25$	M_2 $\gamma = 1\cdot5$	M_3 $\gamma = 0\cdot25$	M_3 $\gamma = 0\cdot50$	M_3 $\gamma = 0\cdot75$
a	13·506 (2·423)	15·982 (2·855)	18·115 (3·230)	−29·181 (3·066)	−31·951 (3·382)	−34·896 (3·633)	−21·024 (2·314)	−28·326 (3·154)	−35·185 (3·953)
λ_0	0·711 (51·646)	0·662 (49·342)	0·619 (48·809)	0·904 (38·976)	0·877 (37·580)	0·851 (37·684)	1·000 (37·589)	0·966 (37·740)	0·934 (37·808)
λ_1	−0·001 (0·344)	−0·001 (0·516)	−0·002 (0·660)	−0·0004 (0·112)	−0·001 (0·340)	−0·002 (0·518)	0·002 (0·655)	0·002 (0·613)	0·002 (0.577)
λ_2	0·001 (1·070)	0·001 (1·340)	0·001 (1·573)	−0·001 (1·411)	−0·001 (1·126)	−0·001 (0.827)	−0·001 (1·723)	−0·001 (1·402)	−0·001 (1·096)
d_1	−10·263 (8·567)	−10·018 (8·519)	−10·112 (8·460)	−12·005 (4·793)	−12·298 (4·919)	−12·589 (5·034)	−10·848 (4·029)	−11·286 (4·196)	−11·696 (4·344)
d_2	−4·560 (3·829)	−4·639 (3·907)	−4·707 (3·965)	−6·056 (2·414)	−6·262 (2·501)	−6·467 (2·581)	−4·932 (1·829)	−5·234 (1·943)	−5·517 (2·046)
d_3	−9·648 (8·032)	−10·006 (8·366)	−10·318 (8·630)	−10·654 (4·270)	−11·739 (4·718)	−12·774 (5·134)	−6·896 (2·568)	−8·294 (3·094)	−9·606 (3·582)
s^2	7·204	7·164	7·163	31·965	31·866	31·937	36·898	36·842	36·942
h	−1·607	−1·557	−1·494	−1·121	−1·105	−1·071	−0·425	−0·353	−0·282
$\dfrac{\lambda_0}{1-\lambda_0} = m^*$	2·46	1·959	1·625	9·417	7·130	5·711	not defined	28·412	14·152

money multiplier, (m_1), is virtually a constant with a strong seasonal pattern, and that m_2 and m_3, both of which have grown substantially over the same period, have had their trends determined
by falling required reserve ratios and rising interest rates. However, the low values of the Durbin-Watson statistic caution against
those conclusions and suggest the presence of further systematic
variability in the money supply process.

Since our basic model allows for partial excess reserve
adjustment on the part of banks, we next turned to an estimation of
that in the form presented in equation (27) but using only one
interest rate, i.e.

$$M = \lambda_0 z - \lambda_1 R^3 z + \lambda_2 r z + \gamma \lambda_0 H - \gamma \lambda_1 R^3 H + \gamma \lambda_2 r H$$

with

$$z = M_{-1} + \Delta H \text{ and } H = G + C$$

Our original idea was to estimate the above as

$$M = a_0 z + a_1 R^3 z + a_2 r z + b_0 H + b_1 R^3 H + b_2 r H$$

and test the hypothesis that

$$\frac{b_0}{a_0} = \frac{b_1}{a_1} = \frac{b_2}{a_2} = \gamma$$

thereby generating an estimate of γ and the three λ's. However,
multicolinearity made that a very imprecise procedure. As an
alternative, we imposed values of γ and estimated the values of
λ_i, in the formulation

$$M = \lambda_0(z + \gamma H) - \lambda_1(R^3(z + \gamma H)) + \lambda_2(r(z + \gamma H)) + \text{seasonals}$$

with λ varying over a coarse grid in increments of $0 \cdot 25$ from zero
to a little beyond the s^2 minimising value. The results of this
exercise for the s^2 minimising and two adjacent values of γ are
set out for all three definitions of money in Table 2.4. Two things
are immediately clear: first, we cannot now reject the null hypothesis of zero autocorrelation in the residuals; and second, the
equations fit remarkably well. It is thus of some interest to inspect
these results rather carefully. The most noteworthy feature of
these estimates is their robustness even in the face of quite large
variations in γ and also the total insignificance of R^3 and r as
explanatory variables. The money supply process, regardless of
the breadth of the definition of money, is, according to these results,
dominated partly by seasonality and partly by a simple dynamic
adjustment process in which, as reserves are created by central
banks, commercial banks endeavour to divest themselves of excess
reserves.

In view of the non-significance of λ_1 and λ_2 we re-estimated
the model, setting those parameters equal to zero and estimating

directly the parameter λ_0 (renamed λ) and γ directly. These
results appear in Table 2.5. The basic story told by these results
is identical to that in Table 2.4 (although there is now a possibility
in the case of M_1 of negative autocorrelation in the residuals).

In terms of the time paths of the multipliers, these results
imply that the narrow money multiplier was fluctuating around its
equilibrium (m^*) value whilst the trend increases in the broad
multipliers m_2 and m_3 represented a process of gradual adjustment to their equilibrium values, m_2^* and m_3^* shown in Table 2.5,
the speed of adjustment being faster the slower the creation of
high-powered money. The implication of this interpretation is that,
even without additional high-powered money growth, the stock of
broad money would have continued to expand substantially had the
fixed exchange rate system not collapsed. For this interpretation
of events to be plausible, it must be the case that at the beginning
of the 1960s the banks felt themselves to be considerably underlent
and excessively liquid. Whilst we have no way of being certain on
this matter, it seems highly plausible that prior to the introduction
of full convertibility and the associated growth and spread of large
scale multinational-multicurrency banks, the banks were indeed
constrained and unable to pursue all the business which they could
profitably undertake. The dating of the introduction of full convertibility (1958) makes this look entirely plausible. It may nevertheless be objected that the process of lending excess reserves was,
according to our estimates, going to take something like a decade
and a half to complete and this is an inplausibly long period. We
think the objection would be wrong for three reasons. First, whilst
one bank can lend its excess reserves, the system as a whole has
to undertake the familiar text-book multiple expansion to eliminate
them. Thus, excess reserves which were lent in a previous period
continue to return. Second, the information required for successful
bank lending is such as to make a relatively slow adjustment highly
plausible. Third, regulations on lending in most countries have
forced banks and borrowers into arrangements which take longer
to work out than would be possible in the absence of restrictions.
For these reasons, although we were surprised to find the results
displayed in Table 2.5, and its implications, we do not find them at
all implausible.

We have now established that the growth of the world money
supply was in an important and predictable way influenced by the
growth of world high-powered money. Control of world high-
powered money could be achieved by detailed control over the
domestic credit policies of each member of the fixed exchange rate
system. Alternatively, if there was a stable relationship between
world reserves and the sum of individual countries' central bank
assets, control of the rate of growth of world reserves would
ensure control of the rate of expansion of world high-powered

Table 2.5 $M = a + \lambda(M_{-1} + \Delta H) + \gamma\lambda H + d_1 + d_2 + d_3$

Dependent variable	a	λ	$\gamma\lambda$	γ	d_1	d_2	d_3	s^2	h	m^*
M_1	8·440 (2·740)	0·767 (7·176)	0·597 (2·350)	0·778	−10·279 (8·653)	−4·386 (3·708)	−9·297 (6·426)	7·230	−2·567a	2·56
M_2	−38·044 (3·005)	0·823 (12·832)	1·315 (3·214)	1·598	−13·069 (5·170)	−6·943 (2·783)	13·380 (3·897)	31·898	−0·625	7·43
M_3	−40·633 (2·015)	0·888 (12·080)	1·064 (1·992)	1·198	−12·463 (4·509)	−6·069 (2·251)	−11·736 (2·869)	37·064	0·238	9·50

Notes

t-values in parentheses.

$$m^* = \frac{\gamma\lambda}{1-\lambda} = \frac{1+\alpha}{\alpha+\beta}$$

$a$indicates presence of autocorrelation

money and therefore of the world money supply. However, a cursory examination of Fig. 2. 5 suggests that there was no well defined relationship between the aggregate of domestic credit policies and the growth of foreign exchange reserves. The correlation between the rate of change of foreign exchange reserves and aggregate central bank domestic credit during the 1960s was 0·03 and confirms that impression. Thus, it appears that even if the Bretton Woods system had allowed for the orderly control of the rate of growth of international liquidity, that would not have prevented central banks, during the 1960s, from pursuing policies of domestic credit expansion not conducive to world price stability.

NOTES

1   The availability of data has led us to define the world as the Group of Ten, i.e. the USA, Canada, UK, France, Italy, West Germany, Netherlands, Belgium, Sweden, Japan. The precise definitions of the data used are given in Appendix 2. 1.

2   These figures refer to the world as a whole and not to the Group of Ten.

3   The implication of our analysis is that the impact effect on the world money supply of domestic credit expansion is not dependent on where it originates. In other words, there is no asymmetry between key and non-key currencies. Swoboda (1973) has presented an analysis of the determinants of the world money supply which does allow for this asymmetry, the value of the world multiplier, then, becoming dependent on, among other factors, the forms in which countries choose to hold their exchange reserves. The importance of Swoboda's more disaggregative approach is an empirical, not an *a priori* matter which we propose to investigate in a subsequent paper.

REFERENCES

Duck, N., M. Parkin, D. Rose and G. Zis (1976), 'The determination of the rate of change of wages and prices in the fixed exchange rate world economy 1956-71', in M. Parkin and G. Zis (eds.), *Inflation in the World Economy* (Manchester University Press).

Gray, M., R. Ward and G. Zis (1974), 'World demand for money', in J. M. Parkin and G. Zis (eds.), *Inflation in the World Economy* (Manchester University Press).

Johnson, H. G. (1972), *Inflation and the Monetarist Controversy* (Amsterdam, North-Holland).

Mundell, R. A. (1971), *Monetary Theory* (Pacific Palisades, Calif., Goodyear).

Swoboda, A. K. (1973), 'Eurodollars and the world money supply: implications and control', in A. K. Swoboda (ed.), *Europe and the Evolution of the International Monetary System* (Geneva, A. W. Sigthoff-Leiden).

—— (1974): 'Monetary policy under fixed exchange rates: effectiveness, the speed of adjustment and proper use', in H. G. Johnson and A. R. Nobay (eds.), *Issues in Monetary Economics* (Oxford University Press).

APPENDIX 2.1

1 Definitions of variables and sources of data

(i) Money supply figures
(*a*) *Narrow money* defined as notes and coin in circulation plus demand deposits. *Source:* OECD, Main indicators, *Historical Abstract 1955-71.*
(*b*) *Broad money* defined for the UK as notes and coin in circulation with the public together with all deposits, whether denominated in sterling or other currencies, held by UK residents in both public and private sectors. For all other countries broad money is defined as narrow money plus quasi-money. *Sources:* for UK, *Bank of England Statistical Abstract* 1969, also *Bank of England Quarterly Bulletin,* various issues. For all others, *International Financial Statistics.*

(ii) Reserve money
Data given in the *International Financial Statistics* were used as the relevant high-powered money for each country. Foreign exchange reserves figures, given in the *International Financial Statistics,* were subtracted from reserve money to derive domestic assets data. In deriving domestic assets, restricted (special) deposits with the central bank were also subtracted from reserve money wherever this was required.
Reserve money is defined as notes and coins in circulation plus banks' deposits with the central bank. *Source:* September issues of *International Financial Statistics.*

(iii) Discount rates
Sources for individual countries:
(*a*) *Japan:* OECD, *Monetary Policy in Japan,* table A, pp. 74-5.
(*b*) *West Germany.* OECD, *Monetary Policy in Germany,* appendix III.
(*c*) *United States: Federal Reserve Bulletin* (February 1972)
(*d*) *United Kingdom: Bank of England Statistical Abstract, Bank of England Quarterly Bulletin.*
(*e*) *Belgium:* K. Holbik (ed.), *Monetary Policy in Twelve Industrial Countries.* Federal Reserve Bank of Boston (for 1962-71) and EEC, *Instruments of Monetary Policy* for 1961
(*f*) *France:* K. Holbik (ed.), *OECD, Main Economic Indicators.*
(*g*) Canada: K. Holbik (ed.), *op. cit.,* pp. 110-11.
(h) *Sweden:* OECD, *Financial Statistics.*
OECD, *Main Economic Indicators, Historical Statistics 1959-69.*
(*i*) *Italy:* OECD, *Financial Statistics.*
(*j*) *Netherlands:* OECD, *Financial Statistics.*
OECD, *Main Economic Indicators, Historical Statistics 1959-69.*

(iv) Required reserve ratios
Sources for individual countries:
(*a*) *Japan:* OECD, *Monetary Policy in Japan,* table B, p. 76.
(*b*) *United Kingdom: Bank of England Statistical Abstract, Bank of England Quarterly Bulletin.*
(*c*) *West Germany: Monthly Report* of the Deutsche Bundesbank.
(*d*) *United States: Federal Reserve Bulletin*
(*e*) *Italy:* OECD, *Monetary Policy in Italy*
(*f*) *France:* K. Holbik (ed.), *op. cit.*
(*g*) *Canada: Bank of Canada Annual Report*

(v) Euro-currencies
Defined as the short-term liabilities of commercial banks in foreign currencies *vis-à-vis* non-residents.
The figures for Euro-currencies relate to the following countries: Belgium, France, West Germany, Italy, Netherlands, Sweden, Switzerland, United Kingdom and Japan. *Source: Bank for International Settlements Annual Reports.*
Figures for Euro-currencies were available only from 1963 onwards. The figures for 1961 and 1962 were estimated on the assumption of equal proportional increase over each quarter with 1958 as the base year.

(vi) Euro-dollar rate
Source: Bank of England Statistical Abstract, Bank of England Quarterly Bulletin.

3 International liquidity and world inflation in the 1960s

Michael Parkin

This paper examines the question: Would control of the growth of international liquidity have been necessary and sufficient for control of the world rate of inflation under the rules of the game embodied in the international monetary system in force between the end of 1958 and mid-1971? It does not analyse questions concerning the inherent survival capacity of the system. An abundant literature and subsequent events point strongly to its weakness in that respect (Williamson (1973)). Nor does it analyse questions concerning the inflationary or deflationary bias of the system *qua* system. Rather, it focuses on the question: If international liquidity had been controlled and expanded less quickly than it was, would the increasingly strong upward trend in world inflation, experienced throughout the 1960s, have been avoided?

The question derives its importance from two considerations. First, although the system now in force is radically different from that of the 1960s, a correct diagnosis of our current inflation, which had its origins in that earlier period, can help to avoid the adoption of inappropriate policies to control inflation. Second, although the fixed rate system has been abandoned, the costs of, and lack of benefits deriving from, variable exchange rates are becoming sufficiently clear for us to hope at least, if not as yet to predict, that a world of greater exchange rate rigidity will eventually re-emerge. If and when that happens, the lessons derived from the failures of the 1960s will be a valuable (though not, of course, infallible) guide to the better construction and control of the new system.

The paper adopts the basic point of view of the Humean tradition in international monetary economics, namely that in a fixed exchange rate system, the forces making for alignment (if not equality) of national inflation rates are so strong that it is neither fruitful nor possible to attempt an explanation of inflation at a national level. Rather inflation is a phenomenon being generated at the world aggregate level by forces which transcend national boundaries. This is not to beg the question of whether monetary and demand factors on the one hand or supranational sociological forces

on the other are the dominant cause of inflation. This question will
be taken up below.

Two principal sources of previous work are drawn on. First,
that of members of the Manchester Inflation Research Programme
(see Duck *et al.* (1976), Gray *et al.* (1976) and Parkin *et al.* (1975)
which has attempted to model the world (proxied by the Group of
Ten) as a single macro-economy, and second, the massive literature
on the demand for reserves surveyed so fully yet concisely by
Williamson (1973).

What follows is organised in six main sections. First, Section I,
the 'facts' about inflation and liquidity growth are presented and
briefly discussed in a purely descriptive manner. Section II develops a broad analytical framework within which it is possible to
pose the detailed empirical questions requiring attention and poses
those questions. Sections III and IV examine the evidence on those
questions, III dealing with the transmission mechanism between the
world money supply and world inflation and IV with the relation
between the world money supply and liquidity. In Section V, brief
attention is paid to what might be called the alternative direction
of causation view, and finally, Section VI presents some tentative
conclusions.

I THE FACTS

The behaviour of the world rate of inflation and growth of international liquidity (for the Group of Ten) are set out in Fig. 3. 1.
The inflation rate displays the well-known upward trend all through
the decade with a particularly strong and persistent upsurge between 1967 and 1970. The trend in international liquidity was running counter to this between 1961 and 1969 but exploded thereafter.
Liquidity growth was much more cyclical than inflation, especially
in the first half of the decade.

Clearly there is little contemporaneous correlation between
these variables. However, that does not imply necessarily that
there is no cause and effect. There is, at a loose level of analysis,
ample reason to suppose that if liquidity changes, through their
impact on the rate of growth of the world money supply, do affect
prices, they will do so through a transmission mechanism which
contains substantial time lags. Hence not only would we find no
contemporaneous correlation but also might find no simple lagged
correlation either. Rather, the behaviour of prices may depend in
a complicated way on a quite long previous history of liquidity
growth. However, without a more explicit formal framework virtually nothing can be said as to the form of such a relationship. Let
us then turn to the development of a framework within which we
can explore the relationship (if any) between liquidity growth and
inflation.

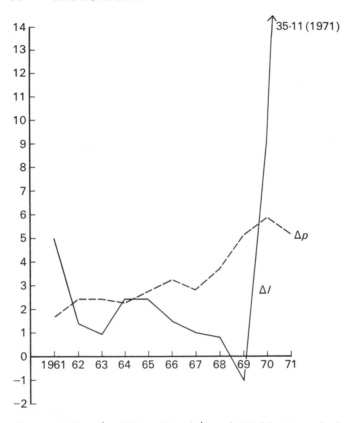

Figure 3.1 $-\dot{R} = ((R_t - R_{t-1})/R_{t-1}) \times 100$ where R_t is average total Group of Ten reserves for year t (source: *International Financial Statistics*).
$-\dot{p} = ((P_t - P_{t-1})/P_{t-1}) \times 100$ where P_t is weighted average retail price index for Group of Ten (weighted by GNP) for year t (source: OECD, *Main Economic Indicators*)

II ANALYTICAL FRAMEWORK

The basic model with which we will work to analyse the relation between international liquidity and world inflation is an entirely conventional one, at least as regards national macro-economic analysis. The model is applied to the world macro-economy with minimal extension and modification, the primary justification being that national prices and interest rates move sufficiently closely together and exchange rates have been sufficiently fixed for the composite goods theorem to permit such aggregation, or, at least, make it no worse than aggregation at the national level.

First, prices of final output are assumed to adjust to excess demand and inflation expectations, i.e.,

$$\Delta p = \alpha x + \Delta p^e, \alpha > 0 \tag{1}$$

where

Δp = actual rate of change of final prices

Δp^e = expected rate of change of final prices

x = proportionate excess demand for goods and services

Second, expectations of inflation are assumed to respond to actual inflation by the error-learning process:

$$\Delta p = \lambda \Delta p_{-1} + (1-\lambda)\Delta p^e_{-1}, 0 < \lambda \leqslant 1 \tag{2}$$

where the subscript -1 indicates a time lag.

Third, the demand for money function is given by

$$m^d = p + \beta(y^* + x) - \gamma \Delta p^e \tag{3}$$

$$\beta > 0, \gamma \geqslant 0$$

where

m^d = logarithm of nominal money demanded

y^* = logarithm of full employment output

(Note: $y^* + x \doteq y$ where y = logarithm of aggregate real income/output.)

Fourth, the stock of money demanded is assumed to equal that supplied, i.e.,

$$m^d = m^s \tag{4}$$

If the money supply was exogenous, this system would yield solutions for the rate of inflation, Δp, and excess demand, x, as second-order difference equations (abstracting from terms in y^*) of the form:

$$\Delta p = a\Delta p_{-1} + b\Delta p_{-2} + c\Delta m + f\Delta m_{-1} \tag{5}$$

$$\Delta x = a\Delta x_{-1} + b\Delta x_{-2} + g\Delta m + h\Delta m_{-1} + k\Delta m_{-2}$$

where

$$a = \frac{2b + \alpha[1 - \lambda(1 - \lambda)]}{\alpha + \beta}; b = -\left[\frac{\beta + \alpha\gamma\lambda}{\alpha + \beta}\right]$$

$$c = \frac{\alpha}{\alpha + \beta}; f = \frac{-\alpha(1 - \lambda)}{\alpha + \beta}; g = \frac{1}{\alpha + \beta}$$

$$h = \frac{-2}{\alpha + \beta}; k = \frac{1}{\alpha + \beta}.$$

The two difference equations generating price change and excess demand will be stable if

$$\alpha\lambda > 0$$

$$4\beta + \alpha(2 - \lambda) + 2\alpha\gamma\lambda > 0$$

$$\gamma\lambda < 1$$

It is clear from the definitions of the range of these parameters that the first two conditions are always satisfied. The third one, therefore, is the critical condition for stability and is directly analogous to that in the continuous time, full employment, perfectly anticipated inflation model of Cagan (1956). The approach to the stable equilibrium will be cyclical if,

$$\frac{4\beta}{\alpha} > \frac{(1 - \lambda)^2}{\lambda} - 2\lambda[1 + (1 - \gamma)\lambda]$$

and will be monotonic with a single over-shoot otherwise.

Since our main purpose is to analyse the relation between international liquidity and inflation, we now go on to examine the determinants of the world money supply and the role of international liquidity in that process. First, the supply of money, which is mainly (though not exclusively) a liability of commercial banks, may be postulated to depend on the supply of high-powered money to the world's commercial banks and, based on a conventional analysis of the demand for and supply of high-powered money, be of the form

$$m^S = \delta h + \phi, \delta > 1 \tag{7}$$

where

$h = $ logarithm of high-powered money

and

$\phi = $ (in principle) a function of reserve opportunity cost and reserve adjustment cost variables.

Now high-powered money (H) (note that capital letters are dollars and lower-case letters are logarithms throughout) is, by definition, the sum of foreign exchange reserves (international liquidity) L and domestic credit (D), i.e.,

$$H = L + D \tag{8}$$

For H to be controllable via control of L, there must exist a stable demand function by central banks for the latter of the form

$$L^d = \Psi H$$

or

$$l^d = \psi + h \tag{9}$$

where $\Psi(\psi)$ is a function of a potentially large number of variables, some of which may be included in the above model but others not.

If

$$l^d = l \tag{10}$$

with l controlled exogenously, then the

$$h = l - \psi \tag{11}$$

and

$$m^s = \delta l + (\phi - \delta \psi) \tag{12}$$

The basic structural equations which constitute our model relating world liquidity to world inflation is summarised as:

$$\Delta p = \alpha x + \Delta p^e \tag{1}$$

$$\Delta p^e = \lambda \Delta p_{-1} + (1 - \lambda) \Delta p^e_{-1} \tag{2}$$

$$m^d = \beta(y^* + x) - \gamma \Delta p^e + p \tag{3}$$

$$m^s = \delta h + \phi \tag{8}$$

$$m^d = m^s \tag{4}$$

$$h = l - \psi \tag{11}$$

where $\alpha, \beta, \gamma, \delta$ are parameters but ϕ and ψ are, in principle, functions of variables not explicitly included in the above system.

We may now, within the framework of the above system, pose the key empirical questions requiring attention if we are to establish whether or not control of international liquidity provides control of inflation.

They are, first, do equations (1) and (2) adequately capture the price—setting behaviour and expectations formation of the world economy or are some important systematic push and sociological factors ommitted? Clearly, if the former, then

$$\Delta p = \alpha x + \alpha \lambda \sum_{i=1}^{\infty} x_{-i} \tag{13}$$

so that the current rate of inflation depends, in a proximate sense, on the entire history of excess demand and on no other variables. In this case, the factors determining excess demand will be the ultimate determinants of inflation and, provided the world displays

additional features to be outlined below, the rate of growth of liquidity is a potential candidate for inclusion in that list. If, alternatively,
there are additional important systematic sociological push forces
ommitted from the price-setting and expectations formation process then, although monetary and liquidity control could influence
prices (provided further conditions enumerated below are satisfied),
it could do so only at the expense of creating excess supply (or
unemployment); and, the stronger the ommitted sociological push
forces, the greater the cost of using liquidity and monetary control
to control inflation.

Second, does there exist a stable demand for money function
of the form set out as equation (3) so that changes in the money
supply lead to changes in excess demand? Variants incorporating
permanent income or partial stock adjustment—or even other variables, provided they move slowly over time—would not create problems. The first two modifications would affect the short-run dynamics of adjustment but not the long-run equilibrium, while the
second might impart gentle long-term trends into the equilibrium
stock of real balances. If there does not exist such a demand for
money function, or if the stochastic variability in that function is
large, then variations in the money stock will not lead to systematic variations in excess demand or inflation, and push-determined
changes in the rate of inflation would not necessarily require a
validating increase in the money supply.

Third, does there exist a stable money supply process as embodied in equations (8) and (11), and what is the nature and behaviour of the additional variables (embodied in ϕ and ψ) upon which
that process depends? If (4) and (8) are good approximations and if
ϕ and ψ are constants, then of course the effects of liquidity on
aggregate money supply are direct. If, alternatively, there are
strong systematic influences in the relation between high-powered
money and total money supply but with offsetting effects in the
relation between liquidity and high-powered money such that the
reduced form equation

$$m^S = \delta l + (\phi - \delta \psi)$$

is not systematically shifted, then again, liquidity and the money
supply will be directly linked. The presence of partial adjustments
and expectational variables (as in the case of the demand for money),
whilst changing the dynamics, would not affect the long-run equilibrium relationships. If, however, the multiplier relation between
high-powered money and total money supply is stable and independent of other systematic influences, but the demand for liquidity
dependent on volatile systematic or random factors (in ψ), then,
whilst control of high-powered money would be sufficient to control
inflation, liquidity control would not. Let us now examine these
empirical questions.

III PRICE SETTING, EXPECTATIONS FORMATION AND THE DEMAND FOR MONEY

The only empirical work on price-setting, expectation formation and the demand for money at a multi-country (world proxy) aggregate level appears to be that of the Manchester Inflation Workshop using aggregate data for the Group of Ten.

Duck *et al.* (1976) estimated for the period 1956-70 a price-setting equation of the form

$$\Delta p = \alpha X + \Delta p^e \tag{1}$$

with the subsidiary hypothesis that

$$\Delta p^e = \lambda \Delta p_{-1} + (1 - \lambda)\Delta p^e_{-1} \tag{2}$$

Estimating λ as the moving average parameter in a Box Jenkins ARIMA $(0, 2, 1)$ model (with a value of 0.31) and entering the resulting Δp^e series in equation (1) gives, for *quarterly* differences (but measured as annual rates of change) the following results (t-ratios in parentheses):[1]

$$\Delta p = 0.500 + 0.204X_{-1} + 0.814\Delta p^e$$
$$(1 \cdot 23) \quad (3 \cdot 58) \quad\quad (6 \cdot 88)$$
$$\overline{R}^2 = 0.533 \quad\quad DW = 2 \cdot 144$$

$$\Delta p = 0 \cdot 100 + 0 \cdot 184X_{-1} + 1 \cdot 000\Delta p^e$$
$$(0 \cdot 72) \quad (3 \cdot 31)$$
$$\overline{R}^2 = 0.513 \quad\quad DW = 2 \cdot 188$$

The first equation was estimated freely and the second by imposing the a *priori* coefficient of unity on Δp^e. It is immediately apparent that this equation gives a powerful approximate explanation of price change. The overall explanatory power (over 50 per cent) is extremely high for the typically very noisy quarterly first difference data and the residuals appear to be free from first-order autocorrelation. The hypothesis that the coefficient on expected inflation is unity cannot be rejected. The speed of response to excess demand (0·2 per cent point per quarter) translates almost exactly to a full per cent point change in Δp in a year per per cent point of excess demand. Although this work does not explicitly search for the potential effects of socio-political push variables it does suggest that if there is any role for them, it is unlikely to be systematic. Thus, on the basis of this study, there is a potential role for monetary policy in the control of inflation and, furthermore, with no implication that the costs in terms of excess supply creation would be excessive. Indeed, if, in the long run, the world (Group of Ten) economy was run at a level of capacity utilisation only slightly below the average of the 1960s, then inflation could eventually be squeezed out. Of course, the greater the degree of underutilisation, the faster would the inflation be reduced.

The study of price-setting behaviour, whilst demonstrating a potential role for monetary policy, does not go far enough to establish the sufficiency of monetary policy. For that, there must exist a stable demand for money function. This was examined by Gray *et al.* (1976) who estimated, again for the Group of Ten, from 1957 to 1971, a series of alternative formulations of that function. The formulation which performed best was as follows (note asymptotic standard errors in parentheses):

$$m^* = 2 \cdot 20 + 0 \cdot 53(y^* + x) + p \\ \quad (0 \cdot 16) \quad (0 \cdot 02)$$

$$m^d = 0 \cdot 42(m^* - m_{-1})$$

$$(0 \cdot 08)$$

$$R^2 = 0 \cdot 986$$

where m^* is the long-run stock equilibrium demand for money and m is narrow money. Attempts to find a role for permanent income failed, with the measured income, partial adjustment combination always dominating. The homogeneity of the demand function was tested explicitly and could not be rejected. Attempts were made to find a role for interest rates and other opportunity cost variables but the parameters always estimated at less than $0 \cdot 03$ and were insignificant with the exception of a sub-sample estimate for the latter forty observations. In that case, the interest elasticity was just significant but only $-0 \cdot 03$, and hence hardly of any importance. Overall, the Gray *et al.* findings seem to point strongly towards there being a stable demand for money function and hence to the necessity of world money supply control for the control of world inflation.

Bringing the above results together, we have

$$\Delta p = 0 \cdot 184 X_{-1} + \Delta p^e$$

$$\Delta p^e = 0 \cdot 31 \Delta p_{-1} + 0 \cdot 69 \Delta p^e_{-1}$$

$$m^* = 2 \cdot 20 + 0 \cdot 53(y^* + x) + p$$

$$\Delta m^d = 0 \cdot 42(m^* - m_{-1})$$

which yields the reduced forms for Δp and x which are very similar to those analytical results given in Section II. They differ because (i) $\gamma = 0$, (ii) x is lagged one period in the price-setting equation, and (iii) the demand for money has a partial adjustment process. The numerical solution to the system for Δp and ignoring y^* is

$$\Delta p = 1 \cdot 66 \Delta p_{-1} + 0 \cdot 75 \Delta p_{-2} = 0 \cdot 82 \Delta m_{-1} - 1 \cdot 07 \Delta m_{-2} + 0 \cdot 34 \Delta m_{-3}$$

This generates a damped cyclical response of prices to a change
in the rate of monetary expansion, the cycles having a period of
five and a half years. The damping is fast, so that after four years
of constant monetary expansion the inflation rate would be in the
neighbourhood of equilibrium. However, the excess demand adjustments precede the inflation changes and are large relative to the
changes in the rate of inflation.

If the behaviour of the world money supply is the crucial
determinant of world inflation, it is of some importance to analyse
the money supply process and its relation to the growth of domestic credit and international liquidity.

IV WORLD MONEY SUPPLY AND INTERNATIONAL LIQUIDITY

The relation between the world (Group of Ten) money supply and
high-powered money has been studied empircially by Parkin *et al.*
(1954). They found for the period 1961-71 that a simple, well-
defined, interest-*in*elastic narrow money supply function, with a
partial adjustment process reflecting partial disposal of excess
reserves, fitted the data well. That function was (ignoring seasonals
which were very strong, with *t*-ratios in parentheses):

$$M^S = 8 \cdot 440 + 0 \cdot 767M_{-1} + 1 \cdot 364H - 0 \cdot 767H_{-1}$$

$$(2 \cdot 74) \quad (7 \cdot 18 \qquad\qquad (7 \cdot 18)$$

$$s^2 = 7 \cdot 23 \quad h = 2 \cdot 56$$

with an equilibrium multiplier of 2·56. Full stock equilibrium
formulations of the quarterly money supply function performed
very badly and a variety of interest rate effects were searched for
without success. In terms of the discussion in Section II, this result implies that ϕ is a constant and that there is a simple long-
run equilibrium relationship between world high-powered money
and the world (narrow) money supply and a simple first order stock
adjustment process leading to that equilibrium.

We now turn our attention to the relationship between international liquidity (reserves), high-powered money and aggregate
money. Here there is a rather considerable empirical literature,
but, fortunately, it has already been surveyed by Williamson (1973).

The main published empirical studies are those by Kenen and
Yudin (1965), Courchene and Youssef (1967), Clark (1970), Kelly
(1970), Archibald and Richmond (1971) and Flanders (1971). These
studies fall into three distinct groups. First, Clark's, Kelly's and
Flanders's models are derived more or less loosely from the
optimising behaviour of central banks and predict that the demand
for reserves will be a function of (*a*) the variability of the balance
of payments, (*b*) the marginal (or average) propensity to import, (*c*)

the opportunity cost of reserve holdings and (*d*) the value of international trade. They use a mixture of cross-section (i.e. cross-country) and time series data. Second, Courchene and Youssef argue that the demand for reserves will be a function of the supply of money and the opportunity cost of reserve holding. They use time series data from 1958 to 1964 for a sample of nine countries. Third, Kenen and Yudin and Archibald and Richmond adopt a purely time series stochastic process approach, and use time series data (1958-62 and 1961-7 respectively) for fourteen individual countries.

There is no shortage of judgements as to the positive nature of the findings. Kelly, for example, concludes that his 'empirical evidence ... lends some support to the idea that reserve holdings are rationally determined and are related to a small set of variables common to all countries over a period sufficiently long to encompass major cyclical swings' (Kelly (1970), p. 666).

There is no need to review the results of these studies in detail, for Williamson (1973) has already done that. What we must do, however, is to ask what bearing they have on the stability of the relationship between reserves and the money supply. Only one study, that by Courchene and Youssef, direcly lends itself to this purpose, although the others do so indirectly. Their empirical results suggest that, at least for nine countries studied (Switzerland, Netherlands, Denmark, Sweden, West Germany, Belgium, Italy, Japan and Australia), over the period 1958 to 1964, the demand for reserves is well explained by the money supply and the opportunity cost of holding reserves (although only in four cases is the latter variable significantly negative). A model which replaces the money supply with imports performs almost, but not quite, as well in seven cases and slightly better in two. Although no formal tests are reported, the differences are almost certainly insignificant. If we accepted the Courchene-Youssef money supply results at face value then we could cut right through the analysis of the relations between total money supply and high-powered money on the one hand and reserves and high-powered money on the other, and so proceed immediately to a multiplier relation between reserves and the total money supply. For the period and countries covered by their study that seems entirely appropriate. How confidently it could be extended to other countries and for a time period beyond 1964 are questions that we consider subsequently.

The optimal central bank behaviour models are more difficult to draw inferences from concerning the controllability of the money supply via aggregate reserves control, for none of them uses monetary variables directly.

Flanders, using cross-sections for the period 1950-65, produces results which suggest that the ratio of reserves to imports is virtually a constant. In the one regression which has reserves as the dependent variable and imports along with many others as

Table 3.1

Dependent Variable log R

	log S (x)	log M/Y	log A	log L	R^2
Country dummies	0·194	0·306	0·112	0·062	
	(6·4)	(2·8)	(7·6)	(3·3)	0·964
Year Dummies	0·578	−0·420	0·196	0·046	0. 882
	(19·2)	(8·8)	(16·0)	(2·9)	

Notes

R = reserves
$S(x)$ = standard deviation of exports,
M/Y = average propensity to import,
A = foreign assets,
L = foreign liabilities.

independent variables, only imports are significant. In other regressions in which the dependent variable is the ratio of reserves to imports, significant coefficients are scarce and explanatory powers of the order of zero.

Kelly uses a pooled cross-section time series for forty-six countries and thirteen years (1953-65) and, with a set of country intercept dummies in one pool and year intercept dummies in another, obtains the results in Table 3.1.

It is clear that Kelly's explanatory power is high. However, there must be a major puzzle and concern at the fact that the coefficient on M/Y is estimated at +0.3 or −0.4 and significant in both cases, depending on whether country or year intercept differences are taken into account. Clearly, there must be an important specification error undermining entirely any confidence we may have in these results.

Clark's study explains cross-section variability of reserves in terms of the marginal propensity to import, *per capita* income and and the variability of payments.

The purely stochastic models of Kenen and Yudin and Archibald and Richmond explain cross-section variations mainly in terms of the stochastic variability of reserve changes, the latter being estimated from time series.

The key factor in all these results, for present purposes (ignoring Kelly, whose results are too puzzling to attempt to draw further inferences from them) is that it is cross-section variability and not time series variability that is being explained, and, further, being explained by variables whose connection with the money supply is at best loose but, more importantly, whose temporal (though not of course cross-section) variability is probably not large.

In terms of our broad analytic framework of Section 2, this amounts to postulating (as an approximation of course) that the demand for reserves over time are *not* systematically related to the money supply at all. Only the study by Courchene and Youssef disagrees with this, and they were studying nine countries, seven of which are extremely small. If we examine the time series of the reserve holding of the Group of Ten over the entire 1960s and its relation to the high-powered money supply, it is clear that the no-association conclusion, and not the Courchene-Youssef conclusion, is strongly supported. Fig. 3.2 illustrates this. The correlation between aggregate reserves and total central bank liabilities is 0·03.

The tentative conclusion to which we are led is that control of world high-powered money may have been necessary and suffi-cient to control world inflation under the Bretton Woods fixed ex-change rate rules, but control of only international liquidity clearly would not.

V DIRECTION OF CAUSATION

Since under the rules of the international monetary system pre-vailing in the 1960s, there was a well-defined causal link between the rate of world monetary expansion (either aggregate or high-powered) and the world inflation rate, and only a loose relationship between reserves (international liquidity) and the monetary aggre-gates, control of the world money (or high-powered money) supply would be necessary and sufficient to control world inflation, but control of only international liquidity would not.

There is one additional matter which requires attention if the conclusion is to be sustained and that is the difficult 'reverse causation' argument. The argument accepts the correlations between prices and the money supply but argues either (*a*) that causation runs from prices to money or (*b*) that pursuit of an unemployment target (excess demand target in the notation of the model of Section II) leads to a simultaneous creation of both in-flation and a validating monetary expansion. There is, of course, the third anti-monetarist position, namely that price (and wage) setting behaviour is proximately influenced both by push forces *and* by demand and expectation variables. One or more of these propositions would appear to lie behind much of the literature reviewed by Williamson on the 'adequacy' of reserves. Let us examine each of them in turn, but in reverse order.

The 'eclectic' view, which would basically accept the model

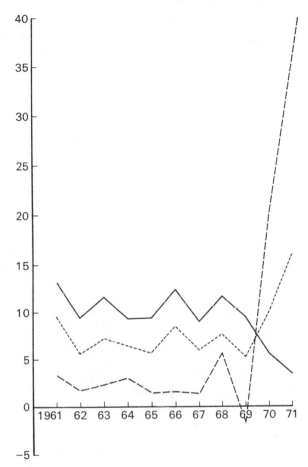

Figure 3.2 Annual rates of change of Group of Ten domestic
assets (solid line), Group of Ten reserves (broken line) and
aggregate Group of Ten base money (dotted line), based on end
of year data (source: *International Financial Statistics*) (%)

set out in Section II, is that the price-setting-expectations formation system is incomplete and omits key push forces. Three things
need to be said about this position. First, it is clearly the safest
one to adopt because, it has not yet been exhaustively tested and
therefore could be right. Second, implicit tests are performed
whenever price and wage equations which ignore such forces are
estimated. They appear to leave little room for such forces.
Third, explicit tests (see e.g. Nordhaus (1970), Ward and Zis (1974)

and for a survey Parkin (1974)) failed to find a convincing role for such factors. One would have more confidence in the various push hypotheses if their proponents stated what evidence would lead to their rejection. So far this task has been left unchallenged to the opponents.

The second view, what may be called the 'joint causation' view, is much more respectable. From detailed knowledge of the way in which governments in all major countries (and certainly the Group of Ten) have behaved, it is almost an indisputable fact that fiscal and interest policies have been used throughout the 1960s to shoot for growth and unemployment targets which, in terms of the model in this paper, are captured in terms of excess demand, x, being the exogenous variable and monetary expansion and prices generated by the chosen path of excess demand. On this view (and it is the author's view), the inflation acceleration of the 1960s occurred because the pursuit of too high an overall level of demand led to inflation and reinforcing—indeed accelerating—inflation expectations and a validating rise in the rate of monetary expansion. Further, and most importantly, however, this interpretation of the 1960s does not deny, indeed it reinforces, the policy prescription of the abandonment of over-full employment real activity targets and their replacement with steady monetary growth targets.

Potentially, the most difficult of all 'reverse direction of causation' propositions and would be one which accepted all the structural equations set out in Section II but argued that prices were determined exogenously by unspecified and unmeasurable push forces; that the price-setting equation (1) should be interpreted as an excess demand determining equation and the supply of money would then adjust passively to satisfy the demand for money, given the exogenous inflation rate and the induced level of excess demand. Fortunately, this view (if advanced) would be easy to reject. The time lags in that price equation completely rule out that particular 'reverse causation' story.

VI CONCLUSIONS

The conclusions are very simple. Under the international monetary rules of the game of the 1960s, control of the world money supply (as high-powered money supply) would have been necessary and sufficient to control world inflation. Control of international liquidity would not.

This is not, of course, to say that liquidity control is irrelevant for other purposes. It is virtually certain that the survival capacity of the system was crucially affected by the highly disparate growth rates of gold, dollars and other domestic assets and points strongly to the need for detailed control of the aggregate world money supply and all its components.

NOTE

1 For full details of data sources, methods and listings see the original papers.

REFERENCES

Archibald, G. C. and J. Richmond (1971) 'On the theory of foreign exchange reserve requirements', *Review of Economic Studies* (April).

Clark, P. B. (1970), 'Demand for international reserves: a cross-country analysis', *Canadian Journal of Economics* 3(4) (November), pp. 577-94.

Courchene, T. J. and G. M. Youssef (1967), 'The demand for international reserves', *Journal of Political Economy* (August).

Duck, N., J. M. Parkin, D. Rose and G. Zis (1976), 'The determination of the rate of change of wages and prices in the fixed exchange rate world economy: 1956-71' in M. Parkin and G. Zis (eds.), *Inflation in the World Economy* (Manchester University Press).

Flanders, M. J. (1971), 'The demand for international reserves', *Princeton Studies in International Finance*, No. 27.

Gray, M. R., R. Ward and G. Zis, (1976) 'World demand for money, in M. Parkin and G. Zis (eds.), *op. cit.*

Kelly, M. G. (1970), 'The demand for international reserves', *American Economic Review* 60 (4) (September).

Kenen, P. B. and E. Yudin (1865), 'The demand for international reserves' *Review of Economics and Statistics*. Reprinted in Kenen, P. B. and L. Lawrence (eds.), *The Open Economy,* New York, Columbia University Press, 1968).

Nordhaus W. D. (1970). 'The world-wide wage explosion', *Brookings Papers* (2), pp. 431-463.

Parkin, J. M. (1974), 'United Kingdom inflation: the policy alternatives,' *National Westminster Bank Quarterly Review* (May), pp. 32-47.

Parkin J. M., I. M. Richards and G. Zis (1975), 'The determination and control of the world money supply under fixed exchange rates 1961-1971', *Manchester School* (September), reprinted as Chapter 2.

Williamson, J. H., (1973) 'International liquidity', *Economic Journal* 83 (331), (September), pp. 685-746.

Ward, R. and G. Zis (1974), 'Trade union militancy as an explanation of inflation. An international comparison', *Manchester School,* (42)1 (March), pp. 46-65.

4 Political origins of the international monetary crisis

George Zis*

I

The purpose of this paper is to draw attention to certain political aspects of the origins and nature of the current international monetary crisis which, perhaps, are important enough to merit consideration in an analysis of the development, breakdown and proposals for the reform of the IMF system.[1] It will be argued that the IMF system ceased to be viable once the balance of economic and political forces prevailing at the time of its creation in 1944 was disturbed. The development of the IMF system between the date of its inception and 1971 will be discussed as being the outcome of changing politico-economic relations among the economies of the non-communist world. The viability of the current proposals for reform will be considered in terms of their consistency with the web of political relations for which they aim at providing a basis.

The paper is organised as follows: Section II sets out the requirements for a smoothly functioning international monetary system of fixed exchange rates. Section III discusses the means by which the IMF sought to fulfil these requirements and evaluates its performance. Section IV outlines the features of the future reformed monetary system upon which international agreement has been reached. Finally, Section V presents some tentative conclusions.

II

A multilateral payments system is a necessary prerequisite if the world economy as a whole and its separate components individually

* I am grateful to D. J. Coppock, D. Laidler, M. Parkin and M. Sumner for very helpful comments on an earlier draft. However, they do not necessarily share the views expressed in this paper, and responsibility for any errors is my own. An abbreviated version appeared under the same title in the *National Westminster Bank Review* (August 1975).

are to derive all the advantages of the specialisation of production permitted by international trade. There must exist a set of internationally agreed arrangements which permit countries to settle their transactions on a multilateral basis. The function of the international monetary system is to provide such a set of arrangements.

It is widely accepted that stability of exchange rates provides a firm foundation for the expansion of international trade. This raises the question of how best this stability can be achieved. To answer this question one needs to examine how exchange rates are determined in the absence of government intervention. In the course of trade transactions importers in, say, Britain offer sterling in exchange for the currency of the country from which they wish to import goods. On the other hand, foreign importers of British goods will offer their domestic currencies in exchange for sterling with which to pay British producers. The demand for and supply of sterling will thus determine the price, i.e. the exchange rate, of sterling in terms of all other currencies. Exchange rate stability acts as an incentive to international trade by promoting certainty with respect to the payments that traders will have to make and receive in their domestic currencies. But what are the necessary conditions for an exchange rate determined by private demand and supply to be stable? Assume that the monetary authorities of, say, Britain increase the rate of growth of the money supply. Economic agents in Britain will then find themselves holding money balances in excess of their desired level. They will, therefore, attempt to eliminate their excess money balances; one way they can do so is through the balance of payments, i.e. they will attempt to exchange part of their excess money balances for goods produced abroad. This will increase the supply of sterling and there is no reason to suppose that the demand for sterling will correspondingly rise in the foreign exchange market. As a result of the increase in the supply of sterling, its international price in terms of all other currencies will begin to fall; that is sterling will depreciate. Now, importers who had concluded contracts prior to the devaluation will have to make payments in terms of sterling larger than would have been the case if the exchange rate had remained unchanged. Uncertainty over exchange rates will therefore act as a retarding factor to the expansion of international trade.[2] One way by which central authorities could remove uncertainty, at least partially, would be to pursue such monetary policies as to promote exchange rate stability. Differences in rates of productivity growth would then be the main source for gradual, small and largely predictable changes in the international value of currencies. However, the degree of monetary co-ordination among central authorities required for the stability of exchange rates determined solely by private demand

and supply of currencies is such as to make such a system an option of no relevance for policy-makers.

If exchange rate stability cannot be achieved through the co-ordination of monetary policies among countries, the only remaining alternative means for achieving it is through the active intervention of central monetary authorities in foreign exchange markets. Monetary authorities purchase/sell their respective currencies as excess supply/demand for them emerges and thus maintain the exchange rate at some predetermined level. A system of fixed exchange rates as a means of achieving stable exchange rates derives its main advantages from the proposition that it is conducive to the expansion of international trade.

For a system of fixed exchange rates to operate smoothly, certain requirements must be met. Firstly, there must exist a money which is internationally acceptable. Central authorities will use this internationally acceptable money to offset any private excess demand/supply of their respective currencies in the foreign exchange market. Furthermore, the system must provide for the adequate growth of the stock of international liquidity, as monetary authorities can be expected to desire a larger volume of foreign exchange reserves as the volume of international trade expands. Secondly, there must exist provisions ensuring a speedy adjustment, i.e. that deficits/surpluses in the balance of payments are rapidly eliminated. Thirdly, confidence in the international value of the major currencies must be promoted.

These three requirements for a smoothly operating fixed exchange rate are closely interrelated. Abundance of international liquidity will act as a disincentive to monetary authorities to initiate such policies as are required for a speedy elimination of balance of payments disequilibria. On the other hand, a shortage of international liquidity will force countries to take immediate corrective steps. If, alternatively, a major country suffers from a persistent balance of payments disequilibrium, confidence in the international value of its currency will be undermined with repercussions spreading throughout the international monetary system.

In summary, then, economic theory suggests there are benefits to be derived from a system of multilateral trade; stability of exchange rates provides the basis for these benefits to be enjoyed; stability can be achieved through a system of fixed exchange rates; a smoothly operating system of fixed exchange rates must provide for the adequate growth of international liquidity, a speedy mechanism of adjustment, and must promote confidence in the international prices of the major currencies. Persistently diverging monetary policies lead to cumulative balance of payments disequilibria; thus, a viable system of fixed exchange rates requires that countries pursue similar rates of monetary expansion.

III

World War II accelerated developments which had their origins in
the 1920s. More specifically, the relative economic decline of the
UK and the emergence of the USA as the dominant power in the
world both gathered momentum. Simultaneously, under the impact
of war, nationalistic tendencies in the USA began to wane while the
UK made the first steps towards accepting the realities of a world
in which British power ceased to reign supreme. The uncertainty
of the inter-war years was gradually being replaced with a quiet
determination to construct a new international order characterised
by co-operation rather than conflict among countries. The isolationist features of the 1930s were giving way to the ideal of multilateralism.

Recognition of the need for international co-operation stemmed from countries' determination to prevent the emergence of
internal economic conditions reminiscent of those of the 1930s.
Governments, and particularly that of the UK pledged themselves to
attach high, if not top, priority to the objective of full employment.
The inter-war years had painfully demonstrated the interaction of
policies aimed at internal and external economic objectives and the
futility of countries' attempts to case their domestic problems
by exporting them. However, though multilateralism was generally
accepted as the goal towards which countries should work, there
was an implicit divergence of views regarding the relative priority
to be attached to the objectives of price stability and full employment.

These were the general principles guiding the participants of
the Bretton Woods conference in 1944 which set up the International
Monetary Fund.[3] Membership of the IMF carried the obligation for
countries to define the price of their currency in terms of gold and
the commitment to maintain a 1 per cent margin on either side of the
declared parity. Adjustment was to be facilitated by permitting
countries to devalue/revalue their currency if confronted by a
'fundamental disequilibrium' in their balance of payments. What
exactly is meant by 'fundamental disequilibrium' has never been
clarified. Since, however, the consent of the IMF was required
before a country could alter its exchange rate, the implication was
that the IMF would play a decisive role in assessing a country's
need to change its parity as a remedy for balance of payments
disequilibrium. Further, in order to promote effective adjustment,
the IMF could declare a currency 'scarce'. In such an event,
countries would be permitted to discriminate against trade with the
country whose currency was declared scarce.

Regarding the liquidity problem, the IMF was to make international credit facilities available to the member countries, and
thus a quota was decided for each. Member countries usually sub-

scribed 25 per cent of their quota in gold and the rest in their own currency. Member countries could purchase currencies from the IMF in exchange for their own currency, the limit being determined by the country's quota and the level of the IMF's holdings of the currency of the country. However, member countries were not granted unrestricted access to IMF facilities. They could automatically borrow only an amount equal to their gold subscription. If they wished to borrow more they had to secure the approval of the IMF Executive Board. For most countries the upper limit of drawings was reached when the IMF's holdings of the currency reached 200 per cent of the country's quota.

IMF Drawing Rights were seen as a supplement to national gold holdings. Increases in international liquidity were to be ensured through increases in member countries' quotas and through the production of new gold. Further, the IMF rules allowed for an increase in the official price of gold, if that was thought desirable, which would be equivalent to an increase in the world stock of international liquidity.

Finally, under IMF rules countries had the right to determine whether controls on short-term capital movements would provide an effective means for maintaining or restoring confidence in the international value of their currency.

It is evident, therefore, that adherence to the rules and regulations incorporated in the IMF system could have been expected to promote a smoothly functioning system of essentially fixed exchange rates. However, throughout the 1960s international monetary crises cast doubts on the viability of the IMF system, and its breakdown in August 1971 came as no surprise. If one were to consider the post-1945 history of international monetary arrangements, would the conclusion follow that fixed exchange rates failed, or would one be led to seek the causes of the international monetary crises in the specific features of the IMF system? For that question to be answered it is necessary to consider in more detail firstly the functions which the IMF was meant to serve and secondly its actual performance in the light of developments that could not be allowed for at the time of its creation.

The specific features of the IMF system reflected a compromise between the alternative plans for post-war international monetary arrangements presented by the UK and the USA during the negotiations leading to the Bretton Woods conference.[4] The other major countries were either incapable of contributing significantly towards the creation of a new international monetary order—e.g. France—or their participation in the negotiations could not be sought—e.g. Germany, Italy and Japan; while the Soviet Union was highly suspicious of any plans that could indirectly lead to its relative position being weakened *vis-a-vis* the capitalist world. Thus it was inevitable that the burden of devising a new inter-

national monetary system would fall on the UK and the USA. Both
countries rejected flexible exchange rates as inimical to the goal
of promoting international trade. However, their views diverged
with respect to the degree of rigidity that was required. That provisions were made allowing countries to devalue/revalue represented a concession to the British position. The UK, having pledged
itself to attaching top priority to the objective of full employment,
was not prepared to undertake commitments which could lead to a
repetition of the post-1925 experience, when in order to maintain
a disequilibrium exchange rate the UK had to suffer high levels of
enemployment. On the other hand the USA favoured a large measure
of rigidity in order to impose a discipline on countries' policies,
the lack of which, combined with the willingness to alter exchange
rates, was diagnosed as the cause of the disintegration of the international economy during the 1930s. The formula which was finally
agreed, i.e. that 'fundamental disequilibrium' in a country's balance
of payments would justify a change in its exchange rate, was ambiguous enough to permit both countries to avoid any explicit international commitment which would be opposed by the legislative
bodies of the two countries. It could almost be argued that the
Bretton Woods negotiators hoped that time would solve the problems arising from the ambiguity of the provisions for exchange
rate changes.

The UK had no doubts regarding the magnitude of aid that the
USA had to extend if post-war reconstruction was to be speedily
effected. It therefore pressed for a large volume of international
liquidity to be made unconditionally available through the IMF which
would permit countries to run (sustained?) deficits with the USA.
The USA, still under the influence of an isolationist mentality—this
being particularly the case with a large number of members of
Congress—was reluctant to agree to providing funds over the
expenditure of which the USA would have little or no control.
Aware of the strength of its economy, the USA pressed for the commitment that barriers to international trade be rapidly dismantled
after the war, special opposition being voiced to the system of
Imperial Preference. The compromise reached was closer to the
USA than to the UK position. The IMF began its operations with a
volume of financial resources which could hardly be described
as adequate. Furthermore, countries were not to enjoy an unconditional access to the IMF resources. Instead, they would have to
submit their policies to IMF scrutiny before they could use the
Drawing Rights allocated to them. On the other hand, the inclusion
of the 'Scarce currency' clause was seen as going a long way towards meeting British demands for safeguards against the sacri-
fice of the objective of full employment under balance of payments
difficulties. The UK was particularly concerned with the possibility
that there would be a shortage of dollars which could force coun-

tries to accept higher levels of unemployment unless they could
either alter their exchange rate or have the right to impose restrictions on imports from the USA. These fears were accentuated when it became evident that the USA would not agree to the
IMF being launched with resources near to what Britain was suggesting. Thus, there was the fear that the IMF would run short of
its dollar holdings, which would induce deflationary policies in
the rest of the world. The 'scarce currency' clause was seen as
a device potentially capable of easing the adjustment problems
that would emerge in the eventuality of a dollar shortage.

The specific features of the IMF system, then, primarily reflected a compromise between the views of the USA and the UK,
and, neither surprisingly nor unexpectedly, both countries sought
the creation of an international monetary system which would best
suit the promotion of their internal economic objectives. In agreeing on a voting system in the IMF which related a country's voting
strength to the size of its quota, both countries secured for themselves a decisive voice in determining the subsequent evolution of
the system. That the principle of one-country-one-vote was not
adopted may well reflect the reluctance of the UK and the USA to
abdicate powers of economic policy-making to an international
institution in which a consensus of opinion among member countries
would be difficult to achieve.

Developments following the end of the war assumed a nature
that was not envisaged by the architects of the IMF system. The
rapid deterioration in the relations between the western countries
on the one hand and the Soviet Union on the other provoked the USA
into making available resources for the reconstruction of European
economies to an amount that could hardly have been anticipated at
Bretton Woods. Marshall Aid, US foreign investment, and military
aid went a long way towards ensuring that the dollar shortage did
not emerge. The structure of exchange rates agreed upon in
1948-9 eased any fears that countries would be unable to sustain their
trade deficits with the US and would as a consequence be forced
to adopt deflationary policies. Fears that unemployment and a
massive US balance of payments surplus would be the main
features of the post-war international economy proved without
foundation. Uncertainties stemming from the Cold War led to a
degree of solidarity and co-operation among the western countries
which obscured their diverging views on international monetary
problems. The supremacy of the USA effectively resulted in the
other countries pursuing passive policies, thus allowing the USA to
determine developments in the international economy. With the
USA assuming the role of economic leader, the IMF was relegated
to relative inactivity.

One of the major functions of the IMF was to provide additional
international liquidity to meet the increases in countries' demand

Table 4.1 Volume and composition of world monetary reserves

Year (end)	Gold *a*		Foreign exchange		Reserve position in IMF		SDRs		Total reserves	
	$ billion	%	$ billion	%	$ billion	%	$ billion	%	$ billion	%
1951	33·9	68.8	13·7	27·8	1·7	3·4	—	—	49·3	100·0
1956	36·1	64·2	17·8	31·7	2·3	4·1	—	—	56·2	100·0
1961	38·9	62·0	19·6	31·3	4·2	6·7	—	—	62·7	100·0
1965	41·9	59·3	23·3	33·0	5.4	7·7	—	—	70·6	100·0
1969	39·1	50·1	32·3	41·4	6·7	8·5	—	—	78·1	100·0
1970	37·2	40·2	44·4	48·2	7·7	8·3	3·1	3·3	92·5	100·0
1971	39·2	30·1	77·9	59·7	6·9	5·3	6.4	4·9	130·3	100·0
1972	38·8	24·5	103·0	65·1	6·9	4·4	9·4	6·0	158·0	100·0
1973	43·1	23·7	120·6	66·4	7·4	4·1	10·6	5·8	181·8	100·0
1974	43·7	20·0	152·5	70·0	10·8	5·0	10·8	5·0	217·9	100·0

Note

a Gold valued at $35 an ounce until December 1971, $38 between 1971 and January 1973, and thereafter at $42·22.

Source: IMF, *International Financial Statistics.*

for a larger volume of reserves as trade expanded. The performance of the IMF in this respect could hardly be considered as
impressive. Further, expectations that world liquidity would
increase through the acquisition of newly mined gold at a rate
compatible with the growing needs of an expanding world economy
proved too optimistic. The gap thus created was filled by the
emergence of the dollar as an international money. USA deficits
became the main source of additional liquidity. Table 4.1 presents
data on the volume and composition of world monetary reserves for
the period 1951 to 1974. During this period world aggregate
reserves increased by $168.6 billion, of which $138.8 billion was
due to the increase in the foreign exchange component, i.e. mainly
dollar balances, of the stock of international liquidity. The IMF's
contribution was negligible, Reserve Positions in the IMF consti-
tuting at the end of 1974 only 5 per cent of the world stock of international liquidity. If we now turn to gold, increases in countries'
gold holdings between 1951 and 1961 amounted to approximately 40
per cent of the total increase in the volume of world reserves. If
this contribution cannot be considered as adequate, developments
since 1961 provide striking evidence of the failure of the IMF
system to fulfil the liquidity requirement of a smoothly operating
system of fixed exchange rates. By 1974 foreign exchange holdings which the creators of the IMF system had hoped would play
only a subsidiary role had grown to constitute 70 per cent of the
world stock of international liquidity.

The emergence of the dollar as a key currency was not the
outcome of some international decision. It simply reflected a
desire to economise on the use of gold. In earlier periods sterling
had emerged as a reserve currency, permitting countries to economise on the use of gold. In the post-1945 world the supremacy of
the USA economy made the dollar the obvious choice as a substitute
for gold which countries were willing to use and accept in settling
their transactions. Confidence in the dollar was based not only in
the strength of the American economy but also on the fact that USA
holdings of gold were so large that countries enjoyed a high degree
of certainty that they could convert any excess dollar balances
they might accumulate into gold at will. Sterling's acceptability as
an international currency rapidly diminished as the UK economy
exhibited signs of increasing weaknesses. The financial expertise
of the City combined with the links between Britain and its former
colonies, however, allowed the UK to slow down the decline of
sterling as a key currency, which, though it eased the UK's difficulties, did not contribute to the stability of the international monetary system.

America's hegemony was not resented so long as there existed
almost a coincidence of interests among the western economies,
whether on economic or political issues. The USA prime objective

was to contain the frontiers of the socialist camp. The enunciation
of the Truman Doctrine in 1948 gave expression to America's
intentions to use its military strength in pursuit of its objective of
preventing any further extensions in the Soviet sphere of influence.
Recognition, however, that military strength was not sufficient to
neutralise internal social tensions in the European countries resulted in the USA eagerly extending aid aimed at the rapid reconstruction of their economies. On their side European countries
gratefully accepted this aid and in return had no hesitation in
paying the price in terms of support for USA international policies.
The relative inactivity of the IMF was not considered as a particularly serious issue. That the main manifestation of this inactivity
was reflected in the failure of the IMF to provide additional international liquidity in line with the expansion of international trade
was not viewed with alarm. That this failure of the IMF was a
major contributory cause of the emergence of the dollar as a key
currency was not recognised as a development endangering the
stability of the international monetary system. The world as a
whole willingly accumulated dollar balances, individual countries
gradually building up their holdings of exchange reserves to their
desired levels.

Would the dollar have emerged as a reserve currency even if
the IMF had provided additional liquidity in line with the expansion
of international trade? Would the international monetary system
set up at Bretton Woods have proved to be more durable had the
dollar not emerged as a key currency? There is no way that a
firm answer could be given to these questions. What, however, can
be said is that, given USA attitudes immediately after the World
War II, the IMF system could not have developed in the way envisaged by its creators. It was a condition imposed by America that
countries receiving USA aid through the European Recovery Programme could not use the IMF facilities.[5] Thus the volume of IMF
transactions, which had totalled $606 million in the financial year
1947-8, fell in the three subsequent years to $119 million, $52
million and $28 million (IMF, 1969). The implication of the USA
imposing its will on the IMF not only caused international friction
but also, and more importantly, signalled USA intentions not to allow
the IMF to develop as an international institution whose policies
would be determined on the basis of international rather than
national USA considerations.

As the transitional period of post-war reconstruction came to
an end in the mid-1950s, the dependence of European economies on
the USA ceased to be as pressing as in the immediate post-war
years. West Germany was accepted as an important member of the
western alliance; on this occasion the burden of reparation payments
was not imposed on her. Thus, defeat did not arouse the domestic
social tensions that it did in the inter-war years. On the contrary,

West Germany was the recipient of substantial USA aid allowing it to enjoy the benefits of an 'economic miracle'. Italy and Japan also became integral parts of the western world, while France's economic performance was successful enough to allow it to survice successive governmental crises during the 1950s; its social system was never in real danger. Countries had successfully prevented the emergence of unemployment. This was achieved in a largely non-inflationary environment, cautious USA monetary policies being responsible for world price stability. In 1958 *de facto* convertibility of the major currencies was established, while the world experienced the benefits of substantial rates of growth in international trade. Indeed, the integrating effects of the economic recovery and of the common policies towards the Socialist camp had proceeded at a rate so fast that the intention of the major European countries to work towards a customs union with the ultimate aim of achieving economic unification, reflected in the creation of the EEC in 1958, was hardly interpreted as an attempt to achieve the impossible. The revival of the western economies, combined with the expectation that prosperity could now be ensured through the mobilisation of resources domestically generated, resulted in individual countries questioning the desirability of the international arrangements that had emerged during the period of heavy reliance on USA aid. The international monetary system was gradually becoming one of the fields in which USA supremacy was being challenged.

As early as 1959, Triffin (1960) argued that the IMF system was inherently unstable. The source of instability was to be found in the co-existence of gold and of the national currency, the dollar, as the main components of international liquidity, combined with the differences in the rates of growth of the two components. As already mentioned, USA deficits had become the main source of increases in international liquidity, but the increases in the dollar component of international liquidity combined with the inadequate increases in gold production resulted in the ratio of USA liabilities to gold holdings steadily deteriorating. Given that a major cause of the emergence of the dollar as a key currency was the large gold holdings of the USA, it followed logically that as this ratio increased the acceptability of the dollar as a reserve currency would be correspondingly reduced leading to a crisis of confidence in the dollar. In other words, the deteriorating reserve position of the USA would gradually generate the expectation that America would be unable to maintain the dollar price of gold. Once such expectations were generated, then countries not only would become increasingly unwilling to accumulate further dollar balances but would also be encouraged to convert existing dollar balances into gold in anticipation of the gains that would accrue to them following a devaluation of the dollar in terms of gold. The gloomy impli-

cations of Triffin's prognostications did not receive the attention
they deserved from the policy-makers.

Confidence in the ability of the USA to maintain the dollar
price of gold at a level which had been fixed as early as 1934 could
not have been sustained for reasons independent of the deteriorating
reserve position of America. The world economy experienced significant rates of growth during the post-1945 period. As one would
expect, this growth led to an increase in private demand for gold.
This increase was reinforced by the fact that with its price fixed
while the prices of other substitute commodities were rising, gold
became relatively cheaper as an industrial input. However, on the
supply side, fixity of price combined with the change in the relative
price of gold in terms of other metals implied that the production
of gold became less profitable. The combination of these developments led to the emergence of private excess demand for gold,
which in turn resulted in the expectation that the central monetary
authorities of the world would sooner or later be forced to raise
the price of gold. The generation of such expectations acted as a
further stimulant to private demand for gold.

In brief, then, the deterioration in the reserve position of the
USA generated expectations of a dollar devaluation in terms of
gold. Furthermore, the emergence of private excess demand for
gold generated expectations that the price of gold would be raised
in terms of all currencies. Criticism of the performance of the
IMF is based not on what it actually did but on what it allowed to
happen by failing or provide for the liquidity needs of an expanding
world economy, i.e. the emergence of the dollar as a key currency
with USA deficits being the main source of additions to international
liquidity.

The governments of the major countries were slow to appreciate that the IMF system as it had actually evolved, based on the co-
existance of gold and dollars as the main international assets, was
in need of urgent and radical reform. Instead, the first expressions
of dissatisfaction stemmed from the advantages accruing to the
USA through its currency being used as an international asset. The
USA was free to pursue its domestic objectives without being constrained by balance of payments considerations. Deficits did not
put pressure on the American authorities to initiate deflationary
policies aimed at the elimination of the balance of payments disequilibrium. In contrast to the USA, countries whose currencies
were not reserve currencies could not sustain balance of payments
deficits for any lengthy period. Given the commitment to fixed
exchange rates, national authorities usually responded to balance of
payments deficits by initiating deflationary measures. In doing so
they had to accept a higher level of unemployment. The asymmetry
introduced into the system by the emergence of the dollar as a key
currency was a source of resentment, first voiced in the beginning

of the 1960s. France was prominent in demanding that USA deficits be reduced and the dollar be stripped of its international role. Indicative of the French views is the following passage from the present President of France, V. Giscard d'Estaing (1969):

> 'For instance, compare the United States and Italy in 1963 and 1964. The deficits of the U.S. started much before the Italian deficits. Italy had to adopt a very hard and very exacting internal economic policy which made its employment, its growth and its foreign trade suffer, all because it had to return to equilibrium within strict time limits. And Italy did return to equilibrium. Yet in the same time period, the corrective mechanism for the reserve currency countries did not work as hard, if at all. It is a one-sided system: the non-reserve currency countries acquire the currencies of others, but not vice versa. And it is an unstable system; past a certain limit there is a feeling of uncertainty concerning its development in the future.'

This 'certain limit' was in effect passed in the second half of the 1960s. In the first part of the last decade the major countries exhibited increasing tendencies to pursue divergent monetary policies. The original EEC countries, and especially West Germany and the Netherlands, in pursuit of their objective of price stability exercised cautious control over the rates of growth of their money supply. The UK, on the other hand, by attaching top priority to the maintenance of full employment while successive governments attempted to win popularity by keeping interest rates low, abandoned control of its money supply, allowing it to grow at whatever rate would ensure low unemployment and low interest rates. In the USA the Kennedy administration decided to lower the level of unemployment, and to achieve this objective it reduced taxes. At the same time the cautious monetary policies of the Eisenhower administrations were quietly abandoned. The divergent monetary policies did not lead to countries having significantly different rates of inflation. That this did not happen was a direct consequence of the fixity of exchange rates. Fixed exchange rates link countries in a way analogous to that in which regions within an economy are linked through the use of a common currency. Instead, divergent monetary policies led to increasing balance of payments disequilibria. Those countries with cautious monetary policies experienced rates of inflation marginally below the world rate and balance of payments surpluses, while countries with relatively expansionary monetary policies endured rates of price increases slightly above the world average, and suffered reserve losses because of balance of payments deficits. Under such circumstances anticipations gradually built up that the prevailing set of exchange rates could not and would not be maintained, and speculative flows of short-term capital began to emerge in the expectation of exchange rate changes. Sterling was the main target of speculators. Coinciding with the growing uncertainty regarding the viability of the IMF system, additional pressures were generated through the attempt of France to assert its independence *vis-a-vis* the USA. This attempt assumed several forms, for example France's decision to leave NATO, to forge links with the Soviet Union independently of its allies, and to proceed with developing its own nuclear power. In the monetary field, France's opposition to the USA assumed the form of converting its dollar balances into gold and pressing for an increase in its price. Progress within the EEC meant that the other member countries took positions on international monetary questions such that France would not be unduly antagonised and as a result place furhter progress towards European economic integration in jeopardy. These developments were themselves a source of uncertainty regarding the future of the international monetary system.

Ad hoc measures taken during the first part of the 1960s were sufficient to contain the speculative pressures that were gradually building up. However, after 1965 these pressures rapidly intensified so that no improvisation could avoid the emergence of an international monetary crisis. Thus after 1965, as a result of private excess demand for gold, central monetary authorities, in their effort to maintain its price, turned from being net buyers to being net sellers of gold. Further and more significantly, the decision of the Johnson administration to finance the escalation of the Vietnam war, and the implementation of domestic social programmes by increasing the money supply rather than by raising taxes, led to an increase in the world money supply and consequently in the world rate of inflation, from which the other major countries could not significantly deviate. The deterioration of the USA balance of payments following its expansionary monetary policies, combined with the acceleration of the world rate of inflation, turned the expectation of a devaluation of the dollar into a conviction that the major countries' central authorities would be forced to increase the price of gold. Speculation reached new heights. In November 1967 the UK devalued sterling; in March 1968 the major countries announced their decision to cease intervening in the private gold market with the aim of maintaining the price of gold at $35 per ounce. Thus the price of gold in the private market was to be freely determined by demand and supply, while for official transactions it would continue to be $35 per ounce. The decision to free the private market for gold provided striking evidence of the divergent views and interests between the USA on the one hand and the rest of the world on the other. The simple laws of demand and supply required that the price of gold be raised; USA governments strongly opposed such a rise. Their opposition allegedly rested on the argument that the

Soviet Union and South Africa would be the main beneficiaries if the price of gold was increased. More convincingly, however, it has been argued that, the dollar price of gold having been elevated to the status of a sacred cow domestically and to a symbol of USA supremacy abroad, no government dared risk the unpopularity that a rise in it would entail. Further, the USA, by opposing an increase in the price of gold, was simply expressing its determination to prevent any gains accruing to countries like France which played an important role in the undermining of confidence in the dollar by converting their dollar balances into gold. The irrelevance of the 1968 gold agreement for the international monetary problems was a manifestation that neither Europe collectively nor the USA were sufficiently strong to impose a solution.

Failure to acknowledge the main weaknesses of the IMF system was also evident during the discussions which led to the decision in 1967 to create a new international asset, the Special Drawing Right. These discussions centred on the question whether or not there was a liquidity shortage. This question is as meaningless as the question of whether or not there is a shortage of money at any point in time in an economy, given the prevailing price level. The real problems facing the international monetary system in the mid-1960s stemmed from the coexistence of two international assets, gold and the dollar, which in turn allowed the USA to determine the world rate of inflation through its monetary policies. The creation of yet another international asset could hardly be expected to contribute towards a solution of the composition problem of international liquidity. If anything, it would complicate the problem further by enlarging the number of available assets between which countries could switch on the basis of differences in the rates of growth of each and thus cause crises of confidence. That the composition problem was being avoided became evident when the SDR scheme was activated in January 1970. The IMF explained that, in deciding the volume of SDRs to be created for the period 1970-2, it had estimated the global needs for additional liquidity during this three-year period. It had then estimated the likely increases in world reserves that would result from USA deficits. The difference between the world 'needs' and the increase in dollar balances was to be made up by SDRs. Thus, despite the creation of a new asset, the international monetary system would still be incapable of providing for orderly increases in international liquidity, since the right of the USA to pursue whatever monetary policies it chose, and thereby largely determine the rate of growth of world reserves, remained unrestricted.

The indecision characterising the deliberations of the major countries in the second half of the 1960s was the outcome of rapidly changing relations among them. The Cold War had ceased to be the inspiration of the western alliance; the USA was involved in a costly war, its allies not only refusing to share the burdens but publicly voicing their opposition. Under these circumstances, it is hardly surprising that the USA extracted resources from the rest of the world through its balance of payments deficits induced by expansionary monetary policies. The further advantage of pursuing such policies was that domestic opposition in the USA to the Vietnam war was confined to a level lower than would have been the case had the war been financed through increased taxation. At the same time the European countries began to face the social consequences of inflation, an inflation that was largely the result of USA policies. Inevitably they became increasingly determined to insulate their economies from external inflationary impulses, rapid progress towards European economic unification being seen as providing the best route to independence. However, there was the sub-set of problems to be faced during the transition period which demonstrated that even among the EEC countries there did not exist an underlying consensus of opinion. The UK, having failed to maintain an international role by replacing the Empire by the Commonwealth, now actively sought EEC membership as a base from which it could exercise influence. All western countries, furthermore, had to adjust to the emergence of Japan as a major economic power and of the bloc of the developing countries which, through sheer numbers, were now determined to assert their interests. Aid to the less developed countries was gradually being accepted as a problem in the reform of the international monetary system. International relations being in a state of turmoil, it is not surprising that no lasting solutions to the problems of the international monetary system could be reached.

Agreement on the SDR scheme, the decision on gold, the devaluation of sterling and the 1968 Basle Agreement providing a guarantee for the gold value of sterling balances, were not sufficient to restore confidence in the IMF system. France's devaluation in 1969 can hardly be justified in terms of its balance of payments position and acted as a signal that countries' commitments to fixed exchange rates were becoming less firm. The same interpretation can be placed on Germany's decision to revalue in 1969 under the pressure of heavy inflows of short-term capital. Speculative pressures intensified. Finally, in August 1971, accelerating inflation, deteriorating balance of payments deficits and a total collapse of confidence in the dollar forced Nixon to announce that the USA was suspending the dollar convertibility into gold. This decision marked the end of the Bretton Woods era and the acceptance by the USA of the fact that it could no longer unilaterally determine developments in the international monetary system.

IV

The crisis that followed the USA decision was 'resolved' in December 1971 when the major industrial countries announced a new set of exchange rates, the USA agreeing to a rise in the dollar price of gold from $35 to $38 per ounce. Further, the IMF announced that member countries' currencies would be allowed to fluctuate within margins of 2·25 per cent instead of 1 per cent on either side of the newly-agreed parities.

In view of what preceded the USA decision to abandon dollar convertibility, it is hardly surprising that the new set of exchange rates and the introduction of increased flexibility failed to restore confidence in the IMF system. The problems arising from the composition of the world liquidity, from the differences in the rates of growth of its different components, from the asymmetry between the dollar and the non-reserve currencies, from world price inflation and from diverging monetary policies, had assumed such complexity that the decisions reached in December 1971 were rendered irrelevant. This irrelevance is epitomised by the decision on the price of gold. The dollar price of gold was fixed in 1934. In the ensuing years, and especially since the mid-1960s, the price of all commodities had increased by varying rates, but none by as little as 8 per cent, which was the agreed rise in the price of gold. Indeed, the price of gold actually fell in terms of the German and Japanese currencies, which were revalued by an amount larger than the 8 per cent devaluation of the dollar. However, policy-makers can be defended against charges of irresponsibility arising from such gross violations of basic economic laws by arguing that, by the end of 1971, such was the balance of power among the western economies and such were the domestic problems of the major countries, that it was not practical to proceed with immediate radical reform. It is to their credit that in December 1971 they demonstrated that, though they could not agree on the reform of the international monetary system, they were determined to commit themselves to that degree of co-operation that would ensure the continuation of multilateralism and would prevent the chaos which characterised the bilateralism of the 1930s.

The inadequacy of the new set of exchange rates in promoting confidence was revealed when, as early as June 1972, the UK authorities announced that they would allow sterling to float. Seven months later, following the announcement of USA balance of payments figures for 1972, foreign exchange markets throughout the world were thrown into turmoil, speculation against the dollar assuming unprecedented dimensions. A further devaluation of the dollar in terms of gold by 10 per cent was not sufficient to restore tranquility in the foreign exchange markets. In March 1973 the EEC countries decided to maintain fixed exchange rates among their currencies but not *vis-a-vis* the other world currencies. The UK and Italy did not participate in this scheme; instead they let their currencies float independently. They were later joined by France. Thus, since March 1973, the world has moved to a system of fluctuating exchange rates, central monetary authorities abstaining from systematic interventions in the foreign exchange markets.

Recognition of the urgency of the need to reform the international monetary system led to the formation in June 1972, of the Committee of Twenty, which was entrusted with responsibility for presenting a set of proposals which would form the basis for a new system. The outcome of its deliberations, *An Outline of Reform,* was presented in summer 1974. By that time the international monetary system had received a new shock in the form of the increases in the price of oil, as a result of which large balance of payments disequilibria emerged and will persist in the immediate short run, with oil producers accumulating foreign exchange reserves in unprecedented amounts. It is, therefore, not surprising that the Committee of Twenty expressed the view that 'it will be some time before a reformed system can be finally agreed and fully implemented'.

However, the views set out in the *Outline of Reform* reflect a substantial measure of agreement among countries on the broad principles to be followed in reforming the IMF system. Freely fluctuating exchange rates were opposed, especially by developing countries. It was, therefore, agreed that fixed exchange rates which can only be altered under certain circumstances and following the approval of the IMF should provide the basis of the new system. This declaration of confidence in a principle which guided also the participants of the Bretton Woods system exhibits a welcome degree of understanding that the IMF system did not collapse because of the fixity of exchange rates. However, it is recommended that countries when confronted with certain well-defined circumstances should be allowed, if they so choose, to let their currencies float for a limited period of time, IMF approval being required for this to occur. On the liquidity problem there is general agreement that the Special Drawing Rights should become the principal international asset, with the role of gold and reserve currencies being gradually reduced. With respect to the adjustment requirement of a smoothly functioning system, countries are unanimous that the burden of correcting balance of payments disequilibria must be shared by both deficit and surplus countries. It is suggested that there be international agreement on the limits between which a country's volume of international liquidity can fluctuate. If any country pursues such policies as to lead to its exchange reserves increasing above or decreasing below the internationally agreed limits, the *Outline of Reform* recommends that the country should be subjected to 'graduated pressures' until it activates measures to eliminate its surplus/deficit. Finally, the suggestion to link aid to developing countries with the method of allocating given increases in international liquidity has attracted widespread support.

There can be no strong objection to the principles of these proposals. However, disagreements emerged and are likely to persist on a number of issues. For example, there is disagreement on the precise role to be played by gold, on the definition of the circumstances in which a country would be allowed to float its currency, on the ways in which the world's 'needs' of international liquidity are to be assessed, on the nature of the 'pressures' to be applied to deficit/surplus countries, and on whether there should be well-defined rules, the violation of which would lead to automatic sanctions, or whether each disequilibrium should be treated as a special case requiring special assessment. Until these disagreements are ironed out the agreements that have been reached are of limited use. Their significance derives from the recognition that the relations which allowed the USA to enjoy certain privileges have broken down necessitating a new international monetary order that reflects the relative decline of USA. Further, there is evidence that the implications for stability of the existance of more than one international asset are better appreciated. That the major industrial countries appear to have accepted the fact that they alone cannot determine the course of world economy and that they have to share the decision-making with the developing countries is a welcome development, consistent with the broad economic aims of the participants in the Bretton Woods conference and reiterated in the *Outline of Reform*.

V

The emergence, development and breakdown of the IMF system is the history of the ascent to, assertion of, and decline from economic supremacy of the USA. The rise and fall of the dollar followed a course similar to that followed by sterling. There are, however, some important differences. The vacuum created by the decline of Britain was rapidly filled by the USA. Today, however, there is no country or bloc of countries that could replace the USA in the western world. Thus, the new international monetary system will have to reflect a set of international relations in which no country's will dominates. It may, therefore, be the case that in the absence of such a dominant power any international monetary system will be doubtful viability. However, a world in which countries share certain aims but do not enjoy identity of interests may provide the minimum conditions required for the emergence of a reformed

IMF as an entity independent of its members, thus providing a basis for international monetary co-operation.

The collapse of the international monetary system in 1931 was followed by economic chaos in which countries sought to ease their problems by exporting them. The collapse of the IMF system, however, has not led to the gains of multilateralism being wiped out. Indeed, countries have sought and secured a degree of monetary co-operation that has ensured that international trade continues to expand. Whether this co-operation is sufficient to maintain a new international monetary system will depend largely on the measure of success that countries enjoy in their attempt to reduce rates of inflation. Under the present system of 'dirty floating', inflation rates have diverged as a result of divergent monetary policies. No system of exchange rates could be expected to survive if countries pursued substantially different rates of monetary expansion. The domestic consequences, however, of a sudden sharp reversal of monetary policies with the aim of promoting convergence would be such as to make such a policy recommendation completely unacceptable to any government. The conclusion therefore follows that the delay 'before a reformed system can finally be agreed and fully implemented' will depend on the extent to which countries attach different priorities to the objectives of full employment and price stability, and on the variance of initial conditions.

NOTES

[1]   Johnson (1972) presents a lucid exposition of problems relating to the reform of the international monetary system.

[2]   Sometimes it is argued by advocates of flexible exchange rates that the forward exchange market provides the means by which traders can protect themselves against exchange rate changes. However, this argument is specious. Forward exchange markets can provide cover usually for a period of three months. What, however, is the burden of the case against flexible exchange rates is that trade as an economic activity would be discouraged under such a system. This argument is fully developed in Lanyi (1969).

[3]   An evaluation of the Bretton Woods conference and of the development of the institutions it established can be found in the collection of essays in Acheson *et al.* (1972).

[4]   Gardner (1969) presents a comprehensive discussion of the negotiations prior and during the Bretton Woods system as well as an evaluation of the development of UK-USA relations during the post-1945 period. This paper has benefitted from Gardner's study.

[5]   I am indebted to D. J. Coppock for pointing out this early manifestation of the USA asserting its will on the functioning of the IMF.

REFERENCES

Acheson, A. L. Keith, Chant, J. F. and Prachowny, M. F. J. (eds.) (1972), *Bretton Woods Revisited* (London, Macmillan).
Gardner, R. N. (1969), *Sterling—Dollar Diplomacy* (London, McGraw-Hill).

Giscard d'Estaing, V. (1969), The international monetary order', in R. A. Mundell and A. K. Swoboda (eds.), *Monetary Problems of the International Economy* (Chicago University Press).

IMF (1969), *The International Monetary Fund 1945-1965* (IMF, Washington, D.C.).

Johnson, H. G. (1972), 'The international monetary crisis', in *Further Essays in Monetary Economics* (London, Allen & Unwin).

Lanyi, A. (1972), 'The case for floating exchange rates reconsidered, *Essays in International Finance,* No. 72 (Princeton, N.J., Princeton University Press).

Triffin, R. (1960), *Gold and the Dollar Crisis* (Yale University Press).

5 A quarterly econometric model of world trade and prices, 1955–71

Michael Beenstock and Patrick Minford *

I INTRODUCTION

The main contribution of the research reported in this paper is an
analysis of the essentially inter-active determination of expenditure, prices and trade in an international setting. Models of real
trade flows are useful in analysing the real effects of expenditure
decisions both within the domestic and foreign sectors of the
countries or regions that are part of the 'world' as conceived for
the purposes of the model under consideration. However, for purposes of determining nominal trade flows and therefore the overall
balance of trade implications of exchange rate changes, it is necessary to construct models that determine not only trade volumes
but also the prices at which this trade is transacted. Models of
this sort are also capable of analysing the international transmission mechanism of inflation.

The capacity to predict the effects of exchange rate changes
is of particular importance at the present time when exchange
rates have undergone several major realignments within a fairly
short space of time. The need for a model of world trade and
prices under such circumstances is self-explanatory. Officials
and economists of each country have tended to calculate the effect
of parity changes without including the effects of their own parity

---

* H.M. Treasury and University of Manchester (on leave of
absence from H.M. Treasury). We would like to acknowledge the
contribution of Tony Bottrill and Jamie Mortimer when the model
was in its earlier stages of development. A special acknowledge-
ment is made to David Rampton who programmed the model and to
Honor Stamler and Michael Davenport who wrote the Almon and
ALS programmes respectively. We are grateful for research
support to H.M. Treasury and to the Hallsworth Fund, University
of Manchester. Views expressed in the paper remain our sole
responsibility (as do any errors); in particular, they do not necessarily reflect the views of H.M. Treasury.

changes on other countries, or the effects of other countries' parity changes on their own country. When only one country changes its parity this simplification may not be too important; however, when an entire spectrum of parities is altered these effects may even become paramount; and under such circumstances an inter-active model of world trade is essential in order to check the appropriateness of the exchange rate realignments.

Not surprisingly, given the enormity of the operation, the history of world trade models is scanty (for a somewhat dated review of the early developments, see Taplin (1967)). However, two recent developments warrant particular attention. The first is the work done at the OECD, where a set of export and import equations in volume terms was estimated, (Adams, Eguchi and Meyer-zu-Schlochtern (1969)). The specification of these equations on the export side included relative prices and the growth of the individual countries' markets. On the import side the specification included relative import prices and a domestic demand term. The main disadvantage of this model was that none of the equations were specified in dynamic form so that the crucial question of the nature of lagged responses in relative price and income movements remained unanswered. Also, the original OECD model did not discuss nominal trade flows because it did not contain a model of price determination in international trade. Since relative prices entered the specification this meant that the model was not particularly useful as a forecasting device, for relative prices would have to be entered exogenously.

Since then the OECD have significantly modified their original model, (Samuelson (1974)). Instead of estimating separate export equations, export volumes are derived from estimated imports by further estimating market share functions based on relative prices; this implies that the elasticity of exports to 'world trade' is assumed to be unity for every country. Export prices are assumed to grow in line with domestic prices within countries, and import prices are derived from the variable weighting function of the geographical distribution of imports. However, these two assumptions are not accepted according to our approach; while in any case this OECD study also suffers from the failure to take account of lags.

The other major development is of course Project LINK, which is essentially an attempt to link national econometric models so that the foreign trade sectors can iterate with each other. Ideally a world econometric model would have fully developed equations for domestic sectors, a feature which the OECD work does not as yet include; Project LINK clearly makes up this deficiency. The question, however, arises as to whether the linking of models based often on different specifications is meaningful, for simulations would work through one country on one basis and other countries on perhaps entirely different bases. If indeed these differences in specification were attributable to fundamental differences in economic structures as between countries there would be no problem. However, it is more likely that they reflect the different economic theories held by the authors. Also, the purely practical problems of gearing model forecasts and simulations together have shown themselves to be considerable. Thus, while the attractions of Project LINK are self-explanatory, the fruits of the project have yet to be fully realised. Nevertheless, we have attempted to find a balance between unwieldy complexity and a total absence of feedback to and from different sectors of the world economy.

The remainder of this paper is divided as follows. Section II describes the theoretical framework within which we have proceeded; Section III describes the structure of the model and estimation methods, and Section IV the data and results. In Section V we draw together the main conclusions of the study.

II THEORETICAL CONSIDERATIONS

In this study we adopt the theoretical approach set out by Hutton and Minford (1975) with certain specialisations; while they were dealing with the case of manufactured exports, we consider that, for the OECD countries, aggregate exports and imports are, at least as a first approximation, susceptible of the same treatment. Without here going into the full reasoning involved (see Hutton and Minford), we now briefly describe the framework we use. The equations are set out formally below in Section III.

We assume that products are in general differentiated within an industry, so that the industrial environment is one of monopolistic competition with free entry, as defined by Chamberlin (1932); this implies the existence of a determinate supply curve, both short- and long-run, with respect to price, for the industry as a whole. It is open to us to aggregate either over industries (ignoring borders) or over countries (ignoring industry differences within each country) or, data permitting, to work at the disaggregated level of country-industry. However, in a general study such as this, the data do not permit the disaggregated approach, while of the two aggregates our interest in country transmission processes clearly dictates aggregation over countries. Consequently, we have a differentiated 'country' product and long-run 'country' supply curve in both exportable and importable sectors of the economy. Finally, we also identify a non-traded goods sector in each country with the same industrial characteristics.

Pricing behaviour by firms is assumed to follow patterns discovered by students of the imperfectly competitive firm, such as Scherer (1970). Because of the costs associated with frequent price changes (including for example the resulting breakdown in pricing 'discipline' within the industry), firms set prices at long-run equilibrium levels and clear the market at these prices by varying stocks, queues, and output. Such behaviour could also be rationalised as the result of speculative awareness by both firms and consumers of the equilibrium price, and consequent willingness to hold stocks (postpone output) and join queues, rather than do business at the current price. It should, however, be distinguished from the normal cost pricing hypothesis in which demand factors play no role.

In the context of this approach, we report below results on price-formation that appear to divide the OECD countries of most importance into two categories, 'price-transmitters', whose export prices are predominantly determined by domestic costs, and 'price-receivers' whose export prices are essentially set by the level of competitors' prices. If this division is correct, it would appear to shed significant light on the origins of international inflation and the nature, and the direction in particular, of the transmission process. As such, it requires elaboration and rationalisation.

The distinction between 'large' and 'small' economies in the theory of international transmission is a familiar one. However, this distinction is insufficient to account for the transmitter-receiver division. We saw earlier that the weight assigned to domestic costs and competitors' prices respectively depends on the relative size of the elasticity of 'supply' and 'demand' with respect to export prices. Assuming that the underlying relationship is in each case an elasticity of substitution, we can, by a familiar formula, express ϵ as $\sigma_s (1-x/GNP)$ and η as $\sigma_d (1-x/WT)$, where x is the volume of exports, GNP is the volume of national output, WT is the volume of world trade, σ_s and σ_d being the substitution elasticities underlying respectively the supply and demand elasticities. Thus, the tendency to be a transmitter is the greater as:

1   σ_s increases, this being a measure of the flatness of the production frontier and indifference curve between exportables and other domestic goods;
2   σ_d decreases, this being a measure of the differentiation of the country's products from competitors' products;
3   the relative importance of the export sector in the domestic economy decreases;
4   the relative importance of the country's exports in world trade increases.

To the extent that as an economy becomes 'larger' it substitutes inter-trade for foreign trade, and simultaneously increases its share in world trade, both (3) and (4) would imply a positive correlation between size and transmitter tendency; and at the extreme we find, not surprisingly, that the USA is wholly a transmitter.

But it is clear that size is not the only determinant of the share of exports both in GNP and world trade, and further that σ_s and σ_d need not be the same between countries; and therefore that the distinction will not correspond to, even though it may imperfectly correlate with, size.

In the absence of data on 'importable' prices, we have been compelled to treat them differently from exportable—i.e. export—prices. We have chosen (not entirely satisfactorily) to aggregate importables with home goods and to assume that substitutability between these two categories (that is, the sum of the elasticities of substitution in production and consumption) tends to infinity, so that the price of the aggregate is the same as the price of the two categories. Thus it is the domestic wholesale price that is entered in the relative price ratio determining import volume, and import prices transmit inflation to the domestic economy (*a*) by entering into domestic costs, and (*b*) by adding to the pressure on domestic resources through the import volume equation.

In principle, we would wish to allow for periods of supply shortage in one of the ways discussed by Hutton and Minford, in particular the distinction of 'supply-dominated' from 'pure demand' periods, the former implying that deliveries are some weighted average of supply and demand factors. However, there were practical difficulties, mainly on the data side, in the way of this and consequently it is assumed that deliveries of traded goods were not limited by supply shortages at all in the estimation period. The only exception is UK exports where we use the Hutton and Minford results. Some experimentation with 'supply' periods for other countries, using industrial production as an (inadequate) proxy for domestic demand for traded goods and its trend as a proxy for capacity in tradable domestic sectors, proved unfruitful; it is therefore possible that in these other countries it was less usual for the pressure of demand to reach the over-high levels often seen in the UK in the post-war period.

Given the assumption that deliveries are demand-determined, the determinants of the demand functions are quite conventionally divided into income and price terms. On the income side, imports are related to industrial production and a trend term (or equivalently, capacity utilisation, being the ratio of industrial production to its trend) corresponding to the underlying and the cyclical elements in income variation. Exports are then recursively related to a weighted average of import volumes into other countries; the resulting 'trade-elasticity' is not constrained to unity on the grounds that while the weights should in principle allow for the differential growth between each country's markets, in practice they are probably insufficiently disaggregated to do so fully and they cannot in any case allow for differential product composition. To allow in certain cases (e.g. Japan) for the apparent effects of

growth independent of income (e.g. through rapid product improvement and innovation), trend terms were also included. Finally, the
condition that the change in world imports is exactly distributed
over exports is ensured by letting one country's exports (those of
the USA) to be determined residually.

On the price side, certain usual restrictions were imposed
with respect to the own and the cross-substitution effects. At the
individual equation level, the 'price' is the ratio of own to competing prices, implying that own and competitors' prices have the
same effect on own trade. Across equations, the restriction that
the own and cross-effects sum to zero for the change in any traded
goods price is satisfied because USA exports are determined
residually. The symmetry restriction on cross-effects was not
however imposed.

The main innovation made, as compared with the usual time-
series equation specification, is to allow for relatively long and
unrestricted lags on the price effects, as previously explored in
Hutton and Minford. The basis for these lags lies in the convolution
of order-delivery delay, information search, adjustment costs and
expectations formation (see Hutton and Minford). Given the possibility of extrapolative factors in expectations formation, it is not
possible to rule out negative terms with any certainty, though
Hutton and Minford report satisfactory results when imposing such
a restriction. We report below several lag structures which contain negative terms.

The main focus of this study is on the trade volume and price
transmission mechanisms. Without wishing to devote massive
resources to the analysis of all the economic areas identified in
this model, we wished nevertheless to 'close' the model in a clear
and plausible manner. For industrial countries, we chose to use a
simple multiplier-accelerator framework for determining real income, and an equally simple model of 'domestic' (that is, wholesale
other than exportable) prices, in which costs and demand pressure
were the reduced form determinants. Monetary factors are in
principle integrated through interest rate effects on real expenditure where interest rates are determined by the demand and
supply for money. In practice it was not possible to include these
factors to any extent because of an absence of empirical evidence
at this stage. However, given the crudity of the domestic sectors,
it is possible and necessary to impose such effects on the exogenous variables.

For less industrial countries and for the non-OECD countries
as a whole, the model was closed by assuming that exports are the
predominant factor in determining GNP. Thus, for 'other OECD',
industrial production, which is the income variable determining
imports, is a lagged function of exports only; and for non-OECD

countries, imports are directly determined in current value terms by lagged exports.

It remains to discuss the export volume and price equations of the non-OECD countries. We treat this bloc as consisting of primary producers, ignoring the industrial element contributed by such countries as Australia (now a member of OECD). According to this first approximation, we constructed a simple model of world commodity supply and demand in which it is assumed, as it is not in the manufactured goods model, that prices clear the market in each period. We suppose that on the supply side the determinants are lagged relative prices (commodities/manufactures) and unspecified trend factors. Demand is determined by relative prices and the current and lagged volume of world trade. The reduced forms that result for commodity price and volume, identified respectively with non-OECD export price and volume, are the equations estimated. Similar reduced forms were estimated for separate equations in world food and world raw material prices which were used to determine the import prices of OECD countries.

In conclusion, at this stage, it is worth emphasising the purpose and nature of this model. It is intended to provide a guide to the channels by which international pressures on an individual country's price level and level of activity are transmitted, and the broad magnitude of those pressures. The pressures may, however, be resisted by domestic policy measures and clearly therefore in simulations great care must be taken in imposing these domestic 'resistance' factors. Furthermore, the model does not attempt to analyse longer term factors, being essentially concerned with cyclical developments and mechanisms. This is apparent from the deliberate failure to identify 'trend' factors with any precision. Subject to these limitations the model may be useful in interpreting the 'conjuncture' of international developments.

III STRUCTURE AND ESTIMATION METHODS

1 Layout and interactive linking

The basic structure of the model owes much to the original OECD trade model. The essential property of this model is that import volumes are determined by relative import prices, industrial production, and trend factors; the allocation of these imports between supplier countries is then determined according to relative export prices, growth of export markets, as well as cyclical and trend variables to pick up features not totally captured by market growth. Exports then feed into domestic output and incomes, and generate further imports so that the cycle of export determination will be repeated once more.

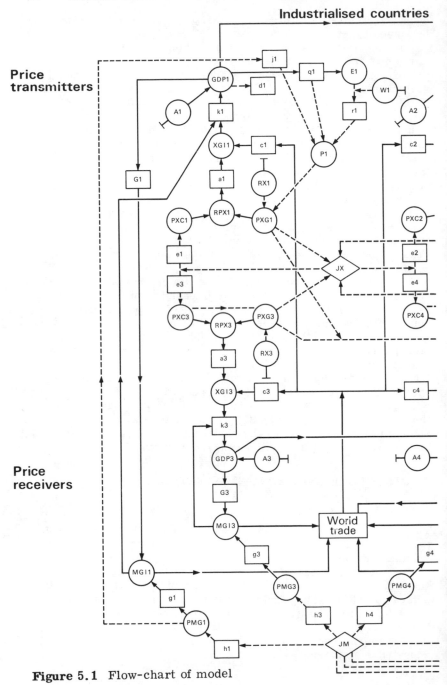

Figure 5.1 Flow-chart of model

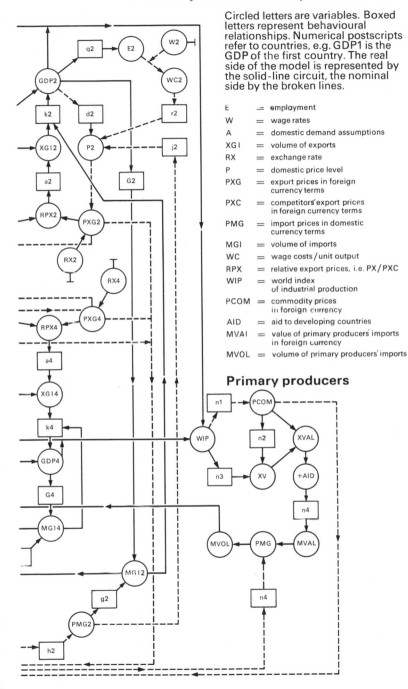

Circled letters are variables. Boxed letters represent behavioural relationships. Numerical postscripts refer to countries, e.g. GDP1 is the GDP of the first country. The real side of the model is represented by the solid-line circuit, the nominal side by the broken lines.

E   = employment
W   = wage rates
A   = domestic demand assumptions
XGI   = volume of exports
RX   = exchange rate
P   = domestic price level
PXG   = export prices in foreign currency terms
PXC   = competitors' export prices in foreign currency terms
PMG   = import prices in domestic currency terms
MGI   = volume of imports
WC   = wage costs / unit output
RPX   = relative export prices, i.e. PX/PXC
WIP   = world index of industrial production
PCOM = commodity prices in foreign currency
AID   = aid to developing countries
MVAI = value of primary producers' imports in foreign currency
MVOL = volume of primary producers' imports

Primary producers

International export prices are also determined on an inter-
active basis as discussed above in Section II. Fig. 5.1 shows
causation going from the transmitter bloc to the receiver bloc, and
it will be noticed that intra-country price transmission takes
place within the receiver bloc since all countries to a greater or
lesser extent compete with each other.

To the extent that the export prices of the receiver countries
affect the import prices of the transmitter countries, their domestic prices and therefore also their export prices, there will be a
feedback relationship between export prices. Also to the extent
that export prices affect exports and so real GDP in the transmitter bloc, there will be a further loop because domestic prices
in the transmitter countries are affected by demand pressures.
Furthermore, industrial production affects commodity prices
which enter into the import costs of the industrial countries,
making an additional loop.

This complex of interactions is summarised on the flow-
chart, Fig. 5.1; the industrialised countries are represented on the
left-hand side of the chart and the primary producers on the right-
hand side. The transmitter countries are situated on the upper
half of the industrialised countries sector and the receivers on the
lower half. To demonstrate the essential interactions of the model,
four industrialised countries are included in the chart. Real interactions are represented by solid lines and price interactions by
broken lines. Variables are circled and parameters are in boxes.
For example, as GDP in country one increases, import volumes
(MGI1) in that country increase through the relationship G1. The
chart shows these imports feeding into total world trade, which is
allocated in terms of export volumes via the relationships c2, c3,
etc. Export volumes are also affected by competitiveness via the
relationships d2, d3, etc.

Apart from the world trade 'junction box' there are two other
points of intersectoral interaction. The 'junction box' denoted by
JX relates the complex of interactions through which export prices
are determined. For example, in the transmitter countries export
prices move in line with domestic prices, as is illustrated by the
link between PXG1 and P1. Export prices in the receiver countries
are affected by PXG1, PXG2, and PXG3 via JX, but PXG3 is affected
also by PXG2. Thus the price receivers transmit export price inflation among themselves as well as receiving it from the transmitters.

The import price 'junction box', denoted by JM, determines
each country's import prices as a weighting of all other countries'
export prices. Thus inflation that is transmitted via JX by the
transmitters can rebound on these countries via JM. Those
countries that were identified as both receivers and transmitters,

e.g. Canada and the UK, are affected by import and export price inflation, i.e. via JX and J̇M.

Finally, the model is inter-active between industrial and primary producers. As output in the industrialised countries rises, both commodity prices and export values in the primary product sector are increased via WIP. Commodity price increases feed back into the system via JM and the additional foreign exchange receipts of the primary producers add to total world trade.

2 Coverage

The model covers all countries except the communist bloc, with the following groupings: Japan, Canada, USA, UK, Italy, France, West Germany, Belgium-Luxembourg, Netherlands, other OECD and all non-OECD (OECD membership as of 1963).

In more recent work (not reported here), the non-OECD sector has been considerably disaggregated, especially between oil-producing and non-oil-producing economies. In the version reported here, it is nevertheless possible to adjust the results without difficulty for events such as the oil price changes.

3 Equation specification

The equations are given in generic form; for particular countries the exact specification will differ. The notation is given at the start of Appendix 5.1 on the model detail.

Each ith country has a national income identity in real terms.

$$Y_i = C_i + IR_i + IH_i + GX_i + XGI_i + XS_i - MGI_i - MS_i$$

The consumption function depends on income and possibly real interest rates:

$$C_i = a_0 + \sum_j a_{1j} Y_{t-j} + \sum_j a_{2j} \left[\frac{RL}{\Delta PE}\right]_{t-j} + U_1$$

Investment will depend on an accelerator relationship and possibly real interest rates:

$$IR_i = b_0 + \sum_j b_{1j} \Delta Y_{t-j} + \sum_j b_{2j} \Delta \left[\frac{RL}{\Delta PE}\right]_{t-j} + U_2$$

Stock-building is usually exogenous to the model; however a typical relationship when given takes the form:

$$IH_i = c_0 + \sum_j c_{1j} \Delta Y_{t-j} + \sum_j c_{2j} \Delta \left[\frac{RL}{\Delta PE}\right]_{t-j} + U_3$$

Government expenditure is assumed to be exogenous; so also are imports and exports of services.

The import function for goods is expressed as:

$$\log MGI_i = d_0 + \sum_j d_{1j} \log IP_{t-j} + \sum_j d_{2j} \log IPT_{t-j}$$

$$+ \sum_j d_{3j} \log RPM_{t-j} + U_4$$

Exports of goods are determined as:

$$\log XGI_i = e_0 + \sum_j e_{1j} \log S_{t-j}$$

$$+ \sum_j e_{2j} \log WBC_{t-j} + \sum_j e_{3j} \log RPX_{t-j}$$

$$+ U_5$$

This completes the real side of the model.

Export prices are assumed to depend on domestic prices and competitors' prices since exportables must compete with domestic production and on foreign markets. Hence when expressed in domestic currency terms we have:

$$\left[\frac{PXG}{RX}\right]_i = f_0 + \sum_j f_{1j} P_{t-j} + \sum_j f_{2j} \left[\frac{RPX}{PXG}\right]_{t-j} + U_6$$

where RPX/PXG is competitors' export prices. Import prices are assumed to be a weighted average of trading partners' export prices and commodity prices:

$$PMG_i = g_0 + \left[\sum_k g_{1k} PXG_k + \sum_r g_{2r} PXC_r\right] RX_i + U_7$$

where the weights sum to unity. In practice because of the f.o.b.-c.i.f. methods of calculation of exports and imports respectively, a constant is specified as well as an error term. Import prices are solved for in the model so that PMG_i is not an independent equation for estimation purposes. PXC_r are commodity prices which are broken down into three categories, food prices (WPF), oil prices (WPO) and raw materials prices ($WPMA$). Because of their political nature, oil prices are considered exogenous. Food prices are given by:

$$\left[\frac{WPF}{WPM}\right]_t = h_0 + \sum_j h_{1j} \left[\frac{WPF}{WPM}\right]_{t-j} + \sum_j h_{2j} WBC_{t-j} + U_8$$

Raw materials prices are determined as:

$$\frac{WPMA}{WPM}_t = m_0 + \sum_j m_{1j} \frac{WPMA}{WPM}_{t-j}$$

$$+ \sum_j m_{2j} WBC_{t-j} + U_9$$

Domestic wholesale prices in the industrial countries are hypothesised to depend on costs and demand pressures:

$$P_i = n_0 + \sum_j n_{1j} CU_{t-j} + \sum_j n_{2j} \left[n_3 \frac{ER.L}{ITP} + (1 - n_3) \frac{MGV}{IPT} \right]$$

$$+ U_{10}$$

(costs being a weighted average of trend unit labour costs and import costs). Earnings in their turn are hypothesised to depend on demand pressure and price expectations:

$$ER_i = p_0 + \sum_j p_{1j} p_{t-j} + \sum_j p_{2j} CU_{t-j} + U_{11}$$

Employment, L, was constrained to depend on industrial production according to:

$$\text{Log } L_i = q_0 + \sum_0^3 q_{1j} \log IP_{t-j} + U_{12}$$

where in accordance with evidence for the UK,[1] $\sum_0^3 q_{1j} = 0.6$.

This closes the circle on the nominal side of the model.

4 Estimation methods

Ideally the model as specified should be estimated using simultaneous equations and possibly limited information methods. The simultaneity arises in the first term of the various lag structures that are implicit in the overall specification. One possibility would be to assume that the system as a whole is block recursive; however, no recourse to this claim is made. Had the estimated lag structures been short, the case for using simultaneous methods would have been a strong one. As it was, lag structures tended to be protracted, in which case, while some simultaneous equations bias no doubt exists, it is most probably too small to be a cause of any serious simultaneous equations bias.

We hypothesised error structures of the form:

$$u_t = \rho u_{t-1} + v_t$$

where v_t was tested for first-order autocorrelation. More generalised ARMA[2] disturbance processes might have been investigated, but in the present form of the model only the first-order autoregressive hypothesis was generally examined.

Lag structures were estimated using the Almon interpolation technique (see Almon (1965)). While this formulation will bias average lags downwards if the tail of the lag structure ($a_\eta + 1$) is wrongly constrained to zero, Almon estimation methods have the advantage of avoiding the specification of lagged endogenous variables on the right-hand side. The ideal of the generalised rational transfer function estimated by hill-climbing procedures entails a knowledge of ARMA disturbance processes which might be regarded as too ambitious given what little knowledge we have of the basic specification of equation systems. Further work is scheduled, however, along these lines.

While the Almon method was used for estimating distributed lags, disturbance processes in the real relationships were estimated by Augmented Least Squares (ALS), whereas those in the pricing sector were estimated by the more familiar Cochran-Orcutt transformation (COT). COT proceeds by taking ρ differences through successive iterations (where ρ is the vector of autoregressive parameters) until adequate convergence is achieved; it is both efficient and unbiased. ALS, discussed in Feldstein (1970), attempts to reduce the inefficiency caused by serial correlation by estimating the residuals in the first stage and specifying the autoregressive process in the second. Here too, iteration in principle continues until a convergence criterion is satisfied. ALS, while less efficient than COT, is more efficient than OLS and is consistent; it also had computational advantages when this work was in progress.

IV DATA AND RESULTS

1 Data

The data for OECD countries was obtained from OECD *Main Economic Indicators;* the source for non-OECD countries was the UN *Monthly Bulletin of Statistics*. The observation period was 1955 (1) to 1971 (4).

The split of trade values between price and volume is in these sources based essentially on unit value indices derived from national sources. Ideally, actual trade prices would be desirable for estimation purposes but in the absence of actual price series it would seem that unit value indices when applied to aggregative data will tend to be as reliable a source of data as can be obtained under the present circumstances. For individual products unit value indices can be regarded as being unreliable (see Kravis and Lipsey (1971)), but when such products are aggregated the error covariance structure should be such as to reduce the percentage error on the index as a whole.

National income data was obtained, where possible, from the OECD source; in the case of the various EEC countries where this was not possible, quarterly data turned out not to be available at all and annual data was used to construct interpolated quarterly series. However, such data was not used for estimation but purely as a benchmark for simulations, the relevant relationships being imposed *a priori*.

2 Import equations

The import relationships are reported in bloc III of Appendix 5.1. In all the main industrial countries apart from Holland both relative price terms and industrial production seemed to display a fairly robust relationship with import volumes, and only in the US case did it seem that capacity utilisation did not affect imports over the observation period. In the Dutch case it is possible that relative import prices did not seem to be significant because import prices have such a large weight in domestic wholesale prices. Improved data might show that relative prices affect imports even in the Dutch case.

The most striking features of the import bloc are the long lags that appear on the relative price term. While for the USA the overall length of this lag was quite short (six quarters), in the Japanese and Belgian cases it was as long as twenty quarters. While it is difficult to explain differences in lag structures between countries, long lags can be accounted for in terms of the component parts referred to in Section II above.

On the whole the relative price elasticities tended to be greater than unity, the principal exception being in the case of West Germany where the elasticity was 0·6, even after ten quarters. In Canada the elasticity was as high as 2·5, and in Belgium, where the overall lag was very long, the long-run elasticity was 2·9. Even for Japan, where commodities form such an important part of total imports, the elasticity was 1·2. The high elasticity in the Canadian case is likely to be accounted for by the high degree of substitution between US and Canadian goods within Canada. It would also appear that Belgian goods are similarly close substitutes with exports of her European neighbours.

Industrial production and its trend play an important role in the determination of imports; this formulation is equivalent to one with industrial production and capacity utilisation, but is preferred because the collinearity between the latter two variables is avoided. In the absence of a semi-logarithmic time trend, the *a priori* sign on the trend of industrial production is of course negative; in Italy, Japan, and Belgium this *a priori* expectation is fulfilled. To the extent, however, that a time trend is included in the specification it will be collinear with industrial production trend (IPT), since IPT is itself derived from a time trend, and it is of course possible for the sign on IPT to be reversed; this is the case in the equations for Germany, France, and Holland. One would expect the lag structures on industrial production to be shorter and in general less complex than their counterparts on the relative import price term; this also is generally the case.

3 Export relationships

The export relationships are reported in bloc I of Appendix 5.1. It will be noticed that US exports are treated as a residual item in the trade matrix. By an iterative procedure a constant term was derived for the US export identity which represented the different data basis for export and imports (especially f.o.b.-c.i.f. differences).

The elasticity on the S variable (world market growth) need not, but is likely to, be unity since a 1 per cent growth in markets must on average lead to a 1 per cent growth in exports. While in fact this elasticity tended to be around unity, in some cases (for example Canada) it was below unity, while in other cases it was slightly above unity.

It is arguable that in the Japanese case the development of exports and the concentration of export production have been such as to exert an exceptional dynamism to Japanese exports. A preliminary investigation in fact showed this S variable to have an exceptionally (and implausibly) high elasticity. To allow for this apparent 'trend' of Japanese market development, a time trend was entered into the specification and it was found that Japanese market penetration and the development of Japanese export production in those goods with high income elasticities accounted for a 10 per cent annual growth rate in Japanese exports over the observation period.

The relative export price elasticities are of particular interest and importance since through them exchange rate changes affect the geographical distribution of imports. The long-run elasticities tended to be greater than untiy and in the Japanese case it was as high as 3, suggesting a very powerful effect of exchange rate changes on the balance of trade. In West Germany and Holland the elasticities were also quite high, at 1·9 in the former case and 2·1 in the latter. Lags tended to be long but robust; on the whole they were considerably longer than the relative price lag on imports. Once again the length of the lag can be understood in terms of a convolution of several lags. It will be noticed that in the case of Japan in particular the lag structure contains humps which once again can be interpreted by speculative factors in demand; the interplay of regressive and extrapolative factors in expected relative prices may create curious patterns in lag structures.

4 Domestic sectors

In blocs **XIX-XXII** equations are reported for various components of domestic demand. The prime purpose of this section of the model is to allow for multiplier effects of changes in real trade flows on the domestic economy, and since movements in the domestic economy feed back into trade flows the specification of domestic sectors provides an additional loop to the system as a whole. For Canada, France, Italy, Holland, and Belgium the consumption relationships were imposed and are essentially standard elementary consumption functions. The German and Japanese consumption equations were estimated and apart from income movements depend on real interest rates in the German case and real movements in the money supply in the Japanese case. Similarly, investment relationships were estimated for West Germany and Japan, the German equation being a simple accelerator model and the Japanese version a mixture of the accelerator and real interest rate effects. While these equations might be of interest in themselves, the main reason behind their inclusion in the model is not any firm belief in their specification but the need to close the system, as discussed earlier.

The consumption and investment relationships for the USA were taken from the Wharton model as was also the relationship for US stockbuilding. For the UK relationships for domestic demand components were taken from the Treasury model (1973 version); for a similar but updated version see H.M. Treasury (1974). For the remaining countries the various components of domestic demand were entered exogenously. In the case of Japanese consumption the money supply appeared as an (exogenous) argument in the consumption function.

In blocs **XIII-XVI** the links from these domestic sectors to industrial production and so to capacity utilisation (and labour demand) are reported. Industrial production is determined quite crudely by the current level of real GDP; the elasticities reported are generally higher than unity. The trend in industrial production is obtained from a (semi-loglinear) regression on time; capacity utilisation follows as the ratio of industrial production to this trend.

5 Pricing behaviour

The export price equations are reported in bloc II of Appendix 5. 2.
Export price 'transmitters' appeared to include Canada, West
Germany, the USA, and the UK; in the case of Canada and the UK
some dependence on competitors' prices was also found to exist.
The price receivers were Japan, France, Italy, Holland, and Belgium. No relationship was found for the rest of OECD, while primary producers' (non-OECD) export prices were found to be determined essentially by a long distributed lag in the world business
cycle as well as by trend factors.

As already stated, import prices are calculated as weighted
functions of relevant export prices and commodity prices so that
inflationary impulses can feed through the system with inflation
in transmitter countries feeding into receiver countries' export
prices and thence back into transmitter countries' import prices.
Since, as can be seen in equation bloc 25 in the transmitter
countries, domestic prices depend in part on movements in import prices, these increases in import prices will generate another
cycle of export price inflation. This export price link has not, to
our knowledge, been investigated before for a wide range of
countries, though theory has clearly posited its existence.

From the point of view of controlling inflation it would seem
that transmitter countries have an advantage *vis à vis* their receiver counterparts in that while their inflation recoils on them
through the import price mechanism, they do not have to contend
with inflationary impulses attributable to the export price mechanism.

Investigations were carried out to see whether in the receiver
countries export prices determined domestic prices; instead of
domestic prices determining export prices as in the transmitter
group, the process should in principle be reversed for the receiver
countries, since in the long run it would not be possible for prices
in the export sector to diverge from those in other sectors when
productivity trends are allowed for. No general evidence to this
effect was found. It is clear however that further investigation of
the transmitter-receiver hypothesis will need to examine this
aspect in more depth.

In the case of all the main OECD countries, the lag structures
for export prices were estimated by using second- or first-order
polynomials. For all countries except Canada time trends were
included in the specification and in those countries where long-
term responses diverged from unity the sign of the time trend
implied a stabilising influence. For example in Italy, where the
long-run elasticity of export prices with respect to competitors'
prices was around 1· 7, the time trend implied an annual fall in
export prices of around 2 per cent. Similarly in France, where the

elasticity was around 0·6 on competitors' prices, the time trend
was positive and suggested an annual growth rate in export prices
of 2 per cent. A similar picture emerges for the USA. However,
when it was decided to drop the time trend from the specification,
the standard errors of estimate fell and the long-run effects of
competitors' and domestic prices were not significantly different.
This suggests that some independent factor either contained in the
time trend or correlated with it exerts an important influence
over international export price behaviour.

In all cases the lags tended to be quite short—of the order of
four quarters to eight quarters—and more often than not the lag
profiles tended to decline in a quasi-linear fashion. The autoregressive expansion however will naturally tend to lengthen the
overall lag.

Because export pricing in the transmitter countries depends
on domestic prices to complete the picture it was necesssary to
determine domestic prices in these countries (Appendix 5.1, bloc
XII). The UK price was entered exogenously into the model. For
the USA, Germany, and Canada prices were found to depend on
costs and on capacity utilisation. However, in the cases of Canada
and Germany the long-run cost elasticity was constrained to unity
and as the R^2 values suggest a tets of these restrictions is likely
to prove to be negative. In the USA domestic prices rise more or
less in line with costs over six quarters; capacity utilisation, while
significant, has only a small elasticity. More interesting are the
equations for Holland and France where domestic prices were
found to be affected by export prices. In the Dutch case in particular this effect was found to be strong, which can be understood
on the grounds that over 50 per cent of Dutch GDP is accounted
for by exports. In France, domestic prices depend on both domestic costs and competitors' export prices when expressed in domestic currency terms.

A preliminary attempt was also made to 'complete the circle'
by estimating wage-price relationships. The investigation showed
that for Canada, the USA, Netherlands, and Belgium the wage-price
relationship was quite strong, but no evidence was found of any
pressure-of-demand effects at this stage. The results are shown
in Appendix 5.1, bloc XVII.

Import prices are calculated from a matrix of fixed weights
(bloc IV) based on 1965 trading patterns. The index numbers could
be improved if these weights were allowed to vary, but this would
increase the iterative nature of the model as it stands. In effect
the matrix provided a very good explanatory basis for import
prices and standard errors tended to be less than 1 per cent.

The commodity price equations for food, raw materials, and
oil feed directly into the import price equations for OECD
countries. Oil, as noted above, is treated as exogenous. Food

prices appear to be essentially autoregressive, suggesting that
a 'hog' cycle may be at work. Raw materials prices were largely
dependent on lagged values of the world business cycle. These
results are reported in Appendix 5.1, bloc XXIII.

6 Identities

The remaining identities required to complete the model are
shown in Appendix 5.1, blocs V-IX. These are mostly self-explanatory. Relative export prices (VII) makes use of a double-
weighting scheme (explained by Adams *et al.* (1969) intended to
take account of shares in 'third markets'. The world business
cycle (VIII) is a weighted average of demand-pressure in OECD
countries, where the weights are the same as for the growth of
export markets (VI) and quite standard.

V CONCLUSIONS

In this study we have attempted to explore the nature of the 'transmission mechanism' in so far as it operates through the volume
and prices of traded goods. We have described a world in which
the markets for manufactured goods are generally characterised
by product differentiation but free entry; stocks, queues and output,
not prices, clear the market. Primary product markets are assumed, apart from oil, to be broadly competitive and to be cleared
by flexible prices. Exchange rates are treated as exogenous
though in principle they could be endogenised by the addition of
capital flow equations, and government reaction functions. We expected to find therefore that the 'price elasticities' (not the elasticities of pure trade theory but of expenditure switching between
countries in response to relative *price levels*) would be high
(generally greater than unity) but non-'infinite' in the relevant
range of price differences; we would not however expect price
differences to be large for prolonged periods, on the grounds that
product differences would in such circumstances become unim-
portant and the elasticities tend to infinity. At the same time we
expected to find long lags in these elasticities for familiar reasons.
Finally, on the price side, we expected to find differences between
countries in the extent to which their own traded goods prices
responded to the international price level. Thus, the 'transmission'
processes we anticipated consisted not only of the familiar 'trade
multiplier' and 'import-cost-push', but also the less well explored
direct response of traded goods prices to international prices and
the second 'multiplier' through expenditure switching effects of
relative price level or exchange rate movements.

   In future work, we hope to set out a number of simulations,
using the model we have described here. At this stage, we simply

note that many of the results reported are broadly consistent with our expectations. However, the model must be taken as intended, namely as an exploration in 'short-term' dynamics (where short is certainly less than ten years and probably no greater than five). It is far from our intention to suggest that the model would be even an approximate guide to asymptotic tendencies. More to the point, we do not attempt to graft on to these dynamic interactions the endogenous interactions implicit in a monetary transmission mechanism, although that is a possibility being explored in further work. In the present formulation, monetary (and fiscal) policy reactions have to be incorporated as exogenous effects on domestic demand and to that extent any simulations of this model that do not incorporate such effects must be interpreted with care. Nevertheless, we believe that even if inevitably incomplete this study sheds some light on important areas of the international transmission mechanism, some of them hitherto relatively neglected.

NOTES

1   See H.M. Treasury (1974).
2   Autoregressive Moving Average error process; for example a Jth order autoregressive and Kth order moving average process would be expressed as

$$u_t = \sum_{j=1}^{J} u_{t-j} + \sum_{k=0}^{K-1} v_{t-k}$$

See Box and Jenkins (1970).

REFERENCES

Adams, F. G., H. Eguchi and F. Meyer-zu-Schlochtern (1969), 'An econometric analysis of international trade', *OECD Occasional Papers*.
Almon, S. (1965), 'The distributed lag between capital appropriations and expenditures', *Econometrica*, 33 (January).
Box, G. E. P. and G. M. Jenkins (1970), *Time Series Analysis: Forecasting and Control* (Holden Day).
Chamberlin, E. H. (1932), *The Theory of Monopolistic Competition* (Harvard University Press, Cambridge, Mass).
Feldstein, M. S. (1970), 'Corporate taxation and dividend behaviour', *Review of Economic Studies* (January).
Hutton, J. P. and A. P. L. Minford (1975), 'A model of UK manufactured exports and export prices', *Government Economic Service Occasional Paper No. 11.*
Kravis, I. and R. Lipsey (1971), 'Price competitiveness in world trade', (National Bureau of Economic Research, New York).
Project Link Working Paper series; see for example: L. R. Klein, C. Moriguchi and A. Van Peeterssen, 'US new economic policy in the world economy: simulation of the international transmission mechanism' (University of Pennsylvania, 1972).

Samuelson, L. (1974), 'A model of international trade', *OECD Occasional Papers*.

Scherer, F. M. (1970), *Industrial Market Structure and Economic Performance* (Rand-McNally).

Taplin, G. (1967), 'Models of world trade', *IMF Staff Papers*, p. 433.

H.M. Treasury (1974), *Economic Assessment Divisions, Treasury Macroeconomic Model Technical Manual*.

APPENDIX 5.1 MODEL EQUATIONS AND ESTIMATION RESULTS

Variable names, numbers and definitions:

A. Countries and their currency unit:

1	C	Canada	Millions of Canadian dollars
2	U	USA	Billions of US dollars
3	J	Japan	Billions of yen
4	G	West Germany	Billions of DM
5	F	France	Billions of francs
6	I	Italy	Billions of lire
7	N	Netherlands	Millions of guilders
8	B	Belgium-Luxembourg	Billions of francs
9	K	UK	Millions of pounds sterling
10	O	Other OECD	Billions of US dollars
11	R	Non-OECD	Billions of US dollars

In what follows, the country to which a variable belongs is shown either by a letter prefix or by a number suffix; e.g. $CXGI$ or XGI_1 is Canadian export volume.

B. Variables

Some variables are not used for all countries. All indices are 1963 = 100.

XGI	Exports of goods volume index
PXG	Price index for exports of goods in dollar terms
XGV	Exports of goods at current prices (millions of US dollars)
XS	Exports of services at constant prices
PXS	Price index for exports of services in dollar terms
XSV	Exports of services at current prices (millions of US dollars)
X	Exports of goods and services at constant prices
INV	Balance of invisibles at current prices (millions of US dollars)
CBV	Current balance (millions of US dollars)
MGI	Imports of goods volume index
PMG	Price index for imports of goods in domestic terms
MGV	Imports of goods at current prices (millions of US dollars)
MS	Imports of services at constant prices
PMS	Price index for imports of services in domestic terms
MSV	Imports of services at current prices (millions of US dollars)
M	Imports of goods and services at constant prices
S	Growth of export markets
RPX	Export prices relative to competitors
WBC	World business cycle

RPM   Import prices relative to domestic wholesale prices
AID   Aid to developing countries
PY   GDP deflator
PE   'Expected' domestic prices
P   Domestic wholesale prices
IP   Industrial production index
IPT   Trend industrial production
CU   Capacity utilisation
L   Index of number employed
RX   Exchange rate (domestic units per billion US dollars)
ER   Index of average earnings per quarter
MO   Money supply
RL   Long-term interest rate (per cent)
RS   Short-term interest rate (per cent)
GX   Government expenditure at constant prices
C   Private consumption at constant prices
IR   Private investment at constant prices
IH   Stockbuilding at constant prices
Y   Gross domestic product at constant market prices
WPF   World food price index (US dollar terms)
WPNF World agriculture non-food price index (US dollar terms)
WPME World metals price index (US dollar terms)
WPMA World raw materials price index (US dollar terms)
WPO   World oil price index (US dollar terms)

C. Equation notation:

Logs are Natural Logarithms; therefore $0 \cdot 01$ in logs $= 1$ per cent approximately. Standard errors bracketed under coefficients. SEE = standard error of estimate; DW = Durbin-Watson statistic. Where these are not shown, the relationship has been imposed as explained in the text.

   Many equations include the residual e, lagged one period, as a regressor. Where, as in most cases, the equation is in logarithmic form, $e = \log x - \log \hat{x}$ where x is the dependent variable and $\log \hat{x}$ is the estimated value of $\log x$ (from an equation in which the lagged residual is *not* present). If the equation is non-logarithmic, $e = x - \hat{x}$.

   Lag coefficients listed (left to right) from first to last lag, thus e.g. $a_i = a_0, a_1, \ldots, a_n$. Bracketed after the list are shown any constraints on the lag structure; for polynomial constraints, polynomial degree and endpoint restrictions (a_{-1}, a_{-n+1}) are shown in that order, eg. $(P, 3; 1, 0)$ indicates a third order polynomial with a_{-1} unrestricted, $a_{n+1} = 0$.

I **XGI** *Exports of goods index*

$$1 \quad C \quad \log (XGI) = 1 \cdot 666 + 0 \cdot 729 \log S + \sum_{0}^{5} a_i \log RPX_{-1}$$
$$(0 \cdot 027)$$

$$+ 0 \cdot 456 \log WBC - 0 \cdot 404 \, e_{-1}$$
$$(0 \cdot 213) \qquad\qquad (0 \cdot 132)$$

$R^2 = 0 \cdot 980$ SEE $= 0 \cdot 048$ $DW = 1 \cdot 92$

where $a_i = -0 \cdot 107, -0 \cdot 179, -0 \cdot 214, -0 \cdot 214, -0 \cdot 178, -0 \cdot 107$
        $(0 \cdot 034) \ (0 \cdot 057) \ (0 \cdot 068) \ (0 \cdot 068) \ (0 \cdot 057) \ (0 \cdot 034)$ $(P, 2; 0, 0)$

(Dummies for auto agreement, 1969 mining strike also included)

2 U $XGI = \dfrac{RX_{2,0}}{k_{x2}} \left\{ \displaystyle\sum_1^{11} \left[\dfrac{km_i}{RX_{i,o}}\, MGI_i \right] - \displaystyle\sum_0^{11} \left[\dfrac{k_{xi}}{RX_{i,o}}\, XGI_i \right] \right\} + e$

(Suffix 0 denotes value in the base period, 1963; k_{xi}, k_{mi} denote the values in 1963 domestic prices of the ith country's exports and imports respectively).

3 J $\log (XGI) = 3\cdot 466 + 0\cdot 020\, t + \displaystyle\sum_0^3 a_i\, \log S_{-i} + \displaystyle\sum_0^{19} b_i\ \log RPX_{-i}$
$\quad\qquad\qquad\quad (0\cdot 005)$

$\qquad\qquad\qquad + 0\cdot 385\ e_{-i}$
$\qquad\qquad\qquad (0\cdot 113)$

where a_i = 0·566, 0·324, −0·191, −0·470
$\qquad\quad$(0·327) (0·268) (0·175) (0·141) $\qquad\qquad\qquad\qquad$ (P, 3; 1, 0)

$\quad b_i$ = −0· 485, −0· 298, −0· 157, −0·055, 0·010, 0·045, 0·053, 0·039,
$\qquad\ $(0· 167) (0· 096) (0· 050) (0·038) (0·047) (0·055) (0·056 (0·054)

$\qquad\qquad$ 0· 008, −0· 035, −0· 086, −0· 140, −0· 193, −0· 239, −0· 275, −0· 295,
$\qquad\qquad$(0· 054) (0· 061) (0· 077) (0· 097) (0· 119) (0· 137) (0· 151) (0· 158)

$\qquad\qquad$−0· 295, −0· 270, −0· 216, −0· 127
$\qquad\qquad$(0· 154) (0· 139) (0· 110) (0· 064) $\qquad\qquad\qquad\qquad$ (P, 3; 1, 0)

$R^2 = 0\cdot 995$ $\qquad$ SEE = 0·042 $\qquad$ $DW = 2\cdot 00$

4 G $\log (XGI) = 0\cdot 306 + \displaystyle\sum_0^5 a_i \log S_{-i} + \displaystyle\sum_0^{16} b_i\ \log RPX_{-i} + 0\cdot 164\ e_{-1}$
$\qquad\qquad\qquad\qquad\qquad\qquad\qquad\qquad\qquad\qquad\qquad\quad (0\cdot 139)$

where a_i = 0·593, 0·351, 0·166, 0·039, −0·032, −0·044
$\qquad\quad$(0·124) (0·041) (0·017) (0·049) (0·058) (0·041) $\qquad\qquad$ (P, 2; 1, 0)

$\quad b_i$ = 0· 325, −0· 286, −0· 250, −0· 216, −0· 184, −0· 155, −0· 129
$\qquad\ $(0· 060) (0· 048) (0· 038) (0· 030) (0· 024) (0· 021) (0· 021)
$\qquad\ $−0· 105, −0· 083, −0· 064, −0· 048, −0· 033, −0· 022, −0· 012
$\qquad\ $(0· 022) (0· 024) (0· 025) (0· 026) (0· 025) (0· 024) (0· 022)

$\qquad\qquad$−0· 006, −0· 001, −0· 001
$\qquad\qquad$(0· 018) (0· 013) (0· 007) $\qquad\qquad\qquad\qquad\qquad$ (P, 2; 1, 0)

$R^2 = 0\cdot 995$ $\qquad$ SEE = 0·026 $\quad$ $DW = 2\cdot 05$

5 F $\log (XGI) = -0\cdot 053 + \displaystyle\sum_0^3 a_i\ \log S_{-i} + \displaystyle\sum_0^9 b_i\ \log RPX_{-i}$

$\qquad\qquad\qquad + 0\cdot 456\ \ \log WBC$
$\qquad\qquad\qquad (0\cdot 378)$

where a_i = 1· 576, −0· 509, −0·382, 0·331
$\qquad\quad$(0· 278) (0· 251) (0·140) (0·236) $\qquad\qquad\qquad\qquad$ (P, 3; 1, 0)

$\quad b_i$ = −0· 454, −0· 393, −0· 322, −0· 244, −0· 165, −0· 092, −0· 030
$\qquad\ $(0· 177) (0· 084) (0· 088) (0· 095) (0· 080) (0· 055) (0· 051)

$\qquad\qquad$ 0·016, 0·040, 0·037
$\qquad\qquad$(0·073) (0·084) (0·065) $\qquad\qquad\qquad\qquad\qquad$ (P, 3; 1, 0)

$R^2 = 0\cdot 989$ $\qquad$ SEE 0·039 $\qquad$ $DW = 1\cdot 82$

6 I $\log (XGI) = -1\cdot 371 + \sum\limits_{0}^{4} a_i \log S_{-i} + \sum\limits_{0}^{16} b_i \log RPX_{-i} + 0\cdot 388\ e_{-1}$
   $\qquad\qquad\qquad\qquad\qquad\qquad\qquad\qquad\qquad\qquad\qquad (0\cdot 113)$

where $a_i = 0\cdot996,\ 0\cdot134,\ -0\cdot070,\ 0\cdot057,\ 0\cdot189$
   $\qquad (0\cdot328)\,(0\cdot250)\ \ (0\cdot220)\,(0\cdot137)\,(0\cdot231)$ $\qquad\qquad\qquad\qquad$ (P, 3; 1, 0)

$\quad b_i = -0\cdot 541, -0\cdot 386, -0\cdot 263, -0\cdot 168, -0\cdot 099, -0\cdot 051, -0\cdot 021,$
   $\qquad (0\cdot 149)\ (0\cdot 098)\ (0\cdot 065)\ (0\cdot 050)\ (0\cdot 047)\ (0\cdot 047)\ (0\cdot 046)$

   $\qquad -0\cdot 008, -0\cdot 006, -0\cdot 013, -0\cdot 026, -0\cdot 041, -0\cdot 055, -0\cdot 065,$
   $\qquad (0\cdot 041)\ (0\cdot 036)\ (0\cdot 033)\ (0\cdot 035)\ (0\cdot 040)\ (0\cdot 047)\ (0\cdot 051)$

   $\qquad -0\cdot 068, -0\cdot 060, -0\cdot 039$
   $\qquad (0\cdot 050)\ (0\cdot 042)\ (0\cdot 026)$ $\qquad\qquad\qquad\qquad\qquad$ (P, 3; 1, 0)

$R^2 = 0\cdot 991 \qquad SEE = 0\cdot 047 \qquad DW = 1\cdot 94$

7 N $\log (XGI) = 0\cdot 349 + 0\cdot 932 \log S + \sum\limits_{0}^{19} a_i \log RPX_{-i} -0\cdot 287\ e_{-1}$
   $\qquad\qquad\qquad\qquad (0\cdot 037)\qquad\qquad\qquad\qquad\qquad (0\cdot 113)$

where $a_i = -0\cdot 414, -0\cdot 364, -0\cdot 316, -0\cdot 272, -0\cdot 230, -0\cdot 191, -0\cdot 154, -0\cdot 121,$
   $\qquad (0\cdot 171)\ (0\cdot 110)\ (0\cdot 072)\ (0\cdot 058)\ (0\cdot 061)\ (0\cdot 067)\ (0\cdot 070)\ (0\cdot 069)$

   $\qquad -0\cdot 091, -0\cdot 065, -0\cdot 041, -0\cdot 021, -0\cdot 004,\ 0\cdot 009,\ 0\cdot 019,$
   $\qquad (0\cdot 064)\ (0\cdot 057)\ (0\cdot 052)\ (0\cdot 052)\ (0\cdot 057)\,(0\cdot 065)\,(0\cdot 079)$

   $\qquad 0\cdot 025),\ 0\cdot 028,\ 0\cdot 026,\ 0\cdot 021,\ 0\cdot 013$
   $\qquad (0\cdot 079)\ (0\cdot 080)\,(0\cdot 074)\,(0\cdot 060)\,(0\cdot 036)$ $\qquad\qquad\qquad$ (P, 3; 1, 0)

$R^2 = 0\cdot 995 \qquad SEE\ 0\cdot 024 \qquad DW = 2\cdot 03$

8 B $\log (XGI) = 0\cdot 608 + 0\cdot 0073t + \sum\limits_{0}^{3} a_i \log S_{-i} + \sum\limits_{0}^{19} b_i \log RPX_{-i}$
   $\qquad\qquad\qquad\qquad\qquad (0\cdot 0057)$

where $a_i = 1\cdot152,\ 0\cdot250,\ -0\cdot243,\ -0\cdot326$
   $\qquad (0\cdot215)\,(0\cdot072)\ (0\cdot121)\ \ (0\cdot110)$ $\qquad\qquad\qquad\qquad$ (P, 2; 1, 0)

$\quad b_i = -0\cdot 194, -0\cdot 167, -0\cdot 142, -0\cdot 119, -0\cdot 097, -0\cdot 078, -0\cdot 060, -0\cdot 044,$
   $\qquad (0\cdot 179)\ (0\cdot 146)\ (0\cdot 116)\ (0\cdot 090)\ (0\cdot 068)\ (0\ 051)\ (0\cdot 041)\ (0\cdot 041)$

   $\qquad -0\cdot030, -0\cdot017, -0\cdot007,\ 0\cdot002,\ 0\cdot009,\ 0\cdot014,\ 0\cdot018,\ 0\cdot019,$
   $\qquad (0\cdot045)\ (0\cdot052)\ (0\cdot059)\,(0\cdot064)\,(0\cdot067)\,(0\cdot067)\,(0\cdot065)\,(0\cdot061)$

   $\qquad 0\cdot019,\ 0\cdot017),\ 0\cdot013,\ 0\cdot007$
   $\qquad (0\cdot054)\,(0\cdot045),\ (0\cdot032)\,(0\cdot018)$ $\qquad\qquad\qquad$ (P, 2; 1, 0)

$R^2 = 0\cdot 992 \qquad SEE = 0\cdot 035 \qquad DW = 1\cdot 74$

9 K $\log (XGI.) = k_9 + \sum\limits_{0}^{3} a_i \log S_{-i} -0\cdot 8 \sum\limits_{1}^{21} b_i \log RPX_{-i}$

   $\qquad\qquad\qquad + 0\cdot 8 \sum\limits_{1}^{4} c_i \log WBC_{-i}$

where $a_i = 0\cdot532,\ 0\cdot415,\ 0,\ -0\cdot298$
   $\qquad (0\cdot133)\,(0\cdot142)\qquad (0\cdot101)$ (a_3 continued to zero)

$$b_i = 0\cdot018, 0\cdot034, 0\cdot049, 0\cdot062, 0\cdot073, 0\cdot083, 0\cdot090, 0\cdot096, 0\cdot101,$$
$$0\cdot103, 0\cdot104, 0\cdot103, 0\cdot101, 0\cdot094, 0\cdot090, 0\cdot083, 0\cdot073, 0\cdot062,$$
$$0\cdot049, 0\cdot034, 0\cdot018 \quad (t\text{-ratio for all } b_i = 8\cdot3) \qquad (P, 2; 0, 0)$$

$$c_i = 0\cdot599, 0, 0\cdot835, -0\cdot835 \quad (\text{constraints } c_1 = 0, c_2 = -c_3)$$
$$(0\cdot282) \quad (0\cdot385) \quad (0\cdot385)$$

$R^2 = 0\cdot996 \qquad \text{SEE} = 0\cdot016 \qquad DW = 1\cdot44$

(Estimated for manufactures only (80 per cent of UK exports); k_9 is an imposed constant, replacing the estimated constant to allow for differences in coverage and valuation).

10 0 $\log (XGI) = -0\cdot257 + 1\cdot056 \log S - 0\cdot566 \log RPX$
$$(0\cdot029) \qquad\qquad (0\cdot333)$$

$R^2 = 0\cdot974 \qquad \text{SEE} = 0\cdot038 \qquad DW = 2\cdot31$

11 R $\log (XGI) = -0\cdot123 - 0\cdot0071\, t + \sum\limits_{0}^{9} a_i \log S_{-i}$
$$(0\cdot0023)$$

$$+ \sum\limits_{0}^{3} b_i \log \left[\frac{PXG\cdot RX}{PMG\; RX63}\right]_{-i}$$

where $a_i = 0\cdot067, 0\cdot179, -0\cdot051, -0\cdot109, -0\cdot069, 0\cdot012, 0\cdot088, 0\cdot132,$
$$(0\cdot101)\,(0\cdot040)\,(0\cdot052)\,(0\cdot034)\,(0\cdot027)\,(0\cdot038)\,(0\cdot035)\,(0\cdot023)$$

$$0\cdot129, 0\cdot080$$
$$(0\cdot036)\,(0\cdot045) \qquad\qquad\qquad (P, 4; 1, 0)$$

$$b_i = -0\cdot541, 0\cdot405, -0\cdot328, 0\cdot142$$
$$(0\cdot218)\,(0\cdot310)\;(0\cdot318)\,(0\cdot235) \qquad\qquad (P, 4; 1, 0)$$

$R^2 = 0\cdot996 \qquad \text{SEE} = 0\cdot017 \qquad DW = 1\cdot60$

II **PXG** *Price index for exports of goods in dollar terms*

For countries 1 to 8.

$$\log (PXG) = a + bt - \log\left(\frac{RX}{RX63}\right) + \sum\limits_{0}^{7} c_i \log\left(\frac{PXG}{RPX}\cdot\frac{RX}{RX63}\right)_{-1}$$

$$+ \sum\limits_{0}^{7} d_i \log P_{-i} + f\, e_{-1} \quad \text{where for country:}$$

	IC	2U	3J	4G	5F	6I	7N	8B
a	$-0\cdot549$	$1\cdot001$	$-1\cdot105$	$0\cdot058$	$1\cdot680$	$-3\cdot120$	$0\cdot045$	$-0\cdot460$
b	—	$0\cdot0034$	$-0\cdot0047$	$-0\cdot0015$	$0\cdot0020$	$-0\cdot0054$	$-0\cdot0024$	$-0\cdot0027$
		$(0\cdot0003)$	$(0\cdot0016)$	$(0\cdot0003)$	$(0\cdot0064)$	$(0\cdot0014)$	$(0\cdot0008)$	$(0\cdot0010)$
c_0	$0\cdot151$	—	$0\cdot362$	—	$0\cdot182$	$0\cdot484$	$0\cdot350$	$0\cdot317$
	$(0\cdot070)$		$(0\cdot091)$		$(0\cdot020)$	$(0\cdot096)$	$(0\cdot075)$	$(0\cdot078)$
c_1	$0\cdot070$	—	$0\cdot302$	—	$0\cdot152$	$0\cdot404$	$0\cdot258$	$0\cdot264$
	$(0\cdot038)$		$(0\cdot075)$		$(0\cdot017)$	$(0\cdot080)$	$(0\cdot0397)$	$(0\cdot065)$

	IC	2U	3J	4G	5F	6I	7N	8B
c_2	0·006 (0·020)	—	0·242 (0·060)	—	0·122 (0·013)	0·323 (0·064)	0·180 (0·008)	0·212 (0·052)
c_3	−0·040 (0·023)	—	0·181 (0·045)	—	0·091 (0·010)	0·242 (0·048)	0·116 (0·013)	0·159 (0·039)
c_4	−0·067 (0·031)	—	0·121 (0·030)	—	0·061 (0·007)	0·161 (0·032)	0·066 (0·027)	0·106 (0·026)
c_5	−0·077 (0·034)	—	0·060 (0·015)	—	0·030 (0·003)	0·081 (0·016)	0·029 (0·032)	0·053 (0·013)
c_6	−0·069 (0·030)	—	—	—	—	—	0·005 (0·030)	—
c_7	−0·044 (0·019)	—	—	—	—	—	−0·004 (0·019)	—
d_0	0·198 (0·135)	0·172 (0·022)	—	0·068 (0·123)	—	—	—	—
d_1	0·198 (0·069)	0·150 (0·020)	—	0·117 (0·061)	—	—	—	—
d_2	0·191 (0·023)	0·129 (0·017)	—	0·150 (0·013)	—	—	—	—
d_3	0·177 (0·032)	0·107 (0·014)	—	0·166 (0·022)	—	—	—	—
d_4	0·156 (0·053)	0·086 (0·011)	—	0·166 (0·044)	—	—	—	—
d_5	0·128 (0·061)	0·064 (0·008)	—	0·150 (0·053)	—	—	—	—
d_6	0·092 (0·055)	0·043 (0·006)	—	0·116 (0·048)	—	—	—	—
d_7	0·050 (0·035)	0·021 (0·003)	—	0·066 (0·031)	—	—	—	—
f	+0·556 (0·113)	+0·478 (0·117)	+0·907 (0·055)	+0·709 (0·094)	+0·333 (0·133)	+0·741 (0·088)	+0·914 (0·054)	+0·735 (0·089)
R^2	0·983	0·988	0·920	0·830	0·970	0·85	0·830	0·840
SEE	0·0126	0·012	0·014	0·012	0·02	0·021	0·009	0·016
DW	2·01	1·85	1·82	2·14	2·13	1·85	2·15	1·99
	(P, 2; 1, 0)	(P, 1; 1, 0)	(P, 1; 1, 0)	(P, 2; 1, 0)	(P, 1; 1, 0)	(P, 1; 1, 0)	(P, 2; 1, 0)	(P, 1; 1, 0)

$$9 \; K \quad \Delta \log (PXG) = 0\cdot 0017 - \Delta \log \left(\frac{RX}{RX63}\right) + \underset{(0\cdot 159)}{0\cdot 321} \, \Delta \log P$$
$$\underset{(0\cdot 0010)}{}$$

$$+ \underset{(0\cdot 153)}{0\cdot 368} \, \Delta \log P_{-1} + \underset{(0\cdot 047)}{0\cdot 145} \, \Delta \log \left(RPX \cdot \frac{RX63}{RX}\right)$$

$$+ \underset{(0\cdot 049)}{0\cdot 129} \, \Delta \log \left(RPX \cdot \frac{RX63}{RX}\right)$$

$$R^2 = 0\cdot 68 \qquad SEE = 0\cdot 005 \qquad DW = 1\cdot 79$$

10 0 Exogenous

11 R $\log (PXG) = 0 \cdot 070 - 0 \cdot 0016 \, t + \log PMG$
$$(0 \cdot 0006)$$

$$+ \; 0 \cdot 636 \log \left(\frac{PXG}{PMG} \; \frac{RX}{RX63} \right)_{-1}$$
$$(0 \cdot 151)$$

$$-0 \cdot 414 \log \left(\frac{PXG}{PMG} \; \frac{RX}{RX63} \right)_{-2} \; + \; \sum_{i=o}^{19} a_i \; \log WBC_{-i}$$
$$(0 \cdot 164)$$

$$- \log \left(\frac{RX}{RX63} \right)$$

where $a_i = $ 0·063, 0·086, 0·101, 0·109, 0·112, 0·112, 0·110, 0·108,
(0·075) (0·060) (0·062) (0·067) (0·069) (0·069) (0·065) (0·061)

0·106, 0·105, 0·106, 0·107, 0·109, 0·110, 0·111, 0·109,
(0·056) (0·052) (0·048) (0·044) (0·042) (0·040) (0·038) (0·038)

0·104, 0·092, 0·073, 0·043
(0·037) (0·036) (0·030) (0·019)   (P, 4; 1, 0)

$R^2 = 0 \cdot 73$ SEE $= 0 \cdot 011$ $DW = 2 \cdot 07$

III MGI *Imports of goods index*

1 C $\log (MGI) = 0 \cdot 551 + 0 \cdot 887 \log IP + 0 \cdot 788 \log CU$
$$(0 \cdot 025) \qquad\qquad (0 \cdot 161)$$

$$+ \; \sum_{0}^{7} a_i \; \log RPM_{-i} \quad \begin{matrix} -0 \cdot 335 \\ (0 \cdot 139) \end{matrix} \quad e_{-1}$$

where $a_i = $ −0·468, −0·444, −0·409, −0·365, −0·312, −0·248, −0·175,
(0·163) (0·084) (0·040) (0·055) (0·077) (0·084) (0·074)

−0·093
(0·046)   (P, 2; 1, 0)

$R^2 = 0 \cdot 980$ SEE $= 0 \cdot 037$ $DW = 1 \cdot 84$

2 U $\log (MGI) = 0 \cdot 520 + 0 \cdot 943 \log IP + \sum_{0}^{5} b_i \; \log RPM_{-i} \; \begin{matrix} -0 \cdot 413 \\ (0 \cdot 140) \end{matrix} \, e_{-1}$
$$(0 \cdot 087)$$

where $b_i = $ −0·112, −0·186, −0·223, −0·223, −0·186, −0·112
(0·023) (0·052) (0·062) (0·063) (0·052) (0·032)   (P, 2; 0, 0)

(Dummy for US–Canadian auto agreement also included.)

$R^2 = 0 \cdot 976$ SEE $= 0 \cdot 057$ $DW = 1 \cdot 82$

3 J $\log (MGI) = 0 \cdot 484 - 0 \cdot 712 \log IPT + \sum_{0}^{3} a_i \log IP_{-i}$
$\qquad\qquad\qquad\quad (0 \cdot 268)$

$\qquad\qquad + \sum_{0}^{19} b_i \log RPM_{-i}$

where $a_i = 1 \cdot 466$, $0 \cdot 495$, $-0 \cdot 527$, $0 \cdot 215$
$\qquad\quad (0 \cdot 377)(0 \cdot 552)\ (0 \cdot 553)(0 \cdot 408)$ (freely estimated)

$\qquad b_i = 0 \cdot 102$, $-0 \cdot 212$, $-0 \cdot 355$, $-0 \cdot 373$, $-0 \cdot 305$, $-0 \cdot 187$, $-0 \cdot 048$, $0 \cdot 087$,
$\qquad\quad\ (0 \cdot 339)\ \ (0 \cdot 159)\ \ (0 \cdot 125)\ \ (0 \cdot 148)\ \ (0 \cdot 151)\ \ (0 \cdot 133)\ \ (0 \cdot 107)(0 \cdot 091)$

$\qquad\qquad 0 \cdot 199$, $0 \cdot 276$, $0 \cdot 307$, $0 \cdot 289$, $0 \cdot 225$, $0 \cdot 122$, $-0 \cdot 008$, $-0 \cdot 148$,
$\qquad\qquad (0 \cdot 097)(0 \cdot 114)(0 \cdot 127)(0 \cdot 128)(0 \cdot 144)\ (0 \cdot 088)\ (0 \cdot 059)\ (0 \cdot 054)$

$\qquad\qquad -0 \cdot 274$, $-0 \cdot 358$, $-0 \cdot 367$, $-0 \cdot 262$
$\qquad\qquad\ (0 \cdot 082)\ \ (0 \cdot 111)\ \ (0 \cdot 118)\ \ (0 \cdot 087)$ $\qquad\qquad\qquad\qquad$ (P, 4; 1, 0)

$R^2 = 0 \cdot 995$ $\qquad$ SEE $= 0 \cdot 035$ $\qquad$ $DW = 1 \cdot 86$

4 G $\log (MGI) = -2 \cdot 818 + 0 \cdot 557 \log IPT + \sum_{0}^{2} a_i \log IP_{-i}$
$\qquad\qquad\qquad\qquad\qquad (0 \cdot 115)$

$\qquad\qquad + \sum_{0}^{9} b_i \log RPM_{-i} + 0 \cdot 237$
$\qquad\qquad\qquad\qquad\qquad\qquad (0 \cdot 112)$ $\ e_{-1}$

where $a_i = 0 \cdot 665$, $0 \cdot 308$, $0 \cdot 086$
$\qquad\quad (0 \cdot 196)(0 \cdot 080)(0 \cdot 131)$ $\qquad\qquad\qquad\qquad\qquad\qquad$ (P, 2; 1, 0)

$\qquad b_i = -0 \cdot 120$, $-0 \cdot 108$, $-0 \cdot 096$, $-0 \cdot 084$, $-0 \cdot 072$, $-0 \cdot 059$, $-0 \cdot 047$, $-0 \cdot 035$,
$\qquad\quad\ (0 \cdot 081)\ \ (0 \cdot 053)\ \ (0 \cdot 032)\ \ (0 \cdot 021)\ \ (0 \cdot 022)\ \ (0 \cdot 027)\ \ (0 \cdot 030)(0 \cdot 029)$

$\qquad\qquad -0 \cdot 024$, $-0 \cdot 012$
$\qquad\qquad (0 \cdot 024)\ \ (0 \cdot 014)$ $\qquad\qquad\qquad\qquad\qquad\qquad\qquad$ (P, 2; 1, 0)

$R^2 = 0 \cdot 995$ $\qquad$ SEE $= 0 \cdot 034$ $\qquad$ $DW = 2 \cdot 04$

5 F $\log (MGI) = -2 \cdot 724 + 0 \cdot 949 \log IPT + \sum_{0}^{5} a_i \log IP_{-i}$
$\qquad\qquad\qquad\qquad\qquad (0 \cdot 270)$

$\qquad\qquad + \sum_{0}^{7} b_i \log RPM_{-i}$

where $a_i = 0 \cdot 593$, $0 \cdot 434$, $0 \cdot 183$, $-0 \cdot 073$, $-0 \cdot 246$, $-0 \cdot 251$
$\qquad\quad (0 \cdot 217)(0 \cdot 079)(0 \cdot 116)\ (0 \cdot 074)\ (0 \cdot 079)\ (0 \cdot 101)$ $\qquad\qquad$ (P, 3; 1, 0)

$\qquad b_i = -0 \cdot 661$, $-0 \cdot 202$, $0 \cdot 014$, $0 \cdot 055$, $-0 \cdot 012$, $-0 \cdot 118$, $-0 \cdot 196$, $-0 \cdot 18$
$\qquad\quad (0 \cdot 167)\ (0 \cdot 067)\ (0 \cdot 074)(0\ 072)\ (0 \cdot 058)\ (0 \cdot 064)\ (0 \cdot 080)\ (0 \cdot 068)$
$\qquad\qquad\qquad\qquad\qquad\qquad\qquad\qquad\qquad\qquad\qquad\qquad$ (P, 3; 1, 0)

$R^2 = 0 \cdot 996$ $\qquad$ SEE $= 0 \cdot 030$ $\qquad$ $DW = 1 \cdot 81$

6 I $\log (MGI) = -3 \cdot 285 - 0 \cdot 243 \log IPT + \sum_{0}^{5} a_i \log IP_{-i}$

$\qquad\qquad\qquad (0 \cdot 204)$

$\qquad\qquad + \sum_{0}^{7} b_i \log RPM_{-i} + \sum_{0}^{15} c_i \, \Delta \log RPM_{-i}$

where $a_i = 0 \cdot 798, \ 0 \cdot 715, \ 0 \cdot 470, \ 0 \cdot 171, -0 \cdot 078, -0 \cdot 170$

$\qquad\quad (0 \cdot 227) \, (0 \cdot 117) \, (0 \cdot 147) \, (0 \cdot 086) \ (0 \cdot 109) \ (0 \cdot 137)$ $\qquad$ (P, 3; 1, 0)

$\quad b_i = -0 \cdot 473, -0 \cdot 259, -0 \cdot 120, -0 \cdot 041, -0 \cdot 005, \ 0 \cdot 001, -0 \cdot 006, -0 \cdot 011$

$\qquad\quad (0 \cdot 895) \ (0 \cdot 252) \ (0 \cdot 271) \ (0 \cdot 365) \ (0 \cdot 323) (0 \cdot 230) \ (0 \cdot 185) \ (0 \cdot 156)$

$\qquad\qquad\qquad\qquad\qquad\qquad\qquad\qquad\qquad\qquad\qquad$ (P, 3; 1, 0)

$\quad c_i = 1 \cdot 199, -1 \cdot 700, -2 \cdot 070, -2 \cdot 321, -2 \cdot 464, -2 \cdot 511, -2 \cdot 474, -2 \cdot 363,$

$\qquad\quad (1 \cdot 161) \ (0 \cdot 915) \ (0 \cdot 731) \ (0 \cdot 597) \ (0 \cdot 501) \ (0 \cdot 428) \ (0 \cdot 369) \ (0 \cdot 317)$

$\qquad\quad -2 \cdot 191, -1 \cdot 970, -1 \cdot 710, -1 \cdot 424, -1 \cdot 123, -0 \cdot 818, -0 \cdot 522, -0 \cdot 245$

$\qquad\quad (0 \cdot 273) \ (0 \cdot 237) \ (0 \cdot 213) \ (0 \cdot 200) \ (0 \cdot 192) \ (0 \cdot 179) \ (0 \cdot 148) \ (0 \cdot 092)$

$\qquad\qquad\qquad\qquad\qquad\qquad\qquad\qquad\qquad\qquad\qquad$ (P, 3; 1, 0)

$R^2 = 0 \cdot 991 \qquad SEE = 0 \cdot 043 \qquad DW = 1 \cdot 77$

7 N $\log (MGI) = -1 \cdot 466 + 0 \cdot 069 \log IPT + \sum_{0}^{3} a_i \log IP_{-i} + 0 \cdot 203$

$\qquad\qquad\qquad (0 \cdot 143) \qquad\qquad\qquad\qquad\qquad\qquad\qquad (0 \cdot 115) \ e_{-1}$

where $a_i = 0 \cdot 911, \ 0 \cdot 192, \ 0 \cdot 428, -0 \cdot 286$

$\qquad\quad (0 \cdot 296) \, (0 \cdot 355) \, (0 \cdot 323) \ (0 \cdot 270) \quad$ (freely estimated)

$R^2 = 0 \cdot 994 \qquad SEE = 0 \cdot 032 \qquad DW = 2 \cdot 00$

8 B $\log (MGI) = -1 \cdot 234 - 0 \cdot 201 \log IPT + \sum_{0}^{3} a_i \log IP_{-i}$

$\qquad\qquad\qquad (1 \cdot 140)$

$\qquad\qquad + \sum_{0}^{19} b_i \ \log RPM_{-i}$

where $a_i = 0 \cdot 491, \ 0 \cdot 449, \ 0 \cdot 354, \ 0 \cdot 204$

$\qquad\quad (0 \cdot 295) \, (0 \cdot 148) \, (0 \cdot 179) \, (0 \cdot 149)$ $\qquad\qquad\qquad$ (P, 2; 1, 0)

$\quad b_i = 0 \cdot 026, -0 \cdot 062, -0 \cdot 095, -0 \cdot 123, -0 \cdot 147, -0 \cdot 168, -0 \cdot 185, -0 \cdot 197,$

$\qquad\quad (0 \cdot 114) \ (0 \cdot 099) \ (0 \cdot 094) \ (0 \cdot 097) \ (0 \cdot 106) \ (0 \cdot 116) \ (0 \cdot 127) \ (0 \cdot 136)$

$\qquad\quad -0 \cdot 206, -0 \cdot 211, -0 \cdot 211, -0 \cdot 208, -0 \cdot 201, -0 \cdot 190, -0 \cdot 174, -0 \cdot 155,$

$\qquad\quad (0 \cdot 143) \ (0 \cdot 148) \ (0 \cdot 150) \ (0 \cdot 149) \ (0 \cdot 145) \ (0 \cdot 138) \ (0 \cdot 128) \ (0 \cdot 115)$

$\qquad\quad -0 \cdot 132, -0 \cdot 105, -0 \cdot 074, -0 \cdot 039$

$\qquad\quad (0 \cdot 098) \ (0 \cdot 079) \ (0 \cdot 056) \ (0 \cdot 029)$ $\qquad\qquad\qquad$ (P, 2; 1, 0)

$R^2 = 0 \cdot 991 \qquad SEE = 0 \cdot 037 \qquad DW = 2 \cdot 31$

9 K $MGI = \dfrac{1}{k_{M9}}$ $\left\{ -135 + (1 \cdot 024 + 0 \cdot 0027t)(0 \cdot 138C + 0 \cdot 055\,GX + 0 \cdot 165 \right.$

$\left. IR + 0 \cdot 178X) + 0 \cdot 288IH \right\}$

10 0 $\log (MGI) = -2 \cdot 550 + 1 \cdot 528 \log IP + 0 \cdot 700 \log CU$
$\qquad\qquad\qquad\qquad\quad (0 \cdot 017) \qquad\qquad (0 \cdot 143)$

$R^2 = 0 \cdot 992$ SEE $= 0 \cdot 037$ $DW = 0 \cdot 72$

11 R $\log (MGI) = -4 \cdot 6 + \displaystyle\sum_{0}^{7} a_i \log (XGI.PXG)_{-i} + AID - \log PMG$

where $a_i = 0 \cdot 14, 0 \cdot 14, 0 \cdot 12, 0 \cdot 12, 0 \cdot 12, 0 \cdot 12, 0 \cdot 12, 0 \cdot 12$

IV PMG *Price index for imports of goods in domestic terms*
For all countries except 9 K.

		Country									
PP_j		1C	2U	3J	4G	5F	6I	7N	8B	10 0	11 R
1	CPXG	0	0·132	0·008	0·004	0·003	0·005	0·003	0·002	0	0·013
2	UPXG	0·530	0	0·178	0·058	0·075	0·088	0·046	0·058	0·038	0·129
3	JPXG	0·018	0·090	0·009	0·003	0·003	0·009	0·005	0·005	0·019	0·105
4	GPXG	0·024	0·071	0·041	0	0·194	0·116	0·236	0·192	0·304	0·095
5	FPXG	0·011	0·033	0·012	0·106	0	0·077	0·063	0·151	0·057	0·062
6	IPXG	0·009	0·033	0·009	0·070	0·074	0	0·042	0·037	0·043	0·040
7	NPXG	0·006	0·014	0·007	0·106	0·053	0·031	0	0·146	0·012	0·017
8	BPXG	0·008	0·026	0·005	0·083	0·087	0·022	0·193	0	0·031	0·017
9	KPXG	0·071	0·074	0·018	0·049	0·054	0·053	0·068	0·074	0·108	0·134
10	OPXG	0·077	0·096	0·020	0·085	0·027	0·126	0·038	0·025	0	0·122
11	WPF	0·111	0·199	0·155	0·193	0·149	0·167	0·124	0·104	0·127	0·158
12	WPMA	0·086	0·165	0·409	0·171	0·176	0·202	0·106	0·159	0·233	0·033
13	WPO	0·049	0·067	0·138	0·066	0·105	0·104	0·076	0·047	0·028	0·025

Weights derived for 1965 from *Foreign Trade Statistics Bulletin,* Series ABC of OECD.

$$\log (PMG) = \sum_{1}^{13} a_j \log PP_j + \log \frac{RX}{RX63}$$

where $PP_j = PXG_j$ for $j = 1$ to 10

$\qquad PP_{11} = WPF$ world food price index

$\qquad PP_{12} = WPMA$ world raw materials price index

$\qquad PP_{13} = WPO$ world oil price index

and a_j is given by

9 K $\log (PMG) = \log PMG + 0\cdot 82 \sum\limits_{0}^{2} k_i \log RX_{-i}$ where $k_i =$

$$0\cdot 7, 0\cdot 2, 0\cdot 1$$

(Where $\log \hat{PMG}$ is exogenous.)

V *Export and import equations and identities*

For all countries 1 to 11.

Exports of goods at current prices (dollars)	$XGV = XGI \cdot PXG \dfrac{k_x}{RX63}$
Exports of services at constant prices (domestic)	XS Exogenous
Exports of services price index in (dollar) terms	PXS Exogenous
Exports of services at current prices (dollars)	$XSV = \dfrac{XS}{RX63} \cdot PXS$
Total exports at constant prices (domestic)	$X = k_x\, XGI + XS$
Imports of goods at current prices (dollars)	$MGV = k_m\, MGI \cdot \dfrac{PMG}{RX}$
Imports of services at constant prices (domestic)	MS Exogenous
Imports of services price index in domestic terms	PMS Exogenous
Imports of services at current prices (dollars)	$MSV = MS \cdot \dfrac{PMS}{RX}$
Total imports at constant prices (domestic)	$M = k_m\, MGI + MS$
Balance of invisibles (dollars)	$INV = XSV - MSV$
Current balance (dollars)	$CBV = XGV - MGV + INV$

Where k_x, k_m denote the values in 1963 domestic prices of each country's exports and imports respectively.

VI S *Growth of export markets*

All countries 1 to 11.

$$S_i = \left\{ \sum_{\substack{j=1 \\ \neq i}}^{11} MGI_j \;\; T_{ij} \right\} \Big/ \left\{ \sum_{j=1}^{11} T_{ij} \right\}$$

where T_{ij} is exports from i to j in 1963.

VII RPX *Relative export prices*

All countries 1 to 11.

$$RPX_i = PXG_i \sum_{\substack{j=1 \\ \neq i}}^{11} \frac{T_{ij}}{\sum_{\substack{k=1 \\ \neq i}}^{11} T_{ik}} \left[\sum_{\substack{k=1 \\ \neq i,j}}^{10} \left(\frac{1}{\frac{T_{kj} \cdot PXG_k}{\sum_{\substack{h=1 \\ \neq i,j}}^{10} T_{hj}}} \right) \right]$$

VIII WBC *World business cycle*

All countries 1 to 11.

$$WBC_i = \left[\sum_{\substack{j=1 \\ \neq i}}^{10} CU_j \, T_{ij} \right] \Bigg/ \left[\sum_{j=1}^{10} T_{ij} \right]$$

IX RPM *Relative import prices*

All countries 1 to 9.

$$RPM_i = \frac{PMG_i}{P_i}$$

X PY *GDP deflator*

All countries 1 to 9.

$$\log (PY) = \log P$$

XI PE *'Expected' domestic price index*

Japan and Germany only.

3 J $PE = \sum_{0}^{7} P_i/8$

4 G $PE = \sum_{1}^{4} P_i/4$

XII P *Domestic wholesale price index*

$$1 \quad C \quad \Delta \log (P) = \sum_{0}^{3} a_i \, \Delta \log CU_{-i} + \sum_{0}^{7} b_i \, \Delta \left(0 \cdot 72 \log \frac{ER.L}{IPT} \right.$$

$$+0 \cdot 28 \quad \left. \log \frac{MGV}{IPT} \right)_{-i} \quad + \quad \underset{(0 \cdot 131)}{0 \cdot 247} \quad e_{-1}$$

$a_i = 0 \cdot 178, \ 0 \cdot 133, \ 0 \cdot 089, \ 0 \cdot 044$
$ (0 \cdot 049) \, (0 \cdot 037) \, (0 \cdot 025) \, (0 \cdot 012)$ (P, 1; 1, 0)

$b_i = 0 \cdot 187, \ 0 \cdot 177, \ 0 \cdot 163, \ 0 \cdot 145, \ 0 \cdot 124, \ 0 \cdot 098, \ 0 \cdot 069, \ 0 \cdot 037$
$ (0 \cdot 060) \, (0 \cdot 033) \, (0 \cdot 006) \, (0 \cdot 011) \, (0 \cdot 021) \, (0 \cdot 026) \, (0 \cdot 024) \, (0 \cdot 015)$

 (P, 2; 1, 0. Constrained estimation $\sum b_i = 1$.)

$R^2 = 0 \cdot 09 \qquad SEE = 0 \cdot 007 \qquad DW = 2 \cdot 02$

$$2 \quad U \quad \log (P) = 0 \cdot 67 + \sum_{0}^{2} a_i \log CU_{-i} + \sum_{0}^{5} b_i \left(0 \cdot 95 \log \frac{ER.L}{IP} \right.$$

$$+0 \cdot 05 \quad \left. \log \frac{MGV}{IP} \right)_{-i} \quad + \quad \underset{(0 \cdot 034)}{0 \cdot 966} \quad e_{-1}$$

$a_i = 0 \cdot 050, \ 0 \cdot 034, \ 0 \cdot 017,$
$ (0 \cdot 020) \, (0 \cdot 013) \, (0 \cdot 006)$ (P, 1; 1, 0)

$b_i = 0 \cdot 254, \ 0 \cdot 212, \ 0 \cdot 169, \ 0 \cdot 127, \ 0 \cdot 085, \ 0 \cdot 042$
$ (0 \cdot 031) \, (0 \cdot 026) \, (0 \cdot 021) \, (0 \cdot 015) \, (0 \cdot 010) \, (0 \cdot 005)$ (P, 1; 1, 0)

$R^2 = 0 \cdot 994 \qquad SEE = 0 \cdot 005 \qquad DW = 2 \cdot 17$

$$3 \quad J \quad \log (P) = 5 \cdot 33 + 0 \cdot 8 \sum_{0}^{7} \log ER_{-i}/8 + 0 \cdot 2 \sum_{0}^{7} \frac{\log PMG}{8} {}_{-i} - \log IPT$$

$$4 \quad G \quad \Delta \log (P) = \sum_{0}^{5} a_i \, \Delta \log CU_i + \sum_{0}^{7} b_i \, \Delta \left(0 \cdot 77 \log \frac{ER.L}{IPT} \right.$$

$$+ 0 \cdot 23 \quad \left. \log \frac{MGV}{IPT} \right)_{-i} \quad + \quad \underset{(0 \cdot 157)}{0 \cdot 202} \quad e_{-1}$$

$a_i = 0 \cdot 112, \ 0 \cdot 093, \ 0 \cdot 074, \ 0 \cdot 056, \ 0 \cdot 037, \ 0 \cdot 019$
$ (0 \cdot 039) \, (0 \cdot 032) \, (0 \cdot 025) \, (0 \cdot 019) \, (0 \cdot 013) \, (0 \cdot 006)$ (P, 1; 1, 0)

$b_i = 0 \cdot 095, \ 0 \cdot 131, \ 0 \cdot 153, \ 0 \cdot 162, \ 0 \cdot 156, \ 0 \cdot 138, \ 0 \cdot 105, \ 0 \cdot 06$
$ (0 \cdot 077) \, (0 \cdot 039) \, (0 \cdot 008) \, (0 \cdot 014) \, (0 \cdot 027) \, (0 \cdot 033) \, (0 \cdot 030) \, (0 \cdot 109)$

 (Constrained estimation $\sum b_i$. P, 2; 1, 0)

$R^2 = 0 \cdot 02 \qquad SEE = 0 \cdot 007 \qquad DW = 2 \cdot 00$

5 F $\log (P) = -0 \cdot 26 + \sum\limits_{0}^{5} a_i \log (PXG.RX)_{-i} + \sum\limits_{0}^{5} b_i \ (0 \cdot 72 \log \dfrac{ER.L}{IPT}$

$+ \ 0 \cdot 28 \log \dfrac{MGV}{IPT}) + 0 \cdot 436 \ e_{-1}$
$(0 \cdot 122)$

$a_i = 0 \cdot 140, \ 0 \cdot 116, \ 0 \cdot 093, \ 0 \cdot 070, \ 0 \cdot 047, \ 0 \cdot 023$
$(0 \cdot 025) (0 \cdot 021) (0 \cdot 016) (0 \cdot 012) (0 \cdot 008) (0 \cdot 004)$ $(P, 1; 1, 0)$

$b_i = 0 \cdot 127, \ 0 \cdot 106, \ 0 \cdot 085, \ 0 \cdot 064, \ 0 \cdot 042, \ 0 \cdot 021$
$(0 \cdot 019) (0 \cdot 016) (0 \cdot 013) (0 \cdot 009) (0 \cdot 006) (0 \cdot 003)$ $(P, 1; 1, 0)$

$R^2 = 0 \cdot 99$ SEE $= 0 \cdot 013$ $DW = 1 \cdot 83$

6 I $\log (P) = 4 \cdot 85 + 0 \cdot 75 \sum\limits_{0}^{7} 0 \cdot 125 \log E\dot{R}_{-i}$

$+ 0 \cdot 25 \sum\limits_{0}^{7} 0 \cdot 125 \log \ PMG_{-i} - \log IPT$

7 N $\log (P) = -12 \cdot 84 + 0 \cdot 0044 \ t + \sum\limits_{0}^{7} a_i \log (PXG.RX)_{-i} + 0 \cdot 773 \ e_{-1}$
$(0 \cdot 0006)$ $(0 \cdot 086)$

$a_i = 0 \cdot 289, \ 0 \cdot 258, \ 0 \cdot 225, \ 0 \cdot 191, \ 0 \cdot 156, \ 0 \cdot 119, \ 0 \ 081, \ 0 \cdot 041$
$(0 \cdot 167) (0 \cdot 103) (0 \cdot 073) (0 \cdot 077) (0 \cdot 088) (0 \cdot 090) (0 \cdot 076) (0 \cdot 047)$ $(P, 2; 1, 0)$

$R^2 = 0 \cdot 97$ SEE $= 0 \cdot 016$ $DW = 1 \cdot 97$

8 B $\log (P) = 4 \cdot 73 + 0 \cdot 53 \sum\limits_{0}^{7} 0 \cdot 125 \log ER_{-i}$

$+ 0 \cdot 47 \sum\limits_{0}^{7} 0 \cdot 125 \log \ PMG_{-i} - \log IP$

9 K P   Exogenous

XIII IP *Industrial production index*
(No standard errors shown for these simple regressions.)

1   C $\log (IP) = -6 \cdot 560 + 1 \cdot 193 \log Y$

2   U $\log (IP) = \ \cdot \ 1 \cdot 024 + 1 \cdot 144 \log Y$

3   J $\log (IP) = -6 \cdot 695 + 1 \cdot 298 \log Y$

4   G $\log (IP) = -0 \cdot 079 + 1 \cdot 022 \log Y$

5   F $\log (IP) = 0 \cdot 02 + 0 \cdot 998 \log Y$

6   I $\log (IP) = -7 \cdot 960 + 1 \cdot 393 \log Y$

7   N $\log (IP) = -8 \cdot 989 + 1 \cdot 428 \log Y$

8   B $\log (IP) = -0 \cdot 774 + 1 \cdot 040 \log Y$

9   K $IP = 3 \cdot 0578 + 0 \cdot 0178\ IH + 0 \cdot 03801\ (0 \cdot 169\ C - 0 \cdot 353\ IR + 0 \cdot 156\ GX + 0 \cdot 413\ X)$

10   O $\log (IP) = 3 \cdot 556 + 0 \cdot 114 \log XGI + 0 \cdot 09 \log XGI_{-1} + 0 \cdot 06 \log XGI_{-2} + 0 \cdot 02 \log XGI_{-3}$

XIV IPT *Trend industrial production index*

(No standard errors shown for these trend regressions.) $t = 1$ in 1960(1).

1   C $\log (IPT) = 4 \cdot 448 + 0 \cdot 0132t$

2   U $\log (IPT) = 4 \cdot 474 + 0 \cdot 0109t$

3   J $\log (IPT) = 4 \cdot 116 + 0 \cdot 0328t$

4   G $\log (IPT) = 4 \cdot 397 + 0 \cdot 0142t$

5   F $\log (IPT) = 4 \cdot 404 + 0 \cdot 0137t$

6   I $\log (IPT) = 4 \cdot 252 + 0 \cdot 0189t$

7   N $\log (IPT) = 4 \cdot 404 + 0 \cdot 0166t$

8   B $\log (IPT) = 4 \cdot 433 + 0 \cdot 0108t$

9   K $\log (IPT) = 4 \cdot 517 + 0 \cdot 0074t$

10   O $\log (IPT) = 4 \cdot 442 + 0 \cdot 0144t$

XV CU *Capacity utilisation*

All countries 1 to 10.

$$CU = \frac{IP}{IPT}$$

XVI L *Index of number employed*

All countries 1 to 9.

For country j $\log (L) = a_j + \sum_{0}^{-3} b_i\ \log IP$

$a_j = 1 \cdot 72, 1 \cdot 57, 1 \cdot 44, 1 \cdot 61, 1 \cdot 54, 1 \cdot 66, 1 \cdot 36, 1 \cdot 53, 1 \cdot 72$

$b_i = 0 \cdot 1, 0 \cdot 2, 0 \cdot 2, 0 \cdot 1$

XVII ER *Earnings per quarter index*

$t = 1$ in 1960(1).

1 C $\Delta \log (ER) = \sum_{0}^{7} a_i\ \Delta \log P_{-i}$

$a_i = 0 \cdot 142,\ 0 \cdot 165,\ 0 \cdot 176,\ 0 \cdot 176,\ 0 \cdot 164,\ 0 \cdot 14,\ \ 0 \cdot 105,\ 0 \cdot 058$
$\quad\ (0 \cdot 075)\ (0 \cdot 053)\ (0 \cdot 047)\ (0 \cdot 050)\ (0 \cdot 050)\ (0 \cdot 050)\ (0 \cdot 041)\ (0 \cdot 024)$ (P, 2; 1, 0)

$R^2 = 0 \cdot 20$ SEE $= 0 \cdot 003$ $DW = 1 \cdot 72$

2 U $\log (ER) = 0.55 + 0.0069\, t + \sum_{0}^{5} a_i\, P_{-i} + 0.659\ e_{-1}$
   $ (0.0003) \phantom{t + \sum_{0}^{5}} (0.099)$

$a_i = 0.246,\ 0.205,\ 0.164,\ 0.123,\ 0.082,\ 0.041$
$ (0.024)\,(0.020)\,(0.016)\,(0.012)\,(0.008)\,(0.004)$ $\hfill$ (P, 1; 1, 0)

$R^2 = 0.998$ SEE $= 0.007$ $DW = 2.13$

3 J Exogenous

4 G Exogenous

5 F Exogenous

6 I Exogenous

7 N $\log (ER) = 0.15 + 0.0171\, t + \sum_{0}^{5} a_i\, \log P_{-i} + 0.612\ e_{-1}$
   $ (0.0007) \phantom{t + \sum_{0}^{5}\log P} (0.104)$

$a_i = 0.264,\ 0.220,\ 0.176,\ 0.132,\ 0.088,\ 0.044$
$ (0.039)\,(0.033)\,(0.026)\,(0.019)\,(0.013)\,(0.006)$ $\hfill$ (P, 1; 1, 0)

$R^2 = 0.998$ SEE $= 0.017$ $DW = 1.95$

8 B $\log (ER) = 3.14 + 0.0129\, t + \sum_{0}^{7} a_i\, \log P_{-i} + 0.613\ e_{-1}$
   $ (0.00055) \phantom{t + \sum_{0}^{7}\log P} (0.107)$

$a_i = 0.263,\ 0.269,\ 0.264,\ 0.248,\ 0.221,\ 0.182,\ 0.133,\ 0.072,$
$ (0.077)\,(0.043)\,(0.023)\,(0.024)\,(0.031)\,(0.034)\,(0.031)\,(0.019)$ $\hfill$ (P, 2; 1, 0)

$R^2 = 0.998$ SEE $= 0.0115$ $DW = 2.33$

9 K Exogenous

XVIII *Monetary and fiscal variables*

MO	Money supply	Exogenous
RL	Long term interest rate	Exogenous
RS	Short term interest rate	Exogenous
GX	Government expenditure	Exogenous

XIX C *Private consumption*

1 C $\log (C) = -0.239 + 0.3 \sum_{0}^{10} 0.7^i \log Y_{-i}$

2 U $C = Y \left(0.1501 + 0.127 \sum_{1}^{4} \left(\dfrac{C}{Y}\right)_{-i} - 0.27 \left(\log Y - \tfrac{1}{4} \sum_{1}^{4} \log Y_{-i}\right)\right)$

$ -0.03\, CU - 0.0104 \sum_{0}^{20} 0.93^i\, C_{-i-1}$

3   J $C = 0.076Y_{-2} + 0.096Y_{-3} + 0.061Y_{-4} + \sum_{2}^{6} a_i \left(\dfrac{MO}{P}\right)_{-i} + 871.3$
           (0.062)   (0.065)   (0.059)

where $a_i = 0.070, \ 0.113, \ 0.072, \ 0.003, -0.040$
        (0.060) (0.042) (0.038) (0.025) (0.041)   (P, 3; 1, 0)

$R^2 = 0.998$ SEE $= 51.0$ $DW = 0.94$

4   G $C = 1.656 + \sum_{0}^{9} a_i Y_{-i} + \sum_{0}^{9} b_i \ (RL - 4 \ \Delta \ \log PE)_{-i}$

where $a_i = 0.200, \ 0.097, \ 0.037, \ 0.011, \ 0.009, \ 0.022, \ 0.042, \ 0.059,$
        (0.030) (0.010) (0.015) (0.017) (0.013) (0.009) (0.011) (0.017)

            $0.063, \ 0.047$
           (0.020) (0.015)   (P, 3; 1, 0)

     $b_i = -0.373, -0.204, -0.085, -0.007, \ 0.037, \ 0.054, \ 0.051, \ 0.037,$
        (0.127) (0.066) (0.055) (0.061) (0.062) (0.059) (0.056) (0.055)

            $0.019, \ 0.004$
           (0.051) (0.035)   (P, 3; 1, 0)

$R^2 = 0.996$ SEE $= 0.42$ $DW = 1.92$

5   F $\log (C) = -0.387 + 0.3 \sum_{0}^{10} 0.7^i \log Y_{-i}$

6   I $\log (C) = -0.182 + 0.3 \sum_{0}^{10} 0.7^i \log Y_{-i}$

7   N $\log (C) = -0.3 + 0.3 \sum_{0}^{10} 0.7^i \log Y_{-i}$

8   B $\log (C) = -0.33 + 0.3 \sum_{0}^{10} 0.7^i \log Y_{-i}$

9   K $C = 0.7 \sum_{0}^{10} a_i \ Y_{-i}$

where $a_i = 0.429, 0.128, 0.094, 0.073, 0.063, 0.054, 0.057, 0.035, 0.018,$
        $0.009, 0.001$

XX   IR   *Private investment*

(Countries 1, 5, 6, 7 and 8: IR exogenous.)

2   U $IR = 4 \cdot 7\, CU + \sum_{0}^{7} a_i\, (0 \cdot 025\, IP_{-i-2} - 0 \cdot 222 RL_{-i} - 0 \cdot 033 RL_{-i-3}$

$\qquad - 0 \cdot 00095 IR_{-i-1} + 0 \cdot 544\, (RL - RS)_{-i-2} + 0 \cdot 007\, (C + IR)_{-i-3}$

$\qquad + 0 \cdot 0082 C_{-i-2}) - 0 \cdot 003 \sum_{0}^{20} 0 \cdot 95^i\, IR_{-i-1} + 0 \cdot 332\, (RL - RS)_{-3}$

$\qquad + 0 \cdot 004\, Y + 0 \cdot 001\, ((C + IR)_{-1} + (C + IR)_{-2}) + 0 \cdot 0395 C_{-1}$

where $a_i = 0 \cdot 074, 0 \cdot 132, 0 \cdot 170, 0 \cdot 183, 0 \cdot 171, 0 \cdot 138, 0 \cdot 091, 0 \cdot 041$

3   J $IR = \sum_{0}^{9} a_i\, \Delta Y_{-i} + 789 \cdot 3 - 96 \cdot 2\, \Delta\, (\dfrac{RL}{4} - \Delta \log PE)_{-2}$
$\qquad\qquad\qquad\qquad\qquad (15 \cdot 2)$

where $a_i = 0{\cdot}317,\ 0{\cdot}650,\ 0{\cdot}892,\ 1{\cdot}065,\ 1{\cdot}116,\ 1{\cdot}107,\ 1{\cdot}022,\ 0{\cdot}865$
$\qquad\quad (0{\cdot}113)\,(0{\cdot}065)\,(0{\cdot}065)\,(0{\cdot}071)\,(0{\cdot}070)\,(0{\cdot}070)\,(0{\cdot}076)\,(0{\cdot}083)$

$\qquad\quad 0{\cdot}639,\ 0{\cdot}350$
$\qquad\quad (0{\cdot}079)\,(0{\cdot}055)$ (P, 3; 1, 0)

$R^2 = 0 \cdot 96$ $SEE = 95 \cdot 55$ $DW = 1 \cdot 19$

4   G $IR = 23 \cdot 39 + \sum_{0}^{14} a_i\, \Delta Y_{-i}$

where $a_i = 0{\cdot}438,\ 0{\cdot}451,\ 0{\cdot}450,\ 0{\cdot}436,\ 0{\cdot}412,\ 0{\cdot}379,\ 0{\cdot}339,\ 0{\cdot}295,$
$\qquad\quad (0{\cdot}114)\,(0{\cdot}069)\,(0{\cdot}046)\,(0{\cdot}001)\,(0\ 044)\,(0{\cdot}047)\,(0{\cdot}052)\,(0{\cdot}060)$

$\qquad\quad 0{\cdot}248,\ 0{\cdot}199,\ 0{\cdot}152,\ 0{\cdot}108,\ 0{\cdot}069,\ 0{\cdot}036,\ 0{\cdot}013$
$\qquad\quad (0{\cdot}071)\,(0{\cdot}082)\,(0{\cdot}090)\,(0{\cdot}093)\,(0{\cdot}089)\,(0{\cdot}073)\,(0{\cdot}045)$ (P, 3; 1, 0)

$R^2 = 0 \cdot 895$ $SEE = 0 \cdot 70$ $DW = 1 \cdot 06$

9   K $IR = 1000 + \sum_{1}^{8} a_i\, \Delta Y_{-i} + 0 \cdot 0088 IR_{-1} + \sum_{3}^{11} b_i\, \Delta IP$

where $a_i = 0 \cdot 057, 0 \cdot 078, 0 \cdot 088, 0 \cdot 087, 0 \cdot 077, 0 \cdot 077, 0 \cdot 058, 0 \cdot 032$
$\qquad\quad b_i = 1 \cdot 295, 2 \cdot 803, 3 \cdot 714, 4 \cdot 105, 4 \cdot 057, 3 \cdot 649, 2 \cdot 950, 2 \cdot 069, 1 \cdot 056$

XXI III *Stockbuilding*

(All countries except 2 and 9: *IH* exogenous.)

2   U $IH = 0 \cdot 102 Y + 0 \cdot 113 Y_{-1} - 0 \cdot 075 Y_{-2} - 0 \cdot 070 Y_{-4} + 0 \cdot 035 C_{-1}$
$\qquad + 40 \cdot 4(P - P_{-2}) - 0 \cdot 083\, IH_{-2}$

9   K $IH = -1200 + (8 \cdot 68 - 0 \cdot 028 t)\, IP_{-1} + 0 \cdot 03 Y_{-1} + 0 \cdot 5 IH_{-1}$

XXII Y *Gross domestic product at constant market prices*
All countries 1 to 9.

$Y = GX + C + IR + IH + X - M$

XXIII *World commodity prices, exchange rates*

1 *WPF* World food price index

$$\log (WPF) = 6 \cdot 935 + 0 \cdot 0053 \, t + \sum_{0}^{5} a_i \log WBC_{11,\,-i} + \sum_{1}^{25} b_i \log WPF_{-i}$$

$$+ \sum_{0}^{5} c_i \log PMG_{11,\,-i}$$

where $a_i = 0 \cdot 217, -0 \cdot 197, -0 \cdot 460, -0 \cdot 572, -0 \cdot 533, -0 \cdot 342$
         $(0 \cdot 322) \ (0 \cdot 173) \ (0 \cdot 154) \ (0 \cdot 183) \ (0 \cdot 178) \ (0 \cdot 119)$ (P, 2; 1, 0)

$b_i = 0 \cdot 033, \ 0 \cdot 015, -0 \cdot 001, -0 \cdot 016, -0 \cdot 030, -0 \cdot 042, -0 \cdot 053, -0 \cdot 063$
      $(0 \cdot 030) \ (0 \cdot 029) \ (0 \cdot 027) \ (0 \cdot 026) \ (0 \cdot 025) \ (0 \cdot 024) \ (0 \cdot 024) \ (0 \cdot 023)$

      $-0 \cdot 071, -0 \cdot 078, -0 \cdot 083, -0 \cdot 087, -0 \cdot 090, -0 \cdot 091, -0 \cdot 091, -0 \cdot 090,$
      $(0 \cdot 023) \ (0 \cdot 022) \ (0 \cdot 021) \ (0 \cdot 021) \ (0 \cdot 020) \ (0 \cdot 019) \ (0 \cdot 019) \ (0 \cdot 018)$

      $-0 \cdot 087, -0 \cdot 083, -0 \cdot 077, -0 \cdot 070, -0 \cdot 062, -0 \cdot 053, -0 \cdot 041, -0 \cdot 029,$
      $(0 \cdot 016) \ (0 \cdot 015) \ (0 \cdot 014) \ (0 \cdot 012) \ (0 \cdot 011) \ (0 \cdot 009) \ (0 \cdot 007) \ (0 \cdot 005)$

      $-0 \cdot 015$
      $(0 \cdot 002)$ (P, 2; 1, 0)

   $c_i = 0 \cdot 558, \ 0 \cdot 305, \ 0 \cdot 116, -0 \cdot 009, -0 \cdot 070, -0 \cdot 067$
        $(0 \cdot 353) \ (0 \cdot 135) \ (0 \cdot 143) \ (0 \cdot 214) \ (0 \cdot 221) \ (0 \cdot 150)$ (P, 2; 1, 0)

$R^2 = 0 \cdot 83$ SEE $= 0 \cdot 029$ $DW = 1 \cdot 64$

2 *WPNF* World agriculture non-food price index

$\log (WPNF) = 0 \cdot 22 - 0 \cdot 00205t + 0 \cdot 957 \log PMG_{11} + \sum_{0}^{4} a_i \log WBC_{11,-i}$
            $(0 \cdot 00016) \quad (0 \cdot 109)$

$+ 0 \cdot 502 \ e_{-1}$
$(0 \cdot 071)$

where $a_i = 0 \cdot 474, \ 0 \cdot 578, \ 0 \cdot 183, -0 \cdot 311, -0 \cdot 505$
         $(0 \cdot 195) \ (0 \cdot 128) \ (0 \cdot 124) \ (0 \cdot 064) \ (0 \cdot 129)$ (P, 3; 1, 0)

$R^2 = 0 \cdot 86$ SEE $= 0 \cdot 017$ $DW = 2 \cdot 06$

3 *WPME* World metal ores price index

$\log (WPME) = 0 \cdot 501 - 0 \cdot 0019 \, t + 1 \cdot 134 \log PMG_{11}$
            $(0 \cdot 0011) \quad (0 \cdot 214)$

$+ \sum_{0}^{19} a_i \log WBC_{11,\,-i} + 0 \cdot 429 \ e_{-1}$
$(0 \cdot 095)$

where a_i = 0·312,   0·469,   0·550,   0·572,   0·552,   0·505,   0·442,   0·373,
            (0·161) (0·111) (0·108) (0·119) (0·126) (0·128)(0·124) (0·118)

         0·307,   0·250,   0·206,   0·178,   0·165,   0·166,   0·177,   0·183,
         (0·111) (0·104) (0·096) (0·089) (0·081) (0·073) (0·067) (0·062)

         0·205,   0·205,   0·180,   0·117
         (0·059) (0·056) (0·049) (0·032)   (P, 4; 1, 0)

4   *WPMA*   World raw materials price index

log $(WPMA)$ = 0·5 log $WPNF$ + 0·5 log $WPME$

5   *WPO*   World oil price index   Exogenous.

    RX   Exchange rate   Exogenous for all countries.

6 The origins of inflation in less developed countries: a selective review

C. H. Kirkpatrick and F. I. Nixson*

I INTRODUCTION

This paper is a selective review of the theoretical and empirical evidence on certain aspects of the post-war inflation experience of less developed countries (LDCs). It is mainly concerned with the factors that are alleged to generate inflationary impulses and the mechanism by which an inflationary spiral comes into being. It does not attempt to provide a comprehensive survey of the many facets of the relationship between inflation and economic development (for a general survey of this relationship, see Thorp (1971)), and it does not directly concern itself with the increases in the world price of traded commodities. Clearly, such price increases are very important (witness the impact of rising oil prices on the LDCs) but they enter the analysis only in so far as the type of development policies pursued by LDCs makes them more vulnerable to this kind of imported inflationary pressure.

After briefly describing the recent inflationary experience of the LDCs in Section II, we discuss in Section III the limited relevance of the analytical framework used in the study of inflation in the developed western economies. It was the rejection of western theories (especially the concepts of 'cost-push' and 'demand-pull') that led to the emergence in the 1950s of the Latin American 'structuralist' school of thought, the main features of which we discuss in Section IV, along with Latin American 'monetarist' criticisms of the 'structuralist' analysis. In Section V we look in greater detail at the alleged foreign exchange bottleneck and its policy implications and contrast it to the monetary theory of the balance of payments. Section VI examines the relationship between policies of import restraint and inflation. In Section VII we consider the question of the 'openness' of LDC economies and

* We would like to acknowledge helpful comments received from Richard Harrington, David Laidler, Philip Leeson, Michael Parkin and George Zis.

this leads us into the discussion of the impact of import-substituting industrialisation (ISI) on the external economic relations and the domestic economic structure of LDCs. In the final section, we present the main conclusions arising from the analysis.

II COMPARATIVE RATES OF INFLATION

A major difficulty in studying the comparative rates of inflation in LDCs is the limited availability of data, and the limitations of such data as are available. The majority of LDCs do not compile GNP deflators so that the cost of living indices and/or indices of wholesale prices are frequently the only price series that are available. Both of these measures are subject to serious defects. The wholesale price index is often an unsatisfactory measure of domestic prices because it is frequently heavily weighted with the prices of imports and exports which tend to be measures of the domestic equivalents of international prices rather than measures of domestic prices. The cost of living index is usually based upon a limited sample of goods and services purchased in the major urban conurbation and is therefore unrepresentative of the consumption pattern of the majority of the population located in the rural areas. In practice, cost of living indices are normally employed, being regarded as the least unsatisfactory of the available measures of domestic price increases.

Table 6.1 shows the average rates of inflation in different groups of countries during the period 1965-73.[1] The figures reveal that throughout this period the average rate of inflation in the LDCs has been substantially greater than the average rate in the groups of industrial and other developed countries. The data also indicate considerable variation in the average inflation rate in different geographical groups of the LDCs, with the highest rate being experienced in Latin and Central America.

III THE RELEVANCE OF 'ORTHODOX' ANALYSIS TO LDCs

The 'orthodox' analysis of inflation is presented in terms of a reversed L-shaped aggregate supply curve and a downward sloping aggregate demand curve. The original Phillips curve hypothesis stated that wage change was caused by excess demand and that the latter could be measured (or proxied) by the inverse of the unemployment rate. This has since been modified to take into account the fact that both sides of the labour market attempt to influence real rather than money wages. It is suggested that the rate of change will equal the expected rate of price change plus an adjustment related to the excess demand for labour (as measured by the level of unemployment) (Parkin (1974)). Expectations are formed by an 'error-learning' process. The reformulated

Table 6.1 Price increases in developed and less developed countries 1965-73 (%)[a]

	Annual average 1965-70	Change from preceding year				
		1969	1970	1971	1972	1973
Industrial countries	4·2	4·7	5·9	5·4	4·8	7·2
More developed primary producing countries	4·9	4·4	6·2	9·0	9·4	13·2
All less developed countries	13·0	9·1	10·5	10·0	13·0	24·0
Africa	4·0	6·0	4·5	6·0	5·0	7·0
Asia	18·0[b]	6·1	9·3	5·0	7·0	19·0
Middle East	3·0	3·4	4·0	5·0	6·0	10·0
Western hemisphere	15·0	15·8	17·0	15·0	21·0	36·0[b]

Source: IMF *Annual Reports,* 1973, 1974

Notes

[a]   For the developed countries, the figures are the average of percentage changes in the GNP deflator of each country, weighted by the US dollar value of their GNPs at current prices in the preceding year. For the LDCs the figures are the average of the percentage changes in the consumer prices indices of each country, weighted by the US dollar value of their GNP in 1972.

[b]   Excluding one high-inflation country, the Asian figure in the first column would be 7 per cent; with a similar exclusion the western hemisphere figure in the last column would be 21 per cent.

Phillips hypothesis predicts that if a (closed) economy is operated with permanent excess demand (i.e. unemployment is permanently below its equilibrium or 'natural' level) inflation will persistently accelerate.[2] The origins of excess demand are to be found in government monetary and fiscal policies. The 'orthodox' theory of inflation in an open economy attempts to integrate the expectations-augmented Phillips curve analysis with the monetary approach to balance of payments theory. We discuss this in greater detail in Section V below.

Over the past decade, economists working on the problems of LDCs have become increasingly wary of uncritically applying concepts and theories which have originated in the economic and institutional setting of western, industrialised economies. Seers (1963) early on pointed out the 'limitations of the special case', emphasising the integrated nature of the industrialised economy and the fragmented nature of the LDC, and Streeten (1972) has warned against '... the simple transfer of fairly sophisticated concepts from one setting to another without close scrutiny of the institutional differences' (p. 127).

One of the principal ways in which errors enter into analysis has been termed 'misplaced aggregation', that is, it is assumed, incorrectly, that dissimilar items can be analysed in terms of a single category (Streeten (1972)).[3] 'Orthodox' theory places emphasis on the concept of the 'natural' rate of unemployment but we must question the relevance of the more basic concepts of 'employment' and 'unemployment' within the LDC context. These concepts, as commonly used, imply a homogenous, mobile, adequately trained, wage-earning labour force willing and able to work and responding to incentives. But as Streeten has argued: 'In a society of isolated communities, some of them apathetic or with religious prejudices against certain kinds of work, illiterate and unused to co-operation, the notion "Labour Force" does not make sense' (Streeten (1972), p. 55).[4]

In all LDCs employment in the 'modern' sector represents a small, but privileged, proportion of the total labour force, strengthened as it usually is by strong trade unions and government legislation (minimum wage legislation, etc.). The great mass of labour is engaged in small-scale, self-employed, low-productivity activities in the "traditional" sectors of the economy (both rural and urban) and may be idle or underutilised for lengthy periods of time. This has been termed disguised unemployment or underemployment but differs from the phenomenon, originally noted by Joan Robinson, of workers being forced to accept less remunerative occupations during periods of economic depression, which is of a temporary nature and is eliminated by an increase in the level of effective demand.[5] Disguised unemployment or underemployment in LDCs refers to the mass of the labour force that is permanently engaged in low-productivity activities and a change in the level of aggregate demand for wage labour has little or no impact on the level of traditional sector underemployment.[6] Concepts such as 'full employment' and the 'natural' rate of unemployment are not meaningful given the disintegrated and fragmented nature of LDC economies.

A second, and perhaps more fundamental limitation of 'orthodox' inflation analysis is the use of the concepts of aggregate demand and supply (another example of misplaced aggregation) and the postulation of a ceiling to aggregate demand in real terms that is set by aggregate supply (Myrdal (1968), appendix 2, section 23). The LDC economy is characterised by factor immobility, market imperfection and rigidities and disequilibrium between demand and supply in different sectors of the economy. Substantial underutilisation of resources in some sectors (for example manufacturing; see Little, Scitovsky and Scott (1970), pp. 93-8) coexists with shortages in other sectors of the economy, and market imperfections (and technological constraints) prevent the movement of resources in response to market signals.[7] In these conditions, it is questionable whether the 'orthodox' interpretation of inflation in terms of aggregate demand and supply can be applied. Myrdal rejects the notion of a single ceiling[8] and argues for the 'structural' or 'structuralist' interpretation of inflation which stresses '... the fragmentation, the disequilibria, and the lack of balance between supplies and demands in different sectors of the economy and between different groups in the community' (pp. 1926-7).

In other words, there is no overall limitation on aggregate supply; limitations are diverse and specific and inflation can be more usefully analysed in the terms of the structural composition of the economy, taking into account the imperfection of markets and the division of the economy into separate or poorly integrated sectors of economic activity. Inflation is then seen as the result of particular sectoral bottlenecks in the economy (we discuss what is meant by 'bottlenecks' in Section IV below) with different types of bottleneck accompanied by '... different types of price rigidities, different supply elasticities, different response mechanisms, different degrees of substitutability on the part of the purchaser, and different distributional effects' (Myrdal (1968), p. 1928).

In Section IV we summarise the 'structuralist' analysis as it has been developed in Latin America. This is not meant to imply that this analysis is relevant only to that area; indeed, Myrdal is referring specifically to South Asia in his discussion of structurally-induced (or 'development') inflation. Likewise the lack of references to African economies indicates that until recently, and for a variety of reasons, inflation was not an immediate problem. We would argue that a 'structural' analysis is relevant to that area, although obviously the relative importance of various sectoral constraints will differ between both countries and continents. Inflation in Latin America has posed the greatest problems and has been most intensively studied. It is for these reasons, and because the analyses discussed make it clear that gross imperfections and fragmentation of markets in LDCs make it inappropriate to analyse inflation in terms of aggregate demand and supply relationships, that we devote the following section (with the exception of the empirical, cross-country studies referred to) exclusively to Latin America.

IV 'STRUCTURALIST' AND 'MONETARIST' EXPLANATIONS OF INFLATION

1 *The theoretical issues*

The debate over the causes and consequences of inflation in Latin America has largely been between two groups loosely labelled 'structuralists' and 'monetarists'.[9] The two groups do not represent coherent schools of thought; rather they each consist of a certain type of approach to the specific problem of inflation and more broadly, economic development in general. Roberto de Oliveira Campos (1967) whilst claiming responsibility for having introduced the expressions, at the same time feels the controversy is a spurious one: He argues that structuralists, if in power, would have to adopt monetarist policies as a short-run measure and that monetarists would, in the long run, accept the primacy of structural change. The monetarist is 'a structuralist in a hurry' and the structuralist is 'a monetarist without policy-making responsibility' (pp. 108-9).

Not everyone would agree with this rather facile dismissal of any fundamental difference (apart from one of time period) between 'structuralists' and 'monetarists'. Felix (1961) notes that there is disagreement not only as to the causes of inflation and the efficacy of stabilisation programmes but, as we have already noted above, there is general disagreement on appropriate development policies. Furthermore, he argues that 'structuralists' are usually 'of the left' while 'monetarists' are 'of the right' of the political spectrum. Seers (1964) summarises the argument as follows:

'it is ... not just a technical issue in economic theory. At the heart of the controversy ... are two different ways of looking at economic development, in fact two completely different attitudes toward the nature of social change, two different sets of value judgements about the purposes of economic activity and the ends of economic policy, and two incompatible views on what is politically possible.' (p. 89)

We will first outline the main features of the 'structuralist' and 'monetarist' analyses before returning to the nature of the controversy.

The 'structuralist' argument (often identified with the UN Economic Commission for Latin America (ECLA)) is that inflation is inevitable in an economy that is attempting rapid growth in the presence of structural bottlenecks or constraints, defined as 'certain fundamental facets of the economic, institutional and socio-political structure of the country which in one way or another inhibit expansion' (Thorp (1971), p. 185). Inflation accompanies the transition of the LDC from an 'outward-oriented' export-based economy to an 'inward-oriented' domestic-market-based economy (ISI being the key feature of this process as we shall see below). Such a transition requires massive changes in the socio-economic structure of the LDC which the price mechanism, operating within very imperfect market structures and with limited resource mobility, is unable to achieve: 'Given the imperfections of the system, the result of attempting major structural change had to be shortages and disequilibria on many fronts' (Thorp (1971), p. 186).

The 'structuralist' analysis is concerned largely with the identification and examination of the alleged structural constraints (what Osvaldo Sunkel (1960) in his seminal work refers to as the basic or structural inflationary pressures). These are generally taken to be: (a) the inelastic supply of foodstuffs; (b) the foreign exchange bottleneck, and (c) the financial constraint.

Before discussing these three constraints in greater detail, we must first be clear as to what is meant by the term 'bottlenecks' and its relation to inflation. Edel (1969) points out that there is no reason in theory why an increase in the price of one commodity should raise the general price level and provoke an inflationary spiral. In an open economy, an increase in imports can keep prices constant and in a closed economy, neo-classical theory would predict that a rise in the relative price of one type of goods (for example food) would lead to a shift in demand to other goods and a re-allocation of the factors of production, leading to the restoration of an equilibrium position. But if the prices of manufactured goods are inflexible downwards, a rise in food prices (with other prices constant) raises the average price level. In turn, if industrial wages are tied to consumer prices, they will rise, leading to an upward movement in industrial prices. The change in relative prices may be insufficient to lead to a shift in demand, and thus an inflationary spiral develops. W. A. Lewis in his 'Closing remarks' in Baer and Kerstenetzky (1964) distinguishes between the factors that start a price rise and the spiral processes that keep prices rising (the above factors plus budget deficits, devaluations and rising import prices) and argues that the inflationary spiral may continue for reasons unconnected with the original cause.[10] In other words, the price increase stemming from the bottleneck is not a once-and-for-all change in relative prices but instead may trigger off an inflationary spiral.[11] However, as we shall see below, an effective propagation or transmission mechanism is necessary for the inflationary spiral to manifest itself.

The structuralists argue that urbanisation and rising incomes have led to a rapidly rising demand for foodstuffs which cannot be met by the agricultural sector. The supply response of the agricultural sector is poor because of the structural constraints within that sector—the domination either by large non-capitalistic latifundia which are not profit maximisers,[12] or by minifundia operating almost at a subsistence level and barely integrated into the larger market economy (Baer (1967), p. 8)—and this inelastic supply constitutes a structural inflationary factor. Sunkel (1960) notes with respect to Chile (the country in which the structuralist analysis originated) that:

> '...the stagnation of global agricultural production cannot be attributed to market, demand and or price conditions, but must be due to factors inherent in the institutional and economic structure of the main part of the agricultural sector itself.' (p. 115)

The 'monetarist' argues that the alleged structural inelasticity of food supplies is not in fact structural at all but rather results from the all-too-frequent administrative control of food prices, imposed by the government in order to protect the urban consumer and avoid growing pressures for wage increases. This interference with the operation of market forces has a disincentive effect on food producers, but this is a distortion induced by administrative controls and is not inherent in the structure of land ownership (Campos (1961), p. 112).

Edel (1969), whose study we shall discuss in greater detail below, tested the agricultural supply bottleneck hypothesis for eight Latin American countries. He did not find a perfect relationship between food supply and inflation but he concluded that the direction of the relationship was the one indicated by the 'structuralist' analysis (inadequate food production meant more inflation, relative rises in food prices, more food imports, and slower growth in other sectors of the economy).

The second major bottleneck identified by the 'structuralists' is the foreign exchange bottleneck, dealt with in greater detail in Section V below. The alleged bottleneck arises because the rate of growth of total foreign exchange receipts (earnings from exports and capital inflows) is not sufficient to meet rapidly rising import demands generated by accelerated development efforts, rapid population growth and attempts to industralise which take place within the environment of imperfect factor mobility, technological limitations and structural imbalances noted above. The structurally induced balance of payments deficit is not cured by devaluation, the latter only adding to the inflationary spiral, and the import constraint is an important stimulus to ISI, the nature and consequences of which we discuss in Section VII. Import shortages and rising import prices trigger off cumulative price rises in a fashion similar to the process described above with respect to the agricultural sector bottleneck. Baer (1967) notes that

'Control of imports ... will create shortages of many form-
erly imported goods. The relative domestic price of these
goods will rise and thus contribute to the inflationary forces
... balance of payments difficulties will sooner or later force
countries to devalue their currencies; this will also have the
effect of an immediate upward push on the price level, especially if imports consist of many consumer goods, including
basic foodstuffs, which the agriculturally inelastic country
might be forced to import.' (p. 9)

It is further argued that instability of export proceeds is inflationary in that when it leads to a reduction in government reven-
ues the government is forced to resort to deficit financing to
maintain relatively inflexible levels of expenditure.

The 'monetarist' counter-argument is that part at least of
the slow growth of exports is policy rather than structurally
induced. Exchange rates are typically overvalued, and development
efforts emphasise 'inward-looking' ISI rather than 'outward-looking' policies aimed at maximising traditional exports and developing new lines. It is further argued that the import quantum has
been maintained, on the average, for Latin America, despite the
alleged external bottleneck, and that therefore there has been no
inflationary decrease in the availability of imported goods.

The third bottleneck, identified by some 'structuralist' writers
but not others, is the lack of internal financial resources. Rapid
urbanisation and the industrialisation effort have increased the
range of necessary government activities, mainly in the sphere of
physical and social infrastructure facilities, but government
revenue has not expanded at a sufficiently rapid rate. Baer (1967)
describes the tax-collecting bureaucracies of Latin America as
'antiquated, inefficient and sometimes corrupt' (p. 10). The necessary reform of these bureaucracies is a long-run problem,
whereas in the shorter run massive infrastructure investment
is an essential condition of more rapid economic growth. The
dilemma is usually solved by recourse to deficit financing, with
inflationary consequences. The problem is compounded by the
low rate of private capital formation and its preference for safe,
non-productive investments (land and property, foreign bank
accounts, etc.) which, it is alleged, forces the government to play
a larger role in capital formation than would otherwise be the
case and does not provide a sufficient volume of investment to
absorb into productive employment the rapidly growing population.[13] In addition to these problems, other writers (for example
Myrdal (1968), pp. 1928-9) argue that bottlenecks in other sectors—
electricity, fuel, imported raw materials, transport, repair facilities and credit facilities—are also of importance in giving rise to
inflationary pressures.

In addition to these basic inflationary pressures, Sunkel (1960) draws attention to so-called exogenous inflation pressures. These would include upward movements in the prices of imported goods and services and major increases in public expenditure arising out of natural disasters or political measures. In addition, we have cumulative inflationary pressures which are induced by inflation itself. In Chile, Sunkel argues that these pressures are an increasing function of the extent and the rate of inflation and they consist of the orientation of investment (already referred to above), expectations, the negative impact of inflation on productivity (including the distortions introduced into the price system by price controls) and the lack of export incentives.

If the structural constraints outlined above are to give rise to price increases, which in turn lead to a rapid and continuous increase in the general price level, it is obvious that there must exist an effective transmission or propogation mechanism which permits the manifestation of the various inflationary pressures. Few 'structuralist' writers (or at least, the interpreters of the 'structuralist' position) pay much attention to this mechanism, yet it is clear that if various groups or classes in society did not attempt to maintain their relative positions in the face of price increases, the chances of an inflationary spiral being generated would be much reduced. In Chile, for example, Sunkel (1960) argues that the propagation mechanism has resulted from the inability of the political system to resolve two major struggles of economic interests, that of the distribution of income between different social classes and that of the distribution of the productive resources of the community between the public and the private sectors of the economy. The propagation mechanism is thus seen as:

'... the ability of the different economic sectors and social groups continually to readjust their real income or expenditure: the wage-earning group through readjustment of salaries, wages and other benefits; private enterprise through price increases, and the public sector through an increase in nominal fiscal expenditure.' (p. 111)

One of the main components of Sunkel's propagation mechanism is the budget deficit (the third major bottleneck referred to above) which leads to an increase in the supply of money. Public expenditure is not easily reduced, and we have already noted the insufficient expansion of tax revenue. The public sector deficit thus represents '... the existence of a number of structural problems which preclude the realisation of a balanced-budget policy' and the propagation mechanism of the public sector inflationary pressures consists of '... the financing of the deficit by loans from the banking system, issuing bonds to the social security institutions, revaluation of monetary reserves and other measures related to the money supply . . . ' (Sunkel (1960), p. 122). For the private sector, 'price increases supported by passive reaction of the monetary and credit system constitutes the propagation mechanism of the inflationary pressures to which the business sector is subjected' (p. 123).

Thus to the 'structuralist' an increase in the supply of money is seen as a permissive factor which allows the inflationary spiral to manifest itself and become cumulative—it is a symptom of the structural rigidities which give rise to the inflationary pressures, rather than the cause of the inflation itself. In other words the increase in the supply of money is a necessary condition for the rise in the overall level of prices, but it is not regarded as a sufficient condition. We return to this point below.[14]

Arising out of Sunkel's analysis of the propagation mechanism is what Thorp (1971) refers to as the 'income shares approach' to inflation. Inflation is seen as the means of reconciling the conflicting objectives of different social groups, with the attempts of weak governments to satisfy all interests inevitably leading to inflation. This is not acceptable as an explanation of the initiation of inflation and is only really an explanation of how various groups attempt to defend their relative economic positions.

It is often assumed that 'structuralist' writers favour inflation as a means of accelerating economic growth, but this is not generally the case. They are concerned with the problem of how to make stability compatible with economic development but they argue that price stability can only be achieved through economic growth, which is a longer-run process. Inflation cannot be curbed in the short run without cost, and although they do not in general question the efficacy of monetary stabilisation policies, they do question the social and economic costs of stability achieved at the expense of full capacity utilisation and economic growth. In other words, inflation is preferred to stagnation.

The Latin American 'monetarist' analysis of inflation is relatively straightforward. Inflation originates in and is maintained by expansionist monetary and fiscal policies, comprising government deficit spending (coupled with the operation of inefficient state enterprises and uneconomic pricing policies), expansionist credit policies and the expansionary exchange operations of central banks. The rate of inflation needs to be drastically reduced (and the concomitant distortions in the economy eliminated) via the curbing of excess demand through monetary and fiscal policies, the control of wage increases and the elimination of subsidised exchange rates, with the help, wherever possible of international financial assistance.[15]

It is important to note that the 'monetarists' do not deny the existence of 'structural' rigidities and bottlenecks in LDCs, but they argue that such bottlenecks are not in fact 'structural' or 'autonomous' in nature. They result from the price and exchange rate distortions which are generated by the inflation itself and government attempts to reduce the rate of price increases (price controls on foodstuffs, overvalued exchange rates, high tariff barriers and direct import controls, etc.). The causal relationship is reversed, and in 'monetarist' eyes the bottlenecks in the economy retarding growth will be eliminated when inflation is brought under control. Furthermore, with a suitably reformed tax structure and with less inflation and perhaps less government intervention, the private sector would be able to play a larger role in the development process, thus reducing the need for government deficit financing. Campos (1967) maintains that the majority of 'monetarists' appear to recognise the 'social priority of development', but insists that stable and sustained growth can best be achieved in an environment of monetary stability.

Campos (1967) argues that 'monetarists' should perhaps be called 'fiscalists' in that the monetarist approach not only includes the use of traditional monetary weapons (the effectiveness of which may be very limited because of the underdeveloped nature of financial markets characteristic of LDCs) but also places emphasis on the use of fiscal policies. He maintains that the effectiveness of monetary weapons is greater in the case of demand inflation than of cost inflation, and this is also the case if the objective is to curb investment rather than consumption. Finally, monetary policies have an asymmetrical effect in that it is easier to promote the expansion of certain selected sectors than it is to enforce the restriction of certain undesirable sectors. Campos concludes that:

'... monetary weapons, though indispensable ingredients in anti-inflationary programs, have to be used in prudent combination with fiscal policies.' (p. 113)

The 'monetarist' analysis leads us directly to the controversy over the need for, and efficacy of, stabilisation policies. The 'monetarist' solution—the removal of budget deficits, the restraint of credit and the elimination of distortions in the market mechanism (especially the establishment of an 'equilibrium' rate of exchange)—forms the basis of IMF-sponsored stabilisation programmes. 'Structuralists' do not deny that monetary variables are partial determinants of inflation (in so far as inflation could not continue for long without monetary expansion)[16] but they are basically concerned with the underlying forces which put such pressure on the monetary authorities as to make the expansion of the money supply almost inevitable. Even if total demand were reduced, the underlying structural inflationary pressures would still persist and short-term stabilisation would in fact be

detrimental to growth because it would prevent the realisation of
the longer-run structural changes essential to the eventual elimination of inflation (Grunwald (1961), pp. 96-7; Thorp (1971), p. 198).

Numerous stabilisation programmes have been imposed upon
various Latin American economies. Thorp (1971, pp. 204-7)
characterises them as 'costly failures' aggravating the basic
inflationary pressures and severely depressing output. In Argentina for example in 1959 (the first year of a severe stabilisation
programme) output fell while prices rose 102 per cent. The
improvement in the following two years originated from an inflow
of foreign exchange, but when that came to an end in 1961 the
underlying structural conditions remained unaltered and the 1959
experience was repeated in 1962-3 (Eshag and Thorp (1965)). Felix
(1964, pp. 392-6) argues that IMF stabilisation programmes worked
against the necessary re-allocation of resources and that '...
they were based on a misappraisal of where some of the leading
difficulties lay, as well as on an erroneous normative perspective'.

The 'monetarists' counter-argument would be that the stabilisation programmes had not been rigorously adhered to. In Chile,
the stabilisation programme introduced in 1956 (the result of the
Klein-Saks Mission of 1954) achieved an initial but short-lasting
success in reducing the rate of inflation. Grunwald (1961) argues
that it was precisely the 'structuralist' aspects of the programme
(for example, tax reforms) that were politically unacceptable, and
the stagnation of economic activity and the rise in unemployment
exerted pressure to ease credit and wage restraints. Sunkel (1960)
notes that the monetary manifestations of inflation became less
marked but

'... the structural, exogenous and cumulative inflationary
pressures remained latent, since the other stabilisation
measures—devaluation and exchange reform, improvement
of agricultural prices and the rise in utility rates—did not
actually counteract these pressures but rather allowed
them free influence on the price system.' (pp. 124-5)

As Thorp points out, the two key factors in the success of a
stabilisation programme are the impact on the external sector
and the ability of labour to maintain its share of national income.
An inflow of foreign capital can alleviate the deflationary impact
of domestic credit restrictions, and the lack of an organised labour
movement (or government repression of that movement) permits
a regressive shift in income distribution which further aggravates
the disequilibrium between the structure of the production and the
composition of demand (Sunkel (1960), p. 126).

Prebisch (1961) maintains that the contraction of economic
activity is the result of a particular type of anti-inflationary
policy, rather than the inevitable result of checking the inflation-

ary process. Campos (1967) is critical of certain aspects of IMF stabilisation programmes,[17] arguing that they need to be more flexible, and Thorp (1971) notes that towards the end of the 1960s the IMF was prepared to co-operate in more unorthodox stabilisation programmes and was beginning to acknowledge the importance of maintaining public investment expenditures.

The 'monetarists' quite rightly point out that the 'structuralists' do not have a coherent, short-run anti-inflation programme to replace IMF-sponsored measures. 'Structuralists' stress the need for economic and social reforms to give greater balance and flexibility to the productive structure and greater social unity. Such measures include lessening the vulnerability of the economy to foreign trade instability, increasing the elasticity of supply of the output of various productive sectors (via government investment in transportation, marketing facilities, irrigation, provision of credit and technical advice) and raising the living standards of the great mass of the population. But they are vague as to what would happen during the transition period when these reforms were working themselves out. Grunwald (1961) argues that it is not surprising that the 'structuralists' do not have such a programme, as they have never been in a policy-making position.[18]

Perhaps of greater importance is the distinction that Felix (1961) makes between those 'structuralists' who would work within the social framework in an attempt to reform it and for whom reconciliation with the 'monetarists' is theoretically possible, and those who would see revolutionary change as an essential condition of development.

As we pointed out at the beginning of this section, the debate over inflation is only one aspect of the debate over the objectives and policies of development in general. 'Structuralists' such as Prebisch (1961) argue that:

> 'The general mistake persists of considering inflation as a purely monetary phenomenon as such. Inflation cannot be explained as something divorced from the economic and social maladjustments and stresses to which the economic development of our countries gives rise. Nor can serious thought be given to autonomous anti-inflationary policy, as if only monetary considerations were involved; it must be an integral part of development policy'. (p. 346)

Campos (1961), on the other hand, argues that the 'structuralists' have failed to distinguish between autonomous and policy-induced bottlenecks, and restates the 'monetarist' (or 'fiscalist') position:

> '... the role of old fashioned monetary and fiscal policy is vitally important. Money factors are not residual but at the

very core of the process. The inflated countries are those that choose incompatible targets'. (p. 73)

There are certainly three criticisms that can legitimately be made of the 'structuralist' analysis (or at least the more popular versions of that analysis). Firstly, their emphasis on two or three bottlenecks and their presentation of a somewhat rigid and mechanical analysis of the operation of the bottlenecks leads to overgeneralisation (often easy to refute with specific examples) and the downgrading in importance of the actual (as opposed to the hypothetical) policy choices that a government is faced with. Within a given socio-political environment, a government is 'forced' to pursue certain policies (inflation is, for example, an 'easier' political alternative than land reform, or a reduction in the consumption of upper-income groups), and although the result may be a policy-induced constraint, it is no less the outcome of a particular economic, political, and institutional structure. We do not agree with Olivera's distinction between 'structural infla-tion' and 'structural proneness' to inflation. We would argue for a broadly defined 'structural' (as opposed to 'structuralist') analysis of inflation and would agree with Sunkel when he states:

> '... inflation does not occur *in vacuo* but as part of a coun-try's historical, social, political and institutional evolution ... *the underlying causes of inflation in underdeveloped coun-tries are to be found in basic economic development prob-lems and in the structural characteristics of the system of production in these countries*.' (Sunkel (1960), p. 108; empha-sis in original)

The second criticism is that too little attention in 'structural-ist' analysis, with the notable exception of Sunkel, has been given to the nature and the role of the propagation mechanism and the expansion of the money supply that accompanies the inflationary process. We have seen that a propagation mechanism is neces-sary to transmit basic inflationary pressures and that an increase in the supply of money is necessary (other things being equal) for the manifestation of inflationary price rises. The 'structuralist' assertion that the increase in the money supply is merely a per-missive factor may tend to obscure the wider socio-economic framework within which this policy option is chosen. Anticipating the discussion of Section IV. 2 below, both schools of thought can accept the proposition that changes in the money supply occur in response to political factors, but the basic question remains as to whether these changes permit or are the actual cause of the infla-tionary process (a question to which some of the empirical studies discussed below address themselves).[19]

The third criticism concerns the distribution of income. Logi-cally, this should be the focus of attention of every 'structuralist' analysis. Most LDCs are characterised by a high degree of inequality (Chenery *et al.*(1974)) which is an important determinant of the pattern of domestic demand and the structure of imports, the composition of industrial output and, through the technology adopted, the creation of employment opportunities.[20] Furthermore, the distribution of economic and hence political power determines the range of policy options any particular government is likely to pursue, and the process of inflation itself significantly alters the economic and political power structure of the inflating economy. The fact that many 'structuralist' analyses abstract from distributional questions weakens both their analytical validity and their general applicability.

2 Empirical tests of the 'structuralist' and 'monetarist' hypotheses

An important test of one aspect of the 'structuralist' analysis has been carried out by Edel (1969) in his empirical study of the alleged food supply bottlenecks in eight Latin American countries. He tests two propositions: (i) that food has lagged behind the required rate of growth, and (ii) that this agricultural lag is associated with inflation, balance of payments difficulties, and stagnation.

The adequacy of food supply is defined as that rate of autonomous growth of production (resulting from the adoption of new techniques, increases in labour force and area of production, etc.) sufficient to satisfy demand without any change in relative prices. Edel found that Mexico, Brazil, and Venezuela outpaced or at least approximately equalled food requirements.[21] Taking into account price changes, he found that the five countries with inadequate growth rates (Chile, Columbia, Peru, Uruguay, and Argentina) all had increasing relative food prices and thus the inadequate growth could not have been a function of price deterioration. He concluded:

'The trend or autonomous rate of growth of food output would thus seem to be a more important determinant of the adequacy of a country's agriculture than the existence of a positive response to prices ... Although it may be incorrect in these countries to speak of "inelastic supply" as the central aspect of the problem, it seems justifiable to speak of "inadequacy" of production trends in Chile, Columbia, Peru, Uruguay and Argentina and to add inelasticity as a factor, perhaps, in the last three.' (pp. 41-2)

He did not find a perfect relationship between food supply and inflation but the evidence justified the conclusion that

'... the direction of the relationship is the one indicated by the structuralist theory that less adequate food production means more inflation, as well as relative rises in the food prices, more food imports, and slower growth in other sectors of the economy.' (pp. 135-6)

Chile, Peru, Argentina and Uruguay in particular showed more clearly evidence of these pressures.

Several factors modified the basic structuralist thesis:

1 Increased foreign exchange earnings allowed imports when production was inadequate (Venezuela and Peru in the early 1960s);
2 The existence of an exportable surplus or a high level of consumption cushioned a country against having to increase imports (Argentina, Uruguay);
3 a change in the distribution of income changed the demand for food (Argentina in 1959), and
4 The possibilities of belt-tightening and the elimination of luxury imports permitted imports to be cut despite the inadequate expansion of food production when foreign exchange was lacking (Columbia).

These factors do not invalidate the 'structuralist' model. Once the *ceteris paribus* conditions are taken into account, the 'production lag' model holds for some Latin American countries. Edel further concludes that the degree of price control on foodstuffs does not appear to be related systematically to agricultural performance for all the countries studied, whereas there is considerable evidence that land tenure and low productivity are related to one another.[22]

Edel considered that Brazil came closest to conformity with the monetarist model, and this conclusion has been strongly supported by Kahil (1973). The four alleged structural constraints that Kahil analyses are the agricultural sector bottleneck, the inadequate mobility of capital, the external sector bottleneck and the effect on demand and costs of rapid urbanisation. His major conclusions are: a rural/urban price spiral was not generated by an inelastic supply of agricultural produce; urbanisation itself has not been responsible for inflationary pressures (specifically, it did not lead to an increase in the purchasing power of migrants); the rigidity of capital supply did not have much influence on the price level; the terms of trade throughout the period studied (1946-63) were more favourable to Brazil than at any time since the mid-1930s, and that the chief cause of increasing balance of payments disequilibria was the stagnation of the export quantum, resulting from inflation and faulty economic policies; and finally, there was no evidence that bottlenecks in transport or energy contributed to rising price levels or

that the lack of labour (especially skilled) pushed up industrial
prices.

Kahil argues that:

'. . . the structural weaknesses of the economy cannot have
played a significant role in the evolution of the price level from
1946 to 1964, and . . . their aggravation towards the end of the
period was more an effect than a cause of the acceleration of
inflation.' (p. 327)

Price rises were caused by large and growing public deficits, a too
rapid expansion of bank credit in the early years, and later unneces-
sarily large and increasingly frequent increases in legal minimum
wages. At the early stages of inflation, these three factors are independent of one another but as inflation accelerates, they interact
in such a way that it is impossible to say which is cause, which is
effect. As price rises become increasingly rapid, '. . . the Central
Bank is *compelled* to supply the public sector with a growing volume
of funds, while the commercial banks are *forced* to expand loans to
the private sector at an accelerated pace, and wages and salaries
have to be raised again and again to restore the rapidly declining
standard of living of workers and employees' (p. 329; emphasis in
original). Thus the basic causes of inflation appear to become mere
parts of the structuralist propagation mechanism—'mere passive
elements in an uncontrollable process which seems to have a life
of its own, and dominates the whole economy' (p. 330).

Having reached a strong monetarist conclusion, Kahil then performs a surprising (and undoubtedly unintentional) *volte-face* and
argues that the factors ultimately responsible for inflation were
political rather than economic. The two main policy aims of the
1950s were rapid industrialisation and the winning of the allegiance
of the urban masses while at the same time serving the interests
of other politically important groups. This, he argues, explains the
incoherent and inflationary nature of many government policies:
'. . . the multifarious and frequently incompatible policy decisions
taken by authorities were largely motivated by their strong determination to achieve their two major objectives simultaneously'
(p. 331). In other words, inflation was the outcome of the attempt by
the State to fulfill its development objectives and grant privileges
(albeit temporary and illusory) to mutually antagonistic groups or
classes.[23] This conclusion is remarkably similar to the one
reached above (and stated in the context of western developed economies by Devine (1974)) and is consistent with the structural
analysis of inflation in LDCs advanced in this paper. In Brazil,
Kahil argues that it was the big industrialists, bankers, merchants,
and contractors who were most favoured by inflation and who were
most likely to resist stabilisation measures. But inflation began to
accelerate at the end of 1958, social and political conflicts inten-

sified, and a combination of economic and political factors eventually precipitated the military coup of 1964.[24]

The study by Harberger (1963) of inflation in Chile has been
the most influential empirical analysis of inflation in the monetarist tradition in Latin America, and subsequent econometric studies
by Diaz-Alejandro (1965), Diz (1970), and Vogel (1974) are extensions of the basic Harberger model.

Harberger's study of Chilean inflation covers the period from
1939 to 1958, during which time inflation was almost continuous and
the wholesale price index and the cost of living index increased
more than eightfold. The approach is basically a monetarist one,
and Harberger tests the hypothesis of a stable demand function for
real balances by regressing the annual rate of price change in the
cost of living index upon the percentage change in money supply
during the present and preceding year and the percentage change in
real income during the present year.[25] Expected changes in the
cost of holding idle balances are allowed for by introducing past
changes in the rate of inflation as an additional independent variable. Harberger also attempts to clarify the role of wage changes
in the Chilean inflation, and wage changes are used as an additional
independent variable in the regression equation. The role of wages
in the inflationary process has been a subject of controversy in
Chile (as elsewhere) with, at the one extreme, 'monetarists' arguing
that wages simply respond in a passive fashion to inflationary
forces which are monetary in origin, while at the other extreme
there is the view that wages are the principal factor in explaining
the rate of inflation, and that once their effect has been taken into
account monetary variables will not add to the explanation of the
inflationary process.

During the whole of the period investigated by Harberger, there
was a form of minimum wage for public sector employees which
was revised upward annually, and was set largely as the result of
political negotiations among parties in the congress. Once a certain percentage increase in this minimum wage had been determined, wage contracts in the industrial sector of the economy
were adjusted at least to match this percentage increase, and private wages tended subsequently to drift upward in response to the
pressures of the labour market and collective bargaining. Harberger argues that in such circumstances wage movements could have
played an active part in the inflationary process.

The empirical results obtained by Harberger would appear to
support the monetarist interpretation, with each of the monetary
variables statistically significant and the inclusion of the wages
variable failing to increase the overall explanatory power of the
monetary variables. However, Harberger is careful not to adopt
the strict monetarist position that would be suggested by a superficial inspection of the results. He argues that:

'These results suggest that one of the major roles of the wage variable was indeed as a "transmitter" of inflation from one period to the next, responding to the monetary expansion of the past period and including monetary expansion in the subsequent period. The wage variable does not significantly alter the predictions . . . and in this sense one does not "need" it. . . . The wage variable does not add significantly to the variation in the rate of inflation explained by monetary factors: in this sense too . . . one does not "need" it. But none of this denies that if wage changes had tended in the period to be unaccompanied by monetary expansion, prices would have none the less responded. Nor does it deny that prior wages rises were an important factor in inducing monetary expansion during the period. It only says that during this period monetary expansions were typically great enough to "finance" prior wage changes, and that on top of this, monetary expansions had independent variations, which also influenced the price level in much the same way as if they had been accompanied by wage changes.' (pp. 246-7)

As previously mentioned, the studies by Diaz-Alejandro, Diz, and Vogel are extensions of the basic Harberger model, and therefore require less detailed discussion. In his study of Argentina, Diaz-Alejandro regresses various indices of inflation (wholesale price index, components of that index, cost of living index) on four independent variables—money supply, real gross domestic product plus merchandise imports, hourly money wage rates in industry, and the exchange rate. All variables are expressed as annual rates of change, with observations covering the period 1945-62. The coefficients are generally statistically significant and have the expected signs. Diaz-Alejandro finds that changes in wage rates are highly correlated with subsequent changes in the money supply, while changes in the money supply do not appear to have a significant influence on subsequent changes in wage rates. He argues that the high rates of inflation combined with the fall in real national product that occured in several periods reflect the existence of cost-push inflation so that the monetary authority is faced with increasing unemployment if it does not permit the money supply to grow in response to increases in wage rates. The author's main conclusion is therefore that the money supply played only a permissive role in Argentina's inflation and was not the underlying cause.

The study by Diz also examines the experience of Argentina, covering the period 1935-62. Two dependent variables are used (wholesale price and cost of living indices), and the independent variables used are: money supply (with two definitions, one including and the other excluding savings and time deposits), real income, an index of nominal wages, the official exchange rate, and a measure of price expectations. In the regression results, the money supply, real income, and expectations coefficients are statistically significant and exhibit the expected sign. The wage coefficients are not significant and the exchange rate coefficients, although significant, suggest a highly inelastic response of prices to changes in the exchange rate. Diz interprets his findings that changes in the money supply have a substantial impact on the rate of inflation as evidence in support of the 'monetarist' analysis of inflation. His conclusions are that:

> 'From 1935 to 1962 the changes in the rate of change in money significantly affected the behaviour of the rate of inflation, through a process of adjustment which involved considerable time. The results indicate that the adjustment of prices to an acceleration of money seemed to require no less than two years and that it involved initial overshooting and later deceleration of prices. Changes in the expected rate of change in prices and real income also affected significantly the rate of inflation. The role of devaluations and wage increases in the Argentine inflationary process was also analysed, but the results show that their influence on the rate of inflation failed to achieve the levels and significance usually attributed to them.' (p. 123)

Vogel has extended the Harberger model to sixteen Latin American countries for the period 1950-69. The dependent variable is the consumer price index, and the independent variables are money supply (currency plus demand deposits), real income (nominal GNP deflated by the consumer price index), and past changes in the rate of inflation (as a proxy for the expected cost of holding real balances). All variables are annual and are expressed as percentage changes. 'Structural' variables, such as wage changes and exchange rate changes are not included in the analysis. The paper reports the results obtained from using pooled data covering time-series and cross-section observations, and for each country separately. The results obtained from the pooled data exhibited a high level of overall explanatory power, and the coefficients of the independent variables exhibited the correct sign and were statistically significant (with the exception of the lagged change in inflation rate variable). The results of the individual country regressions were less favourable, and they revealed considerable differences between countries. The value of the correlation coefficient ranged from 0·87 to 0·00, and some of the coefficients of money supply and real income variables were either statistically insignificant or exhibited an incorrect sign.[26]

On the basis of these results Vogel concludes that:

> 'the most important result of the present study . . . is that a purely monetarist model, with no structuralist variables, reveals little heterogeneity among Latin American countries, in

spite of their extreme diversity. The substantial differences in rates of inflation among these countries cannot under the present model be attributed to structural differences, but must rather be attributed primarily to differences in the behaviour of the money supply.' (p. 113)

Ignoring the question of whether his regression results are sufficiently robust to warrant this conclusion, Vogel misinterprets the structuralist position when he implies that structuralists argue that inflation can be explained by 'structural differences', in isolation from or independently of changes in the monetary environment. Vogel's findings are not inconsistent with the 'structural' interpretation of Latin American inflationary experience (although this is not meant to imply that there would be agreement as to the exact nature of the relationship between changes in the money supply and changes in prices), and adherents to the structural hypothesis would be in full agreement with his conclusion that:

'the importance of the money supply suggests that further research is needed on its determination, particularly since the studies of Harberger, Diaz-Alejandro and Diz indicate that the money supply may not be exogenous in every Latin American country.' (p. 113)

The study by Argy (1970) is an attempt 'to appraise the contribution of structural elements in inflation in developing countries' (p. 73), and it differs from those so far discussed in that it is based entirely on cross-sectional data. The author computed a variety of indices to represent four structural constraints—the foreign exchange bottleneck, the export instability bottleneck, the agricultural bottleneck and the demand shift constraint—for twenty-two LDCs using data averaged over the period 1958-65. Two alternative indicators were used to represent the foreign exchange constraint: the average annual percentage change in net barter terms of trade, and the average import ratio for the period 1954-8. The agricultural bottleneck was tested using two alternative measures of excess demand for agricultural production. For each country, the rate of growth of demand for agricultural output was calculated by assuming that the elasticity of demand with respect to population growth was unity, while the income elasticity of demand was assumed to be 0·6. The first measure of excess demand was taken as the difference between this assumed growth rate of demand and the actual rate of growth of agricultural production in each of the countries in the sample. The second measure was the average annual rate of change in food prices minus the average rate of change in the cost of living for each country. The export instability hypothesis (that, other things being equal, fluctuations in export receipts will tend to create an upward movement in the price level) was tested using two measures of export variability. The first index used was the variance of the annual percentage changes in dollar export receipts. To allow for the possibility of a lag in adjustment, a second index was calculated using the variances for the years 1958-64. The demand-shift hypothesis (that shifts in the sectoral composition of demand will cause an upward movement in the price level) was tested using an index based on the changes in the weights of eight different sectors in each country's economy that occured between 1958-9 and 1964-5. Two further variables were used in the regression analysis: the government deficit rate and the rate of change in the money supply. The variables were tested in a variety of combinations—structural only, monetary only, structural and monetary—using ordinary least squares linear regression analysis. On the basis of the results obtained, Argy concludes that 'the results for structuralist variables are, not surprisingly, poor' (p. 38) and that 'the monetary variables perform very well. In every case the addition of a monetary variable to structuralist variables improved substantially the results' (p. 83).

However, Argy's findings are subject to a number of serious limitations. First, as Argy himself acknowledges, it is extremely difficult to devise appropriate indicators of structural constraints, and the indices used are in most cases of limited value. For example, changes in the sectoral weights may represent changes in the rates of growth of different sectors, rather than shifts in demand; changes in the barter terms of trade may bear little relationship to changes in import capacity; changes in the import ratio are an inadequate measure of the severity of the foreign exchange constraint; the assumptions of unity elasticity of demand for food with respect to the population and 0·6 with respect to income are arbitrary; the relationship between variability in export receipts and inflation will vary significantly between countries depending upon the economic and institutional features of the economy. Second, there is a strong possibility of significant multicollinearity between the independent variables used in the regression analysis. For example, variations in export receipts can be expected to affect the import ratio, changes in sectoral composition will influence agricultural production: furthermore, the change in agricultural prices used in calculating the agricultural bottleneck index will be an important component of the dependent variable. A third, and more fundamental, criticism of Argy's analysis is that his findings, and conclusion that 'monetary variables predominate in accounting for rates of inflation in developing countries' (p. 84), contributes little to our understanding of the basic causes of inflation in LDCs. As we have already seen, little weight can be given to the statistical tests of the 'structuralist' variables, largely because of the difficulty of deriving testable hypotheses from 'structuralist' theory. The fact that monetary variables are found to have a high correlation with the rate of inflation is a result that will cause little surprise to either 'monetarists' or 'structuralists': evidence of correlation fails to provide us with an understanding of the underlying causal relationships that exist between structural constraints, monetary expansion and inflation.

The various studies that have been described in this section of the paper illustrate the immense difficulties that arise in attempting to assess empirically the relative importance of the 'structural' and 'monetary' factors in inflation in LDCs. The studies of Harberger, Diaz-Alejandro, Diz and Vogel illustrate both how different results can arise from an examination of the same time period, and how very different conclusions about the monetarist-structuralist controversy can be reached from essentially similar findings. In the case of Kahil, an initial monetarist interpretation can in fact be shown to be consistent with the structural analysis of inflation. The fundamental problem of distinguishing cause from effect, as distinct from discovering evidence of correlation, has limited the usefulness of existing quantitative investigations (with the exception of Edel's study). Nevertheless, at the very least it can be said that a careful examination of the empirical studies that have so far been undertaken neither discredits nor disproves the structural analysis of the causes of inflation in LDCs.

V THE FOREIGN EXCHANGE CONSTRAINT

An important element in the structuralist interpretation of inflation is the notion of a foreign exchange bottleneck. Many LDCs are faced with persistent balance of payments difficulties which are the result of the rapidly rising import demands implicit in a programme of planned economic development, imperfect factor mobility, and insufficiently rapid growth in foreign exchange receipts.[27] Both demand and supply constraints frequently prevent the LDCs from achieving significant increases in export receipts, the international reserves of most LDCs are at a critically low level,[28] and inflows of external capital do not, with certain notable exceptions, account for a significant proportion of total foreign exchange receipts.[29] Inadequate foreign exchange receipts constitute an effective structural constraint upon the growth and development of the economy, since

> '. . . rapid growth requires a large increase in the supplies of machinery and equipment, raw materials and other manufactured goods that are typically imported in a poor country. The more rapid the rate of growth, the larger the reallocation of labour and capital away from traditional patterns that will be needed to prevent bottlenecks developing. If this reallocation is not sufficiently rapid, shortages of imported goods will provide a limit to further growth quite apart from the investment

limitations. The import limit reflects the inability of the economy to provide the composition of output—from domestic sources plus imports—that is required by its level of income, rate of investment and pattern of consumer demand. In cases of acute shortages of imported goods the economy will be unable to transform potential savings into investment because of insufficient supplies of investment goods.'[30]

The foreign exchange bottleneck argument implies therefore that the typical LDC will experience persistent pressure on its balance of payments, with a permanent tendency for the foreign balance to move into deficit.[31]

The notion of the foreign exchange constraint is contrary to the predictions of the monetary approach to balance of payments theory, which represents a revival of the price-specie-flow theory originally advanced by David Hume. This analysis showed that the amount of money in an economy would be adjusted to the demand for it through changes in the balance of payments, induced by the effects on relative money price levels of excess demands for and supplies of money.[32] The fundamental element in the monetary theory of the balance of payments is therefore the existence of a stable demand for money function, which is determined by the level of real income and the opportunity cost of holding money. If each of these determinants remains constant the monetary approach can be regarded as a theory of the rate of inflation, whereby the price level will adjust to ensure that whatever the stock of nominal money, the level of money in real terms will be equal to the amount demanded. Thus the nominal money supply determines the price level. In an open economy, the supply of money is given by the sum of domestic credit and international reserves: a change in the balance of payments therefore will affect the nominal money supply. In a world of fixed exchange rates where each economy is operating at the full employment level of output, the rate of inflation in the world price level is determined by the rate of expansion of the international money supply (which is equal to the sum of the increase in each country's domestic money supply), and in equilibrium each economy takes this world inflation rate as its own rate of inflation. However, in the short run, inflation rates will differ between countries. These differences can be allowed for by making a distinction between internationally traded and non-traded goods, with the discrepancies in national inflation rates being explained in terms of lags in the transmission of inflationary movements in the traded goods sector to the non-traded sector. The adjustment mechanism can be envisaged by considering an individual economy that is initially in equilibrium with an inflation rate equal to the world rate of inflation, which generates an expansion of domestic credit. The immediate result will be to increase the supply of money and create excess money balances. Demand will then rise as individuals attempt to reduce their increased money balances. Part of this demand will be for traded goods, and since the economy is assumed to be operating at or near to full capacity output level, the increased demand cannot be met from domestic sources of supply and will lead to an increase in imports.[33] Part of the excess money balances will be used in attempting to purchase non-traded goods, resulting in a rise in their domestic prices. This in turn will lead to rises in wages, and a fall in the supply of traded goods to the external market. The balance of payments deficit is thereby accentuated since both exports fall and imports rise with the transfer of resources into the production of non-traded goods.

The effect of the rise in wages and in the price of non-traded goods is to produce a rate of inflation in excess of the equilibrium world inflation rate. Subsequent events are dependent upon whether the authorities reverse or continue with the policy of domestic credit expansion. If the expansion of domestic money supply is reversed, the deterioration in the balance of payments will, through the loss of reserves, lead to a fall in the supply of money. The level of money balances will then be reduced below the desired level, and in an effort to restore the money balances, exports will be increased and imports reduced. There will therefore be an improvement in the balance of payments and a slowing down of the inflation rate back towards the equilibrium, or world, inflation rate. If the authorities do not reduce the expansion of domestic credit, the loss of reserves will force a change in the exchange rate. The effect of devaluation will be to raise the domestic prices of imported goods, thus putting further pressure on domestic prices and wages.

The implications of the monetarist theory for the conduct of the monetary authorities are clear. If the authorities wish to maintain a fixed exchange rate, then the maintenance of the equilibrium in the balance of payments and a steady rate of inflation (equal to the world inflation rate) will require the adoption of a 'passive' monetary policy which allows the supply of money to be determined by the demand for it. Where the authorities expand the supply of domestic credit, and at the same time attempt to maintain an unchanged exchange rate, the result will be an acceleration in the rate of inflation and a deterioration in the balance of payments. The existence of a balance of payments disequilibrium is the result of pursuing a policy of expanding the supply of money that is incompatible with the maintenance of the existing rate of exchange, rather than the result of fundamental or structural imbalances within the domestic economy. The balance of payments pressure can therefore be eliminated (and the rate of inflation reduced) either by a reduction in domestic credit creation or by an abandonment of a fixed exchange rate policy.

It must be acknowledged that certain exponents of the foreign exchange constraint argument have presented the argument exclusively in real terms, and have ignored the monetary environment within which the constraint arises. However, as we argued in Section IV, structuralists do not deny that monetary variables are a necessary condition for the continuation of inflation, but they would argue that the underlying forces, which may be economic, political and social, that have resulted in the monetary authorities' decision to expand the money supply will not be removed or eliminated by the adoption of orthodox monetary policies. In terms of the foreign exchange constraint, structuralists would argue that there is a fundamental difference between the determinants of the level of imports in an advanced economy and in a LDC where the level of imports is frequently closely related to the availability of foreign exchange. In the developed economy where there is considerable scope for substitution between domestically produced and imported commodities, the level of imports will be responsive to changes in relative prices. In contrast, the typical LDC is heavily dependent upon imported goods for which domestic substitutes are not available.[34]

It is also true that the foreign exchange constrain argument has often been presented in an unrealistically rigid manner, implying that the constraint is fixed and cannot be relaxed by deliberate policy measures. As Bruton (1969) has pointed out, a literal interpretation of the foreign exchange bottleneck analysis implies that the importation of non-essential consumer goods is zero, that the imported component of investment is technologically fixed and that exports cannot be increased. None of these assumptions is entirely correct. There is obviously some degree of choice available in the proportion of import capacity that is devoted to the importation of investment goods. Technology is seldom so rigid as to result in the rate of transformation in domestic production being zero. Nor can it seriously be argued that the individual LDC cannot, by adopting appropriate policies, influence the level of its export receipts. Nevertheless, the foreign exchange constraint argument draws attention to the fact that many LDCs have inherited an economic structure that is unable to meet the demands that are imposed by the need for economic development. A lack of domestic substitutes coupled with a reliance upon imported technology has resulted in a heavy dependence upon imported investment goods and raw materials. Leff and Netto (1966) make the point with respect to Brazil:

'In Brazilian conditions, the marginal propensity to import, m, means something very different than it does in economies with more ample foreign exchange supply. In other economies, imports are determined by the level of income, relative prices of domestic and imported products, and the exchange rate, subject to the constraint that imports be less than or equal the supply of foreign exchange. In such conditions, the marginal propensity to import can be considered a function of national income. In Brazil, however, the constraint imposed by the availability of foreign exchange intervenes long before the desired level of imports in reached . . . within a considerable range, imports would be much higher were it not for the foreign exchange availability constraint. Consequently, the import co-efficient, M/y, is simply the ratio of foreign exchange receipts to national income.' (pp. 227-8)

Leff (1967) has argued that in discussing the economic consequences of limitations of import supplies, a distinction should be made between a 'demand-diverting' effect and a 'supply-constraining' effect. That is, one effect of import limitations is to divert demand from imported suppliers to domestic suppliers. At the same time however, a lack of raw materials and other inputs imported from abroad may inhibit the ability of domestic producers to respond to the increased demand for their products, so that a shortfall in foreign exchange receipts will have a serious depressive impact on the level of domestic economic activity. Thus, while it is logically correct to argue that, given a fixed exchange rate, there is a rate of domestic credit expansion that will ensure equilibrium in the balance of payments, this view ignores the underlying distortions, imperfections and structural rigidities that exist within the less developed economy, and which ensure that the actual level of imports will frequently be less than that required to achieve the economic development of the economy. Chenery (1969) has made this point in the following way:

'It has become customary to . . . regard . . . limited success in increasing exports or curtailing imports as . . . evidence of bad policy . . . [However] the limits to government action are set by its diagnosis of the problem, the likely response of the economy, and the polical acceptability of the results. . . . A diagnosis of past causes of balance of payments disequilibrium . . . is important primarily for the guidance that it provides as to future possibilities for improved performance. Whether or not disequilibrium in the payments balance could have been avoided by having a higher peso-dollar exchange rate for the past ten years does not determine whether the current problem in country X is structural. The effects of an over-valued rate or other misguided policies are incorporated in the existing distorted structure of production and trade. The fact that it requires a reallocation of investment and other changes extending beyond the short run to expand the trade limit makes the problem structural, whatever its origin.' (pp. 446-7)

The view that denies that LDCs face a fundamental or structural balance of payments disequilibrium in many instances amounts to arguing that 'the problem would not exist if countries had followed ideal policies in the past. Whether or not this is true, it is not particularly relevant to a description of actual policy alternatives.' (Chenery (1969), p. 447). The persistence of the foreign exchange constraint, as evidenced by the persistent balance of payments pressures experienced by many LDCs has encouraged the adoption of policies aimed at its removal. The widespread pessimism that exists in LDCs concerning the prospects of obtaining a significant increase in foreign exchange from the export of primary products has resulted in a concentration upon policies that attempt to relieve the foreign exchange bottleneck by reducing the economy's dependence on imported commodities.[35] This response to the foreign exchange constraint has taken two main forms. In the short run, policies have been directed at releasing foreign exchange for 'essential' imports by reducing the volume of consumer goods imports. This has been attempted by the use of import controls, quotas, duties, and exchange rate changes (as discussed in Sections VI. 1 and VI. 2). In the longer run, policies have been directed at the substitution of domestic production for imported commodities through the process of import-substituting industrialisation (as discussed in Section VII. 2). The adoption of these policies has had two related, but unanticipated, results. First, they have not in general reduced the foreign exchange constraint: rather, as we shall argue in subsequent sections of the paper, they have frequently increased the economy's dependence on imported commodities. The second result of adopting these policies has been to accentuate the inflationary pressures that result from the structural bottlenecks in the economy. Therefore we turn now to an examination of each of these types of policy-response to the foreign exchange constraint, placing particular emphasis on their implications for the rate of inflation.

VI IMPORT RESTRAINT AND INFLATION

1 Import controls and inflation

A characteristic feature of economic policy in many LDCs is the widespread use of import controls. This structure was initiated in most countries in response to the economy's balance of payments difficulties, and policy was therefore initially aimed at restricting inessential consumer goods imports rather than encouraging the establishment of domestically produced substitute commodities, with the result that protective effects were incidental rather than planned. Nevertheless, the result has been to give the highest protection to these commodities that are considered to be non-essential for the growth of the economy.[36] The introduction of import controls will result in an initial increase in the domestic price level, either as a direct result of the import tariffs or indirectly through the black market prices created by the administrative controls. However, the inflationary impact of import controls will vary with the type of control that is employed. If import tariffs which do not limit the volume of imports are used, and if the level of the tariffs is constant, then the imposition of the tariff will simply mean that the commodity will be supplied at a higher constant domestic price: the price will rise with the introduction of the control but there will be no further inflationary impact. However, as we have already argued, in most LDCs the potential demand for imports exceeds the available supply. As a result, import controls and quotas that limit the volume or total value of imports are used, the result being to create domestic shortages which lead to the inflation of the domestic prices of imported goods. Where domestic substitutes are available, their prices will tend to increase in line with those of imported commodities. The increase in prices will lead to demands for increased money wages, and, by means of the propagation mechanism and increases in money supply, inflation will become established.[37] Since most LDCs rely heavily upon discretionary import controls that limit the total volume or value of imports, the impact of the widespread adoption of quantitative import controls in LDCs has, in general, been to add to domestic inflationary pressures.

2 Devaluation and inflation

Orthodox analysis would suggest that a persistent balance of payments disequilibrium is evidence that the exchange rate should be devalued to the level at which there is equilibrium between the demand and supply of foreign exchange without import controls: devaluation is seen as a policy substitute for restricting imports by controls. This view, based on the standard analysis of currency devaluation, fails to take into account many of the features that are typical of LDCs, and that limit the impact of devaluation on their foreign exchange situation.

One explanation of the reluctance of policy-makers in LDCs to use devaluation as a tool of economic management is the fact that the foreign exchange rate may be used to pursue many objectives other than the clearing of the foreign exchange market.[38] The objectives may include the encouragement of import-substituting industrialisation, improving the barter terms of trade, avoidance of an increase in the domestic costs of imports or external debts denominated in foreign currency, altering the distribution of income among broad sectors or classes in the economy.[39] Faced with inadequate means of achieving the multiple objectives of economic policy, it need not be considered irrational to use the exchange rate as an indirect instrument with which to pursue these aims. Most LDCs therefore have some combination of an open and a supressed payments deficit, and, as a result, when the decision to devalue is ultimately taken or forced upon the policy-makers, the nature and impact of the exchange rate alteration is considerably more complex than a simple adjustment of the exchange rate.

The reluctance to devalue is frequently due to pessimism with regard to the potential contribution of devaluation to an easing of the foreign exchange constraint in LDCs. For a number of reasons, the price elasticity of demand for both imports and exports is likely to be low. The first point to be noted is that the elasticity of demand for imports is likely to be low where imports consist largely of raw materials, capital and intermediate goods, the volume of which will be unresponsive to relative price changes.[40] Second, to the extent that devaluation is accompanied by the removal or relaxation of import controls and quotas, the domestic final price of imported commodities may be reduced and consumption increased. Third, in so far as the incomes of exporters are increased, their consumption of imports or import-intensive domestic commodities will increase.[41] On *a priori* grounds, therefore, it seems unlikely that devaluation will have the effect of significantly reducing the value of imports.[42] The burden of adjustment therefore rests largely upon the response of the export sector.

The response of the export sector to the currency devaluation can be expected to be more variable, but nevertheless there are a number of *a priori* reasons for supposing that, in general, the devaluation is unlikely to result in a substantial increase in export receipts. The export receipts schedule is a function of both domestic supply conditions and foreign demand conditions. The price elasticity of demand for many primary products and raw materials is low: in part this may be due to the low proportion of raw material cost in final output, or it may be due to the imposition of quotas or taxes upon these commodities by the importing country. There are also grounds for believing that the supply within the LDCs may be unresponsive to changes in relative prices. We have already referred to the importance of the agricultural sector bottleneck in many LDCs which may prevent any significant increase in the production of agricultural exports. Where the export commodity is a major item of wage goods within the domestic economy there is a greater possibility for an immediate increase by reducing domestic consumption, but this is likely to result in increased inflationary pressures originating in wage and price movements in the urban sector.[43] A re-direction of manufactures from the domestic to the external market not be easily accomplished. First, the previous pattern of highly protected ISI is likely to have led to the establishment of a relatively high-cost inefficient sector whose products are uncompetitive in world markets. Second, even where manufactures can be competitively exported at the new rate of exchange, the opening up of new export markets requires the establishment of new marketing networks and the identification of consumer tastes and preferences. Furthermore, the export of manufactures from LDCs is subject to substantial trade barriers in the developed countries' markets.[44]

There are therefore good reasons for being pessimistic about the import and export elasticities in LDCs, and for believing that devaluation may fail to make a significant contribution to the removal of an existing trade deficit. On *a priori* grounds it seems unlikely that devaluation alone will reduce the foreign exchange constraint that exists in many LDCs. Since devaluation cannot be expected to alter the value of either exports or imports substantially, it cannot free the LDCs from the necessity of import controls. Devaluation is therefore not an alternative to import controls.

The effect of devaluation in LDCs upon the rate of inflation is more difficult to establish from *a priori* reasoning. The immediate effect of the devaluation will be to increase the c.i.f. price of imported goods, expressed in domestic currency. But if the devaluation is accompanied by a relaxation of import controls, the scarcity rents that previously accrued to those who obtained import licences will be reduced, and depending on the degree of devaluation as compared with the measure of import liberalisation, domestic prices of imports may fall somewhat. On balance however, it seems more likely that the domestic prices of imports will rise after devaluation. Since most imports consist of intermediate and capital goods, the higher import costs will increase the final cost of manufactured goods. The devaluation may also be used as a 'cover' for increasing the price of non-traded goods and services: for example, a devaluation has frequently been accompanied by a programme of increased consumer charges for public utility services. In those economies where labour is organised, the increased prices will lead to demands for increased money incomes. If these pressures are met by increases in domestic credit, there will be increased inflationary pressure and further deterioration in the balance of payments.

To summarise, it has been argued in this section that the foreign exchange constraint that exists in many LDCs compels the adoption of import controls and devaluation, aimed at the restraint of non-essential imports. The implementation of these policies can be expected to have two major effects, both of which are negative. First, they are unlikely to lead to any substantial reduction in the foreign exchange constraint. Second, they may be expected to contribute to an increase in the rate of inflation.

VII 'OPENNESS', IMPORT-SUBSTITUTING INDUSTRIALISATION AND INFLATION

The prominance given to discussion of the foreign exchange constraint concept in the development literature is a recognition of the 'open', dependent nature of the majority of LDCs. The failure of import-restraining policies significantly to reduce the foreign exchange constraint has encouraged the adoption of policies aimed at reducing the 'openness' and dependence of the economy by substituting domestic production for imported commodities through the establishment of import-substituting industrialisation. We begin this section with a brief but critical discussion of the measure of 'openness' that is commonly used in the literature. We then proceed to outline the pattern of import-substituting industrialisation that is occuring in the majority of LDCs, its impact on the 'openness' of the economy, and its relationship to inflation.

1 'Openness' and Inflation

Iyoha (1973) has used cross-country regression analysis to test the monetarist hypothesis that where an economy is closely integrated with other economies by international exchange relationships, domestic excess demand can be met, at least in the short run, by an increased import surplus, thus reducing the pressure on the domestic price level. This 'spillover' hypothesis is tested by examining the relationship between the 'openness' of the economy, as measured by the ratio of imports to national income, and the rate of inflation. The observed negative correlation between these two variables is interpreted as evidence in support of the hypothesis that, in an open economy, domestic inflationary pressure spills over into the balance of payments, thus necessitating less price inflation.

In attempting to transfer this 'spillover' hypothesis to the LDCs, Iyoha has seriously misinterpreted the relationship that exists between inflation and the balance of payments in most LDCs. A fundamental criticism of Iyoha's analysis relates to the casual relationship that he envisages between 'openness' and inflation in the LDCs. We are in agreement with Iyoha when he states that '. . . most developing economies are open, and . . . rapid inflation can be a serious obstacle in the process of economic development' (pp. 31-2). But we feel that he has seriously misinterpreted the nature of this 'dependence' and has, as a consequence, utilised an inappropriate definition of 'openness' in his analysis of inflation. We will discuss each of these criticisms separately.

As we have already seen, many LDCs are faced with balance of payments pressures which constitute an effective structural constraint upon the growth of the domestic economy, and the possibility of absorbing potential inflationary pressures through an increasing import surplus is therefore severely limited. As a result, and contrary to Iyoha's argument, the import surplus is not the dependent factor that responds to changes in the pressure of internal demand, but rather it constitutes a structural constraint upon the growth of the economy and contributes to the rate of inflation. The typical LDC does not have a choice between the rate of inflation and the magnitude of the balance of payments deficit: the rate of inflation is, in part, determined by the foreign exchange constraint. The degree to which an individual LDC is constrained by the foreign exchange bottleneck can be established only by detailed examination of the particular characteristics of its economy. It is highly unlikely that a single measure, such as the import ratio, will provide a reliable indication of the magnitude of this constraint and, at the very least, it is necessary to examine the composition of imports to establish the extent to which 'less essential' imports can be reduced.

The import-income ratio is used by Iyoha as a measurement of the degree of 'openness' of a LDC's economy. But the use of this ratio is subject to a number of criticisms and it is very difficult to give an unambiguous interpretation of movements in this coefficient (Robock, 1970). A reduction in the coefficient does not necessarily imply a reduction in the absolute value or quantity of imports, and both imports and the import coefficient are closely related to the availability of foreign exchange.[45]

A LDC will probably (though not necessarily) experience a falling import coefficient if it is pursuing a policy of ISI, but of far greater significance than a low or falling coefficient is the change in the composition of imports that arises during the ISI process. We discuss this phenomenon in greater detail below and will also comment on the impact of ISI policies on domestically generated inflationary pressures. For the present, it is sufficient to state that if, as we believe to be the case, inflation in most LDCs originates in (although is not exclusively caused by) long-run sectoral bottlenecks and imbalances in the economy, the reduction of inflation will necessitate the adoption of policies aimed at altering the fundamental structure of the economy. An implicit assumption of the 'spillover' hypothesis is that the impact of domestic excess demand is reduced by the importation of consumer goods. However, a development strategy aimed at eliminating inflation must lead to the removal of the inflation-generating structural constraints. Priority must therefore be given to altering the structure of imports in favour of those goods that are essential for the transformation of the LDC.[46]

Iyoha admits to the weakness of his own case when at the end of his paper he states that '. . . the import-income ratio is not a good measure of the true openness of the economy' (p. 37). He argues that changes in imports can result from policy decisions and that '. . . the import value is the thing that can be changed at

will, the only degree of freedom.' We will argue below that this is
unlikely to be the case, especially for those countries deeply involved in ISI policies and which are unable to face the domestic
consequences of a cut in imports. Our analysis of the relationship
between ISI and inflation will provide a more plausible explanation
of Iyoha's empirical results. But of greater importance than this
is the fact that Iyoha, even though admitting to the poor quality of
his 'openness' variable, does not hesitate to conclude that, if true,
his results have far-reaching implications for development policy:

> 'Specifically it will have implications for the optimal trade
> policy ("inward-looking" vs "outward-looking" policies) and
> the optimal capital accumulation strategy. If rapid inflation in
> fact discourages domestic capital accumulation and if increased
> capital accumulation is needed for development, it will turn out
> that an outward-looking trade policy resulting in more open-
> ness is optimal.' (p. 36)

We will strongly dispute this conclusion below. As a more general
criticism, the results derived from cross-sectional data cannot be
used in this manner to infer the optimal relationship between the
import ratio and inflation in a particular economy over time.
Cross-sectional data do not necessarily indicate the trend that will
be followed by any economy over time and one of the most frequent
criticisms of this approach is that very different patterns of change
are observed when time series data are used (Aaron (1967)).

2 *Import-substituting industrialisation and inflation*

The vast majority of LDCs are pursuing policies of ISI. Typically
this begins with the manufacture of consumer goods for which a
domestic market is already well established, although such production usually takes place behind high protective tariff barriers. As a
result of this development, the import of finished consumer goods
is reduced but the commodity composition of imports changes towards raw materials, semi-finished imputs and capital goods.[47]
One of the main results of this change in import structure is to increase the proportion of domestic value added which is supported
by, and dependent on, imports, and this factor introduces an inflexi-
bility into the import structure and generates a trade dependency
markedly different from the one that existed prior to the implementation of ISI (Winston (1967)). In this new situation, a decline in
export proceeds not counterbalanced by a net inflow of foreign capital leads to forced import curtailments and industrial recession.
Looked at from a different angle, 'non-essential' consumer goods
imports are converted into 'essential' raw material and intermediate and capital goods imports, needed to maintain domestic production and employment. The import structure may not become

completely inflexible and a certain amount of room for substitution
between different categories of imports may still exist, but in general the LDC becomes more dependent on foreign trade and more
vulnerable to foreign influence and actions. W. Baer (1972) comments that it is ironic that '. . . the net result of ISI has been to
place Latin American countries in a new and more dangerous dependency relationship with the more advanced industrial countries
than ever before'. Another observer concludes that:

> '. . . the economic structure that the ISI approach to develop-
> ment spawns is no more flexible and adaptable than the one
> that is sought to be replaced . . . [it] . . . is so incompatible
> with the rest of the system that adjustments to changes in
> demands, in technology, in any part of the routine are accom-
> plished painfully if at all.' (Bruton (1970))

Two further considerations merit brief mention. Foreign private capital has been extremely important in establishing import-
substituting industries in the majority of LDCs, and the need to
finance the repatriation of interest, profits, management fees, etc.,
constitutes a growing, and relatively inflexible, burden on the balance of payments. A second feature of the ISI process is that it
tends to get stuck at the stage of consumer goods substitution. Instead of achieving a smooth transition from consumer goods to
intermediate goods and finally to capital goods production, we observe what D. Felix (1964) has referred to as the 'premature wid-
ening' of the productive structure. The fragmented market, the
greater risks and uncertainly associated with capital goods production and the reliance on an imported, capital-intensive technology combine to build into the system a bias against the development of intermediate and capital goods industries (which reduces
the possibilities for the development of an indigenous technology
which in turn might reduce the dependence on imports) and the
usual result of the ISI strategy is the establishment of an industrial
sector characterised by high cost and inefficient operation, large
scale excess capacity and whose continued existence depends upon
high levels of protection (Little, Scitovsky and Scott, 1970).

The available evidence points overwhelmingly to the fact that
the LDC, pursuing a policy of ISI, increases its dependence on the
external sector. The import coefficient may be constant or falling,
but of greater significance is the change in the composition of imports and the rigidity introduced into the import structure. The
economy's increased dependence on imported inputs increases the
likelihood of inflation being imported through rising international
prices of essential capital and intermediate goods (Sunkel's exogenous inflationary pressures).[48] Furthermore, fluctuations in export receipts may tend to result in an upward movement of the
price level.[49]

Even if we ignore the increased vulnerability of the ISI econo-my to externally generated inflationary pressures, the ISI process itself can be expected to add to domestic inflationary pressures.[50] The structuralist explanation of inflation, as we have seen, centres on the slow growth of agricultural output and the slow growth in the capacity to import. Shortages and rising prices provide opportuni-ties for ISI, but at the same time ISI adds to inflationary pressures in the following ways: it does not, in general, relieve the balance of payments constraint (that is, it does not increase the capacity to im-port, at least in the short run); the changed structure of imports, noted above, leaves little scope for reduction or reorganisation; ISI turns the domestic terms of trade against agriculture and thus re-duces the rate of growth of agricultural output below what it would otherwise have been (and the lack of investment in agriculture fur-ther exacerbates this problem); the concentration on ISI has an ad-verse effect on exports, aggravated by the neglect of agriculture and the overvalued exchange rate, and the creation of a high-cost, inefficient and monopolistic manufacturing sector adds to infla-tionary pressures. ISI, as practised in LDCs over the past few years, can thus aggravate the major rigidities in the economy that are the basis of the structuralist view of inflation.[51]

We also reject as a gross oversimplification the distinction between 'outward-looking' and 'inward-looking' development poli-cies.[52] Import substitution, as currently practised, even if it re-duces the import coefficient, does not reduce the external depen-dence of the LDC or promote self-sufficient development. The foreign exchange constraint is not alleviated and the economy be-comes heavily dependent upon foreign capital, skills and technology. In other words, ISI has produced results contrary to those expected by its early advocates. Even if it is accepted that the expressions 'inward-looking' and 'outward-looking' are meaningful, the impres-sion still remains that they are in some sense mutually exclusive. This is not the case. ISI by itself has not proved to be a viable development strategy. Such a strategy must aim at structural changes permitting self-sustaining growth and should include, *inter alia*, measures aimed at the domestic production of goods previous-ly imported, the exploitation of existing and the development of new export opportunities, the transformation of agriculture and the es-tablishment of a fully integrated industrial sector. The far-reaching significance and complexity of such measures are not adequately encompassed by the expressions 'inward-looking' and 'outward-looking'.

To summarise, ISI aggravates the inflationary tendencies that already exist in the LDC and, by changing the structure of imports, increases the vulnerability of the economy to 'imported' inflation. As a result of ISI, the concepts of openness and dependence require reformulation.

VIII CONCLUSIONS

Our objectives in this paper are threefold. Firstly, we have critically examined the relevance and usefullness of western concepts and 'orthodox' theory to the analysis of the inflationary process in LDCs. We have argued that these concepts and theories are not directly applicable, and their transfer into a different economic and institutional setting is likely to lead to faulty analysis and incorrect policy prescriptions.

Following on from this, our second objective has been to present a concise summary of the state of the debate between the two main schools of thought concerning the origin and nature of inflation in LDCs. The theoretical and empirical contributions have originated largely, although not exclusively, in Latin America, but we argue that a structural approach to the problem of inflation is applicable (indeed essential) to all LDCs.

We distinguish between 'structural' and 'structuralist' analyses in order to focus attention on the broader socio-economic institutional framework which LDC governments both influence and are a part of, and within which development objectives are pursued and policies are formulated, rather than concentrating on specific alleged structural constraints, usually not applicable to all LDCs. Within this framework, the nature of the transmission or propagation mechanism (including necessary increases in the money supply) is of crucial importance. If specific groups or classes within society are unable to regain their previous position relative to other groups after an inflationary increase in prices has led to a deterioration in their real living standards, relative price changes will not lead to an inflationary spiral. They will, of course, lead to a redistribution of income, and the relationship between inflation and income distribution is vital to any understanding of inflation in LDCs. Jackson, Turner and Wilkinson (1972, pp. 31-2) note the relationship in Argentina, and Baer (1973) presents data illustrating the movement towards even greater inequality that has taken place in Brazil in the period 1960-70 (for example, the top 5 per cent of the population have increased their share from 27·4 per cent to 36·3 per cent and the share of the bottom 40 per cent has fallen from 11·2 per cent to 9·0 per cent). Evidently, inflation can be 'cured' or at least brought under some degree of control given a sufficiently strong (and repressive) government.

Two additional conclusions are perhaps implicit in the analysis. Firstly, the problem of inflation cannot be separated from the problems of underdevelopment and development. An asocial and ahistorical analysis obscures the real issues involved and incorrectly reduces a complex economic and socio-political problem to a 'straightforward' technical one. Secondly, broad generalisations and aggregate cross-country studies are of limited value. Sunkel

(1960) has stressed the specific nature of each country's inflationary process and we can do no more than strongly endorse that position.

NOTES

1   Adekunle (1968) examined the rate of inflation in developed and less developed countries during the period 1949-65. The average annual rate was 3·7 per cent in the developed countries and 10·0 per cent in the LDCs. The figures also revealed significant differences in the average rate for different geographical groups of LDCs, with an above average figure for Latin and Central America.

2   The 'natural' rate of unemployment is not thought of as being constant and is expected to vary; it is determined, *inter alia*, by the rate at which the economy reallocates labour, demographic variables, and the efficiency of the labour market; see Parkin (1974a), pp. 12-13.

3   'Almost all concepts formed by aggregation suitable for analysing Western economies must be carefully reconsidered before they can be applied to underdeveloped economies. "Capital", "income", "employment", "unemployment", "price level", "savings", "investment", presuppose conditions which are absent in many underdeveloped countries' (Streeten (1972), p. 55).

4   Modigliani and Tarantelli (1973) in their generalisation of the Phillips curve analysis to a 'developing country' (Italy in the post-war period) explicitly recognise the heterogeneity of the labour force and distinguish between (a) 'employed' labour—that fraction of the labour force currently absorbed in the productive process, (b) 'trained unemployed' labour—that fraction already integrated in the production process but currently looking for a job, and (c) 'untrained unemployed' labour—that fraction that lacks previous experience in the industrial sector. It is, to say the least, debatable that Italy could be considered a 'developing economy' and the analysis does not address itself to the main issues raised in this section.

5   'It is natural to describe the adoption of inferior occupations by dismissed workers as disguised unemployment' (Robinson (1936)).

6   For a critical appraisal of the concept and theory of underemployment, see Myrdal (1968), vol. III, appendix 6.

7   Balogh (1961) notes: 'This fractioning of the economic structure produces two equally unfavourable results. It leads, in the first place, to an unsuitable allocation of factors, and, in the second place, it renders the system inelastic and incapable of responding to economic stimuli considered "normal" in more highly developed countries' (p. 52).

8   He argues that in LDC's '. . . immobilities, inflexibilities, indivisibilities, imperfections, monopoly elements, and weak or non-existent response mechanisms fragment the market into a great number of separate demands and supplies with little hope of substitution on the side either of consumption or production. The concept of a "ceiling" can hardly be used for something that is compressible, can be pushed up to a different extent in different places, is craggy and of uneven height, and is called into existence as well as conjured away by elevators in other parts of the building' (Myrdal (1968), p. 1926).

9   It must be emphasised that the term 'monetarist' in this context refers to Latin American authors. Many western economists, writing within a 'monetarist' framework would find the Latin American 'monetarist' analysis somewhat naive and unsophisticated.

10   The analysis by Sjaastad (1976) of the use of inflation by governments as a vehicle for increased taxation is also of relevance in this respect.

11   '. . . In the economies of South Asia price rises, particularly if they occur in isolation without other policies, do not tend to allocate the scarce commodity while the scarcity lasts, nor do they tend to remove the scarcity. Simply defined, a "bottleneck" would exist where the price that would equate demand to supply is substantially higher than production costs. . . . Price increases that, in a different institutional setting, would be confined to a few items and carry their cure with them, will in an underdeveloped country tend to spread to other items and be self-defeating' (Myrdal (1968), p. 1929).

12   Balogh (1961) argues that it is not accurate to state that the owners of the latifundia and minifundia act irrationally. Large scale land-owners are interested in the maximisation of their incomes over time, constrained by the minimisation of effort and risk (both economic and political); the small farmers and sharecroppers have little interest in improvement: 'Their lack of capital and access to credit at reasonable terms makes risks connected with improvement unbearably high. Should anything go wrong, even their wretched existence would be jeopardised' (p. 57).

13   Felix (1961) argues that '. . . Latin American countries entered their industrialisation era burdened with a domestic capitalist class of limited investment horizons and weak propensities to accumulate, and a low and regressive tax structure which hampered public capital formation' (p. 85).

14   Olivera (1964) does not accept the recourse to deficit financing as a structural bottleneck. He argues that it is not useful to describe as 'structural' an inflation which results from the difference between *ex ante* savings and *ex ante* investment. He terms this 'structural proneness to inflation' rather than 'structural inflation'. Thorp (1971) has some sympathy with this viewpoint but feels that those who argue thus separate themselves from 'structuralists' proper (pp. 189-90).

15   Myrdal (1968) attacks the idea of a straightforward relationship between deficit finance and inflation, and maintains that the size of the deficit does not provide a yardstick measuring the effects of the budget on inflation. He gives three reasons for this view:

> '(i) Expenditures, taxes, and loans vary and have varying effects on the timing, direction, and size of demand and supply in different domestic markets and also on all of these factors in relation to foreign transactions; simple aggregation is therefore misplaced. (ii) The effects of the budget cannot be separated from the effects of a number of other policies that do not appear in the budget; this would imply illegitimate isolation. (iii) The budget covers only a small part of the whole economy, and therefore many important areas are left in the dark' (p. 2025).

16   '. . . the structuralist should not deny that monetary variables in some sense determine inflation. Structuralists may write at times as if inflation is a totally non-monetary phenomenon—but implicit in their analysis must be the assumption that the monetary system is having to respond to pressure, in order that a given rate of growth and level of employment be achieved' (Thorp (1971), p. 193).

17   Campos's main criticisms are: (i) the IMF's approach was too aggregative and failed to distinguish between consumption and investment expenditures and to identify bottleneck sectors where investment would have to be maintained or accelerated, (ii) underestimation of the effects of trade fluctuations, (iii) inflexible attempts to achieve internal and external balance simultaneously, (iv) underestimation of political problems associated with stabilisation programmes (pp. 117-20).

18   It is clear that the successful implementation of 'structuralist' policies would require a degree of political organisation and commitment entirely lacking in the great majority of LDCs at the present time. It is also unlikely that they would possess the technical and administrative skills needed to implement a sophisticated reform programme, although this should not be taken as an argument against attempting such reforms.

19   Devine (1974) makes the similar point within the developed economy context: 'The expansion of the money supply is essentially a sympton rather than a cause, of inflation. It is either the *result* of the state seeking to make expenditures that socio-political pressures make necessary and that these same pressures prevent from being financed by taxation or by borrowing from the private sector; or it is the *result* of the state being obliged to accommodate pressures elsewhere in the economy for fear of the socio-political consequences that would follow if it did not.'

Furthermore, it is of interest to note that in a recent discussion, (IEA, (1974)) Milton Friedman stated that 'I always speak of the change in the money supply as a proximate cause, and say that the deeper causes must be found in what are the explanations for the rise in the money supply' (p. 101). E. J. Mishan in his review of the IEA volume (*Times Literary Supplement*, 18 April 1975) perceives the cause of inflation as residing in the 'apparent irreconcilability of current aspirations with current institutions' and suggests that the difference between the monetarist and other schools of thought is largely one of semantics. It should be clear from what we have already said that we do not accept the latter conclusion, at least with respect to LDCs. The clearest difference between the monetarist and structuralist schools of thought and one where the issue is obviously not one of semantics is to be seen in the controversy over the necessity and desirability of policies aimed at economic stabilisation.

20   Manufactured goods consumed by the upper income groups—for example, durable consumer goods—are more likely to be produced by capital-intensive methods of production. In other words, the choice of product determines the choice of technique. See Streeten and Stewart (1969); Stewart in Streeten (1973).

21   There were special circumstances to explain the three cases: foreign exchange availability in Venezuela, land reforms in Mexico, and the exploitation of an 'open' frontier in Brazil.

22   Myrdal (1968) comments: 'Prices of agricultural products and government price policies play, of course, a vital role in determining the course of agricultural output in the West, and naturally Western economists who happen to touch on the problems of underdeveloped countries often naively assume that these countries could stimulate agricultural production by raising farm prices. Western experts who have studied the South Asian agricultural situation are more careful. Like their South Asian colleagues, they do not count much on price support as a means of raising agricultural production' (vol. II, pp. 1257-8).

23 Kahil notes that it did not matter if government policies were inflationary: 'On the contrary, the continuous increase in prices must have played an essential role in concealing from the public eye the amounts, and frequently the source and destination, of the substantial resources which were ceaselessly transferred from one section of the population to the other, whether by means of budget deficits, of the rapid but highly selective expansion of bank credit, of the complicated and everchanging foreign exchange regulations, or by any other means.

Furthermore, the privileged groups to whom resources were transferred generally realised, or were made to realise, that their gains resulted from government action, whereas those whose interests were sacrificed through the price mechanism, with a view to making these gains possible, tended to attribute their losses . . . to the action of specific groups. . . In no other way could sacrifices, temporary or permanent, have been imposed on one group to permit government largesses to another' (p. 331).

24 For an analysis of the economic and political background to the coup, see Arreas (1972).

Brazil is usually quoted as the one country that has successfuly eliminated a very high rate of inflation (90-100 per cent in 1964) without social chaos and, through 'monetary correction' and indexation, has learnt to live with an inflation rate of approximately twenty per cent per annum. The implications for the post-1964 distribution of income are examined in the conclusion. We may note here that the 'economic miracle' may be nearing its end and rapid rates of inflation once again making an appearance. See for example; *The Guardian,* 7 June 1974;*The Sunday Times,* 7 July 1974; *The Financial Times,* 26 April 1974 and 17 June 1974.

25 Harberger also uses the wholesale price index and various components of the wholesale and consumer indices as the dependent variable. He also uses both quarterly and annual data.

26 Vogel also tested a modified version of the Harberger model which included pooled data on lagged real income (to test the permanent income hypothesis) and an additional lag on the money supply (to test Harberger's findings that the rate of inflation is influenced by the money supply of only the current year and the preceding year) as additional independent variables. The inclusion of these additional lagged variables did not increase significantly the explanatory power of the estimated equations ($\bar{R}^2$ increased from 0·82 to 0·84). The inclusion of the lagged income variable as a proxy for permanent income did not improve the situation—in fact, the coefficients of income lagged one year were significantly positive rather than negative. The inclusion of an additional lagged observation of money supply reduced the coefficients on the lagged money supply variables, and the coefficient on money supply lagged two years became negative and significant.

27 The magnitude of the LDCs' trade gap is discussed in Stein (1971), Agosin (1973), and Stein (1973).

28 The ratio of reserves to imports for all developing countries (excluding the major oil exporters) fell from 0·32 in 1960 to 0·29 in 1970 (Agosin (1973), table 11), which is significantly below the 'critical' 0·33 reserves—imports ratio (i.e. four months' supply of imports).

29 In 1971 the total net resources flow (i.e. Official Development Assistance, other official flows, private export credits, private investment and grants and loans from multinational agencies) to LDCs amounted to a per capita receipt of $9·2 (OECD (1973), table 23). Reuber (1973) states that the 'rapid growth and development of the international market for portfolio in-

vestment has, to date, been largely concentrated in developed countries and has not been reflected to anything like the same extent in securities issued directly by private and public borrowers in the LDCs' (p. 54).

30   Chenery and Strout (1966), p. 682. The similarity of the 'gap-analysis' of foreign aid requirements and the foreign exchange constraint interpretation of inflation in LDCs is discussed in Cochrane (1972). The concept of a foreign exchange constraint, and in particular the strategic role that it assigns to imported investment goods, is critically examined by Wall (1968).

31   It is important that a distinction be made between the notion of a foreign exchange constraint and the balance of payments deficit. The former concept relates to an *ex ante* situation, whereas the balance of payments deficit is an *ex post*, or realised, situation which is dependent upon the amount of external finance available. The existence of a small or zero balance of payments deficit is therefore not necessarily evidence of the absence of a foreign exchange constraint.

32   This section draws heavily on Laidler and Nobay (1974) and Parkin (1974).

33   The view that in open economies, variations in the pressure of domestic demand will 'spill over' into the balance of payments is examined by Triffin and Grubel (1962), Whitman (1969), and Iyoha (1973), all of whom consider the relationship between the degree of openness of the economy (as measured by the import ratio) and variations in domestic inflationary pressures.

34   The dependence of LDCs upon imported investment goods does not appear to be a function of the size of the economy. Adams (1967), found that, whereas for developed countries the import coefficient of investment fell from an average of 36·3 per cent for small countries (population less than 20 million) to 9·5 per cent for large ones, suggesting increasing self-sufficiency in the production of capital goods as size increases, the corresponding decline for LDCs was only from 43·4 per cent to 32·9 per cent (p. 149, table 5).

35   There is considerable controversy as to the extent to which the LDCs have underestimated the potential gains to be obtained from the adoption of 'outward-looking' export-orientated policies. Johnson (1967) argues that '. . . emphasis on the denial of trade opportunities tends to divert attention from the equally important question of ability to take advantage of trade opportunities and to generate the mistaken belief that trade policy changes by developed countries offer a magic new route to painless development' (p. 65). Kravis (1970) examined the post-war export performance of LDCs and concluded that 'the poor performance of many LDCs in world export markets is the direct result of adopting an "inward-looking" economic strategy, thus giving rise to a self-fulfilling prophesy'. However, irrespective of the appropriateness of the policies adopted, for the purposes of this paper it is sufficient to note that in practice most LDCs have adopted 'inward-looking' strategies.

36   Little, Scitovsky, and Scott (1970) examined the average level of effective protection in a number of LDCs, and concluded that: '. . . this amount of protection has not arisen because the authorities ever thought that so much was necessary or advisable. It has come into being largely because most countries have used import quotas, and to a lesser extent tariffs, as a means of keeping their external payments in balance, or as a means of allocating scarce imports in wartime. . . . It is not denied that quotas have been put on and tariffs raised independently of balance of payments arguments; and this specifically for protective reasons. But even

so the bulk of the growth of the protective system in most of our countries has arisen as a result of quantitative control of imports originally imposed mainly for balance of payments reasons' (p. 175).

[37] This sequence of events is very similar to that envisaged by the monetarist school. The essential difference concerns the 'cause' of the inflation. The structural approach envisages the foreign exchange constraint giving rise to domestic shortages and relative price increases, which are followed by increases in domestic credit and inflation. The monetary analysis argues that the balance of payments disequilibrium arises as a result of the expansion of the money supply, which in turn leads to inflation.

[38] The complexity of the devaluation decision in LDCs is emphasised in Cooper (1973).

[39] The pursuit of these objectives will frequently involve the use of multiple exchange rates.

[40] Cooper (1971) has argued that devaluation in LDCs may be deflationary, since higher money payments for imports will withdraw purchasing power and thereby reduce expenditures on domestic goods.

[41] Felix (1968) has argued that the redistribution of income that resulted from devaluation in Argentina led to a change in the pattern of demand towards imports and import-intensive domestically produced commodities.

[42] A recent IMF study of the effect of devaluation in non-industrial countries showed that in the majority of the countries studied, '. . . in the post-devaluation period . . . the rate of growth of imports actually exceeded the pre-devaluation growth rate' IMF (1974), p. 54.

[43] This situation may be contrasted with developed countries where there is a wide range of domestically consumed manufactures that are actual or potential exports, and as a result there is greater scope for achieving short-term increases in export supply by diverting output from the home to the foreign market.

[44] The much-publicised Generalised System of Preferences is unlikely to result in a substantial improvement in market conditions for manufactured exports from LDCs—see Murray (1973) and Cooper (1972).

[45] The quotation from Leff and Netto given above illustrates this point with respect to Brazil. Robock (1970), p. 359, further argues that there is likely to be some minimum limit to the level of imports, determined, *in ter alia*, by resource endowment, exploration success, technological trends affecting the utilisation of resources, the size of the country and its stage of development, economic structure and rate of growth.

[46] It is possible that a LDC could import consumer goods (e.g. food) in order to reduce inflation and to release domestic resources for the making of capital goods, but this is an option unlikely to be open to many LDCs. Myint (1969) has questioned the wisdom of policies which concentrate on import-substitution at the consumer goods end of the production spectrum, arguing that the LDCs' comparative advantage may lie in the production of capital rather than consumer goods. As we shall argue in the next section of the paper, ISI as currently practised in most LDCs does not lead to the elimination of the structural constraints mentioned in the text.

[47] For an analysis of the falling share of consumer goods imports, see Bhagwati and Wibulswasdi (1972). Helleiner (1972) gives data indicating the compositional changes that have taken place in the imports of Brazil, Nigeria, Mexico, Argentina, and Tanzania.

[48] Sunkel (1960). The acceleration of inflation in many LDCs in 1971-2 has been largely ascribed to 'the extraordinary inflation of import prices in

terms of many local currencies, attributable in part to the December 1971 realignment of exchange rates' (IMF, (1973)). Furthermore, it should be pointed out that if world inflation was faster than inflation generated solely by domestic factors, then the openness of the economy (as defined by Iyoha) would be positively correlated with inflation.

49   The evidence linking export instability with inflation is inconclusive. See: MacBean (1966); Argy (1970); Maynard·(1962).

50   See Felix (1961) and Grunwald (1961), especially p. 113.

51   Furtado (1970) also places emphasis on the interrelationship between the ISI process and the generation of inflation. ISI requires rapid structural changes if it is to succeed as a development strategy, but such changes have not been forthcoming and in addition to the conventional structural constraints, Furtado draws attention to the inadequcy of infrastructure, the short term inadequacy of labour (lack of skilled labour and industrial entrepreneurs), the inadequacy of fiscal systems and increased financial commitments aggravated by government policies aimed at increasing investment.

52   Robock (1970) refers to the choice between ISI and export promotion as a 'false dichotomy'. The 'inward-looking'-'outward-looking' distinction has also been questioned by a number of prominent economists. See Streeten (1973).

REFERENCES

Aaron, H. (1967), 'Structuralism versus monetarism: a note on evidence', *Journal of Development Studies* (January).

Adams, N. A. (1967), 'Import structure and economic growth: a comparison of cross-section and time-series data', *Economic Development and Cultural Change,* vol. 15 (January).

Adekunle, J. O. (1968), 'Rates of inflation in Industrial, other developed and less developed countries, 1949-65', *IMF Staff Papers*.

Agosin, M. R. (1973), 'On the Third World's narrowing trade gap: a comment', *Oxford Economic Papers* (March).

Ahmad, Z. (1970), 'Inflationary process and its control in less developed countries', in E. A. G. Robinson and M. Kidron, *Economic Development in South Asia* (London, Macmillan).

Argy, V. (1970), 'Structural inflation in developing countries', *Oxford Economic Papers* (March).

Arraes, M. (1972), *Brazil: The People and the Power* (Harmondsworth, Penguin Books).

Baer, W. (1967), 'The inflation controversy in Latin America: a survey', *Latin American Research Review* (Spring).

— (1972), 'Import substitution and industrialization in Latin America: experiences and interpretations', *Latin American Research Review* (Spring).

— (1973), 'The Brazilian boom 1968-72: an explanation and interpretation', *World Development,* vol. 1, No. 8 (August).

Baer W., and Kerstenetzky, I. (1964), Inflation and Growth in Latin America (Homewood, Ill., Irwin).

Balogh, T. (1961), 'Economic policy and the price system', *UN Economic Bulletin for Latin America* (March), reprinted in T. Balogh, *The Economics of Poverty* (2nd ed. London, Weidenfeld & Nicolson, 1974).

Bhagwati, J. N. and Desai P. (1970), *India, Planning for Industrialisation—Industrialisation and Trade Policies since 1951* (Oxford University Press).

Bhagwati J. N., and Wibulswasdi C. (1972), 'A statistical analysis of shifts in the import structure in LDCs', *Bulletin of the Oxford University Institute of Economics and Statistics* (May).

Bhatt, V. V. (1970), 'On inflation and its control', in E. A. G. Robinson and M. Kidron (eds.), *Economic Development in South Asia* (London, Macmillan).

Bruton, H. J. (1970), 'The import-substitution strategy of economic development: a survey', *Pakistan Development Review*.

— (1969), 'The two-gap approach to aid and development: comment', *American Economic Review* (June).

Campos, R. de O. (1961), 'Two views on inflation in Latin America', in A. O. Hirschman (ed.), *Latin American Issues: Essays and Comments* (New York, The Twentieth Century Fund).

— (1967), *Reflections on Latin American Development* (Austin, Tex., University of Texas Press).

Chenery, H. (1969), 'The two-gap approach to aid and development: a reply to Bruton', *American Economic Review* (June).

Chenery, H. and Strout, A. (1966), 'Foreign assistance and economic development', *American Economic Review* (September).

Chenery, H. B. *et al.* (1974), *Redistribution with Growth* (London, Oxford University Press).

Cochrane, S. H. (1972), 'Structural inflation and the two-gap model of economic development', *Oxford Economic Papers* (November).

Cooper, R. N. (1971), 'Devaluation and aggregate demand in aid-receiving countries', chapter 16 in J. N. Bhagwati *et al.* (eds.), *Trade, Balance of Payments and Growth, Papers in International Economics in Honour of C. P. Kindleberger* (Amsterdam, North-Holland).

— (1972), 'The European Community's system of generalised tariff preferences: a critique', *Journal of Development Studies* (July).

— (1973), 'An analysis of currency devaluation in developing countries', chapter 9 in M. B. Connolly and A. K. Swoboda (eds.), *International Trade and Money* (London, Allen & Unwin).

Devine, P. (1974), Inflation and Marxist theory', *Marxism Today* (March).

Diaz-Alejandro, C. F. (1965), *Exchange-rate Devaluation in a Semi-Industrial Country: The Experience of Argentina 1955-61* (Cambridge University Press, 1965).

Diz, A. C. (1970), 'Money and prices in Argentina 1935-62', in D. Meiselman (ed.), *Varieties of Monetary Experience* (Chicago, Ill.).

Donnithorne, A. (1974), 'China's anti-inflationary policy', *The Three Banks Review*, No. 103 (September), 1974.

Economic Commission for Latin America (ECLA) (1962), *Economic Bulletin for Latin America* (October).

Edel, M. (1969), *Food Supply and Inflation in Latin America* (New York, Praeger).

Erb, G. F. and Schiavo-Campo, S. (1969), 'Export instability of development and the economic size of less developed countries', *Bulletin of the Oxford University Institute of Economics and Statistics*, vol. 31, No. 4 (November).

Eshag, E. and Thorp, R. (1965), 'The economic and social consequences of orthodox economic policies in Argentina in the postwar years', *Bulletin of the Oxford University Institute of Economics and Statistics* (February).

Felix, D. (1961), 'An alternative view of the "monetarist"-"structuralist" controversy', in A. O. Hirschman (ed.), *Latin American Issues: Essays and Comments* (New York, The Twentieth Century Fund).

— (1964), 'Monetarists, structuralists and import-substituting industrialisation' in W. Baer and I. Kerstenetzky (eds.), *Inflation and Growth in Latin America* (Homewood, Ill., Irwin).

— (1968), 'The dilemma of import substitution—Argentina', in G. F. Papanek (ed.), *Development Policy—Theory and Practice* (Cambridge, Mass., Harvard University Press).

Furtado, C. (1967), 'Industrialisation and inflation', *International Economic Papers*, No. 12.

Grunwald, J. (1961), 'The "structuralist" school on price stabilisation and economic development: the Chilean case', in A O. Hirschman (ed.), *Latin American Issues: Essays and Comments* (New York, The Twentieth Century Fund).

Harberger, A. C. (1963), 'The dynamics of inflation in Chile', in C. Christ *et al., Measurement in Economics: Studies in Mathematical Economics and Econometrics in Memory of Yehudi Grunfeld* (Stanford University Press).

Harvey, C. (1971), 'The control of inflation in a very open economy: Zambia 1964-9', *Eastern African Economic Review*, vol. 3, No. 1 (June).

Helleiner G. K. (1972), *International Trade and Economic Development* (Harmondsworth, Penguin Books).

Institute of Economic Affairs (1974), *Inflation: Causes, Consequences, Cures* (London, IEA).

International Monetary Fund (1972), *Financial Statistics*, vol. XXV.

— (1973), *Annual Report* (Washington D.C.).

— (1974), *Financial Survey* (18 February).

Iyoha, M. A. (1973), 'Inflation and "openness" in less developed economies: a cross-country analysis', *Economic Development and Cultural Change* (October).

Jackson, D., Turner, H. A., and Wilkinson, F. (1972), *Do Trade Unions Cause Inflation?* (Cambridge University Press).

Johnson, H. G. (1967), *Economic Policies Towards Less Developed Countries* (London, Allen & Unwin).

Kahil, R. (1973), *Inflation and Economic Development in Brazil, 1946-63* (Oxford, Clarendon Press).

Kravis, I. B. (1970), 'Trade as handmaiden of growth: similarities between the nineteenth and twentieth centuries', *Economic Journal* (December).

Laidler, D. and Nobay, A. R. (1974), 'Some current issues concerning the international aspects of inflation' (mimeo).

Leff, N. H. (1967), 'Import constraints and development: causes of the recent decline of Brazilian economic growth', *Review of Economics and Statistics*, vol. XLIX.

Leff, N. H. and Netto, A. D. (1966), 'Import substitution, foreign investment and international disequilibrium in Brazil', *Journal of Development Studies* (April).

Little, I., Scitovsky, T., and Scott, M. (1970), *Industry and Trade in Some Developing Countries* (London, Oxford University Press).

MacBean, A. I. (1966), *Export Instability and Economic Development* (Cambridge, Mass., Harvard University Press).

Maizels, A. (1968), Review of A. I. MacBean (1966), *American Economic Review* (June).

Maynard, G. (1962), *Economic Development and the Price Level* (London, Macmillan).

Modigliani, F., and Tarantelli, E. (1973), 'A generalisation of the Phillips curve for a developing country', *Review of Economic Studies*, vol. L(2), No. 122 (April).

Murray, T. (1973), 'How helpful is the generalised system of preferences to developing countries?', *Economic Journal* (June).

Myint, H. (1969), 'International trade and the developing countries', in P. A. Samuelson (ed.), *International Economic Relations*, (London, Macmillan).

Myrdal, G. (1968), Asian Drama: *An Inquiry into the Poverty of Nations* (Harmondsworth, Penguin Books).

OECD (1973), *Development Co-operation, 1973 Review* (Paris, OECD).

Olivera, J. H. G. (1964), 'On structural inflation and Latin American Structuralism', *Oxford Economic Papers* (November).

Parkin, J. M. (1974), 'Inflation, the balance of payments, domestic credit expansion and exchange rate adjustments', in R. Z. Aliber (ed.), *National Monetary Policies and the International Financial System* (Chicago University Press).

— (1974a), 'Inflationary policy in the UK: an evaluation of the alternatives', *National Westminster Bank Review*, (May), pp. 32-47.

— (1975), 'The causes of inflation: recent contributions and current controversies', in R. Nobay and M. Parkin (eds.), *Current Economic Problems* (Cambridge University Press).

Prebisch, R. (1961), 'Economic development or monetary stability: the false dilemma', *Economic Bulletin for Latin America*, vol. 6, No. 1; Reprinted in I. Livingstone (ed.), *Economic Policy for Development* (Harmondsworth, Penguin Books, 1971).

Reuber, G. L. (with M. Crookell, M. Emerson and G. Gallais-Hamonno), (1973), *Private Foreign Investment in Development* (London, Oxford University Press).

Robinson, J. (1936), 'Disguised unemployment', *Economic Journal* (June).

Robock, S. H. (1970), 'Industrialisation through import substitution or export promotion: a false dichotomy', in J. W. Markham and G. F. Papanek (eds.), *Industrial Organisation and Economic Development* (Boston, Mass.).

Seers, D. (1962), 'A theory of inflation and growth in under-developed economies based on the experience of Latin America', *Oxford Economic Papers* (June).

— (1964), 'Inflation and growth: the heart of the controversy', in W. Baer and I. Kerstenetzky (eds.), *Inflation and Growth in Latin America* (Homewood, Ill., Irwin).

— (1963), 'The limitations of the special case', *Bulletin of the Oxford University Institute of Economics and Statistics*, vol. 25, No. 2; reprinted in Martin, K. and Knapp, J. (eds.), *The Teaching of Development Economics* (London, Frank Cass & Co, 1967).

Sjaastad, L. A. (1976), 'Why stable inflations fail', in J. M. Parkin and G. Zis (eds.), *Inflation in the World Economy* (Manchester University Press).

Stein, L. (1971), 'On the Third World's narrowing trade gap', *Oxford Economic Papers* (March).

— (1973), 'On the Third World's narrowing trade gap', *Oxford Economic Papers* (March).

Stewart, F. (1973), 'Trade and technology', in Streeten (1973).

Streeten, P. (1972), *The Frontiers of Development Studies* (London, Macmillan).

— (ed.) (1973), *Trade Strategies for Development* (London, Macmillan).

Streeten, P. and Stewart, F. (1969), 'Conflicts between output and employment objectives in developing countries', *Oxford Economic Papers* (July).

Sunkel, O. (1960), 'Inflation in Chile: an unorthodox approach', *International Economic Papers*, No. 10.

Thorp, Rosemary (1971), 'Inflation and the financing of economic development', in K. Griffin (ed.), *Financing Development in Latin America* (London, Macmillan).

Triffin, R. and Grubel, H. (1962), 'The adjustment mechanism to differential rates of monetary expansion among the countries of the European Economic Community', *Review of Economics and Statistics* (November).

Turner, H. A. and Jackson, D. A. S. (1970), 'On the determination of the general wage level, a world analysis: or "unlimited labour for ever" ', *Economic Journal* (December).

Vogel, R. C. (1974), 'The dynamics of inflation in Latin America 1950-1969', *American Economic Review*, vol. LXIV (March).

Wall, D. (1968), 'Import capacity, imports and economic growth', *Economica* (May).

Whitman, M. V. N. (1969), 'Economic openness and international financial flows', *Journal of Money, Credit and Banking* (November).

Winston, G. C. (1967), 'Notes on the concept of import-substitution', *Pakistan Development Review* (Spring).

7 The relation between wage inflation and unemployment in an open economy

Andrew Horsman*

I

How does the behaviour of the labour market in an open economy differ from that in a closed economy? There can be little doubt about the importance of this question. On the one hand wage inflation and unemployment (which in the spirit of Phillips we take to characterise the behaviour of the labour market) are certainly among the most controversial and widely discussed of current economic problems , and the believed causes of their behaviour among the most important determinants of public policy. But on the other hand formal and informal analyses of the labour market usually ignore the influece of the open economy, except for some reference to import prices, while nevertheless acknowledging in other contexts the importance of that influence. These other contexts include; first, the concern in the UK over the stop-go cycle in which swings in unemployment are clearly related to the balance of payments; second the observation that the devaluation of sterling in 1967 preceded a wage explosion of almost unprecedented size; and third the evident fact (well documented by Nordhaus [14]) that the rates of wage inflation in most western economies appear (from time to time at any rate) to follow remarkably similar paths, so much so that Duck et al. [4] speak of a world Phillips curve. It is high time we had a well-developed Phillips curve analysis that is firmly rooted in the context of an open economy. The aim of this paper is to provide such an analysis and so to answer the question with which we began.

Three important conclusions of this analysis may be anticipated. First, it provides a strong theoretical basis not only for single country Phillips curves but also for the world Phillips curve discussed in purely empirical terms by Duck et al. Second,

---

* I am greatly indebted to the editors of this volume for much helpful guidance, advice and criticism. Responsibility remains mine.

it demonstrates very clearly the nature and causes of the international links among wage inflation rates and of the problem of
stop-go cycles in the labour markets. Third, like other analyses
based on normal theories of behaviour it deduces the existence
of a so-called natural rate of unemployment, and discusses the
very strong implications of this for the behaviour of the labour
market of an open economy. Since the existence of this natural
rate is still in dispute, we show that UK data for the 1960s strongly
confirm that there is indeed no long-run trade-off between unemployment and wage inflation and that the natural unemployment
rate in the UK is close to 2 per cent.

We approach an open-economy analysis of the labour market
as follows. An efficient division of labour in economics suggests
the extension of some current closed-economy model rather than
construction *de novo*. For this purpose we need an analytically
tighter and more appealing model than the standard Keynesian one.
A set of *ad hoc* and now discredited generalisations from the
empirical Phillips curve will not do.

Fortunately, it is now realised that rigorous reasoning about
wage inflation and unemployment is possible provided it is pre-
dicated upon an assumption of imperfect information in the labour
market (see, for example, Friedman [6], or Phelps *et al.* [15] *pas-
sim*), so that a choice of unemployment represents a choice of
investing time in gathering information about wages. For unless
workers are perfectly informed as to how fast the average wage
is changing they can only guess at how well a particular wage
compares with the average. The slower the average is rising
compared with the speed at which it is believed to be rising, for
example, the more it will be thought by workers that wages are too
low and the more they will be induced to choose unemployment in
order to look for the higher wages that are believed to exist.

This reasoning enables us to relate movements in the level of
unemployment to movements in the rate of wage inflation to produce our desired theoretical model of the Phillips curve. Its most
convincing and thorough presentation is by Mortensen [13], and we
accordingly adopt that model for extension in order to study the
labour market of an open economy,

II

By adopting this model we have begged one important question
that faces any theory of the labour market. Are we to suppose
that trade unions are of major importance and that the supply of
labour is characterised by monopoly, or that the market behaves as
if they were of minor importance and the supply of labour were
atomistic ? This paper makes the latter assumption and, without

joining battle with the proponents of the former, we may make a
few points to justify this choice. First, the former view is, of
course, a typically Keynesian one, and we have already chosen to
reject the Keynesian model of the labour market. Second, it is
normally advanced on the grounds that otherwise such phenomena
as the coincidence of rising unemployment with rising wage inflation are not explicable, which claim this paper shows to be wrong.
Third, there are grave difficulties both in ascribing wage inflation
to the exercise of monopoly power (see, for example, Johnson [10])
and in giving any meaning to the concept of trade union militancy
(see Purdy and Zis [17]). Fourth, there is no acceptable evidence
from empirical studies of any major role for trade unions (see
Purdy and Zis [18] for a critique of the attempt by Hines [8] to
furnish such evidence). We accordingly invoke Ockham's razor
and decide that since there is no need to make use of the union
monopoly hypothesis we shall avoid it.

By the same principle we consider, where possible, monetary
effects to the exclusion of real ones, assuming constant such things
as the underlying nature of markets, the real growth rate, equilibrium international relative prices; and we avoid the added complication of imperfect information in product markets (as considered
by, for example, Phelps and Winter [16]) because this is not necessary for explaining the facts under observation whereas imperfect
information in the labour market is necessary. Likewise, although
it is necessary to consider a difference between the true size of
various quantities (such as the rate of wage inflation) and what
people believe their size to be, it is not necessary in addition to
consider different estimates of the same magnitude by different
agents.[1] Thus all expectations in the model are assumed to be held
in common by all agents. Further, the assumed constancy of
equilibrium international relative prices means that the equilibrium
rate of change of the exchange rate (the domestic currency price
of foreign currency) equals the excess of the domestic over the
world inflation rate, and we assume that if the exchange rate were
freely floating it would in fact change at this rate. We neglect any
difference between real growth rates at home and abroad. Finally
we assume that the open economy under consideration is small
in relation to the rest of the world and is unable to influence international prices and markets, but that some goods (the so-called
non-tradables) have domestically determined prices, so that under
a fixed exchange rate the domestic inflation rate is *not* constrained
to equal the world rate.

III

Mortensen conducts his analysis by postulating that imperfect
information requires workers to conduct continuous random

sampling of the wages distribution, and this sampling is assumed
to take both time and real resources and to be easier when unemployed than when employed. Once we admit imperfect information we banish the concept of a market wage rate at which firms
can instantaneously hire any desired number of men. Instead a
given differential between the wage offered by a firm and the
average wage will lead to a finite rather than an infinite rate of
change of that firm's labour force, since workers will form different judgements from their sampling about the size of this differential and since knowledge of its existence will spread only
slowly. It takes time therefore for the firm to increase or reduce
its labour force to any particular size. Each firm's profit maximisation is thus constrained by this dependence of the rate of
change of its labour force upon the wage it offers relative to the
market average and upon the difference between workers' estimate of the rate of wage inflation and the true rate.

The implication of this is twofold. It constrains the behaviour
of firms, of course, in a way that we shall discuss shortly. But
it also implies that the rate of change of *aggregate* employment
and hence (given the size of the labour force) the rate of change of
unemployment is a function of the difference between the actual
rate of wage inflation and workers' estimate of it. Mortensen
shows that this relationship is of the form

$$\dot{u} = f(u, \dot{w} - \dot{w}^e, \sigma^2) f_1 < 0, f_2 < 0, f_3 > 0 \tag{1}$$

where u is the rate of unemployment, w the logarithm of the average wage, and a dot signifies a time derivative, where $\dot{w}^e$ is what
workers believe is the current rate of wage inflation, and where
σ^2 is the variance of the wages distribution (and is in effect a
proxy for the unavoidable but probably constant imperfection of
information inherent in the market).[2]

This equation clearly bears some relation to the Phillips
curve. First it implies a long-run relationship between u and $\dot{w}$
that is vertical at what Friedman [6] calls the natural unemployment rate u^N, the unique solution to

$$f(u^N, 0, \sigma^2) = 0$$

Second by virtue of the signs f_1 and f_2 it implies that

$$\partial \dot{w}/\partial u < 0$$

so that there exists a downward-sloping $(u, \dot{w})$ relation, the Phillips
curve, which is displaced vertically by movements in $\dot{w}^e$. This
curve, however, is not a structural equation in $\dot{w}$, as Lipsey [12]
thought, but is derived from a structural equation in $\dot{u}$ when the
restriction $\dot{u} = 0$ is imposed. Striking confirmation that this is the
Phillips curve can be found in Desai [2] who argues that the estimation method used by Phillips amounts to estimating the curve cor-

responding to $\dot{u} = 0$ taken from the structural equation

$$\dot{u} = g(u, \dot{w})$$

Moreover Irving Fisher [5] long ago argued that $\dot{u}$ is the relevant dependent variable. If we accept this we can assert from Mortensen that at last we know the true nature of the Phillips curve: it is an equilibrium *supply* relationship showing how much labour will be withheld (unemployment chosen) at each different level of unanticipated wage inflation.

This is clearly one of the relations we shall want in our open economy model. It is equally clearly an incomplete description of the labour market since it is derived from supply considerations only, and we must next consider the demand for labour by firms. As noted above this is the result of profit maximisation constrained by the imperfection of information. The result, Mortensen shows, is that since there is no longer a single market wage each firm must choose the wage it will offer relative to what it believes is the average wage, and that when all firms do so they give rise to an aggregate relationship of the form

$$\dot{w} - \dot{w}^e = h(u, V) h_1 > 0, h_2 > 0 \qquad (2)$$

where $\dot{w}^e$ is what firms believe to be the current rate of wage inflation and where V is the reciprocal of the average real wage multiplied by an index of productivity. We now have an equation in $\dot{w}$ as well as one in $\dot{u}$, and the complete model in equations (1) and (2) forms the model to be extended to apply to an open economy.

The following is a sketch of one way in which this can be done. A full, not to say laborious, exposition of this method is to be found in my doctoral thesis [9].

IV

The extension is done in two obvious steps, dealing with the choices of workers and the choices of firms respectively.

In an open economy workers face the extra option, besides those of taking domestic jobs and being unemployed, of emigrating, and we might expect this option to be more frequently chosen the greater are foreign compared with domestic real wages. International (and interregional) real income differentials in excess of transport costs have proved a tiresome problem for neo-classical economics, and invoking a presumed immobility of labour is not so much a solution as another name for the problem. But with our assumption of imperfect information the problem is clearly much less worrying. We accordingly envisage the decision whether or not to emigrate to be considered by some but not by all the workers (and by a greater proportion of the unemployed than of the employed), and to be based on varying estimates of the ratio of domestic to foreign average real wages as well as on the varying domestic wage offers received. The speed with which any firm can change its labour force then depends additionally upon this ratio, which we denote by C (and the constraint on its profit maximisation is accordingly altered, with effects to be considered shortly), and so the rate of change of aggregate employment is a function as before as $u, \dot{w} - \dot{w}^e$ and σ^2 and now also of C. But we cannot go straight from this rate of change of employment to the rate of the change of unemployment, the open economy equivalent of equation (1), since the rate of change of the labour force now depends on the rate of net immigration.

In accordance with what was said at the start of the last paragraph we view workers' choices as resulting in a rate of emigration that clearly depends upon the rate of unemployment—the greater it is the more likely is emigration to be considered—and on C and $\dot{w} - \dot{w}^e$—since they make immigration more or less attractive. The rate of immigration is of course the rate of emigration from the rest of the world (multiplied by the ratio of the foreign to the domestic labour force), which by an exactly parallel argument depends on u^*, C^* and $\dot{w}^* - \dot{w}^{e*}$ (where asterisks denote values for the rest of the world, and where $CC^* \equiv 1$). We have therefore instead of equation (1)

$$\dot{u} = F(u, \dot{w} - \dot{w}^e, \sigma^2, u^*, \dot{w}^* - \dot{w}^{e*}, C) \tag{3}$$

$$F_1 < 0, F_2 < 0, F_3 > 0, F_4 > 0, F_5 < 0, F_6 > 0.$$

and the natural unemployment rate u^N from $F(u^N, 0, \dots) = 0$ is greater the greater are σ^2, u^* and C and the smaller is $\dot{w}^* - \dot{w}^{e*}$.

Now the influence of u^* on u^N is clearly small enough to make $\partial u^N / \partial u^* < 1$. Since by a similar argument the rest of the world's natural employment rate u^{*N} is greater the greater is u and with $\partial u^{*N} / \partial u < 1$, there exists a unique world equilibrium or natural rate of employment $u_w{}^N$ which rules when both the domestic economy and the rest of the world are at their natural rates. In such a situation only the parameters C, σ^2 and σ^{2*} in equation (3) and its equivalent for the rest of the world remain free to vary. The effects of the σ^2 s is trivial—any increase in the inherent imperfection of information in the labour market increases natural unemployment—but that of C is more interesting. If world unemployment is at $u_w{}^N$ then an increase in C increases u^N but reduces u^{*N} (since an increase in C is a reduction in C^*). The greater a country's real income per head compared with the rest of the world's, therefore, the *greater* its share of the world's natural unemployment (because the more it encourages immigration into and discourages immigration from its unemployment stock). Furthermore, a change in C changes the size of $u_w{}^N$ as well as its distribution, and (although this cannot be rigorously demonstrated unless the real characteristics of the labour market are the same in each country—see [9]) it is likely, and certainly plausible, that $u_w{}^N$ is at minimum when $C = 1$. That is, the greater the international inequality of real *per capita* income, the greater the world's natural unemployment rate.

Finally, if we are prepared to make use of the construct of an average world rate of unanticipated wage inflation, then from equation (3) and the corresponding equation for the rest of the world it follows that the rate of change of world unemployment is a function of world unemployment and world unanticipated wage inflation. This relationship can be expressed in an equation which is a direct analogue of equation (3)—the Phillips curve—for the whole world, and which can therefore be seen as providing a theoretical basis for the empirical work on the world Phillips curve by Duck *et al.*[4].

We turn next to the demand side of the labour market and discuss the effects of the openness of the economy on the behaviour of firms. One effect has already been noted, namely that the constraint expressing the speed at which each firm can change the size of its labour force now depends upon the additional parameter C, the ratio of domestic to foreign average real incomes. But more importantly for its implications for the behaviour of firms, some assumption is now needed about the course of international relative prices. On the simplest such assumption, that domestic prices are world-determined and that the domestic price level is therefore identically equal to the world price level multiplied by the exchange rate, no variations in relative prices are possible and the behaviour of firms is only trivially affected by the openness of the economy.

To produce an analysis of greater explanatory power than this we use the now familiar concepts of tradable and non-tradable goods, goods with respectively foreign and domestically determined prices.[3] This allows us to build a model in which relative price effects from the rest of the world have a substantial influence (except in equilibrium) on firms' wage-setting behaviour.

Postulating for each firm a production function relating labour input to net output of tradables and of non-tradables, we view the firm as choosing its wage rate subject to this production function and its labour-supply constraint given the prices P of non-tradables and $E\Pi$ of tradables (where Π is the world price level and E is the domestic currency price of foreign currency). On this view the influence of the open economy is felt through the relative price $E\Pi/P$. And since each firm's maximisation problem is an inter-temporal one (on account of the constraint on the rate of change of its labour force) it must act on expectations of the future behaviour of these price levels and of the exchange rate.

Thus expected inflation rates and the nature of the exchange rate regime become of critical importance.

We consider the two cases of fixed and freely floating exchange rates. As mentioned above, it is assumed that a freely floating exchange rate will move so as to maintain equilibrium in international relative prices, that is to maintain (with a suitable definition of units)

$$P_d = E\Pi \tag{4}$$

where P_d is the domestic price level, which we assume for convenience to be

$$P_d = (E\Pi)^a P^{1-a} \tag{5}$$

Then from (4) and (5)

$$P = E\Pi = P_d$$

so that all relative prices are constant and the openness of the economy has no effect on the firm's behaviour. Equation (2) therefore stands unchanged in the case of a flexible exchange rate (except for the addition of C as an argument of the function h, which we shall now ignore by assuming C constant).

Under a fixed exchange rate, however, it is plain from equation (4) that unless P_d and Π are expected to inflate at the same rate the exchange rate will in general be in disequilibrium, and will be expected to require adjusting from time to time. The effect of the fixity of the exchange rate is thus to make firms expect the relative price $E\Pi/P$ to fluctuate continuously about its equilibrium value of unity. If we suppose firms to be unable to do better than to act on expectations of a constant future world inflation rate ($\dot{\pi}^e$, where the lower-case letter denotes the logarithm of its upper-case counterpart) and a constant future rate of inflation of the price of non-tradables ($\dot{p}^e$), then this relative price is expected to change at a constant rate $\dot{\pi}^e - \dot{p}^e$ between future exchange rate changes and to jump up (down) at an expected devaluation (revaluation) from below (above) unity to above (below) (since a devaluation is a *rise* in E).

The firm's profit-maximising choice of wage (relative to the market average) will in general be different, then, at different current levels of this relative price $E\Pi/P$, at different expectations of its future rate of change ($\dot{\pi}^e - \dot{p}^e$), and at different expectations of the extent of its future fluctuation. These are therefore three extra arguments of the function h in equation (2).

Since the last of these three influences is unobservable, the analysis as it stands is consistent with any observed behaviour and so uninteresting. To make it operational we introduce the subsidiary hypotheses: first, that firms act on the expectation that

exchange rate changes will occur when the level of foreign exchange reserves reaches its 'normal' minimum (maximum), to be
identified empirically with the level of reserves at the last devaluation (revaluation); and second, that the rate of change of reserves
(which we denote by B, for the balance of payments) is believed to
be an increasing function of the ratio of the actual to the equili-
brium exchange rate $E/\overline{E}$ and to be zero when $E = \overline{E}$. $\overline{E}$ is given
from (4) as P_d/Π so that from (5)

$$E/\overline{E} = (E\Pi/P)^{1-a} \tag{6}$$

and therefore the rate of change of reserves is believed to be an
increasing function of $E\Pi/P$ and to be zero when this relative
price is unity—for example

$$B = k \, \log \, (E\Pi/P) \tag{7}$$

Then, given the current level of $E\Pi/P$ and given its expected rate
of change $(\dot{\pi}^e - \dot{p}^e)$, the first expected devaluation is further ahead
and the extent of the decline by then of the relative price $E\Pi/P$
is greater the greater is the difference R between current and
'normal' reserves. If we hypothesise finally that the *size* of each
future exchange rate change is expected to be closely related to
the extent of the disequilibrium it corrects (so that, for example,
a currency overvalued by x per cent relative to its equilibrium
value will be devalued so as to be undervalued by x per cent), then
from (6) this determines the extent of the expected fluctuation in
the relative price $E\Pi/P$. Therefore once we know current $E\Pi/P$
and R, and $\dot{\pi}^e - \dot{p}^e$, the entire expected future path of the exchange
rate and hence of $E\Pi/P$ is determined. Thus the effect of a fixed
exchange rate is to enlarge equation (2) so that $E\Pi/P$, $\dot{\pi}^e - \dot{p}^e$ and
R are arguments of the function h.

In an open economy, therefore, the behaviour of firms is such
that equation (2) becomes

$$\dot{w} - \dot{w}^e = H(u, V, \{B, \dot{\pi}^e - \dot{p}^e, R\}) \tag{8}$$

where the three variables in braces are relevant under a fixed,
but not under a flexible, exchange rate, and where B—the balance of
payments—has replaced $E\Pi/P$ by virtue of (7). As before, $H_1 > 0$
and $H_2 > 0$; but the signs of H_3, H_4 and H_5 depend on the effects
on the firm of changing relative prices and are *a priori* undetermined: an increased price of tradables relative to non-tradables
may increase or diminish the firm's demand for labour. I show
in [9] that the sign of H_5 is totally ambiguous but that H_3 and H_4
at any rate both have the same sign. The analysis that follows
the next section will assume that they are both negative, but it
will be shown to be broadly unaffected if they are both positive.

V

Our model is now complete in equations (3) and (8). But before we go to the trouble of investigating its dynamic behaviour it is worth looking more closely at one of its features in particular, namely its prediction that in the long run no trade-off is possible between inflation and unemployment and that unemployment must instead be at the natural rate regardless of the inflation rate. Since this proposition is not universally accepted despite its clear basis in simple economic rationality, and since if it is false there can be little point in examining the dynamics of our model, and since furthermore if it is true the question of the size of the natural rate becomes of critical importance, it is of interest to test empirically for the existence of the natural rate and (if it exists) for its size. In this section we present some evidence on both questions by deriving estimates of the Phillips curve, equation (3), from quarterly UK data for the 1960s.

This involves us in all the usual problems. First the form of the function F in equation (3) is undetermined; but from [9] or [13] we can at least give it the slightly more specific form

$$\dot{u} = a_0 + a_1 u + (a_2 + a_3 u) f (\dot{w} - \dot{w}^e)$$

(ignoring as ever the variables σ^2, C, u^* and $\dot{w}^* - \dot{w}^{*e}$). *Faute de mieux* we specify f to be linear, and so the equation is

$$\dot{u} = b_0 + b_1 u + b_2 (\dot{w} - \dot{w}^e) + b_3 (\dot{w} - \dot{w}^e) u \qquad (9)$$

Since unemployment is at the natural rate when $\dot{u} = 0$ and $\dot{w} = \dot{w}^e$, an estimate of the ratio $-b_0/b_1$ will provide an estimate of the natural rate. To test for its *existence* we must first re-specify the equation as

$$\dot{u} = b_0 + b_1 u + b_2 \dot{w} + b_2' \dot{w}^e + b_3 \dot{w} u + b_3' \dot{w}^e u \qquad (10)$$

and then test the restrictions

$$b_2 + b_2' = b_3 + b_3' = 0 \qquad (11)$$

The degree of confidence with which our data lead us to accept these restrictions will then be the degree of confidence with which we assert that (10) takes the form (9) and that there is therefore no long-run trade-off between inflation and unemployment. If we accept the restrictions (11) we should then impose them and estimate (9) which will give us an estimate of the natural rate.[4]

The data used for the estimation are described in Appendix 7. 1 and are conventional except in the case of $\dot{w}^e$. For this we use the series constructed by Carlson and Parkin [1] for households' expectation of inflation plus an estimated average rate of productivity growth. Rates of change are constructed as four times first differences (remember that $\dot{w}$ is the rate of change of

the logarithm of the average wage). Equations (3) and (8) form a
simultaneous system; but it is fortunately a recursive one, and so
ordinary least squares may be used without risk of simultaneous-
equation bias.

The estimates are presented in Table 7.1. Ten cases are
reported and will be distinguished as we go along. Case (i) is
the straightforward ordinary least squares estimate of (10).
Ignoring the poor t-ratios and R^2 and F_1 statistics, note that the
restrictions (11) are almost exactly met. This is confirmed by a
formal F test of (11): the computed F_2 statistic of $0\cdot0014$ with two
and thirty-six degrees of freedom is a very great deal too low
to enable (11) to be rejected at any level of confidence. If we
therefore impose the existence of the natural rate and estimate
(9) we get the results of case (ii), which are much more encouraging. The F_1 statistic enables us to reject the hypothesis of a null
parameter vector with 95 per cent confidence, the t-ratios are
greatly improved, and both $\hat{b}_0$ and $\hat{b}_1$ are well determined and imply a natural unemployment rate of $0\cdot0196$ or just under 2 per cent.

This is such a strikingly low result—if 2 per cent unemployment is the result of not intervening in the labour market a good
deal of the basis of current policy needs rethinking—that we should
test whether it is sensitive to changes in specifications and
estimation methods. Case (iii) reports estimates of (ii) using
the construction

$$\dot{w}_t = 4(W_{t+1} - W_{t-1})/(W_{t+1} + W_{t-1})$$

instead of

$$\dot{w}_t = 4 \log W_t/W_{t-1}$$

(where W is the average wage). Once again the restrictions (11)
are almost exactly met, and the F_2 test statistic is $0\cdot05$ which
again cannot reject (11). If we impose (11), case (iv) shows that
$\hat{b}_0$ and $\hat{b}_1$ have t-ratios exceeding 3 and imply a natural unemployment rate of $0\cdot0213$ or just over 2 per cent. Use of the construction

$$\dot{w}_t = 2(W_{t+1} - W_{t-1})/W_t$$

yields results virtually indistinguishable from cases (iii) and (iv),
and use of

$$\dot{w}_t = 4(W_t - W_{t-1})/W_t$$

is virtually indistinguishable from cases (i) and (ii). Thus the
method of constructing the $\dot{w}$ variable does not influence the estimate of the natural rate.

Next, since the Durbin-Watson statistics in cases (i)-(iv) are
all in the inconclusive range, consider the correction of approximating the parameter r of first-order autocorrelation by $1 - \frac{1}{2}DW$,

Table 7.1

Case	Coefficient b_0	b_1	b_2	b_2'	b_3	b_3'	u^N	R^2	DW	F_1	F_2
i	−0·016 (0·52)	0·80 (0·60)	−0·27 (1·49)	0·28 (0·60)	10·93 (1·59)	−11·75 (0·60)		0·21	1·70	1·87	0·0014
ii	−0·014 (2·47)	0·74 (2·86)	−0·27 (1·55)		10·95 (1·65)		0·0196	0·21	1·71	3·29	
iii	−0·024 (0·78)	1·19 (0·89)	−0·71 (2·15)	0·71 (1·28)	29·45 (2·10)	−29·98 (1·27)		0·24	1·74	2·33	0·05
iv	−0·023 (3·09)	1·09 (3·48)	−0·70 (2·18)		29·12 (2·14)		0·0213	0·24	1·75	4·05	
v	−0·009 (0·26)	0·54 (0·38)	−0·23 (1·37)	0·14 (0·30)	9·75 (1·51)	−6·53 (0·33)		0·20	1·92	1·72	0·02
vi	−0·014 (2·13)	0·74 (2·53)	0·23 (1·40)		9·56 (1·55)		0·0188	0·20	1·91	3·01	

vii	−0·001 (0·03)	−0·14 (0·09)	−0·44 (2·11)	0·33 (0·56)	18·79 (2·25)	−11·32 (0·46)		0·19	1·86	1·68	0·39
viii	−0·01 (1·76)	0·59 (1·99)	−0·46 (2·27)		19·79 (2·44)		0·0198	0·17	1·85	2·62	
ix	0·02 (0·86)	−0·22 (0·20)	−0·26 (2·12)	−0·25 (0·73)	8·34 (1·95)	8·67 (0·60)		0·69	1·88	8·75	1·81
x	−0·008 (1·35)	0·74 (2·90)	−0·19 (1·66)		6·81 (1·65)		0·0192	0·64	1·93	10·27	

Notes

Figures in parentheses are t-ratios.

Data period: 1961(2) to 1971(3).

$u^N = -b_0/b_1$ except in case (x); see text.

F_1 is the test statistic for the hypothesis of a null parameter vector.

F_2 is the test statistic for the hypothesis $b_2 + b'_2 = b_3 + b'_3 = 0$.

and regressing $\dot{u}_t - r\dot{u}_{t-1}$ on $1 - r, u_t - ru_{t-1}, \dot{w}_t - r\dot{w}_{t-1}$ and so on.
The resulting estimates of (10) and (9) with $\dot{w}$ constructed as in
cases (i) and (ii) are then shown in cases (v) and (vi). The DW
statistics are improved, but it is apparent that little else is altered.
The restrictions (11) can again not be rejected by the F_2 statistic
of 0·02, and the implied natural unemployment rate is 1·88 per cent.
A similar correction for possible autocorrelation in the results
of cases (iii) and (iv) yields an F_2 statistic of 0·16 which, although
higher than before, is still unable to reject (11), and the estimate
of the natural rate is 2·09 per cent. We may conclude, then, that
first-order autocorrelation, even if it is present, has no effect on
the estimate of the natural rate.

Next we note that equations (9) and (10) are continuous differential equations on which we have used the classical least
squares technique. If instead we use the method suggested by
Wymer [19] for a recursive differential equation system, the results shown in cases (vii) and (viii) are obtained. This method
involves replacing each independent variable x_t by $\frac{1}{2}(x_t + x_{t-1})$
and constructing $\dot{u}$ and $\dot{w}$ as four times first differences. Since we
have been using these latter constructions anyway, the difference
is not great and the results of cases (vii) and (viii) again confirm
the restrictions (11) and give an estimate of the natural unemployment rate of 1·98 per cent. It appears that the difference between
discrete-time and continuous-time regression models is also not
a problem.

Finally, if we repeat the regressions of cases (i) and (ii) but
with seasonal dummy variables, and correct as before for the
strong positive autocorrelation that emerges, cases (ix) and (x)
show that this produces a considerable increase in the R^2s at the
expense of reducing our confidence in the restrictions (11). Nevertheless the F_2 statistic of 1·81 cannot reject these restrictions.
But with seasonal dummies in the equation the intercept is constrained to fluctuate seasonally, and so too therefore is the natural
unemployment rate. Our theory gives us no reason for expecting
this to be the case. It is nevertheless not implausible in view of
the marked seasonal behaviour of unemployment; and if we accept
this view the implied seasonal pattern of the natural unemployment
rate is 1·12 per cent in the first quarter, 3·23 per cent in the
second, 1·96 per cent in the third and 1·33 per cent in the fourth,
an average of 1·91 per cent.

In summary, then, we may observe that our data, however we
treat them, strongly support the existence of the natural rate and
imply that its value in the UK during the 1960s was close to 2 per
cent. With this result established we can now go on to examine its
implications for the dynamic behaviour of the labour market.

VI

Since on our assumptions the behaviour of the market is the same in a floating exchange rate open economy as in a closed economy, our aim in this paper, to illustrate the differences in behaviour between an open and a closed economy, can be achieved by illustrating the differences between the behaviour of the market under fixed and under floating exchanges rates. Following normal practice we conduct the analysis in terms of the behaviour of u and $\dot{w}$ and examine the influences on these of certain disturbances. To do so we must consider the nature of the equilibrium to be disturbed.

We define a full $(u, \dot{w})$ equilibrium as one in which u and $\dot{w}$ are constant and all expectations are fulfilled. Thus from equation (3) we require $\dot{u} = 0$ and $\dot{w} = \dot{w}^e$, whence we know from our earlier discussion of the Phillips curve that in equilibrium unemployment must be at the natural rate. From equation (8) we require $\dot{w} = \dot{w}^e$ and $\dot{v} = 0$ (where $v = \log V$) and in addition, in the case of a fixed exchange rate, $\dot{p}^e - \dot{\pi}^e = \dot{p} - \dot{\pi}$ and R and B must be constant. Now V is the price of non-tradables relative to (effective) labour and hence changes at the rate

$$\dot{v} = \dot{p} + \dot{y} - \dot{w} \tag{12}$$

where $\dot{y}$ is the rate of growth of output per head. R is the excess of current over 'normal' reserves, and so its (absolute) rate of change is B. And B according to equation (7) changes at the rate

$$\dot{b} = \dot{\pi} - \dot{p} \tag{13}$$

under a fixed exchange rate.

In a closed economy or a flexible-rate open economy, therefore, full equilibrium requires

$$\dot{u} = 0, u = u^N, \dot{w} = \dot{w}^e = \dot{w}^e, \dot{w} = \dot{p} + \dot{y} \tag{14}$$

and in a fixed exchange rate open economy full equilibrium requires in addition

$$B = 0, \dot{p} = \dot{\pi} = \dot{p}^e = \dot{\pi}^e \tag{15}$$

We now illustrate such equilibria graphically and conduct dynamic experiments about them in $(u, \dot{w})$ space.

In Fig. 7.1 equation (3) is represented by the Phillips curve AA, that is to say the locus $\dot{u} = 0$. Since this is an equilibrium relationship we need to know the directions of motion the market will follow when it departs from AA. From (3) $\partial \dot{u}/\partial u < 0$, so that $\dot{u} < 0$ to the right of AA and $\dot{u} > 0$ to the left. These directions are marked by the arrows D in Fig. 7.1. Movements in $\dot{w}^e$ displace AA vertically by the amount of such movements.

Equation (8) is represented by the line GG, which is upward-sloping since $H_1 > 0$—that is, the behaviour of firms is such as

to lead to a positive relationship between w and u.[5] This curve
shifts with movements in $\dot{w}^e$, V, B, $\dot{p}^e - \dot{\pi}^e$ and R.

Now GG is clearly different in nature from AA, for it is not
an equilibrium relationship and the market must always lie on it.
Since the market must lie on AA in equilibrium, full equilibrium
will be at the point of intersection of the two curves, E_0 in Fig. 7.1,
when the curves are not shifting. This graphical representation
clearly satisfies (14) and (15).

We make some final comments on the nature of this equilibrium. By virtue of our assumptions a flexible exchange rate ensures that the rate of inflation of the price of non-tradables ($\dot{p}$) is
identically equal to that of tradables ($\dot{\epsilon} + \dot{\pi}$) and to the general
domestic inflation rate ($\dot{p}_d$). Notice here that the same equalities
hold under a fixed exchange rate, not identically but in equilibrium.
Note too that only in equilibrium does the rate of wage inflation
equal the rate of price inflation plus the rate of productivity
growth. Note finally that implicit throughout this discussion of
full equilibrium is the usual presumption that in equilibrium the
rate of domestic monetary expansion differs from the domesti
inflation rate only by the real growth rate times the real income
elasticity of demand for money.

We now consider disturbances to this equilibrium arising from
changes in the rate of domestic monetary expansion, changes in
the world inflation rate, and changes in the exchange rate.

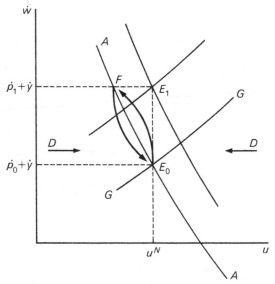

Figure 7.1

The effect in our model of an increase in the rate of domestic monetary expansion $(\dot{m})$ must fall on $\dot{p}$, the rate of inflation of the price of non-tradables. We side-step the undoubted problems of lag structures in linking $\dot{m}$ to $\dot{p}$ and for the purposes of illustrating the dynamics of the labour market consider directly the effects of changes in $\dot{p}$.

We deal first with the case of a flexible exchange rate. In this case an increase in $\dot{p}$ from $\dot{p}_0$ to $\dot{p}_1$, according to (14), shifts the full $(\dot{w}, u)$ equilibrium from $(\dot{p}_0 + \dot{y}, u^N)$ to $(\dot{p}_1 + \dot{y}, u^N)$, that is, from E_0 to E_1 in Fig. 7.1. In other words, as is well known from Friedman [6], the locus of possible full equilibria among which the authorities can choose is the line vertical at the natural unemployment rate. Now how does the market adjust to the new equilibrium at E_1? If $\dot{w}^e$ and $\ddot{w}^e$ do not change, then from (12) the increase in $\dot{p}$ makes $\dot{v}$ positive (since at E_0 $\dot{v} = 0$), so that, having been constant at E_0 V begins to rise. From (8) $\partial \dot{w}/\partial V > 0$, and so the curve GG begins to shift upwards, taking the market above the Phillips curve and (in view of the arrow D) causing u to start to fall. The market thenfollows a path like the upper arrow from E_0 to F where it stabilises, since at F $\dot{v}$ is again zero. If $\dot{p}$ falls again to $\dot{p}_0$ the lower arrow is followed back to E_0.

Clearly F cannot be a full equilibrium, because $\dot{w}$ exceeds $\dot{w}^e$. Suppose, then, that $\dot{w}^e$ and $\ddot{w}^e$ do not stay constant. If $\ddot{w}^e$ rises this merely causes the curve GG to rise, which it is doing anyway, and

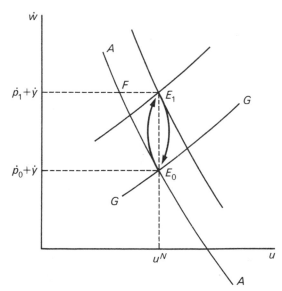

Figure 7.2

neither the path of adjustment nor the points F and E_1 are
affected. But if $\dot{w}^e$ rises as $\dot{w}$ rises, presumably with a lag, then
at some point along the upper arrow in Fig. 7.1 the Phillips
curve AA will begin to shift upwards and to cause the arrow to
turn to the right. Thus in Fig. 7.2 the new equilibrium at E_1 is
approached via the left-hand arrow; and if $\dot{p}$ is reduced again to
$\dot{p}_0$ the market returns to E_0 along the right-hand arrow. These
arrows reflect the familiar proposition that the effect of monetary
policy on unemployment is a temporary one only.

It is apparent, therefore, that, depending on whether $\dot{w}^e$ is
approximately constant (as is plausible for the sample period
used by Phillips) or whether it responds fairly quickly to changes
in $\dot{w}$ (as is plausible for more recent years), the model is able to
explain both the anti-clockwise loops observed by Phillips (Fig.
7.1) and also in Fig. 7.2 the clockwise loops and the apparent
vanishing of the Phillips curve with which (as Grossman [7] notes)
we are now more familiar.

But it is crucial to note that only under a flexible exchange
rate or in a closed economy is it the case, as claimed by Friedman,
that the locus of possible full equilibria is the line vertical at the
natural unemployment rate. Under a fixed exchange rate, unless
there is a change in the world inflation rate, there is only one
possible point of full $(\dot{w}, u)$ equilibrium, namely $(\dot{\pi} + \dot{y}, u^N)$, regardless of the rate of domestic monetary expansion.

Suppose now that this fixed exchange rate equilibrium at E_0
in Fig. 7.3 is disturbed by a rise in $\dot{p}$ from $\dot{\pi}$ to $\dot{p}_1$. From (13) this
makes $\dot{b}$ negative, and a falling B shifts the curve GG. From (8)
$\partial \dot{w} / \partial B = H_3$ which we have assumed to be negative. Thus when $\dot{p}$
exceeds $\dot{\pi}$ so that B is falling, GG tends to shift upwards. Since the
rise in $\dot{p}$ makes $\dot{v}$ positive as well, both forces work together to
raise GG, and the market moves either towards point F (as in
Fig. 7.1) or, if $\dot{w}^e$ rises, towards point H (as in Fig. 7.2). Notice,
however, that at F and H $\dot{w}$ is above $\dot{p}_1 + \dot{y}$. This is because by the
time $\dot{w}$ reaches $\dot{p}_1 + \dot{y}$ and from (12) $\dot{v}$ becomes zero, $\dot{b}$ is still
negative (from (13) $b = \dot{\pi} - \dot{p}_1$) and is still causing GG to shift upwards and $\dot{w}$ to rise; but as soon as $\dot{w}$ rises above $\dot{p}_1 + \dot{y}$ $\dot{v}$ becomes
negative and begins to exert downward pressure on GG, pressure
that grows as $\dot{w}$ rises. There soon comes a point where this downward pressure just balances the upward pressure exerted by the
constant $\dot{b}$, and the market stabilises at F or H where $\dot{w}$ is slightly
above $\dot{p}_1 + \dot{y}$. The words 'soon' and 'slightly' reflect a judgement
that except in an extremely open economy the effect of $\dot{v}$ will
heavily outweigh that of an equal $\dot{b}$.[6]

The important point here, however, is that neither F nor H can
be a full equilibrium, and the market cannot remain permanently at
either point—not on account of the behaviour of firms and workers
but for external reasons. For at F or H $\dot{b}$ remains constant and

$(\dot{\pi}_0 + \dot{y}, u^N)$ to $(\dot{\pi}_1 + \dot{y}, u^N)$, that is, from E_0 to E_1 in Fig. 7.4. To trace the path of adjustment to E_1 we note from (13) that an increase in $\dot{\pi}$ makes $\dot{b}$ positive and begins to depress the curve GG in Fig. 7.4. As soon as $\dot{w}$ falls below $\dot{\pi}_0 + \dot{y}$ $\dot{v}$ becomes positive, and 'soon' arrests the fall in GG, so that the market moves towards a point F 'slightly' below E_0 on the Phillips curve.[7] But since $\dot{b}$ remains positive, the balance of payments is in growing surplus, and this can be corrected only if the authorities raise $\dot{p}$ from $\dot{\pi}_0$ to above $\dot{\pi}_1$ in order to make $\dot{b}$ negative. The same difficulties as before then prevent an easy approach to E_1, the only point of full equilibrium, and the severity of the stop-go problem is doubly emphasised. For in the previous case, where the disturbance was in the monetary expansion rate, the stop-go cycle could have been avoided merely by the authorities' refraining from altering $\dot{p}$ in the first place—which calls for political willpower but not for technical ability (beyond the undoubted skill needed to control $\dot{p}$ by $\dot{m}$). But in this case, where the disturbance is in the world inflation rate, considerable technical skill is required of the authorities if they are to restore equilibrium, and our observation of the stop-go cycle suggests that they may simply not possess that skill. For unless they can monitor movements in the world inflation rate perfectly and can ajust $\dot{p}$ instantaneously so as always to equal it—yet another impossible task—then when $\dot{\pi}$

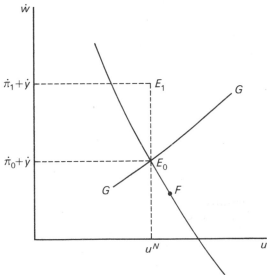

Figure 7.4

changes they cannot choose but to embark on a stop-go cycle
which may be almost impossible to break.

It is worth noting here that if the disturbance in $\dot{\pi}$ is indeed
accompanied by an equal change in $\dot{p}$, which might be interpreted as
the authorities' following the rules of the gold-standard game and
maintaining rigidly-fixed exchange rates, then $\dot{b}$ remains identically zero and the only effect is that of $\dot{p}$ on $\dot{v}$ through equation (12).
The market thus behaves exactly as in the case where a flexible
rate open economy or a closed economy is disturbed by a change
in $\dot{p}$ only. In other words, the relevant analytical distinction is not
the fourfold one of closed economy, flexible exchange rates, fixed
rates, and rigid rates, but the twofold one of fixed rates and the
rest. This reflects the obvious point that the system of fixed
exchange rates between nominal currency units in an inflationary
world (as opposed to both flexible and rigid rates) is in fact a
guarantee of disequilibrium.

Consider finally the effect on the labour market of a devaluation—to which we might expect the authorities to have resort when
confronted by the difficulties of breaking a stop-go cycle and
restoring equilibrium under fixed exchange rates. Now whatever
the effect of a devaluation is it is plainly not to overcome the
cycle. For the source of the cycle is a divergence between $\dot{p}$ and
$\dot{\pi}$, and a devaluation affects only the *level* of the relative price
$E\Pi/P$ and not its rate of change. Of course a devaluation may
turn a deficit into a surplus, but if the rate of change of the balance
of payments in equation (13) is unchanged then the effect will be to
transform a growing deficit into a diminishing surplus which (if
nothing else is done) will eventually become a growing deficit
again, and the pre-devaluation position will be restored. An exchange rate change can thus have a short-run effect only and cannot be a substitute for the difficult (and perhaps impossible)
monetary management required to break a stop-go cycle and
restore equilibrium.

What is this short-run effect of a devaluation? To answer
this we must return to our model of the behaviour of the firm.
For a devaluation is an instantaneous jump in the relative price
$E\Pi/P$, and the foregoing dynamic analysis of the labour market
under a fixed exchange rate has been based (naturally) on the
assumption that the exchange rate is not changing and that $E\Pi/P$
changes only when there is a difference between $\dot{p}$ and $\dot{\pi}$.

Unfortunately it turns out (see [9]) that it is not possible in
general to predict the *direction* of the effect of a devaluation on
the firm's choice of wage. Nevertheless it is possible to make the
following general point. The firm in our model is required by
its labour-supply constraint to make a profit-maximising choice
of relative wage, that is to say, of a wage relative to what it
believes is the average. This relative wage is what the devaluation

effects, and if it is changed in the same direction for all or a preponderence of firms, then to the extent that each firm realises it to be impossible for all to offer (say) a higher wage relative to the average, there is the clear possibility of a very large and perhaps unstable response of the average wage to a devaluation. The analysis can therefore accommodate without difficulty any observation that a devaluation (such as sterling's in 1967) is followed by a wage explosion.[8]

VII

This paper has developed a model that illustrates clearly the considerable differences between an open and a closed economy as regards the labour market. Three very broad policy implications emerge. The first is the obvious but crucial point that in devising policies to act on wage inflation and/or unemployment the authorities must not work either explicitly or implicitly with a model that ignores the open economy. The second is the rather less obvious point that when deciding on appropriate exchange rate policies the authorities must not overlook their influences on the labour market and in particular on fluctuations in unemployment. The third is that neither labour market policies nor exchange rate policies must ignore the fact of the existence in the UK of a natural unemployment rate of around 2 per cent.

Other more detailed conclusions include the fact that unemployment fluctuates around the natural rate only because workers are not perfectly informed about the current rate of wage inflation when it is fluctuating. Moreover, imperfect information is also the reason why the natural unemployment rate is above zero. Given these two facts the interesting question arises of whether the government should subsidise the provision of labour market information, and if so to what extent. A further interesting question is whether the indexation of wages would help to minimise fluctuations in unemployment. Our analysis seems to suggest that if it would and if it were feasible then the appropriate measure would be the index-linking of wage rates to the average level of wages rather than to the price level. This question is of particular importance in a fixed exchange rate open economy, since such an economy is unlikely to be able to avoid considerable swings in price and wage inflation rates due to fluctuations in the balance of payments, and these will cause corresponding and possible severe fluctuations in unemployment which would disappear only if labour market information were made perfect. It is clear, finally, that governments that wish to avoid such stop-go cycles altogether must either improve their skill at monetary management, to an extent that may well be impossible, or else abandon the maintenance of a fixed exchange rate or persuade the world to adopt non-inflationary policies.

NOTES

1   For some questions, of course, this may be important, as for example the question of the distributional effects of inflation, but these are not our concern here.

2   The analysis takes the existence and shape of the wages distribution as given and assumes that it is not affected by the inflation rate in the short run and does not degenerate in the long run.

3   For other examples of this construct see Dornbusch [3] or Jones [11] among many others.

4   Note that this will be to ignore all influences that may cause the natural rate to vary through time. In so far as it is at least possible that such things as changes in unemployment benefits have had a not insignificant effect, the estimates presented below should be treated as first approximations only.

5   This is because, other things being equal, a reduction in employment (an increase in u) moves each firm to an employment level further below or closer above its eventual or steady-state employment level. This increases the profit-maximising rate of increase (or reduces the optimum rate of decrease) of each firm's labour force and hence increases its optimum wage relative to the market average—see [9] and [13].

6   We can now demonstrate that if H_3 is positive rather than negative the analysis is broadly unaffected. For if $H_3 > 0$ GG tends to shift downwards when $\dot{b} < 0$ and $\dot{v}$ will be 'slightly' positive rather than 'slightly' negative at the point where its effect just balances that of $\dot{b}$. This means that at F and H in Fig. 7.3 $\dot{w}$ is 'slightly' less than $\dot{p}_1 + \dot{y}$, but this is of no qualitative significance.

7   As before, if H_3 is a positive rather than a negative, F is 'slightly' above rather than 'slightly' below E_0.

8   The above diagrammatic analysis has other interesting implications which are strictly out of place in a comparison of open with closed economies but which may be found spelt out in [9]. They include the impossibility both of maintaining unemployment permanently below the natural rate and of reducing inflation without causing a temporary rise in unemployment; and also the ineffectiveness of incomes policies (interpreted as attempts to influence $\dot{w}$ by acting on $\dot{w}^e$). Moreover if we interpret a cost inflation as one generated by an exogenous rise in $\dot{w}^e$ subsequently validated by monetary expansion, and a demand inflation as one generated by an initial rise in the monetary expansion rate, the analysis provides a simple and clear way of distinguishing between these sources of a rise in the equilibrium inflation rate.

REFERENCES

[1] Carlson, J. A. and J. M. Parkin, 'Expected inflation', *Economica* NS, XLII (1975).
[2] Desai, M., 'The Phillips curve: a revisionist interpretation', *Economica* NS, XLII (1975).
[3] Dornbusch, R., 'Devaluation, money and non-traded goods', *American Economic Review*, LXIII (1973).

[4] Duck, N., J. M. Parkin, D. Rose and G. Zis, 'The determination of the rate of change of wages and prices in the fixed exchange rate world economy, 1956-1972', in J. M. Parkin and G. Zis (eds.), *Inflation in the World Economy* (Manchester University Press, 1976).

[5] Fisher, I. M., 'A statistical relation between unemployment and price changes', *International Labour Review,* XIII (1962).

[6] Friedman, M., 'The role of monetary policy', *American Economic Review,* LVIII (1968).

[7] Grossman, H. I., 'The cyclical pattern of unemployment and wage inflation', *Economica* NS, XLI (1974).

[8] Hines, A. G., 'Trade unions and wage inflation in the United Kingdom, 1893-1961', *Review of Economic Studies,* XXXI (1964).

[9] Horsman, A. A., 'On the dynamics of wages and unemployment in an open economy' (unpublished Ph.D. thesis, University of Manchester, 1975).

[10] Johnson, H. G., 'Inflation: a 'monetarist' view', in his *Further Essays in Monetary Economics* (London, Allen & Unwin, 1972).

[11] Jones, R. W., 'Trade with non-traded goods: the anatomy of inter-connected markets', *Economica* NS, XLI (1974).

[12] Lipsey, R. G., 'The relation between unemployment and the rate of change in money wage rates in the United Kingdom, 1862-1957: a further analysis', *Economica,* NS, XLI (1974).

[13] Mortensen, D. T., 'A theory of wage and unemployment dynamics', in E. S. Phelps (ed.) [15].

[14] Nordhaus, W. D., 'The worldwide wage explosion', *Brookings Papers on Economic Activity,* 2 (1972).

[15] Phelps, E. S. (ed.), *Microeconomic Foundations of Employment and Inflation Theory,* (New York, Norton, 1970).

[16] Phelps, E. S. and S. G. Winter, 'Optimal price policy under atomistic competition', in E. S. Phelps (ed.) [15].

[17] Purdy, D. L. and G. Zis, 'On the concept and measurement of union militancy', in D. Laidler and D. Purdy (eds.) *Inflation and Labour Markets* (Manchester University Press, 1974).

[18] Purdy, D. L. and G. Zis, 'Trade unions and wage inflation in the UK: a reappraisal', in D. Laidler and D. Purdy (eds.), *op. cit.*

[19] Wymer, C. R., 'Econometric estimation on stochastic differential equation systems', *Econometrica,* XL (1972).

APPENDIX 7.1

The sources of the data used are as follows.

u: the wholly unemployed as a porportion of themselves plus estimated employees. The figures are averages for each quarter, for Great Britain only *(Department of Employment Gazette)*

W: for the average wage we use the index of basic weekly wage rates for all manual workers in all industries and services, to base end-of-January 1956 = 100. The figure for the first quarter is as of the end of January and so on *(Department of Employment Gazette)*.

w^e: households' expected rate of inflation derived by Carlson and Parkin [1] from Gallup survey data, plus an average rate of change of output per head, 0·03223, computed as the coefficient of an ordinary least squares regression of the logarithm of A (see below) on time.

A: for real output per head we use an average over the three months of
each quarter of the ration of the index of industrial production
(Monthly Digest) to the index of employees in employment in production industries *(Department of Employment Gazette)*.

8 The determinants of price and wage inflation: the case of Italy

Franco Spinelli*

In Italy today there is the widespread belief that unless the problem of inflation is solved the entire economic and political system is in danger of collapse. During 1974 the disruptive effects of inflation (running at an annual rate of 25·25 per cent) have become so evident that it is no longer necessary to attempt to convince anyone of its importance and of the necessity to work towards the formulation of a satisfactory solution to it. Solving the problem of inflation, however, requires that its causes be correctly diagnosed. Since the beginning of the 1960s, the Italian economic literature on inflation has been dominated by the union militancy hypothesis. The proposition that the rate of change of money wages depends on the level of unemployment, current or recent past variations in the cost of living index, and some measure of strike activity (which is supposed to measure the autonomous impact of unions on the process of wage determination) has emerged as a sort of conventional wisdom. As a result, the rate of growth of the money supply is not generally regarded as a relevant variable when considering the determinants of the rate of inflation.

In view of the popularity of the trade-union-pushfulness hypothesis and the relatively little attention paid to demand management and monetary policy, it is clearly of importance to establish the relative significance of union militancy and the other factors in the generation of inflationary pressures. This is the purpose of the present paper.

First we consider the wage-push hypothesis in some detail both on *a priori* grounds, when we examine the relationship between the behaviour of various strike variables and that of the phenom-

* I wish to thank Professor Michael Parkin for supervising this study and George Zis for helpful discussions. I am also grateful to Professor Giancarlo Mazzocchi of the Catholic University of Milan for valuable comments on earlier drafts and for providing financial support. For any error that may be present in the paper, the author alone bears responsibility.

enon they are supposed to measure, i.e. union pushfulness, and on purely empirical grounds when we fit wage equations in which every possible measure of strike activity is included among the regressors. As a result of this analysis we come to the conclusion that the union militancy hypothesis is not supported by the empirical evidence and therefore we discard it as a basis for the explanation of inflation in Italy during the last fifteen years.

We then consider an alternative view, the excess demand expectations-augmented theory of wage and price determination. Here we examine whether or not excess demand exerts a significant influence on the rate of change of both wages and prices. Also we investigate the nature of the trade-off between inflation and excess demand, paying particular attention to the existence or otherwise of a long-run trade-off. Additionally we analyse and establish the role of the rate of inflation in the rest of the world in the determination of wages and prices in Italy. The main conclusions we reach are that excess demand exerts a significant influence on both wages and prices but that the trade-off appears to be a short-run phenomenon only. Italy has, in the institutional environment of the 1960s, had a natural rate of non-agricultural unemployment of about 4·5-4·7 per cent. The world rate of inflation appears to affect the process of determination of domestic prices directly through inflationary expectations and, statistically, this influence becomes strong and significant towards the end of the 1960s; moreover the inflationary expectations based on the world rate of inflation are found to adjust much faster than those based on purely domestic factors.

THE FACTS

As a prelude to attempting to discriminate between the two competing views about Italian inflation, let us establish and examine the facts. In Fig. 8.1 we have plotted the rate of price and wage inflation (based on the retail price and on the minimum wages in the manufacturing industry indices) along with total unemployment. In Fig. 8.2 we present the number of hours lost in strikes (as a broad indicator of industrial unrest) and the rate of change of the ratio of the money supply (narrow money) to Gross National Product at constant prices. [1]

The period up to the end of the 1950s was characterised by a high rate of unemployment, fairly low rates of domestic money expansion, and the presence of a weak and divided trade union movement which may partly explain a low level of industrial unrest. The general price level was rather stable, the rate of inflation being only about 2 per cent per annum. The wholesale price index was falling at an average rate of 0·6 per cent per year. Since the end of the 1950s however this picture changed sharply:

there was a big jump in the rate of money expansion and towards 1962 the Italian economy was driven into a situation of over-full employment. [2] In 1963 the unemployment rate reached its minimum value of 2·5 per cent and, in view of the structural characteristics of the Italian labour market, this implies a high level of excess demand. [3] Further, since the autumn of 1960, the trade unions have shown themselves to be ready for more militant action. In the 1962-3 wage round there was a sharp rise in the level of strike activity. During these years the Italian economy went through the first serious inflationary episode, the rate of change of the retail price index accelerating from 2 per cent in 1961 to 7·4 per cent in 1963. The pre-crisis rates of both wage and price inflation were restored in 1965-6, following a period of deflation associated with a sharp reduction in both the rate of domestic money creation (11·6 per cent in 1962, 6·9 in 1963, 3·7 in 1967) and the rate of accumulation of foreign reserves (+ 14 per cent in 1962(4), −22 per cent in 1964(1)). [4] Since the response to mild reductions in the levels of unemployment at the end of the 1960s and unprecedented industrial unrest (in particular in 1970) the Italian economy has experienced two wage explosions. The first raised minimum wages by 17·5 per cent in 1970 and the second by 24·4 per cent in 1973. During these years the rate of money creation reached excessively high levels; for three consecutive years, from 1970 to 1972, M_1 was expanded at an average rate of just under 20 per cent per annum. The rate of price inflation continuously accelerated from 1·2 per cent in 1968 to 10·9 per cent in 1973. In 1974 the retail price index was rising at a rate of 25·25 per cent per year and the Italian economy was being driven into a hyperinflation. Again, as in 1963, the rate of money creation was savagely reduced (even below the limits drawn up by the IMF) and the downward spiral that followed from that is part of the history of the present days.

From this brief description of the facts it is evident that there are two possible hypotheses that one could follow in a study of the proximate determinants of the Italian inflation. On one side, after taking into consideration the quite exceptional situation that determined the 1970 wage explosion, one could set up a three-equation model, the first equation of which describes the impact of the rate of money expansion on the levels of unemployment and unused capacity, the second the effects of excess demand and expectations on wage and price inflation, and the third the mechanism by which inflationary expectations are generated. Further, through a careful analysis of the effects of disequilibrium inflation on the distribution of income in real terms and of the attempts to realise the real income increases which people have been denied by unanticipated inflation, one could also shed some light on the possible endogenous causes of industrial unrest. [5] And indeed if we

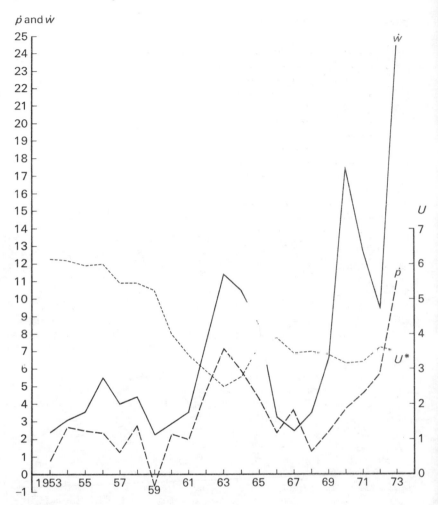

Figure 8.1 Values of $\dot{p}, \dot{w}$ and $U, 1953\text{-}73$. Total unemployment is on a double scale.

look at Figs. 8. 1-3 we see that the monetarist analysis we have just described seems to be confirmed by the events of the Italian economy of the last two decades. Alternatively one could look at the association between strike activity and inflation (which is also evident from the three figures) and come to the conclusion that, independently of market forces, wages may be pushed up by unions and these are to be blamed for the phenomenon of rising prices

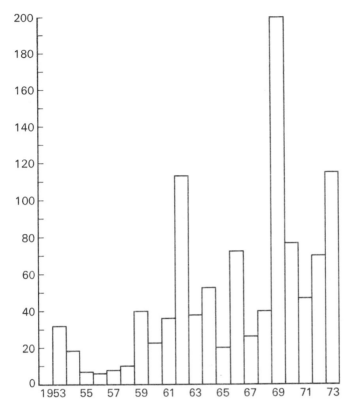

Figure 8.2 Time lost in strikes (million hours per year)

since prices are believed to be determined through a mark-up
mechanism and to be unaffected by the level of excess demand in
the market for goods. So, in this second type of analysis, the
sequence of events is completely reversed and the money supply
simply validates the rate of inflation generated by union militancy.

This latter view has been adopted by the majority of Italian
economists. At the beginning, the debate was dominated by the
Bank view according to which the rate of wage inflation is exogenously determined by union pushfulness and the money supply simply
validates the price inflation that follows from that. Modigliani and
La Malfa (1967) disagree on this latter point and recognise that a
sharp contraction in the rate of money expansion is among the
major causes of the deflation of the middle of the 1960s but, again
in line with the standard Keynesian tradition, they maintain that the
rate of wage inflation is largely exogenous to the system. After

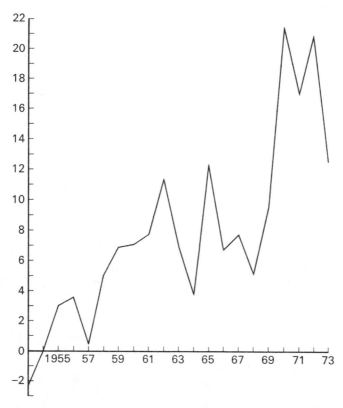

Figure 8. 3 Rate of change of M_1 (%)

saying that 'On the whole we are inclined to think that the high rate
of inflation of 1962-1963 is to be explained as a cost-push phenomenon. . . ', they quite naturally end up by invoking some kind of
incomes policy as a superior alternative to the control of the
growth rate of the money supply in moderating inflation. Battara
(1967), with a rather sophisticated analysis that was confirmed
years later by Brunner *et al.* (1973), goes a long way in undermining these positions but his study has been almost totally ignored.
Towards the end of the 1960s the faith of Italian economists in the
union militancy hypothesis was reinforced both by the events of
the 'hot autumn' which apparently showed a greater capacity by the
trade union movement to achieve its goals and by the bad fit which
was usually obtained in standard Phillips-curve-type analyses. As
a result of this Sylos Labini (1970, 1972), Ferri (1971), Valcamonici
(1973), Del Monte (1973) and Ferretti (1974) augmented the Phillips

curve with the number of hours lost in strikes and found that this variable played a significant role in their explanation of wage inflation.

The general conclusion we can draw from all these studies is that there is a direct relationship between union militancy and inflation, with the direction of causation running from the former to the latter, implying that even in a world on a fixed exchange rate inflation can be considered as a national social phenomenon. And the policy prescription which follows is that because union behaviour is largely independent of market forces, inflation may be brought under control mainly by implementing some sort of incomes policy and not through aggregate demand and monetary policies. Also that the solution to the problem of rising prices in the world economy requires a set of co-ordinated price freezes.[6] But before accepting these conclusions and policy implications, two sets of questions are worth raising. On purely empirical grounds, the obvious question is related to the significance of the strike variable in a wage equation fitted for the period including the very recent years. Further, we address the questions: what is the actual meaning of the variables used as proxies for union pushfulness? Why should we use the number of hours lost in strikes as the Italian economists do instead of the number of strikes (as in Ashenfelter, Johnson, and Pencavel (1972), Godfrey (1971), Taylor (1972, 1973, 1974)) or the number of workers involved in strikes? What kind of correlation is there between individual measures of strike activity? We now turn to these questions.

STRIKE ACTIVITY VARIABLES AND UNION PUSHFULNESS

There are many reasons for feeling uneasy about variables like the number of men involved in strikes (N), the time lost because of industrial disputes (HL), and the number of strikes (S). If we use N for example when we aggregate, a very long strike involving a certain number of workers receives the same weight as a very short stoppage involving the same number of strikers. Also the historical series of data are heavily influenced by the trend in the employment and a higher number of men involved in strikes could be generated either by increased militancy or, more simply, by an increase in the total number of workers employed in the sector or industry we are considering. Besides we cannot even take N as a good proxy for the amount of lost production, because problems related to the average degree of specialisation of workers on strike and to the capital intensiveness of the production processes inevitably arise and cast serious doubts on the homogeneity of our data.

The number of hours lost in strikes is the variable that has been used by the Italian economists. None of them has justified this choice. Sylos Labini (1972) for instance says: 'Several indices of union "pushfulness" have been devised but, to my knowledge nobody has yet tried to use the number of man-hours (or man-days) lost owing to strikes. I did so and the results were positive.' Ferri (1971), on the other hand, suggests that the proper variable to be used is the rate of change of the proportion of the unionised labour force and that because of the lack of these data he is going to use HL. But it would seem that the attraction of HL lies in that it is considered to be a good proxy for the costs firms have to bear in terms of lost production, and therefore it must be a relevant variable in determining the results of a dispute. The first point we want to make is that, as has long been noticed, 'the working days lost can be only a crude indication of the economic loss sustained by stoppages, since 5, 000 working days lost may differ in their consequences according to how they are caused, for example, by a five day stoppage of 1, 000 men or by a twenty-five day stoppage of 200 men' (Evans and Galambos (1966)).[7] However, the main objection we want to raise is that in the settlement of a dispute, past costs are also important because they contribute to the determination of expectations about future costs and those are the main variable we have to look at. And how can we handle past costs and expectations about the future costs of a dispute without referring to a precise model of wage bargaining in which claims, offers, present costs and expectations of future costs interact *and* in which the particular problem of how to handle employers' resistance is explicitly analysed? It is often alleged that wage bargaining may be analysed as a case of bilateral monopoly. But apart from the fact that this approach has serious drawbacks[8] the impact of the demand side of the labour market on the settlement of a dispute and on the volume of industrial unrest is completely ignored. Employers are assumed to be passively waiting the end of the dispute in order then to determine the amount by which prices are to be raised. Furthermore, HL is a naive proxy for the impact of workers' behaviour on the bargaining process, since when we speak of 'hours lost' we imply that the time spent striking would otherwise have been spent working. But, as Hyman (1972) points out, some strikes are merely substitutes for curtailment of work which would otherwise take the form of layoffs.[9] Evidence in support of this point has come from an analysis of industrial unrest in Britain's car industry: the time lost tends to be very high in periods of recession when the production could not be sold anyway. 'To have strikes is not perhaps the most rational form to fill in a slump, but it is more interesting and sociable than some other forms of idleness, and helps to keep workers from drifting away to other jobs' (Turner *et al.* (1967)). All this is rather important because it shows that, as soon as we take into consideration the possible attitudes on the demand side of the labour market, severe doubts emerge regarding the adequacy of strike activity as a measure of workers' pushfulness.

Further arguments are developed by Fisher (1973) who argues that, in order to be able to evaluate the impact of strike activity on the results of a dispute through the amount of lost production'... one would wish to know the degree of speed up of jobs and output before stoppages and subsequently we would like to have some indicator of the intensity of utilisation of men and equipment before, during and after the stoppage. In this context working to rule may be as damaging as an actual strike although not recorded in any of the customary measures.'[10] The interesting aspect of this point is that it brings into play the evolution through time of the strategy of the trade union movement. We must not forget that the variable which is central to all the discussion is union militancy and that strikes are only one of the possible ways by which militancy becomes manifest. In Italy phenomena like work to rule, overtime bans, rallies through the cities, occupation of firms or of public buildings, intervention of local or central government are a common occurrence. Only a few years ago these forms of pressure were unknown or seldom used and it is not unreasonable to say that, at least in part, they have replaced the normal strike activity and that the relationship between *HL* or any other measure of strike activity and union militancy is far from stable.[11]

We remain with the last alternative proxy: the number of stoppages. The Italian statistical sources do not distinguish between strikes and lockouts and this is a first serious drawback. But even if they did, the actual data would not be more meaningful. 'The only essential difference between a strike and a lockout is that the union takes the first step in one case and the employer in the other' (Ross (1948)). Of course to take the first step need not indicate special aggressiveness. Purdy and Zis (1974) maintain that it is practically impossible to distinguish between strikes and lockouts because 'it takes two to make a fight'. Fisher (1973) goes further when arguing that 'the lockouts not only lead directly to the closure of the plant thereby undermining profitability unless inventories are adequate, but foment ill-will between workers and management on a scale that is generally unwarranted if the enterprise is to remain in existence and continue to benefit from the services of much of the same sources of labour. Employers' pressure when confronted by some unacceptable measure of performance is more likely to take a form that induces direct action by workers through resort to the strike'. More or less the same point is made by Hyman (1972) who notices that one of the reasons for which strikes are far more common than lockouts is that the employers have the right to alter conditions unilaterally; workers who object to changes introduced by management have to take the initiative in stopping work. Again, from all these considerations we can easily see that, as soon as we start considering both workers' *and* employers' attitudes, it is no longer clear whose militancy we are referring to when we look at the various measures of industrial unrest, and consequently there emerges a problem regarding the sign we should expect *a priori* on the strike variables in a wage equation. Finally, we have to remember that a stoppage is not recorded unless it lasts for more than one hour and this means that, particularly since 1969, a remarkable number of very short stoppages, mainly caused by the militancy of the stop floor, are simply not recorded.

In addition to these *a priori* considerations there is the further important question about the empirical relationship between N, HL, and S. Given these three measures of strike activity, is there a stable and high correlation between them? If we discover such a correlation then at least the problem of the choice would be a spurious one; if this is not the case, however, i.e. if N, HL and S do show individually different behaviours through time, then they cannot all be adequate proxies for the same phenomenon, namely trade union pushfulness; and one should then justify the choice of any particular measure of strike activity. In Fig. 8.4 we represent the strike activity in the Italian manufacturing industry since the end of the 1950s. The three sub-periods have been chosen in such a way that the total HL (i.e. the volume of the three solids) is more or less the same. By looking at the shapes of the solids we notice that even over a period of a decade the relative contribution of S to HL decreases first and then rises again. The contrary happens to the average number of men involved in strikes. Alternatively, we could look at how the correlation coefficients between the three alternative measures changed over time. By considering two different periods we have obtained the matrix of simple correlation coefficients shown in Table 8.1.

The data speak for themselves. First, the correlations are rather

Table 8.1

	N		HL	
	1954–68	1954–73	1954–68	1954–73
N	1·00	1·00		
HL	0·72	0·88	1·00	1·00
S	0·65	0·53	0·56	0·45

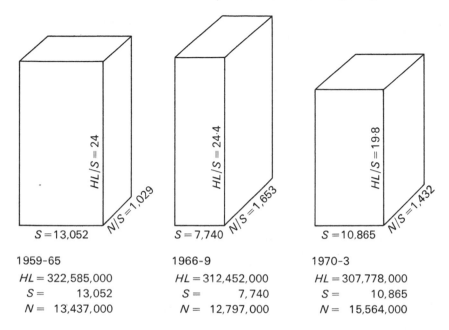

Figure 8.4 Industrial unrest in the Italian manufacturing industry

low. Moreover the inclusion of five new observations is sufficient to alter the relationship between the three proxies of union milit-ancy. The problem relating to choosing one in preference to the other two is evident. On what basis can we make a choice? Before this question can be answered adequately, further work is required.

STRIKE ACTIVITY VARIABLES AND WAGE EQUATIONS

We now turn to the problem of the statistical significance of strike variables in wage equations. We fitted many equations using as a dependent variable both minimum wages and earnings in the Italian manufacturing industry and in the entire industrial sector. As a proxy for excess demand in the labour market, we have alterna-tively used the total unemployment rate and the non-agricultural unemployment rate and the unemployment in the industrial sector. Besides HL, N, and S we have also considered two further measures of strike activity: the average number of hours lost in strikes per striker (IHL) and the Evans-Galambos index (EG). Each equation has been fitted to two different periods of time, 1954-68 and 1954-73, in order to see whether or not the events since the 'hot autumn' significantly affect the estimated values of the parameters in

favour of the union militancy hypothesis. For space reasons we
do not present all our results.

The equations we have been fitting are of the form:

$$\dot{w} = f(U^{-1}, \dot{P}, SA)$$

where U is the unemployment variable, $\dot{P}$ is the variation in the
cost of living index and SA the measure of strike activity.

In Table 8.2 we present the results for the period 1954-73.[12]
The dependent variable is the annual rate of change of earnings in
the manufacturing industry. Given that these results are similar,
these equations do not require detailed comments. The coefficients
on the cost of living variable assume quite reasonable values which
also appear to be significant. With the exception of equation (4) the
same happens for the unemployment variable. All the five measures
of strike activity turn out to be insignificant. In Table 8.3 we report some of the results relating to the entire Italian industrial
sector. Because of the lack of data on industrial unrest, these
equations can only be fitted to the period 1960-73 and, if this builds
a bias in our results, that must be in favour of the militancy hypothesis (considering that the acceleration of the industrial unrest
goes back to the beginning of the 1960s). But, in spite of this, the
results seem to be even worse for that hypothesis. Both when the
dependent variable is the rate of change of money wages (equations
(6) to (10)) and when it is the rate of change of earnings, the unemployment variable is highly significant, while the strike variables are not significant in all the equations *and* wrongly signed in
three of them. Finally notice that in all the equations of Tables
8.2 and 8.3 the *DW* statistics seem to indicate the presence of
autocorrelation in the residuals, and this could be interpreted as
further evidence that the model of wage determination we have
estimated is mis-specified.

At this stage it is necessary to reconcile our results with
those obtained in previous studies. In doing this we will in particular consider the study by Sylos Labini (1972) which inspired
all the subsequent work on these aspects of the debate on inflation.
The main points of that analysis, which was originally based on the
period 1951-68, are as follows:

1. In his basic model the rate of change of earnings in the manufacturing industry is regressed on the unemployment and on the
cost of living; the number of hours lost in strikes is included as a
further regressor. This raises the value of the explained variance
and, at the same time, generates an insignificant coefficient on
unemployment.

2. The problem of multicollinearity between U and HL is resolved in this way: 'After calculating the regression between hours
lost and unemployment I took the deviations between calculated

Table 8.2 Manufacturing industry, 1954–73

Dep	Constant	DIS^{-1}	VCL	HL	IHL	N	S	EG	$\bar{R}^2$	DW
$\dot{e}$ (1)	−3·236775 (1·?04461)	30·42871 (2·178517)[a]	1·253508 (3·291785)[a]	0·0001876 (0·9488348)					0·69705	1·24885[b]
$\dot{e}$ (2)	−3·838134 (1·536551)	34·77660 (2·38432)[a]	1·214755 (3·15405)[a]		0·02865383 (0·2803055)				0·68096	1·33350[b]
$\dot{e}$ (3)	−3·44041 (1·49400)	31·31407 (2·272601)[a]	1·213028 (3·183181)[a]			0·0004975 (0·8570024)			0·69346	1·25773[b]
$\dot{e}$ (4)	−4·415523 (1·858092)	24·28690 (1·474735)	1·236310 (3·302790)[a]				0·00192134 (1·1209821)		0·70274	1·47350[b]
$\dot{e}$ (5)	−3·666892 (1·605144)	28·61612 (1·919983)[a]	1·275577 (3·354379)[a]					0·0097004 (0·958531)	0·69680	1·33366[b]

Notes to Tables 8.2 and 8.3

$\dot{e}$ = annual rate of change of earnings.
DIS = non-agricultural unemployment.
HL = hours lost in strikes.
IHL = hours lost in strikes per striker.
N = number of strikers.
S = number of strikes.
EG = Evans-Galambos index.
[a] indicates the *t*-statistic is significant at the 5 per cent level.
[b] indicates the *DW* statistic lies in between the significance points.
[c] indicates the presence of positively autocorrelated residual.

Table 8.3 Total industry, 1960-73

Dep	Constant	DIS^{-1}	VCL	HL	IHL	N	S	EG	$\overline{R}^2$	DW
$\dot{w}$ (6)	-12·11685 (2·085356)[a]	67·79418 (2·387938)[a]	1·013450 (2·107012)[a]	-0·00001412 (0·837015)					0·72816	1·14424
$\dot{w}$ (7)	-11·77208 (1·86332T)[a]	62·77045 (2·119644)[a]	0·9650099 (1·876680)[a]		-0·0011888 (0·008280)				0·70629	1·25722
$\dot{w}$ (8)	-12·33742 (2·049669)[a]	62·32633 (2·187490)[a]	0·8935132 (1·263465)			0·000267128 (0·5545225)			0·71505	1·40999
$\dot{w}$ (9)	-10·35515 (1·616496)	64·74267 (2·260820)[a]	1·020920 (2·052746)				-0·0007956 (0·5887593)		0·71613	1·18844
$\dot{w}$ (10)	-12·02186 (0·6056603)	61·72702 (2·128551)[a]	0·9509918 (1·911071)[a]					0·00297072 (0·2897869)	0·70873	1·30788
$\dot{e}$ (11)	-15·01442 (2·306620)[a]	83·87641 (2·637227)[a]	0·8537638 (1·584452)	0·0000063 (0·356563)					0·73810	0·71620
$\dot{e}$ (12)	-17·68333 (2·800527)[a]	77·48495 (2·617974)[a]	1·050996 (2·045029)		0·1930215 (1·345140)				0·77445	0·56768
$\dot{e}$ (13)	-15·73131 (2·406556)[a]	85·73109 (2·770673)[a]	0·7995272 (1·453022)			0·00027712 (0·5298127)			0·74201	0·79618
$\dot{e}$ (14)	-18·16564 (2·75273)[a]	81·62967 (2·767057)[a]	0·7581108 (1·479691)				0·001698 (1·216912)		0·76824	1·04516
$\dot{e}$ (15)	-15·77184 (2·459022)[a]	83·16345 (2·708023)[a]	0·8324452 (1·579730)					0·00833163 (0·7674729)	0·74872	0·82056

and actual hours lost as the additional explanatory variable for the wage equation. The idea is as follows. If the number and duration of strikes were mechanically related to the degree of unemployment with no room left for trade unions' discretionary power, then there would be no need to include such a variable in addition to unemployment and the cost of living and the correlation between hours lost and unemployment would be equal to unity. But this is not so, mainly because there is no such mechanical relation and trade unions do have discretionary power. Since we are interested in a measure of this power we can take the deviations between these two variables. The substitution of this new variable for the original data of hours lost leaves the multiple correlation coefficient unchanged but the coefficient of the inverse of the unemployment rises and the t-statistics again become very significant'.

3. 'In Italy major strikes took place in 1966 but the new contracts in connection with which workers struck became operative only in 1967. We therefore assigned to 1966 the normal deviation (i.e. zero) and carried over to 1967 the 1966 deviation. '

We are now going to examine these three points in the light of the more recent experience. We start by fitting the basic model for the period up to 1973 and we obtain:

$$\dot{e} = -3 \cdot 57948 \quad + 37 \cdot 00411 \ U^{-1} + 1 \cdot 245527 \ VCL$$
$$(9 \cdot 577218) \quad (3 \cdot 059666) \quad (3 \cdot 237488) \tag{11}$$

$$\overline{R}^2 = 0 \cdot 69882 \qquad DW = 1 \cdot 01826$$

When we add HL as a further regressor (see equation (1) in Table 8. 2), contrary to Sylos Labini, we observe neither an increase in $\overline{R}^2$ nor the insignificance of the unemployment variable. The zero-order correlation between HL and the inverse of non-agricultural unemployment is 0·5 only.

As far as point 2 is concerned there is no need to comment in detail on the mis-specification of the parameters which is generated by the adopted procedure. Instead what we would argue is that in the light of the more recent experience this point makes much less sense. Among all the possible measures of the strike activity, HL shows the least stable relationship with unemployment and this raises serious problems with the 'discretionary power' of the unions as defined by Sylos Labini. In fact when we fit HL on unemployment over the period 1953–73 we obtain:

$$HL = -0 \cdot 00013 + 0 \cdot 000030 \ U^{-1}$$
$$(0 \cdot 5400) \quad (2 \cdot 7504)$$

$$R^2 = 0 \cdot 28677 \qquad DW = 2 \cdot 27770$$

The explained variance is now very low, 28 per cent against a value of 62 per cent obtained by Sylos Labini over the period up to 1968, and it is hard to believe that the remaining variance is to be attributed totally to the discretionary power of the unions. In such a situation clearly either one should think of using a different measure of strike activity[13] or, more preferably, the discretionary power of the unions should be redefined after carefully spelling out *all* the economic variables (not only unemployment) that can contribute to the explanation of industrial unrest.

Finally let us consider point 3. The problem Sylos Labini is raising may well exist and we cannot ignore it. However, its solution is too *ad hoc* to be acceptable. In fact if a problem of lag is involved in the sense that there is a significant and systematic time interval between industrial unrest and wage increases, it may be solved by taking the lagged values of the strike variable over the entire period of the analysis (as Ferri (1971) does) *unless*, through a detailed analysis of the history of the wage rounds, one shows that the lag has not been systematic and therefore only few observations must be shifted. This particular analysis is carried out neither by Sylos Labini nor by Del Monte and is not surprising that the years in which a lagged value of industrial unrest is considered do not correspond in their studies: Sylos Labini shifting the 1966 observation, Del Monte the 1962 and 1969. Because we want to avoid *ad hoc* formulations and because, given that we are operating on annual data, it would anyway be impossible to avoid a certain amount of mis-specification in the lags involved, we believe that the most correct procedure consists in taking the lagged value of the strike activity for the entire period of the analysis. The particular variable we are going to consider is given by the residuals of the regression of *HL* on unemployment (*RHL*) as suggested by Labini. This yields:

$$\dot{e} = -1\cdot82330 + 31\cdot02081\ U^{-1} + 1\cdot13199\ VCL$$
$$\quad\ \ (0\cdot99294)\quad (3\cdot2560)\qquad\quad (3\cdot8527)$$

$$\quad\ + 0\cdot00005\ RHL_{-1}$$
$$\qquad\quad (3\cdot506918) \tag{12}$$

$$\bar{R}^2 = 0\cdot8187 \qquad DW = 1\cdot5696$$

The strike variables turn out to be significant and we also see that the explained variance is much higher than that of equation (11). In spite of this we can hardly consider these results favourable to the union militancy hypothesis. We know that the 1970 wage round took place in quite exceptional circumstances and that, in a wage equation, sensible results can be obtained only if among the regressors we include a dummy taking value one in that year. In equation (12) the variable *RHL* is exactly playing the role of that dummy and this becomes evident when in Fig. 8.5 we compare the fitted values of equations (11) and (12) and we notice that the improvement in the proportion of explained variance is *exclusively* related to the 1970 observation. As a further proof of this we fitted an equation in which the variable *RHL* is replaced by a dummy taking value one in 1970 and zero otherwise. The result was:

$$\dot{e} = -1 \cdot 86614 + 23 \cdot 85934\ U^{-1} + 1 \cdot 367546\ VCL$$
$$\quad\ (1 \cdot 0588) \qquad (2 \cdot 454) \qquad\qquad (4 \cdot 7730)$$

$$+ 10 \cdot 83141\ d$$
$$\quad\ (3 \cdot 7695) \tag{13}$$

$$\overline{R}^2 = 0 \cdot 83045 \qquad DW = 1 \cdot 60112$$

The substitution of time lost through strikes with a dummy variable slightly improves the fit. From Fig. 8.5 we see that there is hardly any difference between the fitted values of equations (12) and (13). Finally, when we fitted a wage equation in which both the dummy and the lagged values of the residuals of the regression of *HL* on unemployment were included among the regressors, neither turned out to be significant. The result was as follows:

$$\dot{e} = -1 \cdot 704262 \quad + 25 \cdot 79116\ U^{-1} + 1 \cdot 2811993\ VCL$$
$$\quad\ (0 \cdot 9472738) \qquad (2 \cdot 542517) \qquad\quad (4 \cdot 141662)$$

$$+ 0 \cdot 00002\ RHL + 0 \cdot 7042598\ d$$
$$\quad\ (0 \cdot 8367325) \qquad (1 \cdot 307825)$$

$$\overline{R}^2 - 0 \cdot 82643 \qquad DW = 1 \cdot 64749$$

In the light of this discussion it is rather interesting to note that in the latest version of the complete macroeconomic model set up by Sylos Labini (1967)[14] the strike variable is replaced by a dummy. The explanation given for this substitution is that it helps to keep things simple, a hardly persuasive explanation. Even less convincing is the way in which the dummy is handled. The author simply says that 'It assumes values different from zero in those years when the militancy of the unions has been particularly intense'. We are told that these years are 1962-3 and 1970, a choice that is difficult to apprehend given the information contained in Fig. 8. 2-3. However, this procedure amounts to saying that the effects of the strike activity are not systematic and that the reported statistical significance is due to only three observations. But this is only half of the story. If we look at Fig. 8.5 we see that a better fit is achieved when the dummy variable assumes a value of zero for 1962 and 1963 (compare the fitted values of equations (12) and (13)), this implying that the significance of the strike variable entered with a lag and the improvement in the fit are to be associated with the 1970 observation *and with that alone*.

Our general conclusion then is that, in the long run, there is no systematic and significant influence of the strike activity on the Italian rate of wage inflation and that the union militancy hypothesis is to be rejected as a basis for a sensible explanation of the inflationary phenomena experienced in Italy during the last fifteen

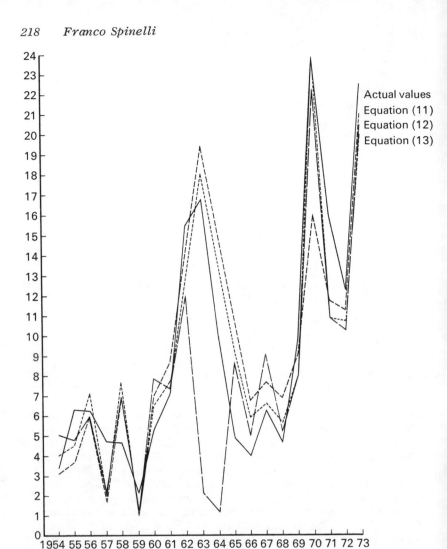

Figure 8.5

years. The policy implications that follow from this conclusion
are quite clear. If it is the case that wage inflation can be explained in terms of trade-union-pushfulness as a phenomenon
autonomous of market forces, then incomes policy may be a potent
anti-inflationary weapon. However, the empirical evidence we
have surveyed points in the opposite direction and strongly denies

any usefulness in augmenting the Phillips curve with some measure of strike activity. Therefore reliance on some sort of incomes policy as the *major* anti-inflationary weapon cannot be justified.

THE ROLE OF EXCESS DEMAND AND EXPECTATION IN THE PROCESS OF DETERMINATION OF PRICES IN ITALY

The literature on the determinants of inflation in Italy has been characterised by:

1   a concentration on the determinants of wage inflation, usually incorporating the assumption of money illusion;
2   when a price equation is included in a study, it is estimated separately and builds on the mark-up hypothesis; any direct influence of excess demand upon the rate of price inflation is frequently excluded or is supposed to work on the long-run mark-ups only, and frequently no role is assigned to inflationary expectations;
3   the openness of the Italian economy and its direct consequences on the rate of domestic inflation through the expectations generated by inflation in the rest of the world is ignored.

It is not our task to discuss in detail the reasons why this happened. [15] We will simply note that this approach stems from the three assumptions of an exogeneous rate of wage change, that economic agents do not distinguish between real and monetary variables and the ability of the monetary authorities to act independently though maintaining fixed exchange rates. Against this theoretical background we are going to test the hypotheses that:

1   excess demand exerts a significant influence on the determination of both wage *and* price changes;
2   both in the market for goods and in that for labour no money illusion is at work so that no long-run trade-off between inflation and unemployment is available to policy-makers;
3   that expectations are generated on the basis of both the domestic and the world rate of inflation.

Our work will make use of the Cross-Laidler model of price behaviour and of the standard Friedman-Cagan wage equation.

The hypothesis we are going to formulate says that the rate of price inflation is to be explained in terms of excess demand and inflationary expectations. This latter variable is supposed to be generated by an error-learning mechanism based on the past history of inflation. Formally:

$$\dot{p} = \alpha X_{-1} + \dot{p}^e_{-1} \tag{1}$$

where X is the excess demand and, of course, $\dot{p}^e$ is the expected rate of price inflation generated according to:

$$\dot{p}_t^e = \lambda\dot{p}_t + (1 - \lambda)\dot{p}_{t-1}^e \quad 0 < \lambda < 1 \tag{2}$$

The dependent variable in equation (1) is the rate of change of the retail price index, and X is proxied by the deviations of actual to full employment real output. Notice that all these variables are expressed in natural logs.

By substituting (2) into (1) and applying the usual Koyck transformation we obtain the estimating equation:

$$\dot{p}_t = \alpha X_{t-1} - \alpha(1 - \lambda)X_{t-2} + \dot{p}_{t-1} \tag{3}$$

By estimating equation (3) we shall be able to answer two of our questions, those relating to the role of excess demand on the rate of price inflation and the absence of money illusion in the market for goods. Fitted to the period 1954-72 (later on it will be clear why we stop at 1972), equation (3) yields:

$$\dot{p} = \underset{(2 \cdot 704447)}{0 \cdot 726423} X_{-1} - \underset{(2 \cdot 208253)}{0 \cdot 609038} X_{-2} + \underset{(7 \cdot 167390)}{0 \cdot 9393408} \dot{p}_{-1}$$

$$\overline{R}^2 = 0 \cdot 81686 \qquad DW = 1 \cdot 68308 \tag{4}$$

Considering we are not dealing with an equation that is intended to give the 'best fit' we see that the explained sum of squares is relatively high. Moreover, all the coefficients are significant and satisfy our *a priori* requirements of a positive coefficient on X_{-1}, a negative (and inferior in the absolute value) coefficient on X_{-2} and of a unitary coefficient on the rate of past inflation. In other words, excess demand does exert a significant influence on the rate of inflation and there is no long-run trade-off. An interesting question that arises relates to the way in which the estimated parameters change when our model is fitted to a different time period. Notice that we are not talking about the 'stability' of the estimated parameters but about the way in which they change because we do expect them to change. In fact our analysis is concerned with the way in which economic agents are supposed to behave in the face of inflation *and* it is based on a period of two decades during which the Italian economy moved from ten years of price stability into a situation of an accelerating inflation. Monetarism has always made a strong appeal to the rationality of economic agents who are supposed to learn from past experience and errors, and this, in terms of the model we are dealing with, seems to imply that as we move towards the end of the period we are considering we should find that the estimated coefficient on the expected rate of inflation becomes higher, asymptotically approaching unity.

The results we obtained seem to support this *a priori* reasoning. In fact while the estimated coefficient on the expectations variable is around 0·8 when the model is fitted for the period up to the middle of the 1960s, it rises consistently as observations from the end of the decade are included. This appears to be the message of the results below:

1954-68 $\dot{p} = 0{\cdot}8289758\, X_{-1} - 0{\cdot}6540344\, X_{-2} + 0{\cdot}8403859\, \dot{p}_{-1}$
  (2·932262)   (2·276988)   (6·000076)

$\bar{R}^2 = 0{\cdot}80398 \qquad DW = 1{\cdot}88941$ (5)

1954-69 $\dot{p} = 0{\cdot}8297532\, X_{-1} - 0{\cdot}6781061\, X_{-2} + 0{\cdot}857121\, \dot{p}_{-1}$
  (3·017809)   (2·456604)   (6·352678)

$\bar{R}^2 = 0{\cdot}80738 \qquad DW = 1{\cdot}93924$ (6)

1954-70 $\dot{p} = 0{\cdot}8512666\, X_{-1} - 0{\cdot}7049097\, X_{-2} + 0{\cdot}8684956\, \dot{p}_{-1}$
  (3·217829)   (2·671305)   (6·713147)

$\bar{R}^2 = 0{\cdot}81885 \qquad DW = 1{\cdot}86269$ (7)

1954-71 $\dot{p} = 0{\cdot}8618767\, X_{-1} - 0{\cdot}7104063\, X_{-2} + 0{\cdot}8797723\, \dot{p}_{-1}$
  (3·415492)   (2·792056)   (7·084182)

$\bar{R}^2 = 0{\cdot}83613 \qquad DW = 1{\cdot}96210$ (8)

The estimated coefficient takes a further jump when the model is fitted for the period up to 1972 (see equation (4)).

In spite of all these encouraging results there are reasons to be unsatisfied with the model embodied in equation (3). The first is that, although the estimated coefficient on the expected rate of inflation in equation (4) is not significantly different from the unity value our theory would predict, when we constrain it to assume such a value we get:

$\dot{p} = 0{\cdot}6997174\, X_{-1} - 0{\cdot}6599187\, X_{-2}$
  (2·732539)   (2·702409)

$\bar{R}^2 = 0{\cdot}27751 \qquad DW = 2{\cdot}85958$ (9)

The parameter values are different from those of equation (4). Second, the value of λ implied by the estimated parameters of equation (4) is 0·16 and this is clearly too low a value if we consider that we are working with annual data. Third, we are dealing with a closed economy model. This last objection is the most serious, and we believe the first and most important step we have to take in order to improve upon the original model is to modify it in such a way that we can capture at least part of the effects of the world economy on the Italian rate of price inflation. The world has essentially been on a fixed exchange rates regime over the period of our analysis, and economic theory suggests that in such a situation inflation in a small open economy is determined at the world level rather than at the national level. In the long run inflation rates are equalised across countries on fixed exchange rates, though in the short run national rates of inflation can deviate from the world rate. There are many ways in which we can capture at least partly the effects of the world economy on the Italian rate of inflation. In order to be able to keep the analysis as simple as possible following Cross and Laidler, we are going to make the hypothesis that expectations are based on both the domestic and the world rates of inflation. The model we apply is as follows:

$$\dot{p} = \alpha X_{-1} + E$$

$$E = m\dot{p}^e{}_{-1} + (1 - m)\dot{\Pi}^e{}_{-1}$$

$$\dot{p}^e = \lambda\dot{p} + (1 - \lambda)\dot{p}^e{}_{-1}$$

$$\dot{\Pi}^e = \lambda\dot{\Pi} + (1 - \lambda)\dot{\Pi}^e{}_{-1}$$

where $\dot{\Pi}$ is the rate of inflation in the rest of the world.

The estimating equation becomes:

$$\dot{p} = \alpha X_{-1} - \alpha(1 - \lambda)X_{-2} + [1 - \lambda(1 - m)]\dot{p}_{-1} + \lambda(1 - m)\dot{\Pi}_{-1} \tag{10}$$

A priori we expect to obtain a considerable improvement in the fit and the coefficients on the two price variables should sum to unity. The results over the period 1954-72 are:

$$\dot{p} = 0{\cdot}8067115\, X_{-1} - 0{\cdot}4891213\, X_{-2} + 0{\cdot}5777028\, \dot{p}_{-1}$$
$$\quad (3{\cdot}336115) \qquad\quad (1{\cdot}955006) \qquad\quad (2{\cdot}925967)$$

$$\quad + 0{\cdot}4313406\, \dot{\Pi}_{-1}$$
$$\quad\quad (2{\cdot}272048)$$

$$\bar{R}^2 = 0{\cdot}85476 \qquad DW = 1{\cdot}84918 \tag{11}$$

All the parameters are highly significant and the sum of the estimated parameters on the two expectations variables is indeed 1·00, which is stronger evidence in favour of the natural rate hypothesis. Furthermore, if we compare the explanatory power of equations (4) and (11) we see that the open economy model performs much better.

It is of interest to investigate the differences between the two models. We know that the interdependence among national economies has been greatly increased during the 1960s owing to different kinds of agreement that generated a reduction or abolition of tariffs throughout the world (GATT) and the formation of EFTA and EEC, and also owing to the development of an international capital market based on the Euro-dollar. Moreover, from our previous analysis, we have seen that in the Italian economy inflationary expectations seem to start playing a relevant role during

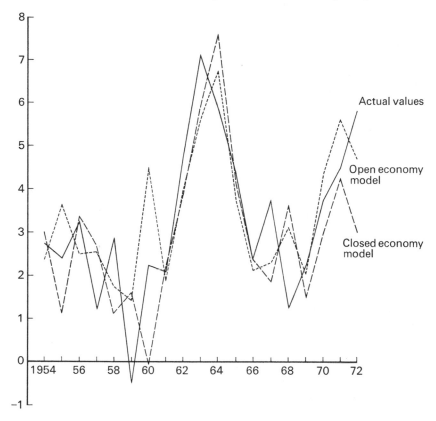

Figure 8. 6

the second half of the 1960s, a period of low unemployment and
high inflation at the world level. So, it seems reasonable to expect
that the improvement in the fit associated to the open economy
model should be concentrated on the period following the mid-
1960s. In Fig. 8. 6 we have plotted the actual against the estimated
values of equations (4) and (11) and we can easily see that up to
1965-6 the performance of the two models is practically the same
but that since then the open economy model performs much better.

These results are confirmed statistically when we try to
identify the value of the parameter m which measures the relative
weight of $\dot{p}^e$ and $\dot{\Pi}^e$ in the formation of total expectations. Although
the model is clearly overidentified there is no need to use a non-
linear programme in order to be able to determine the values of

the structural parameters. What we have to do is rearrange equation (10) into:

$$\ddot{p} = \alpha X_{-1} - \alpha(1 - \lambda)X_{-2} + \lambda(1 - m)[\dot{\Pi}_{-1} - \dot{p}_{-1}] \tag{12}$$

which is also of interest as the dependent variable is now the rate of acceleration of inflation, which turns out to be explained by the excess demand and the gap between the world and the domestic rate of inflation. This equation has been fitted to different periods of time and the results are as follows:

1954-68 $\ddot{p} = 0.92902\, X_{-1} - 0.5515784\, X_{-2} + 0.45555\,[\dot{\Pi}_{-1} - \dot{p}_{-1}]$
                (3·329962)   (1·942132)   (1·680396)

$\overline{R}^2 = 0.42766$ $DW = 2.25580$ $\tag{13}$

1954-69 $\ddot{p} = 0.9312695\, X_{-1} - 0.552125\, X_{-2}$
                (3·488111)   (2·022449)

                $+ 0.45931\,[\dot{\Pi}_{-1} - \dot{p}_{-1}]$
                (1·808599)

$\overline{R}^2 = 0.44502$ $DW = 2.43995$ $\tag{14}$

1955-70 $\ddot{p} = 0.8923180\, X_{-1} - 0.565672\, X_{-2}$
                (3·619463)   (2·145119)

                $+ 0.4057765\,[\dot{\Pi}_{-1} - \dot{p}_{-1}]$
                (1·817765)

$\overline{R}^2 = 0.55752$ $DW = 2.82180$ $\tag{15}$

1954-72 $\ddot{p} = 0.810285\, X_{-1} - 0.4826319\, X_{-2}$
                (3·510625)   (2·116452)

                $+ 0.427862\,[\dot{\Pi}_1 - \dot{p}_{-1}]$
                (2·408035)

$\overline{R}^2 = 0.46342$ $DW = 2.71385$ $\tag{16}$

When the equation is fitted up to the middle of the 1960s no significant role is played by the gap between the two rates of inflation, but in 1968 the t-statistic on this variable is just under the significance level and from 1969 it will fall in the significance region. This obviously confirms our previous considerations and, if we want to have an idea of the difference in terms of explanatory power between the closed and the open economy model in explaining the rate of change of the Italian rate of inflation we can compare equations (16) and (9).

Let us now take a closer look at equation (16). From it we can derive the values of the structural parameters of the model which turn out to be:

$\alpha = 0.810$ $\lambda = 0.404$ $m = -0.06$

Part of our dissatisfaction with the results of the closed economy model was that it generated a value of λ equal to 0·16 and this was clearly implying too low a speed of adjustment of expectations. We now have a value of 0·407 and, although still rather low, it makes much more sense. On the other hand the value of m is clearly unreasonable and in contrast with our *a priori* requirements. As far as the negative sign is concerned it must be due to the precision with which the parameters are estimated and in fact, when the appropriate constraints are imposed and a non-linear programme is used, m turns out to be equal to zero; that is, it tends to assume the lowest possible value, thereby confirming the results obtained by Cross and Laidler.

A zero value for the m parameter clearly implies that expectations of inflation are based entirely on the rate of inflation in the world-wide economy and that, consequently, the past and present history of the domestic inflation plays no role at all. Of course this is not inconsistent with the monetary approach to inflation in a world economy on a fixed exchange rates regime or at least with its extreme version. In spite of this we cannot accept a value of m equal to zero as reasonable because we cannot see how the Italian economic agents, when forming expectations and fixing prices, can pay attention to what is happening at the world level only. After all there have been frequent and remarkable gaps between the Italian and the world rates of inflation and in similar circumstances, no matter how open an economy is, there must be people who, either because they simply deal in non-traded goods or because they do not know what is happening to the world rate of inflation, form their expectations purely on domestic considerations or, in any case, they cannot be supposed to ignore the domestic retail price index. Given the actual situations in which both Italy and the rest of the world were operating up to the collapse of the Bretton Woods system, we do believe that the world rate of inflation did play a significant, perhaps dominant, role in the formation of expectations; but we do feel that domestic inflation must have had some role to play, and that clearly this role is not captured by the model as it stands now.

It is not difficult to see that the Cross and Laidler open economy model, by imposing a constraint that undoubtedly helps to keep things as simple as possible, generates this particular result which we cannot easily accept. We have already noticed that the inclusion of the rate of world inflation raises the estimated value of the adjustment coefficient λ (0·407 against 0·16). Could it not be the case that expectations based on the world rate of inflation adjust much faster than those based on purely domestic considerations? We fitted an equation in which the domestic rate of inflation does not appear among the regressors, i.e.

$$\dot{p} = \alpha X_{-1} - \alpha (1 - \lambda) X_{-2} + \dot{\Pi}^e{}_{-1}$$

and we obtained a value of 0·78 for the estimated parameter. It the face of this kind of evidence, we have reformulated the Cross and Laidler open economy model in such a way that the two types of expectation can adjust at different speeds. Formally:

$$\dot{p} = \alpha X_{-1} + E$$

$$E = m\dot{p}^e_{-1} + (1 - m)\dot{\Pi}^e_{-1}$$

$$\dot{p}^e = \lambda_1 \dot{p} + (1 - \lambda_1)\dot{p}^e_{-1}$$

$$\dot{\Pi}^e = \lambda_2 \dot{\Pi} + (1 - \lambda_2)\dot{\Pi}^e_{-1}$$

We have fitted this model to the period 1955-72 and the estimated values of the structural parameters turned out to be:

α	m	λ_1	λ_2
0·78350	0·787 20	0·20228 $\longrightarrow$	1. 00
(0·1955)	(0·1702)	(0·05415)	

The parameter m assumes a completely different value and the two speeds of adjustment differ dramatically. Expectations based on purely domestic considerations bear a weight of 0·78 and adjust slowly, while Π^e turns out to carry a low weight and to adjust within twelve months. In the light of these values for the structural parameters we could say that the weight of one obtained by Cross and Laidler on Π^e was simply picking up part of the effect due to the very high speed of adjustment of these expectations, and this was happening because that speed, by the structure of the model itself, was forced to assume too low a value, indeed some weighted average of the two quite different rates at which $\dot{p}^e$ and Π^e seem to adjust.

Is a weight of 0·22 underestimating the importance of the world rate of inflation? We would say yes but only in a very limited sense. We have already noticed that in the second half of the 1960s the short-run trade-off has been worsening and that this could be attributed to the fact that the Italian economic agents were more and more aware of the problem of inflation. But between 1966 and 1969 the actual rate of inflation has been oscillating around a value of 2·5 per cent, and this does not seem to be a rate in the face of which one may become aware of inflation. Instead during these years the rate of inflation in the world economy has been progressively accelerating from 2·5 per cent to over 5·5 per cent, and it seems reasonable to say that if people were becoming more and more aware of the problem of distinguishing between real and nominal variables, that happened mainly because inflation was exploding at the world level. In this sense only, a weight of 0·22 underestimates the importance of the world rate of inflation. However, we are not trying to capture this kind of impact. When we say that economic agents by looking at the events in the world economy learn to anticipate inflation or, better, learn that inflation is a quite serious problem, we are not saying that they believe the world rate of inflation will be imported at some particular speed and extent. It is exactly in the light of the last point that the weight on Π^e must be evaluated, and we would say it is not unreasonable.

There is a further argument that makes us believe that the results associated with our formulation of the open economy are more sensible. At the world level there has been a trough in the rate of inflation in the first quarter of 1967 and the Italian rate of inflation marked a trough in the first quarter of 1968, just twelve months after, just as an estimated coefficient equal to one seems to predict. It would be difficult to explain this short time lag on the basis of an adjustment parameter of 0·40 obtained from the Cross and Laidler formulation of the model.

Our conclusions are as follows. First, the impact of excess demand on the rate of inflation is clear. Second, both from the closed economy model and, even more strongly, from the open economy version, we have obtained results that exclude the possibility of choosing any particular combination of excess demand and inflation in the long run. The estimated values of 0·93 (equation (4)) and 1·00 (equation (10)) leave little doubt about the fact that we are facing a vertical Phillips curve and that the trade-off is a short-run phenomenon only. Third, we have shown that the fit of the model improves and the structural parameters assume more reasonable values when we make the hypothesis that expectations are formed on the basis not only of purely domestic considerations but also of the rate of inflation in the world economy and that, therefore, they provide one of the mechanisms through which international inflationary pressures are transmitted. Finally, some items of evidence relating to the domestic considerations carry a higher weight but adjust at a much lower speed.

THE LONG-RUN TRADE-OFF AND THE ITALIAN WAGE EQUATION: 1953-73

In this section we seek the answers to the following questions:

1   Given that expectations seem to play a relevant role in the inflationary processes, what is the mechanism on the basis of which expectations are formed?
2   Is there a long-run trade-off between unemployment and wage inflation?

In order to answer these two questions we start by considering the standard wage equation fitted by Italian economists. It postulates that the rate of change of earnings (in the industrial sector) is explained by the inverse of the non-agricultural unemployment rate, the present rate of inflation, the inclusion of which is simply due to the presence of escalator clauses in the Italian wage agreements, and a dummy taking value one in 1970. By applying ordinary least squares to such a model we get:

$$\dot{e} = -0\cdot003516 + 0\cdot210432 \ U^{-1} + 1\cdot09516 \ \dot{p} + 0\cdot0983964 \ d$$
$$\quad (0\cdot24641) \quad (2\cdot40581) \qquad\quad (3\cdot751069) \quad (3\cdot839031)$$

$$\bar{R}^2 = 0\cdot83769 \qquad DW = 1\cdot25665 \tag{1}$$

We notice that in this model the problem of autocorrelation in the residuals is rather serious; this casts doubts on the validity of the model embodied in equation (1). That coefficient on $\dot{p}$ turns out to be unity. This is an important finding because when we consider the estimated values of the same parameter (on the cost of living now) of the equations of Tables 8. 2 and 8. 3 we observe that even when both the dependent variable and the period of the analysis are different we obtain a coefficient which is not significantly different from one. Further the unity coefficient we have obtained in equation (1) is interesting because it is a result which goes against the results of Italian economists. In fact, when a Phillips curve has been fitted, often the estimated parameter turned out to be well over $1\cdot00$, indeed between $1\cdot15$ and $1\cdot35$, and this was of course recognised to pose serious problems of interpretation. At the same time it was argued that because of the fact that escalator clauses act as only partial compensation for the increase in the cost of living and because they only apply to minimum wages which represent approximately 70 per cent of actual earnings (the dependent variable in our equation (1)), the estimated coefficient on the price variable should lie in the region of $0\cdot6$-$0\cdot7$. In this context the parameter estimate we obtained is clearly more satisfactory and, above all, it makes much more economic sense.

But this does not imply that we are not unsatisfied with the model embodied in equation (1). In our view the presence of the rate of inflation among the regressors is due not so much to the escalator clauses as to the fact that workers form expectations about the future rate of inflation. In this light, equation (1) is to be interpreted as a reduced form of a model which says that wages depend on excess demand and expectations and that these, by definition, are equal to the present rate of inflation. We do not think this is a correct hypothesis and the question we are going to raise is as follows: what kind of an expectations-generating scheme is it sensible to formulate?

The first model, an alternative to that embodied in equation (1), is based on the Hicksian concept of extrapolative expectations. People are supposed to look at both the present rate of inflation and at its present rate of acceleration. Again the system is assumed to ignore past errors. Formally this expectations-generating mechanism is as follows:

$$\dot{p}_t^{\,e} = \dot{p}_t + \phi(\dot{p}_t - \dot{p}_{t-1}) \tag{2}$$

Where ϕ is to be different from zero, we want to differentiate this from the previous hypothesis. Instead, as far as the sign of ϕ is concerned it is not possible to formulate any *a priori* requirement because it obviously depends on whether or not economic agents expect recent trends in the inflation rate to persist. The estimating wage equation will be:

$$\dot{e} = a_o + a_1 U^{-1} + a_2 \dot{p} + a_3 (\dot{p} - \dot{p}_{-1}) + a_4 d$$

By applying ordinary least squares we obtained:

$$\dot{e} = 0 \cdot 000058 + 0 \cdot 235187\, U^{-1} + 0 \cdot 8819022\, \dot{p}$$
$$(0 \cdot 004098)\quad (2 \cdot 638578)\qquad\quad (2 \cdot 20057)$$

$$+ 0 \cdot 4549021 (\dot{p} - \dot{p}_{-1}) + 0 \cdot 09156 d$$
$$(1 \cdot 260476)\qquad\qquad (3 \cdot 49459)$$

$$R^2 = 0 \cdot 83006 \qquad DW = 1 \cdot 41889 \tag{3}$$

The present rate of inflation is insignificant and the overall fit is not increased. Moreover, the DW statistic is still too low. On the basis of these results it is impossible to claim that the expectations-generating mechanism as described by equation (2) is a sensible and superior alternative to that embodied in equation (1).

We can now turn to consider the standard error-learning hypothesis first formulated by Cagan and then successfully used, with few exceptions, in the empirical literature of the excess demand expectations augmented models of wage determination. The Cagan-Friedman model is well known and there is no need here to work out the fitted equation; we will simply report and discuss our results. The structural parameters of the model are defined as follows:

α = intercept
β = coefficient on the unemployment variable
γ = coefficient on the dummy variable
η = coefficient on the expected rate of inflation
λ = adjustment parameter of the expectations-generating scheme.

They have been estimated with a non-linear programme[16] and the results are as follows:

α	β	γ	η	λ
−0·0084149	0·23355	0·095991	1·1385	0·66348
(0·018805)	(0·11250)	(0·024642)	(0·38121)	(0·15400)

$$R^2 = 0 \cdot 87188 \qquad DW = 1 \cdot 70130 \qquad F = 27 \cdot 246$$

(Standard errors in parentheses)

The DW statistic although it is now less reliable, owing to the presence of the lagged dependent variable among the regressors in the reduced form equation) seems to denote that the problem of auto-correlated residuals is not so serious as in the previous models we have estimated. All the parameters, excluding the intercept, are strongly significant, and the coefficient on the expected rate of inflation is not significantly different from one. Indeed there is not much difference between these parameters and those obtained in equation (1) and this is obviously due to the fact that we are dealing with annual data, while the estimated value of λ would suggest that a considerable part of the adjustment of the expecta-tions takes place within twelve months. Notice however, that a value of λ equal to 0·66 implies that the length of the adjustment process does involve a space of time of more than two years, and therefore equation (1) was indeed based on a mis-specification of the true lag structure of the model. At this point we simply add that when the value of the parameter on the expected rate of infla-tion has been constrained to be equal to one, the remaining para-meters turned out to be much the same as those obtained with a free estimate. And the exact result was as follows:

α	β	γ	η	λ
—0·008896	0·24577	0·094686	1·00	0·67834
(0·018275)	(0·082507)	(2·26640)		(0·15106)

$$R^2 = 0·84980 \qquad DW = 1·71830 \qquad F = 26·25$$

Before drawing general conclusions we performed a further experi-ment. We sought the answer to the question: does the rate of infla-tion in the rest of the world significantly affect the process of wage determination in the Italian labour market directly through inflationary expectations? We have called E the total expectations and we assumed that it is the sum of the expectations formed on the basis of both the domestic and the world inflation rates. Formally:

$$E = m\dot{p}^e + (1 - m)\dot{\Pi}^e$$

$$\dot{p}^e = \lambda\dot{p} + (1 - \lambda)\dot{p}^e_{-1}$$

$$\dot{\Pi}^e = \lambda\dot{\Pi} + (1 - \lambda)\dot{\Pi}^e_{-1}$$

The structural parameters of the model have been estimated as follows:

α	β	γ	η
—0·014774	0·25223	0·093789	1·1263
(0·019430)	(0·11609)	(0·025016)	(0·38026)

λ	m
0·68251	1·15100
(0·13335)	(0·34856)

$$R^2 = 0·88117 \qquad DW = 1·82985$$

There is not a substantial improvement in the fit, and the estimated parameters are not significantly different from those of the closed economy model. Moreover the value of m turns out to be not significantly different from one, and this seems to reinforce the conviction that in the wage-bargaining process people would act essentially on the basis of purely domestic considerations.

At this stage some conclusions can be drawn. We have considered a naive model postulating that wage inflation depends on excess demand and expectations and that these, by definition, are equal to the present rate of inflation. This model was rejected because it was clearly based on a mis-specification of the true lag structure of the expectations generating scheme. We then considered the extrapolative expectations hypothesis which was also rejected because of its inconsistency with the facts. Finally the standard Friedman-Cagan model was implemented and it was shown to produce sensible results. In particular the estimated value of the parameter λ is such than the generating scheme of the expectations in the Italian labour markets can be described by:

$$\dot{p}^e_\epsilon = 0.66\dot{p}_\epsilon + 0.34\dot{p}^e_{\epsilon-1}$$

and the length of the adjustment is well above the twelve months implied by equation (1).

But the more important result which confirms the conclusion we have already drawn at the end of the previous section on the price equation is that the coefficient on the expected rate of inflation, by being not significantly different from one, seems to undermine the Keynesian standard view that in the long run there is a trade-off between excess demand and unemployment. This implies there is some 'equilibrium' or 'natural' rate of unemployment beyond which the costs in terms of inflation of a further expansion of aggregate demand will be enormous. The natural rate of non-agricultural unemployment appears to lie in the region between 4·5 and 4·7 per cent, which is of course a high value with respect to those experienced by other countries. But we must also add that, given the structural characteristics of the Italian labour market, there are ample possibilities for implementing policies especially aimed at reducing the value of the natural rate.

How can we reconcile these results with those obtained by Modigliani and Tarantelli (1972), who argue that the trade-off has become more and more favourable in the sense that less unemployment is required in order to obtain any particular rate of inflation? The answer is that the reconciliation is not possible because the two studies look at two different aspects of the general problem of inflation. We agree with these two authors only when they say that we need a better proxy for the state of pressure in the labour market, although, as we will point out later on, we do not believe that the improvement in the skill and competitiveness of the labour

force is the major argument we have to consider in order to formulate such a proxy. We cannot agree with them when they maintain that their arguments can play a relevant role in the explanation of the inflationary processes in the Italian economy. The
study by these two authors is to be interpreted as a piece of economic history in the sense that it highlights *one* aspect of the relationship between the growth process and inflation and, more precisely, the impact of the changing structure of the unemployment
on the rate of wage change. In this limited sense only their conclusion that the trade-off has improved is correct. This of course
does not exclude the concept that, when forces other than the
change in the skill and competitiveness of the labour force are
taken into due consideration, that conclusion is to be reversed.
And in fact this is precisely the message from the study by
Valcamonici (1973), who also pursues a structural view of the
inflationary processes but who argues that, if one considers the
changing structure of the entire economy, one cannot but conclude
that the trade-off has been worsening. One cannot study one of the
possible determinants of the natural unemployment rate and then
jump to the conclusion that the natural rate does not exist.

   In the light of this last point it is even more interesting to see
a certain similarity between the conclusions of our study and those
of Valcamonici. He writes that, beginning from some 'Break Point'
along the Phillips curve, '. . . it is likely that unacceptable rates of
inflation would be generated if, in order to alleviate unemployment,
aggregate policies are used.' It is not difficult to see the similarity
between our concept of 'natural rate' and Valcamonici's 'Break
Point Rate'. And it is also remarkable that, numerically, there is
no significant difference between the two rates, the former being
between 4·5 and 4·7, the latter 4·45 per cent. The difference is
negligible and may well be accounted for partly by the fact that
some of the data used in the two studies are not the same and by
considering that our analysis also covers the years 1970-3 which,
being characterised by the presence of strong pressures by unions,
must have witnessed an increase in the value of the natural rate.
So, in spite of the difference in the two analyses, their conclusions
are rather the same and seem to suggest that beyond a certain
level of unemployment inflation will become difficult to control.

POLICY PRESCIPTIONS AND FINAL CONSIDERATIONS

In this paper we started by considering the union militancy hypothesis which represents a sort of conventional wisdom among a
great number of Italian economists. The analysis was carried out
on both *a priori* and pure empirical grounds and the conclusion we
reached was that the hypothesis was unsatisfactory and that there
was no systematic influence of the strike activity on the rate of

wage inflation. Rejection of incomes policy as a potent anti-inflationary weapon rests on the empirical results that we have presented. At this stage the necessity of an alternative hypothesis capable of coping with the recent phenomenon of accelerating inflation and on the basis of which policy prescriptions could be formulated was evident. We considered the empirical relevance to the Italian economy of the excess demand expectations-augmented theory of wage and price determination. Our conclusions are as follows. First, excess demand exerts a significant impact on price and wage changes. Second, we cannot proceed on the assumption that Italy is a closed economy. There is room for discussion about the more appropriate way in which the influence of the world rate of inflation can be captured; it is felt, however that the inclusion of some index of the price of the imported goods is not a satisfactory procedure. The third point we made is that inflationary expectations appear to be generated according to an error-learning mechanism and that more than two years are required in order to adjust to a different rate of inflation. This particular conclusion was reached at the end of an analysis in which the performance of the Cagan hypothesis was compared to that of the two naive models. The fourth and most important point is that no money illusion seems to be at work in the Italian markets for goods and labour and that consequently the long-run Phillips curve is vertical. The policy implications that follow from this are quite clear. Given that in the short run there is a Phillips curve for any particular rate of expected inflation, the target of a constant rate of inflation can be achieved only if the employment of resources is at its natural level. A reduction in the rate of inflation can be obtained only through a temporary creation of excess supply and a subsequent reduction in the expected rate of inflation. The longer the period of time over which we can implement our anti-inflationary programme, the lower will be the cost in terms of unemployed resources. And it is precisely in the context of the discussion on the effects of the absence of money illusion that we can appreciate the mistake made by the Italian policy-makers since the early 1970s. They were looking for growth and they believed that, by causing inflation and devaluation through a huge expansion of the money supply, they could guarantee higher levels of profits and investments to the firms. This policy, which was essentially based on the assumption that creditors in the financial markets and workers in the labour markets were suffering from money illusion and that only entrepreneurs could anticipate inflation, was bound to fail miserably and to generate zero growth and unprecedented rates on unemployment and inflation in 1974 and 1975.[17]

NOTES

1   The statistical sources are given in the appendix at the end of this study.
2   Notice that while at the time of the first acceleration in the rate of money creation (1958 and 1959) the rate of total unemployment is well over 5 per cent and the non-utilised capacity in the industrial sector around 11 per cent, in 1961 and 1962, when there is a further jump in the rate of domestic money expansion, the unemployment rate is around 3 per cent and the non-utilised capacity 5 per cent only. With this we simply want to stress that, in terms of potential effects on the rate of inflation, the two stages of the process of acceleration in the expansion of the money supply must not be confused. We also want to notice that, when in 1965 the rate of money expansion reaches an even higher level, the non-utilised capacity will be well over 15 per cent. This can help in understanding why no serious inflation followed this last event.
3   The effects of this are evident in the fact that while in general during periods of sharp rise in minimum wages the wage drift tends to assume negative values, the 1962-3 wage round was characterised by a high and positive wage drift (+3·8 per cent in 1962 and +3·5 per cent in 1963).
4   The impact of this sharp cut in the rate of money expansion on the 1965-6 depression is also emphasised in Brunner *et al.* (1973).
5   In recent years it has become evident that both unemployment *and* inflation affect the volume of industrial unrest. For a discussion on this point see Laidler (1973) and Fisher (1973).
6   Examples of this view may be found in OECD (1970) and (1973).
7   As a partial answer to the problem they raise, these two authors work out an index which is based on all the three measures of the strike activity. Formally the Evans-Galambos index is an unweighted arithmetic mean of three ratios as follows:

$$EG_t = \frac{100}{3} \left\{ \frac{S_t}{S_0} + \frac{HL_t/HL_0}{E_t/E_0} + \frac{N_t/N_0}{EG/E_0} \right\}$$

where S_0 HL_0 and N_0 are respectively the number of strikes, the time lost and the men involved in strikes in the year base and E_t/E_0 is the employment index. At first sight this index could appear a rather sophisticated measure of union militancy but if we look in particular at the equal weights given to the three ratios, we cannot but conclude it is a very crude measure. And in fact Knowles (1966) in his comment to the study by Evans and Galambos criticises the index because, he says, its three components do not seem likely to be of equal importance in any particular context and their relative importance will almost certainly differ in different contexts. This aspect has been pointed out to me also by Professor Michael Parkin, who argued that it would be more correct to postulate that wage inflation depends on union militancy and that this is a linear function of three separate variables. This in fact would enable us to find out the appropriate weights with which S, N and HL are to be entered in the determination of the index. This exercise would obviously generate a vicious problem of multicollinearity among the strike variables and it is hard to believe we could correctly identify their separate effects. However, it is clearly arbitrary to assume *a priori* that these effects are the same.
8   On this point see Purdy and Zis (1974).
9   The reader can also see Kornhauser *et al.* (1954).

10 The same view was expressed in the Donovan Report (1968).

11 Besides, we see that some of these phenomena can be quantified and that consequently the problem of the choice of the appropriate regressor is even greater.

12 In both tables the 1973 rate of change in earnings is determined on the basis of the first six months.

13 In this context HL appears to be a less satisfactory proxy than for instance the number of strikes that are more heavily and systematically influenced by the level of unemployment.

14 We are referring to the study by Del Monte (1973).

15 For a detailed analysis on this point see Laidler and Nobay (1973).

16 The programme is the BMDX 95 of the University of Manchester.

17 It is also interesting to notice that more or less the same type of economic policy started being implemented in the UK in 1970 by the Heath administration and that the effects have been equally disastrous. For an interesting discussion on this point see *British Economic Policy 1970-1974* (Hobart Paperback), IEA, 1974.

REFERENCES

Ashenfelter, O. C., G. E. Johnson and J. H. Pencavel, 'Trade unions and the rate of change of money wages in United States manufacturing industry', *Review of Economic Studies* (1972), pp. 27-54.

Battara, P., 'Ancora su la congiuntura e la politica monetaria Italiana', *Moneta e Credito* 1967, pp. 51-85.

Brunner, K., *et al.* 'Fiscal and monetary policies in moderate inflation: case studies of three countries', *Journal of Money, Credit and Banking* (1973), pp. 312-53.

Carlson, J. and M. Parkin, 'Inflationary expectations', Economica (1975).

Cross, R. and D. Laidler, 'Inflation, excess demand and expectations in fixed exchange rate open economies: some preliminary results', in M. Parkin and G. Zis (eds.), *Inflation in the World Economy* (Manchester University Press, 1976).

Del Monte, C., 'Un modello econometrico per l'economia Italiana utilizzato a fini previsivi', *Rassegna Economica* (1973), pp. 69-140.

Donovan, Lord, Chairman, Royal Commission on Trade Unions and Employers' Associations. *Report* (London, HMSO, 1968).

Ercolani, P., 'Analisi quantitativa per la programmazione di breve periodo. Salari', *Isco*, documento No. 8 (1971).

Evans, E. W. and P. Galambos, 'Work-stoppages in the United Kingdom, 1951-1964: a quantitative study', *Bulletin of the Oxford University Institute of Economics and Statistics* (1966), pp. 33-40.

Ferretti, M., 'Gli effetti delle differenze regionali di disoccupazione sulla inflazione salariale in Italia'. *Rassegna Economica* (1974), pp. 729-70.

Ferri, P., *La disoccupazione in un processo di sviluppo economico* (Giuffre', 1971).

Fisher, M., *Measurement of Labour Disputes and their Economic Effects* (OECD, 1973).

Godfrey, L., 'The Phillips curve: incomes policy and trade-unions effects', in H. Johnson (ed.), *The Current Inflation* (London, Macmillan, 1971).

Hyman, R., *Strikes* (London, Fontana, 1972).

Knowles, K. G. J. C., Comment (on Evans and Galambos), *BOUIES*, (Feb. 1966).

Kornhauser, A. *et al. Industrial Conflict* (London, McGraw-Hill, 1954).

Laidler, D., 'Information, money and the macroeconomics of inflation', *The Swedish Journal of Economics* (1974), pp. 26-41.

Laidler, D. and R. Nobay, 'Some current issues concerning the international aspects of inflation', paper presented at the third Dauphine Conference on International Monetary Economics, 1974.

Modigliani, F. and G. La Malfa, 'Inflation, balance of payments deficit and their cure through monetary policy: the Italian example', *BNL Quarterly Review* (1967), pp. 3-47.

Modigliani, F. and E. Tarantelli, 'A generalisation of the Phillips curve for a developing country', *Review of Economic Studies* (1972), pp. 203-23.

Purdy, D. and G. Zis, 'On the concept and measurement of trade union militancy', in D. Laidler and D. Purdy (eds.), *Labour Markets and Inflation* (Manchester University Press, 1974).

Ross, A. M., *Trade Union Wage Policy* (Berkely, Calif., 1948).

Sylos Labini, P., 'Prices, distribution and investment in Italy, 1951-1966: an interpretation', *BNL Quarterly Review* (1967), pp. 295-315.

— 'Forme di mercato, sindacati e inflazione', *Rassegna Economica* (1970).

— *Sindacati, inflazione e produttivita* (Laterza, 1972). The English version of this work is now available in *Trade Unions, Inflation and Productivity* (Saxon House, 1974).

Taylor, J., 'Incomes policy, the structure of unemployment and the Phillips curve: The United Kingdom experience'. in M. Parkin and M. Sumner (eds.), *Incomes Policy and Inflation* (Manchester University Press, 1973).

— 'Wage inflation, unemployment and the organised pressure for higher wages in the United Kingdom 1961-71'.

— *Unemployment and Wage Inflation* (London, Longmans, 1974).

Turner, H. A. *et al.*, *Labour Relations in the Motor Industry* (London, Allen & Unwin, 1968).

Valcamonici, R., 'Modificazioni strutturali, disoccupazione ed inflazione nella industria Italiana: una analisi empirica'. *Note Economiche* (1973).

Vinci, S., 'Il funzionamento del mercato del lavoro in Italia. Una analisi comparata delle varie interpretazioni' Portici (relazione) 1972.

APPENDIX 8. 1

Statistical sources

1   Retail price index: *Bollettino mensil di statistica.*

2   Index number of minimum contractual wage rates: *Annuario Istat* and *Bollettino mesile di statistica*. In 1966 the sample on the basis of which this index is calculated has been changed. Our data include family allowances.

3   Index number of earnings: *Bollettino mensile di statistica*. In 1965 the sample has been changed. Firms with less than ten employees are not considered in the determination of the index.

4   Industrial unrest: *Bollettino mensile di statistica.*

5   Non-agricultural unemployment rate: these data are from Del Monte (1973).

6   Cost of living index: *Bollettino mensile di statistica.*

7   Money supply: OECD, *Main Economic Indicators* for the period 1955-73 and *Bollettino della Banca d'Italia* for 1953 and 1954.

9 World influences on the Australian rate of inflation

Peter D. Jonson*

I INTRODUCTION

Australia is a small open economy with both economic and non-economic trends strongly influenced by the rest of the world, and not least her rate of inflation. But in their writings on the inflation issue contemporary Australian economists, and until recently her policy-makers (although not all of their policy advisers) have tended to play down the implications of openness and to operate with largely closed economy models. This approach was probably fostered by the long period from the end of the Korean War boom to the late 1960s, when the influence of the rest of the world appeared, superficially at least, to be small and diminishing. In the recent past, however, the world-wide inflation influenced Australia perhaps as pervasively, if not as dramatically, as during the Korean experience, and the most surprising feature of much recent analysis is the persistence of beliefs that inflation in a small country which maintains a fixed exchange rate is domestically generated. This paper is designed to redress the balance. It examines post-war experience in broad outline, surveys the available single-equation econometric evidence on wage and price determination, and finally discusses the findings of a complete model simulation study of the recent Australian inflationary take-off.

The current analysis owes much to the writings of so-called 'monetarist' economists, and in particular those of Keynes, Johnson (1971, 1972a, b, c) and Parkin (1972), and the present writer's general theoretical presumption is best stated at the outset. From November 1949, when Australia followed sterling in devaluing

* I would like acknowledge, without delegating responsibility for any errors, the helpful comments on earlier drafts by H. G. Johnson, J. M. Parkin, J. F. Henderson, W. E. Norton, D. W. Stammer, C. R. Wymer and G. Zis. The assistance of G. J. Thompson in providing the revised wage equations presented below is also gratefully acknowledged.

relative to the US dollar, until the middle of 1971 the $A/$US
exchange rate varied only slightly, and the revaluation in the period
to December 1972 was relatively minor.[1] Given that many other
currencies were pegged to the $US, one would expect the influence
of cycles of activity and prices in the rest of the world to be
marked, and that domestic economic policy would be strongly
related to the balance of payments. This does not of course mean
that the Australian inflation rate was pegged to the American rate,
or the world average, in the short run, only that over the longer
run it had to be broadly compatible. The possibility of running
down or building up reserves, and changing trade and capital controls introduces some short-run independence, even with fixed exchange rates, and allows domestic influences such as the vagaries
of climate, economic policy, or decisions of wages tribunals to
have an independent short-run influence on the inflation rate.

Analysis of the period since the major revaluations of the $A
relative to the $US and in particular since the independent revalu-
ations of December 1972 and September 1973 which substantially
changed the trade weighted exchange rate is not as complete as
that for the earlier period of largely fixed exchange rates. But a
continued high rate of inflation during 1973 and 1974 illustrates
that such analysis is seriously needed. This paper is intended to
suggest one way in which this analysis should proceed. It also
emphasises the world influences in recent experience, and particularly in generating the Australian inflationary take-off of the early
1970s.

II POST-WAR INFLATION EXPERIENCE: AN OVERVIEW[2]

At the onset of the Korean War the Australian price level, as measured by the retail price index, had been rising by just under 10
per cent per annum for three years. In 1951 the annual inflation
rate[3] rose to a peak of 22·5 per cent; with the collapse of the boom,
and especially of wool prices (historically a key variable for
Australia), foreign reserves began to fall suddenly. After winning
an election in which it perhaps understandably stressed political
rather than economic issues, the government introduced what was
widely believed to be a 'horror budget'. Waterman (p. 88) concludes that apart from any psychological effects of this budget, its
influence was certainly minor compared with the external factors,
which reduced domestic demand considerably, and resulted in the
introduction of import licensing early in 1952. The next few years
were relatively stable, with consumer prices rising on average
less than 3 per cent per annum and the ecomomy displaying no
clear cyclical pattern, as the external factors were relatively
stable and largely offset by skillful domestic policy variations
within the balance of payments constraint. (Waterman, p. 145).

Expansionary fiscal policy from mid-1957, reinforced by a fairly short-lived export boom in 1958, sparked a domestic boom. This was dampened by the relaxation of import controls and then the slackening of British and American economic activity. One result was a drastic decline in foreign reserves from February 1960, and interestingly enough Waterman observes (p. 172) that the rate of inflation began to fall *before* the slackening of output and employment. Despite the indications of slackening demand, a credit squeeze was engineered in November 1960, and ushered in a severe recession which, given the stable external situation, helped provide domestic price stability for three years. Perkins (1967, p. 8) argues that the November measures were taken since there could be no 'reasonable confidence' that the deflationary policy measures introduced earlier in 1960 would arrest the fall in reserves and check the boom, and this judgement again illustrates the pervasive influence of external variables and constraints.

The Australian price stability of 1961-3 and the American and British recovery contributed to a strengthening of exports (Perkins (1967), p. 30), and when the economy approached full employment in 1964, stimulated by this rise in exports and a sharp increase in government spending in 1963, it was with a strong balance of payments for the first time since the Korean boom. Monetary policy was tightened, and Perkins (1967, pp. 24-6) praises the authorities for raising interest rates relatively early in the boom, in contrast to their sluggish response in earlier cyclical episodes. Mundells's theoretical work, [4] however, suggests that the main effect of this is probably to contribute to an increase in capital inflow, and recent empirical work by Porter (1973) provides evidence of the relevance of this reaction for Australia.

The five years following the downturn in 1964 are in some respects similar to those from 1961 to 1963, with the economy in approximate balance although with a higher level of utilisation of resources and a higher rate of inflation, averaging approximately 3 per cent per annum. By 1969 the world inflation began to influence Australia, [5] with a strong build-up of foreign reserves accompanying a domestic boom. One reason for the time taken for the world inflation obviously to influence Australia, which also masked recognition of its effects, was the prolonged slump in wool prices which prevented any rise in the export price index until 1972. Early in 1972 wool prices began to rise dramatically, with the index moving from 61 in December 1971 to 260 in March 1973 (1966/7 = 100) and between the same two quarters the export price index rose from 95 to 150. But although these traditional indicators of the impact of world inflation were not giving their usual signals from 1969 to 1971, the volume of exports was rising strongly, and imports were increasing relatively slowly, in part owing to the relatively slow growth of Australian prices. The tra-

ditional response of tight domestic stabilisation policies succeeded
in raising unemployment considerably in the short run, and in
raising capital inflow in the longer run. The rise in the unemployment rate temporarily reduced inflation, further strengthening the
balance of payments and contributing to speculative capital inflows
in expectation of a revaluation of the exchange rate. In the event
the exchange rate was not revalued until shortly after the General
Election of 1972 in which the conservative parties were defeated
for the first time in twenty-three years. The incoming labour
government almost immediately revalued relative to the $US, and
further revaluations were effected in February 1973, when Australia did not follow the $US devaluation, and in September when
a further revaluation took place. The government also announced
a general 25 per cent tariff cut in July, almost immediately after
the consumer price index for June revealed an annual rate of
inflation of 8·5 per cent (or over 13 per cent measured relative to
the previous quarter).

As an indication of the net result of these various influences
it is worth noting that the volume of money (currency plus demand
deposits) rose by 26 per cent in the fiscal year to June 1973, compared with 9 per cent in the previous year. This is difficult to
explain except as a (not fully understood) disequilibrium phenomenon, [6] as the growth of demand at the current prices cannot
account for it. As an offsetting factor, the exchange rate, from
November 1949 until December 1972 A$1 = US$1·191, was by the
end of September 1973 A$1= US$1·488, although the trade-weighted
exchange rate had not changed nearly so dramatically. Indeed,
Porter (1973) has calculated that the rate of monetary expansion,
and by implication the rate of inflation, would have been 'two or
three times greater' without revaluation.

Debate on the causes of the Australian inflation has understandably been intensive. The employee organisation has presented the world inflation argument at recent national wage cases, and
their opposition have relied on the traditional cost-push arguments.
Indeed the Federal Treasurer of the previous conservative government referred to H. G. Johnson as a 'discredited academic', although a newspaper report on the debate pointed out that in view of
some of the empirical work that is discussed below this was an
indefensible position.[7] The ex-Treasurer's dismissal of world
influences is however supported by many influential academic and
public service economists: for example the Treasury's 1972
White Paper on the state of the economy concluded that 'much
the greater part' of the inflationary take-off 'is left to be explained
in terms of domestic influences' (Commonwealth of Australia
(1972), p. 22). And an academic survey of the existing empirical
work concluded that: '... the available econometric evidence
points to the important role of cost pressures, mainly domestic,

in our inflationary processes, but it also recognises a subordinate role for demand pressures, again mainly domestic' (Simkin (1972) p. 476). This conclusion was recently reaffirmed by Arndt (1973, p. 41), and so for some economists at least is apparently unshaken by the empirical evidence appearing since Simkin's survey was written.

The recent policy changes indicate that the present government partly accepts 'monetarist' arguments, although it sponsored a referendum designed to give it powers to legislate to control prices and incomes directly. The referendum (held in December 1973) was defeated, and one feature of the campaign was newspaper letters for and against, each signed by prominent economists.[8] Notable among those advocating a 'no' vote was J. M. Parkin, whose earlier paper to the ANZAAS conference had recalled that in 1936 L. F. Giblin, a distinguished Australian economist, called for a price level rule to be administered by an authority independent of parliament.[9] Parkin amended this to advocate that the government 'charge the Central Bank with the pursuit of a money stock target and, by implication, the abandonment of interest rate and exchange rate targets' (1973a, p. 25).

III SINGLE EQUATION STUDIES

An examination of the available econometric studies of wage and price determination will set the stage for the simulation tests reported in the next section. The Australian work has been briefly compared with that for Canada, the United Kingdom and the United States by Parkin (1973a). The Australian wage determination system is unusual in that a considerable role is played by Commonwealth and State wages boards. These wages boards determine the value of 'award wages', and econometric studies of Australian wage and price determination have almost always included award wages as an explanatory variable,[10] until recently an exogeneous one. The award wage decisions are widely publicised and in fact establish legal minimum wages for a wide range of workers. Thus the award wage series sets the tone for wage determination in general and, depending as it does on past and expected price and productivity changes, seems best interpreted as the Australian wage expectations generating mechanism. A recent paper by Parkin (1973b) has set out a detailed theoretical justification of this interpretation, with some empirical work that will be discussed below. The paper shows that the test of whether there is a long-run trade-off between inflation and unemployment is whether the sum of the weights on award wages and foreign prices is less than or equal to unity.

One important study by Pitchford (1968) produced an equation for the (quarterly) rate of change of consumer prices using data for 1947-68. Pitchford did not specify separate equations for prices and earnings, but combined these into a single equation in which the explanatory variables were, most importantly, labour demand pressure, and changes in minimum hourly (award) wages, adjusted for the terms of trade, import prices and export prices, with the numerical influence of the latter term very small. One, two- and three-quarter lags are imposed on each variable, with the best fitting combinations determined experimentally, being two quarters for labour market demand pressure, one and two quarters for adjusted award wages and three quarters for import and export prices. Apart from the aggregation and imposition of non-zero lags, the main weaknesses of this study are its treatment of award wages as exogeneous, and the use of import and export prices as representing the full direct effects of world prices on Australian prices, although the competitive effects of non-traded but potentially tradable goods are excluded by the latter assumption.

The point estimate of the sum of weights on the awards variable and the foreign price variables in Pitchford's equation is 0·46, significantly different from unity, and implying the existence of a long-run trade-off between inflation and unemployment in Australia. This is a similar result to that obtained by Solow (1969) for the United States, although without the emphasis on price expectations of the latter work.

Other influential studies of Australian wage and price determination include Hancock's study (1967) of 'earnings drift', Nevile's well-known macroeconometric model (1970) and Nieuwenhuysen and Norman's paper (1971) on price determination. All include award wages as exogenous variables, and all imply a long-run inflation-unemployment trade-off. Nevile's book in fact contains an extensive discussion of the 'choices' implied by the alleged trade-off. All also include demand pressure variables, and the last also includes an indirect tax variable and a minor effect from import prices. None stresses the possibility that their demand pressure variables might be influenced by the rest of the world, and so foreign influences were completely de-emphasised. The important role of award wages tempted people into suggesting that the arbitration system be used in the implementation of an incomes policy, and there has been considerable fruitless discussion of rules for the wages tribunals to follow.[11]

The assumption that award wages are exogenous is both pervasive and misleading in Australian discussions of inflation. This assumption is presumably made because award wages are strongly influenced by an annual national wage case and other strategic wage cases in which employer, employee, and government representatives all submit cases, but a panel of judges decide the outcome. Literary contributions have however sometimes noted the role of past price changes in determining awards,[12] and econometric studies have recently attempted to explain award wages more precisely.[13] These studies, the most recent of which is discussed in some detail below, do much to dispose of the cost-push hypotheses for Australian inflation, as it turns out that the Arbitration Commission has largely acted like overseas labour markets.

A more ambitious study of wage and price determination by Higgins (1973), which included simulation analyses of the whole model within which his wage-price sector was embodied, represented in many ways a significant advance in the state of the art, but did nothing to shake the belief in a long-run trade-off. Indeed, Higgins defines his awards variable so as to eliminate the apparent 'absorption of award increases into drift' (Higgins (1973), p. 124) which is said to be partly or entirely an arithmetic phenomenon. The redefined variable (which is one hundred times the absolute annual change in awards divided by earnings lagged four quarters) is much smaller than the simple annual percentage change in awards, and thus takes on a larger coefficient than that variable in his earnings equation, the sum of weights on the current and lagged values being 0·975. Higgins also includes the rate of change of domestic prices as a proxy for price expectations, and obtains a coefficient of 0·157. The theoretical model underlying this work is therefore rather different from that underlying the results discussed below, and if one believed that awards were exogenous there would be a considerable trade-off implied by Higgins' results. There are no direct foreign influences in Higgins' wage equations, and so foreign influences were once again largely ignored.

And although Higgins specifies an endogenous explanation for award wages, he published a simulation in which the basic wage decision was treated as exogenous and altered by 1 per cent. This result was taken by Simkin as confirming the predominant importance of 'domestic cost pressure' in Australia, although in Higgins' work, and other work surveyed, demand variables play an importance of 'domestic cost pressures' in Australia, although in Higgins' prices are also directly represented, although not strongly. And, as already stressed, awards are not exogenous.

We now discuss in somewhat greater detail the most recent work on wage and price determination in Australia. The most logical order is to explain award wages, then earnings given awards, and then prices given earnings.

Award wages

Award wages are strongly influenced by the decisions of the Commonwealth Arbitration Commission, with Commonwealth decisions directly applying to almost half the Australian work force and flowing on rapidly to State awards. In addition, consent agreements negotiated between employer and employee but registered with the Commission are heavily influenced by the key central decisions.

The most strategically important decision is provided in the annual national wage case, and so Jonson, Mahar, and Thompson (1973) explain the national wage or basic decision ($\dot{b}$) with an annual model for the years 1959-72. This period included two years when the case was adjourned (1962, 1963) and two years when a 'no increase' decision was made (1960 and 1965). In the other years the results varied in impact on the change in award wage from 2·3 per cent (in 1967) to 6·0 per cent in 1971, the large increase that lent such superficial plausibility to the cost-push explanations for the current inflation in Australia.

To suggest explanatory variables for the national wage decisions, Jonson *et al.* examined the reasons given by the bench when explaining its decisions. Many factors were mentioned at different times, but most consistently discussed were price rises since the last increase in the national wage and productivity movements. Following the work of Higgins (1973), decision-specific variables were constructed that allow for the change in prices and productivity since the last increase in the national wage. Productivity is notoriously difficult to measure, and the Commission at one stage enunciated the principle of making major productivity adjustments at fairly regular intervals, and there is some evidence in the judgements that the larger-than-usual increases in award wages in 1959, 1964, and 1970 were the result of such productivity adjustments. These were of course years of relatively high economic activity and, especially 1964 and 1970, of a strong balance of payments position and so it is quite possible that these considerations influenced the timing of the major productivity adjustments. This refinement has not however been introduced into the model, and the timing of these adjustments remains formally exogenous. There is also evidence that some productivity adjustment is made each year.

There is one other interesting exogenous influence on award wages that has been identified by Hancock (1971). In 1964 there was a minority judgement opposing the increase given, and in 1965 the judges that were in the minority in 1964 were in the majority. The no-increase decision in 1965 was smaller than usual, and in 1966, as Hancock so delicately points out, the President of the Commission 'refrained from appointing two of the three majority judges of 1965'. Hence a dummy variable was included to represent the influence of the composition of the bench in that year. It has been suggested that the bench might have reversed the 1965 decision in 1966, and allowing for this possibility has improved the basic wage equation significantly. To summarise: the explanatory variables in the annual model of national wage decisions are:

$\dot{p}_x$ = the percentage change in the consumer price index since the last increase in the national wage.[14]

$\dot{q}_x$ = the percentage change in aggregate productivity since the last increase in the national wage.

$\dot{q}_z$ = the percentage change in aggregate productivity since the last major productivity adjustment to the national wage.

d = a dummy variable to represent the special composition of the bench in 1965, with value 1 in 1965, -1 in 1966 and zero otherwise.

The equation, which is estimated over the period 1959-72, is:

$$\dot{b} = 0·60 + 0·162\ \dot{p}_x + 0·317\ \dot{q}_x + 0·264\ \dot{q}_z - 2·23\ d \qquad (1)$$
$$\phantom{\dot{b} = }(1·1) \quad (1·5) \quad\quad (2·0) \quad\quad (5·0) \quad\quad (3·2)$$

$$\text{SEE} = 0·93 \qquad \bar{R}^2 = 0·813 \qquad DW = 1·70$$

In explaining award wages with a quarterly model, the basic decision variable ($\dot{b}$) explained by equation (1) is included as an explanatory variable in the award wage equation. Other variables include a measure of price expectations based on a poll of manu-facturers[15] ($\dot{p}^e$), a decision-specific variable to represent the influence of past price changes on another key decision, the metal trades margins decision ($\dot{p}_y$) and the lagged dependent to allow crudely for a lag in the adjustment of awards to their determinants. The dependent variable, the annual rate of change of award wages, is denoted $\dot{w}_A$. The equation, estimated over the period 1960(1)-1972(2), is

$$\dot{w}_A = 0·80 + 0·452\ \dot{p}^e + 0·695\ \dot{b} + 0·120\ \dot{p}_y + 0·331\ (\dot{w}_A)_{-1} \qquad (2)$$
$$\phantom{\dot{w}_A = }(2·1) \quad (5·2) \quad\quad (8·2) \quad\quad (3·5) \quad\quad (4·5)$$

$$\text{SEE} = 1·01 \qquad \bar{R}^2 = 0·885 \qquad D = 2·1$$

D is the Durbin statistic, and its value indicates the presence of serial correlation in the above equation. A possible explanation of this is the institutional propensity to give (or negotiate, in the case of consent agreements) 'round' amounts (e.g. $2 or 2·5 per cent), when the underlying determinants are presumably more continuous. This introduces an error into each observation, and, given the annual rate of change formulation, tends to produce runs of positive or negative residuals. Hence it is argued that conventional indi-cators of serial correlation are likely to be biased and thus do not necessarily indicate the absence of a meaningful explanatory vari-able from the equation, or other mis-specification. It is clear however that the classical assumption of random residuals is not tenable, and it must be accepted that the econometric inference is less than rigorous and thus the resulting estimates of variance must be treated with caution.

Accepting the estimated coefficients however, the results

appear plausible. The long-run coefficients on the basic-decision variable is close to unity (the point estimate being 1·04) and the average lag just under half a quarter. The coefficient on price expectations seems reasonable, although there is some offset from the negative and significant constant. Equations (1) and (2) thus establish an explanation of award wages stressing the strong influence of expected and past price changes, with an important role also played by the occasional major productivity adjustments, and current productivity movements via each national wage decision.

Average weekly earnings

An earnings equation was also developed by Jonson *et al,* in which short lags on award wages and world prices together represent expected price changes. Lagged productivity changes are also included, and three demand pressure variables: a four-quarter average of the ratio of registered vacancies to registered unemployment, the rate of change of that variable, and the current rate of change of Australia's foreign reserves. The first two variables are somewhat unconventional measures of labour market demand pressure. The third is included on the grounds that it represents a strategic variable which employers and employees take as indicating the likely future course of aggregate demand, and thus of excess demand for labour. Although a formal theoretical model was not worked out, it is clear that what might be called 'super-rational expectations', with the private sector second guessing government policy reaction on the basis of its knowledge of past government reaction patterns and the behaviour of policy targets, could well be incorporated into models of price and output dynamics.[16] The change in the balance of payments position proved however to be a somewhat controversial variable, although it is interesting to note that Laidler (1973, p. 388) has independently suggested (in a closed economy context) that 'expectations about the time path of aggregate demand and not just its current level, affect the rate of inflation'.[17] In any case, the direct influence of the reserves variable is numerically small, although it seems to improve the significance of some of the more traditional explanatory variables.

To summarise, the explanatory variables are:

V/U = four-quarter average of the ratio of registered vacancies to registered unemployment.
$\dot{V}/U$ = the percentage change in V/U
$\dot{r}$ = the annual percentage change in foreign reserves.
$\dot{w}_A$ = the annual percentage change in award wages.

$\dot{p}_w$ = the annual percentage change in world prices, defined as an average of the consumer price indices of the USA, and the UK and Japan, Australia's three major trading partners. The country indices were weighted by their respective real GDP in \$US.

$\dot{q}$ = the annual percentage change in aggregate productivity.

The dependent variable is denoted $\dot{w}$, and the preferred equation for the period 1960(1) to 1972(2) is:

$$\dot{w} = 0{\cdot}183 + 2{\cdot}28 \ V/U + 0{\cdot}008 \ V/U + 0{\cdot}019 \ \dot{r} + \sum_{i=0}^{2} W_i \ (\dot{w}_A)_{-i} \quad (3)$$

$$(0{\cdot}3) \qquad (2{\cdot}5) \qquad\quad (2{\cdot}1) \qquad\quad (2{\cdot}1)$$

$$+ \sum_{i=0}^{2} V_i \ (\dot{p}_w)_{-i} + \sum_{i=0}^{2} S_i \ (\dot{q})_{-i}$$

SEE = 1·20 $\overline{R}^2 = 0{\cdot}830$ DW = 1·53

The weights on lagged values, which were each estimated by a single Almon variable, thus constraining them to be monotonically declining, are:[18]

Lag	W_i	V_i	S_i
0	0·417	0·195	0·195
1	0·184	0·087	0·087
2	0·046	0·022	0·022
Sum	0·647	0·304	0·304
	(6·3)	(2·3)	(2·0)

The most interesting feature of this equation is seen by adding the sum of weights on lagged award wages and world prices; it is 0·951, not significantly different from unity and confirming the 'no-trade-off' result has been observed for other countries and 'the world', including other open economies[19] and which was foreshadowed by the intuition of Friedman (1968) and the theoretical work of Phelps (1965). This result is especially plausible as it disposes of the collective irrationality implied by the money illusion in the labour market apparently illustrated in earlier work.

Parkin (1973b) has reworked this equation in conjunction with his attempt to estimate the natural rate of unemployment in Australia. In brief, he replaced the ratio of registered job vacancies to unemployed in turn by their difference and by the inverse of the unemployment ratio (N/U), and dropped the foreign reserves variable. He also explicitly imposed the constraints suggested by the theoretical development that the sum of the coefficients on current and lagged world prices and productivity changes be equal, and, when added to the sum of coefficients on award wages, should sum to unity (although he also presents the unrestricted estimates, which, like those of Jonson *et al.*, are not significantly different from the contrained ones). His results confirm the no-trade-off result, and his 'expectations-augumented Phillips curve' is:

$$\dot{w} = 0\cdot038 + 2\cdot111 \ N/U + 0\cdot019 \ \dot{N}/U + \sum_{i=0}^{2} W_i \ (\dot{w}_A)_{-i} \qquad (3')$$

$$(0\cdot1) \qquad (1\cdot9) \qquad (3\cdot1)$$

$$+ \sum_{i=0}^{2} V_i (\dot{p}_w)_{-i} + \sum_{i=0}^{2} S_i \ \dot{q}_{-i}$$

$$\text{SEE} = 1\cdot20 \qquad \overline{R}^2 = 0\cdot830 \qquad DW = 1\cdot49$$

with $\sum W_i = 0\cdot811, \ \sum V_i = \sum S_i = 0\cdot189.$

$$(11\cdot5) \qquad\qquad (2\cdot7)$$

Unfortunately, neither from the above equations nor from the other versions that Parkin examined is it possible to infer the natural rate of unemployment for Australia. Furthermore, an econometric analysis of the relationship between $V-U$ and N/U and $\dot{N}/U$ revealed a close relationship but did not help determine the natural rate of unemployment, although it suggested a lower bound of $1\cdot5$ per cent. He thus proceeded to examine visually the three unemployment-inflation cycles between 1960 and 1973, and concluded that the natural rate must now be between $1\cdot5$ and $2\cdot0$ per cent, say $1\cdot75$ per cent. The data for the period 1960-5 however, appears to be inconsistent with that figure, and Parkin concludes that it was possibly as high as $2\cdot5$ per cent, and points to the need for further work to specify the determinants of a variable natural unemployment rate. One could also add that it could well be fruitful to extend the estimation period to cover a longer period, including the Korean experience.[20]

Price determination

The literature on price determination is in a rather less satisfactory state than that on wage determination as is indicated by the recent survey by Nordhaus (1972). The existing Australian work exhibits the same lack of certainty, although there is considerable work in hand.

The disaggregated price equations currently in the Reserve Bank model[21] explain the *level* of prices in terms of demand pressure, average weekly earnings, a measure of expected price changes and, where appropriate, indices of sales tax rates. Lags in adjustment are accounted for by inclusion of the lagged dependent variable, and it is typically very significant and takes a very high weight which implies long adjustment lags. Multiplicative seasonal dummy variables are generally also significant.

In other versions of these equations unit labour costs or normal unit labour costs replace average weekly earnings and perform equally well, and in an aggregate equation for the GNE deflator import prices are significant.

Now although there are criticisms of the form of these equations, in particular of the specification in levels, and the treatment of the indices of sales tax as an additive variable, it is clear that they fit closely over their historical period (1959-69). And in the equation for the deflator for gross national expenditure the implied long-run coefficient on average weekly earnings is above one half which, together with a further contribution from import prices (which, as argued above in connection with wage determination, is not the ideal variable anyway), implies a point estimate of the long-run effects of these variables of 0·87, supporting the no-trade-off hypothesis suggested by the earnings equations presented above. To illustrate, equation A6 from Norton *et al.* (1971) is reproduced below, the notation being:

p_e = implicit deflator for gross national expenditure
p_m = implicit deflator for imports of goods and services
w = average weekly earnings
V = registered job vacancies, a proxy for goods market demand pressure
S_i : seasonal dummy variables

$$p_e = 6·33 + 0·99\ S_1 + 0·45\ S_2 + 0·77\ S_3 + 0·692\ (p_e)_{-1} \qquad (4)$$
$$(3·2)\qquad(2·8)\qquad(4·8)\qquad(11·5)$$
$$+ 0·0112\ V_{-1} + 0·168\ w + 0·072\ p_m$$
$$(2·4)\qquad\quad(5·2)\qquad\quad(2·0)$$
$$\text{SEE} = 0·250 \qquad \overline{R}^2 = 0·999 \qquad D = 0·63$$

The essential feature of the wage-price sector discussed above is that it exhibits little or no long-run trade-off between inflation and unemployment. Although it is vitally important to look at the whole system and the exogenous shocks impinging on that system, the results presented give a considerable direct role to world prices in the adjustment of Australian wages and prices; indeed world prices are the only unambiguously exogenous variable influencing Australian wages and prices. Domestic prices, price expectations, excess demand and policy reaction all interact in a manner that is difficult to summarise without a complete macroeconometric model. Nevertheless, Fig. 9·1 summarises the linkages discussed above, although it should be stressed that the lines of causation depicted are only those discussed above. There are many others linking these variables in the whole system.

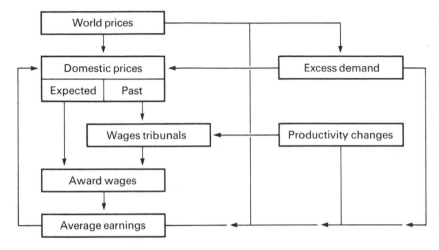

Figure 9.1 The Australian wage-price sector

IV A WHOLE MODEL TEST OF RECENT EXPERIENCE

There are, however, in addition to the proximate effects of world prices, the indirect effects of world conditions on domestic wage and price determination to consider, and in particular the effects via domestic income flows and the domestic money supply of fluctuations in exports, imports and capital flows in response to world conditions and the resulting domestic policy response. The following discussion is based on the international transmission mechanisms incorporated in the Reserve Bank of Australia model[22] (RBA1), although it is intended to be general.

In a fixed exchange rate regime, inflationary world developments strengthen the balance of payments of small open economies while directly raising domestic prices, and so reduce the tendency for anti-inflationary policy action to be taken.[23] A rise in exports and slower growth of imports directly increases incomes and thus demand, and also adds to the money supply and private sector wealth. The increase in wealth raises demand, in the RBA1 model, demand for durable goods and housing expenditure. An increase in capital inflow, which as argued by Porter (1973) was one response to tight domestic monetary policy designed to offset the domestic boom resulting from the strengthening current account in recent experience, also adds to the money supply, although the effects of this on demand are offset by an increase in foreign liabilities of Australians.[24] The initial rise in demand is reinforced by an accelerator mechanism which is built into RBA1's investment equations. When the indirect and lagged effects of an increase in world demand are added to the direct effect on prices and wages examined above, we can see how the eventual whole system effect of changing inflation in the rest of the world will exceed the impact effect.

By contrast, the reactions to a domestically generated inflation, given a fixed exchange rate, will tend to offset the initial inflationary impact. Consider a larger than usual increase in award wages; this initially raises real wages, and hence unemployment rises,[25] with an immediate dampening effect on earnings to offset the initial rise in award wages. And to the extent that Australian prices do rise more quickly in response to a wages (or macroeconomic policy) shock, the balance-of-payments deteriorates, with further feedbacks to dampen domestic inflation.

It is worth noting that if the exchange rate was freely floating, the above conclusions about the whole system responses to world or domestically generated inflation would be reversed. A rise in the world inflation rate would be accompanied by an appreciation of the exchange rate, which would tend to reduce domestic demand and thus help to offset the inflationary shock. But a domestically generated inflation would tend to depreciate the exchange rate, which would add to demand pressures and raise world prices domestically, so exacerbating the inflation. With a floating exchange rate, domestic sources of inflation become far more potent. But in Australia over the period considered here, the exchange rate was fixed and so we would expect world inflationary influences to the far more important than domestic ones.

A recent article by Jonson (1973a) set out to test the relative contribution of the world inflation and of the larger than usual increase in award wages in 1971 to the sharp increase in the Australian inflation rate from 1970. The test utilised the RBA1 model modified to incorporate a version of the wage equations described above.[26] The model also contains several disaggregated price equations similar to the aggregate one presented above but not containing import prices. These price equations exhibit what are probably implausibly long adjustment lags, and this, plus the absence of government reaction functions, meant that the simulation tests produced a greater impact on employment and a smaller impact on inflation than seemed entirely plausible. Limitations of computer core space necessitated that one variable, private capital inflow, be made exogenous, but since this was one of the variables to be varied in the tests, this seemed acceptable.

The tests consisted of examining the influence of exogenous changes in some variables on the endogenous variables of the model. The model is first solved using actual values of the exogenous variables, and generated values for the lagged endogenous variables, (with a non-stochastic, dynamic simulation). Comparing the control solutions for the endogenous variables with their

historical values provides one measure of the overall performance
of the model, and the revised version of RBA1, like its predecessor,
performs well in this respect.[27] The control solution provides the
bench-mark against which to compare the solution from simulations using different values for some exogenous variables, or
imposing exogenous shocks to endogenous variables. The strategy
was to simulate the influence of the recent world inflation, and of
the 1971 wages shock on the model at the equivalent time in the
previous business cycle, i.e. from 1965, to infer by analogy their
relative effects on the recent inflationary take-off in Australia.

The world inflation

From mid-1969 Australia's exports (value and volume), capital inflow and import prices all rose strongly above what was a fairly
steady trend from 1959-69. It was argued that these rises, which
were large relative to the standard error of the earlier trend
relationship, were mainly a consequence of the world inflation.
This was supported by a literary discussion which used recent
econometric work, for example that on capital flow by Porter
(1973), to back the argument. It would obviously be more satisfactory if the model incorporated well-specified equations for
exports and capital inflow, and the shocks imposed were to the
exogenous determinants of those variables. The necessary equations were not however available, and it is clear that the above
trend growth of the external variables cannot be a consequence of
'domestic cost pressures', or domestic demand pressures for that
matter.

The shocks imposed on the external variables were approximately proportionate to the amount by which these variables were
above their 'normal' values in 1970-1973(2); the normal values
being defined by a regression of the logarithm of each variable on
time and seasonal dummy variables for the period 1959-69. These
regressions produced good fits, with the divergences from 1969
being very large relative to the standard error of the trend relationship. For example, the shock imposed on the volume of exports
was +8·0 per cent in the fourth quarter of the simulations, and
rose fairly smoothly to +12·9 per cent by the sixteenth quarter
(equivalent to 1973(2) in historical time). There was a similar
rise on the value of exports, and the import price index was 5·1
per cent above its trend value by quarter sixteen. Capital inflow
rose much more sharply, being up 21·4 per cent after four quarters,
121·5 per cent after eight, 27·8 after twelve, but was then 22·7 per
cent *below* the historical trend by quarter sixteen, when the December 1972 revaluation and capital controls were beginning to bite.

The wage shock

Recall that in the 1970 national wage case there was a large increase given, an increase that lent considerable weight to the cost-
push argument in Australia. The extent to which this could be
characterised as 'larger than normal' was defined for the simulation test by the contribution of the major productivity adjustment,[28]
which the work by Jonson *et al.* suggested contributed almost 4 percentage points to the increase in award wages in 1971. Treating this
as a legitimate independent contribution to inflation is bending over
backwards to the cost-push argument, since, as argued above, it
is a normal adjustment, the timing of which may well depend on the
state of demand and the balance of payments.

This point aside, the results are devastating to the cost-push
argument. The influence of each shock or set of shocks[29] on key
endogenous variables such as nominal and real gross national
product, consumer prices and unemployment was recorded; after
eight quarters, the period of maximum impact from the wages
shock, there is 0·52 per cent added to the annual rate of inflation
by that shock. This is less than a quarter of the 2·25 per cent
added by the world inflation shock, which is the sort of order of
magnitude that the earlier theoretical discussion would lead us to
expect for the fixed exchange rate case. Together with the 0·31
per cent contributed by the above trend rise in cash benefits, the
world inflation and wages shocks add slightly over 3 per cent to
the rate of inflation by quarter eight. By quarter sixteen, when the
December 1972 revaluation and capital controls were reducing
the impact of the world inflation somewhat, the external shocks
are still contributing 61 per cent of the just over 4 per cent rise
in the inflation rate above its control solution value. When added
to the normal (control solution) value for the annual inflation
rate in the mid-1960s (about 2·5-3 per cent), this produces an
inflation rate of approximately 7 per cent. As noted above, the
actual inflation rate in Australia in the second quarter of 1973
(equivalent to quarter sixteen in the simulation) was 8 per cent
per annum.

Thus, although the basic model used is far from ideal in
several respects, the results would appear to go a long way towards
explaining by analogy the recent Australian inflationary take-off,
and to demonstrate that it owes overwhelmingly more to the world
inflation than 'domestic cost pressures'. The results also demonstrate the elementary theoretical point that domestic factors can
influence the Australian inflation rate in the short run with a
fixed exchange rate. And as a floating exchange rate will float
downward if domestic credit expands too rapidly, the article
concluded by stressing that a floating exchange rate is a necessary
but not sufficient condition for inflation control in Australia (as
in other open economies).

V CONCLUDING OBSERVATIONS

Inflation has been a major policy issue in Australia, as in other countries, for several years now. Inflation—or the consequence of misguided attempts to control it— will continue to be a major policy problem in the foreseeable future.

Discussion of the problem is, however, frequently bedevilled by confusion of cause and effect; thus, wage increases are cited as the cause of inflation while the evidence shows them to be just one effect in an interacting cycle. The confusion is compounded by failure to think through the logical implications of the special factor explanations that are perennially popular; thus, even if a special institutional factor such as the Australian arbitration system does give a major exogenous shock to domestic wages, the impact on employment and the balance of payments acts to reverse this effect on the domestic inflation rate, unless the exchange rate is adjusted to validate the shock. By comparison to the all-too-common non-explanations, there is a logical, coherent explanation for the recent Australian inflationary take-off, one that is supported by the available empirical evidence. It is also an explanation that fits the experience of many other countries, and stresses the interdependence of individual countries in a world economy.

Debate on the causes of inflation is not merely a storm in an academic teacup. Unless the problem is understood by policy-makers there is the possibility of major policy errors which could well have serious consequences for economic welfare. Understanding offers the possibility of learning to live with a relatively constant inflation rate, or of gradually reducing the rate towards zero (or some non-zero rate different to the present one). In view of the importance of the issue, it is perhaps appropriate to conclude on a methodological note. We know from economic theory that the trend rate of inflation in a small open economy like Australia's will be determined by the world rate of inflation if her exchange rate is fixed, and that this trend is modified by changes in the exchange rate. But to understand the details of the short-run fluctuations around that trend, and thus the contribution of various factors to these fluctuations over any time period, it is not sufficient to examine wage and price equations independently of the whole system. What is required is some whole system test (such as the simulation analysis discussed above), with careful identification of and allowance for the exogenous sources of inflation.

NOTES

1   The pre-Smithsonian $A was pegged to sterling, and varied relative to the $US with the pound (except that Australia did not devalue with the UK in 1967). In December 1971, Australia pegged its dollar to the $US, although there have been three revaluations of the $A relative to the $US since then.

2   The following overview was facilitated by the discussions of Waterman (1972) and Perkins (1967 and 1971).

3   At the time of the Korean War boom there was widespread appreciation of the international source of the inflation. For one example which called for a floating exchange rate as an anti-inflationary device, see Copland (1951).

4   See Mundell (1962). The monetary approach to balance-of-payments analysis presented in Johnson (1972b) also stresses reactions via the current account.

5   As will be demonstrated more completely in Section IV.

6   Factors which could help explain it are expectations about the revaluations of the $A, and an increase in uncertainty about future economic stability.

7   Haupt (1973). See also *Hansard*, 28 March 1973, pp. 787-8.

8   Discussed by Jay (1973).

9   Parkin (1973a). Giblin's views seem to have paralleled those of Henry Simons, as discussed by Friedman (1967). It is also interesting to note that in 1923 Keynes compared India's relatively 'unstable' exchange rate and stable prices in 1919-22 with England's relatively stable exchange rate and unstable price level. Keynes wanted the Bank of England to be responsible to 'regulate but not peg' the price of gold to maintain 'the stability of sterling prices' (Keynes (1923), p. 190).

10   It is worth noting however, that the latest published version of the Reserve Bank of Australia model, discussed in Norton and Henderson (1972) does not include award wages in its equation (No. 14) for the *level* of average weekly earnings. In that equation the determinants of (the level of) award wages were substituted for award wages, although when one moves to a more sensitive rate of change formulation, this substitution does not appear to be viable.

11   See the survey in Corden (1968, ch. 1).

12   See for example Hancock (1971), Nevile (1972) and Nieuwenhuysen (1970).

13   See Schott (1971), Ironmonger (1971), Higgins (1973) and Jonson, Mahar, and Thompson (1973).

14   These decisions-specific variables allow for the publication lag of the relevant statistics, and are constructed on assumptions spelt out in Jonson *et al.* (1973).

15   Developed and explained by Danes (1973). The original work by Jonson *et al.* used an alternative measure of price expectations, based on statements about inflation made by an influential financial newspaper, but as the new variable performs somewhat better in the awards equation, the version using this variable is presented here.

16   And a study of Australian government policy reaction reveals a consistent focus on the state of the balance of payments (Jonson (1974)).

17   A direct test of this hypothesis would be to construct some direct measure of expected excess demand and use it (in the earnings equation in the present case) and also explain it.

18   This assumption was checked by estimation of less restricted versions.

[19]   See Parkin (1974) for a theoretical rationalisation and a survey of the existing evidence. It should be noted that the coefficient estimates are slightly different to those published in Jonson *et al.* because of a minor data revision. The main effect of the data revision was to make the unrestricted estimates of ΣV_i and ΣS_i equal to the third decimal place.

[20]   And in this respect Pitchford's article is instructive.

[21]   See Norton and Henderson (1972), and also Norton, Schott and Sweeney (1971), and Hawkins, Kelly, and Lightfoot (1972), for the extra results discussed here. Similar results are reported by Higgins (1973), although he used direct estimation of the lag structure, and finds demand pressure less important.

[22]   See Norton and Henderson (1972) for a full description of the model.

[23]   For a study of Australian policy reaction functions which establish the role of external and internal policy targets over the period 1959-71 see Jonson (1973b).

[24]   The distinction drawn by McKinnon (1969), who points out that an increase in exports raises outside money and an increase in capital inflow raises inside money is reflected in the RBA1 model.

[25]   In RBA1 employment and unemployment depend on real wages and output aggregate.

[26]   Which were estimated to 1969(4), and which contained import prices in place of world prices.

[27]   For the control solution of the earlier version, see Norton and Henderson (1972, pp. 18-22).

[28]   Represented by $\dot{q}_z$ in equation (1) above.

[29]   There was also an inflationary contribution from 'larger than usual' changes in government policy variables, in particular a large rise in cash benefits to persons which was almost certainly influenced by the strong balance of payments.

REFERENCES

Arndt, H. W., 'Inflation: new policy prescriptions', paper presented to the 45th ANZAAS Congress, Perth, August 1973; revised version in *Australian Economic Review* (third quarter, 1973).

Copland, D. B., 'Australia and international economic equilibrium', *Economia Internazionale* (1951).

Corden, W. M., *Australian Economic Policy Discussion, a Survey* (Melbourne University Press, 1968).

Danes, M. K., 'The measurement and explanation of inflationary expectations in Australia', Reserve Bank of Australia, Research Discussion Paper No. 30 (October 1973).

Friedman, M., 'The monetary theory and policy of Henry Simons', *Journal of Law and Economics* (October 1967), reprinted in M. Friedman, *The Optimum Quantity of Money* (London, Macmillan, 1969).

— 'The role of monetary policy', *American Economic Review* (March 1968).

Hancock, K. J., 'Earnings drift in Australia', *Journal of Industrial Relations* (1966).

— 'Wage policy and inflation: Australia's experience under compulsory arbitration', *Australian Economic Review* (fourth quarter, 1971).

Haupt, R., 'Inflation policy split', *Australian Financial Review* (13 June 1973).

Hansard (Australian Parliamentary Debates) (28 March 1973), speech by Rt. Hon. B. M. Sneddon, and especially pp. 787-8.

Hawkins, R. G., Margaret R. Kelly and R. E. Lightfoot, *Factor Demands, Stocks and Prices: An Inter-related Approach* (Sydney, Reserve Bank of Australia, Occasional Paper No. 3H, December 1972).

Higgins, C. I., 'A wage-price sector for a quarterly Australian model', paper presented to the Conference of Econometricians (August 1971); reprinted in A. A. Powell and R. A. Williams (eds.), *Econometric Studies of Macro and Monetary Relations* (Amsterdam, North-Holland, 1973).

Ironmonger, D. S., *The Institute Model: A Progress Report,* paper presented to the Second Conference of Economists, Sydney (August 1971).

Jay, C., 'Come Back, John Maynard Keynes. 33 economists need you!', *Australian Financial Review* (7 December 1973).

Johnson, H. G., 'The inflation crisis', *International Currency Review* (August 1971).

— 'Inflation: a "monetarist" view', in H. G. Johnson, *Further Essays in Monetary Theory* (London, Allen & Unwin, 1972).

— 'The monetary approach to balance-of-payments theory', *Journal of Financial and Quantitative Analysis* (March 1972).

— *Inflation and the Monetarist Controversy* (Amsterdam, North-Holland, 1972).

Jonson, P. D., 'Our current inflationary experience', *Australian Economic Review* (second quarter, 1973) (this is a revised version of a paper presented to Third Conference of Economists, Adelaide, May 1973).

— *Reaction Functions and Stabilization Policy in Australia, 1959-71; An Objective Analysis,* Reserve Bank of Australia, Research Discussion Paper No. 28 (June 1973).

Jonson, P. D., K. L. Mahar and G. J. Thompson, 'Earnings and award wages in Australia', Reserve Bank of Australia, Research Discussion Paper No. 27; revised version (August 1973), forthcoming in *Australian Economic Papers*.

Keynes, J. M., *Tract on Monetary Reform* (London, 1923).

Laidler, D. E. W., 'The influence of money on real income and inflation', *Manchester School* (December 1973).

McKinnon, R. I., 'Portfolio balance and international payments adjustments', in R. A. Mundell and A. K. Swoboda (eds.), *Monetary Problems of the International Economy* (Chicago, Ill., University of Chicago Press, 1969).

Mundell, R.A., 'The appropiate use of monetary and fiscal policy for internal stability', *International Monetary Fund Staff Papers* (March 1962).

Nevile, J. W., *Fiscal Policy in Australia* (Melbourne, Cheshire, 1970).

— 'Options for internal economic policy', *Economic Papers* (September 1972).

Nieuwenhuysen, J. P., and N. R. Norman, 'Wages policy in Australia: issues and tests', *British Journal of Industrial Relations,* vol. 8 (1971).

Nordhaus, W. D., 'Recent developments in price dynamics', in O. Eckstein (ed.), *The Econometrics of Price Determination* (Washington, D.C., 1972).

Norton, W. E., and J. F. Henderson, 'A model of the Australian economy: a further report', Sydney, Reserve Bank of Australia, Occasional Paper No. 3G (March 1972).

Norton, W. E., Kerry E. Schott and K. M. Sweeny, 'Employment and prices', Sydney, Reserve Bank of Australia, Occasional Paper No. 3F (1971).

Parkin, J. M., 'Inflation, the balance of payments, domestic credit expansion and exchange rate adjustments', paper prepared for the Conference on National Monetary Policies and International Financial System, Racine, Wisconsin, 1972 (University of Manchester mimeo).

— 'Inflation: the policy options', Giblin Memorial Lecture, presented at the 45th ANZAAS Congress (August 1973); reprinted in *Search* (October 1973).

— 'The short-run and long-run trade-offs between inflation and unemployment in Australia', *Australian Economic Papers* (December 1973).

— 'Inflationary expectations and the long-run trade-off between inflation and unemployment in open economies', in J. M. Parkin and G. Zis (eds.), *Inflation in the World Economy* (Manchester University Press, 1976).

Perkins, J. O. N., *Anticyclical Policy in Australia 1960-1966* (Carlton, Melbourne University Press, 1967).

— *Macroeconomic Policy in Australia* (Carlton, Melbourne University Press, 1971).

Phelps, E. S., 'Anticipated inflation and economic welfare', *Journal of Political Economy* (February 1965).

Pitchford, J. D., 'An analysis of price movements in Australia, 1947-68', *Australian Economic Papers* (December 1968).

Porter, M. G., 'The interdependence of monetary policy and capital flows in Australia', paper presented to the Third Conference of Economists (May 1973), forthcoming in *Economic Record*.

Schott, Kerry, *Can We Predict Sir Richard?*, Economic Society of Australia and New Zealand, New South Wales Branch, Economic Monograph No. 322 (June 1971).

Simkin, C. G. F., 'Inflation in Australia and New Zealand; 1953-71', *Economic Record* (December 1972).

Solow, R. M., *Price Expectations and the Behaviour of the Price Level* (Manchester University Press, 1969).

Waterman, A. C. M., *Economic Fluctuations in Australia, 1948 to 1964* (Canberra, Australian National University Press, 1972).

10 Inflation in a small, fixed exchange rate open economy: a model for New Zealand

V. B. Hall*

This paper presents a preliminary simultaneous equation model capable of explaining New Zealand's post-war inflation. It is a model consistent with New Zealand having been a small fixed exchange rate[1] open economy subject to very extensive controls over its balance of payments' current account items, and an impressive array of controls capable of affecting capital account items.

The intensity of application of these controls[2] has varied considerably, but to a greater or lesser degree they have existed throughout the post-war period.

If such an array of controls over external transactions had been neither existent nor effective, then some form of monetary approach to the balance of payments and inflation theory may have been appropriate for inclusion within the model. This would have required that in the long run New Zealand's rate of inflation be determined by the world inflation rate, and that its domestic monetary policy be subservient to the world inflation rate and its chosen fixed exchange rate.

However, it is generally agreed that the controls, and especially those relating to import and export licensing, have been both tightly administered and effective. Accordingly, some considerable measure of independence from world inflation rates and more particularly from international private capital movements must be assumed for both New Zealand's rate of inflation and monetary policy. The model presented below therefore reflects this view rather than emphasises international monetarist lineage.

In a preliminary model for New Zealand's inflation, it was

* This is a revised version of the paper entitled 'A preliminary model of New Zealand's post-war inflation' which appeared in the *Economic Record* (March 1974). Valuable critical comments by Dr Roderick Deane are gratefully acknowledged. For recent less technical accounts of New Zealand's post-war inflation, see Simkin [14] and Hall [9].

thought desirable to incorporate six dependent variables: the
retail price level, the actual wage rate, the minimum wage rate,
the demand for labour services, the supply of labour services, and
the level of real output. Influences exogenous to the model are
the level of import prices, the level of real government expenditure, the level of real exports, and the supply of money. Open
economy influences are thus felt directly through the import
price level and the level of real exports, and indirectly through
significant current account balance of payments effects on the
supply of money.

The resulting preliminary model is presented in structural
form in Section I, and in estimation form in Section III. In Section
II, the model is explained first in an *ad hoc* fashion with special
reference to further certain important characteristics of the New
Zealand economy, and then some of its microeconomic implications
are examined. The results obtained from econometric estimation
using annual data and the methods[3] of ordinary least squares
(OLS) and two-stage least squares (2SLS) are critically examined
in Section IV, and attention is then given in Section V to some of
the model's dynamic properties and its predicting power.

Finally, principal conclusions are summarised in Section VI.

I THE STRUCTURAL MODEL

The structural model in deterministic form is

$$\left[\frac{P_{r,t}}{P^b_{i,t}}\right]^{\frac{1}{\alpha_1}} = \frac{W_{a,t}}{(1 - \frac{1}{\alpha_1 \varsigma_1})v(1-c)f\overline{v}e^{\frac{-\rho - \mu\rho.t}{v}} Y_{s,t}^{\frac{1+\rho}{v}} L_{d,t}^{-(1+\rho)}} \tag{1}$$

$$\frac{W_{a,t}}{W_{a,t-1}} = A\left[\frac{W_{m,t}}{W_{m,t-1}}\right]^{\beta_1} \left[\frac{L_{d,t}}{L_{s,t}}\right]^{\beta_2} \tag{2}$$

$$W_{m,t} = B\left[P_{r,t}\right]^{\gamma_1} \left[\frac{Y_{s,t}}{L_{s,t}}\right]^{\gamma_2} \tag{3}$$

$$\frac{L_{d,t}}{L_{d,t-1}} = \left[\frac{\{Y_{s,t}^{\frac{-\rho}{v}}(1-c)^{-1}f\overline{v}e^{\frac{\rho}{v}\frac{\mu\rho.t}{v}} - c(1-c)^{-1}(K_0e^{kt})^{-\rho}\}^{\frac{-1}{\rho}}}{L_{d,t-1}}\right]^n \tag{4}$$

$$L_{s,t} = \left[C \left[\frac{L_{d,t}}{L_{s,t}} \right]^q e^{xt} \right]^{1 - \epsilon_3 + \epsilon_4} (L_{s,t-1})^{\epsilon_3} (L_{s,t-2})^{-\epsilon_4} \tag{5}$$

$$Y_{d,t} = F \left[\frac{M_{d,t}}{P_{r,t}} \right]^{\zeta_1} G_t^{\zeta_2} E_t \frac{3}{2}^{\zeta_3} \tag{6}$$

$$Y_d = Y_s \tag{7}$$

$$M_d = M_s \tag{8}$$

where

P_r = retail price level,
P_i = import price level,
W_a = actual or ruling wage rate,
t = time,
Y_s = supply of real net output,
L_d = demand for labour,
W_m = minimum or award wage rate,
L_s = supply of labour,
Y_d = demand for real net output,
M_d = demand for money,
G = real net government expenditure,
E = real exports,
M_s = supply of money.

A, B, C, F are constants; the parameters $c, \rho,$ and n are subject to the restrictions $0 < c < 1, \rho \geq -1, 0 < n \leq 1$; and all other parameters are positive.

The variables P_i, t, G, E, and M_s are assumed to be exogenous.

II EXPLANATION OF THE STRUCTURAL MODEL

The relationships between the variables appearing in the above model could have been formulated and interpreted in a number of different ways, depending on the degree of *ad hoc* or theoretic justification one is prepared to accept. Different *a priori* views about the functioning of the New Zealand economy could also have led to different relationships.

To justify the particular relationships of Section I both the *ad hoc* and theoretic approaches are to some extent relied on. In an *ad hoc* manner, an outline is made of the rationale behind construction of a model of eight equations and some comments are provided on each of the six non-definitional equations. Then it is shown, within a static[4] framework, what microeconomic behaviour patterns could lie behind the equations.

1 Ad hoc explanation

The basic reasoning for proceeding with an eight equation model in which six non-definitional equations explain the six jointly dependent variables P_r, W_a, W_m, L_d, L_s, and $Y(=Y_s=Y_d)$ was as follows: Few would now doubt that any simultaneous equation model relating to inflation should include at least one price and at least one wage equation. With respect to the incorporation of a wage influence, for the greatest part of the post-war period, the nature of New Zealand's wage-fixing structure has been such that two wage equations can be justified—one to explain the actual or ruling rate and the other to explain the minimum or award rate. Previous research (Brownlie and Hampton [2], Hall [5], [7]) has shown that the excess demand for labour services (i.e. the demand for labour services less the supply of labour services) has been significant in explaining actual wage rate changes, and that changes in productivity (i.e. in real net output per man) have been significant in explaining changes in the minimum wage rate. It thus became necessary to develop three further equations in order to explain the demand for labour services, the supply of labour services, and the level of real net output, because it was not considered satisfactory to treat any of the three as exogenous. The reasons for including equations (7) and (8) will become apparent from the discussion in the rest of Section II.

In developing the six non-definitional equations, account was taken wherever possible of the limited amount of econometric research available on the New Zealand economy.

At the time this research was undertaken, little quantitative or substantive econometric work had been published on price determination in New Zealand.[5] In addition, data deficiencies and the lack of success in finding a satisfactory representation of, or proxy for, excess demand in the commodity market[6] have prevented the incorporation of any reasonably sophisticated modified mark-up approach or a commodity excess demand variable.

The actual wage equation is essentially a labour market equation, and it has been a feature of New Zealand's post-war economy that complete clearing of this market has consistently not been achieved.[7] The minimum wage equation has been Arbitration-Court dominated: it is, however, now open to question[8] whether the Court's influence will remain dominant in the future. If this is not to be so then it is unlikely that the dual wage determination hypotheses represented in equations (2) and (3) will remain valid for forecasting purposes.

In equation (4), because the required data are not available, the CES production function exhibiting Hicks-neutral technical progress and non-constant returns to scale has the level of real net fixed capital proxied by the expression $K_0 e^{kt}$.

For the purposes of this annual model, it has been appropriate[9] to assume in equation (5) that the supply of labour has been adjusted in the longer run to demographic influences such as the natural increase in the labour force and net immigration, and in the shorter run directly to labour market movements. The former is proxied by the variable t and the latter by the current excess demand for labour services.

The treatment of real net output in equations (6) and (7) can be explained with reference to the representative market identity.

$$Y_s \equiv Y_d + dU \tag{9}$$

and the representative market definition

$$Y_d = C + dK + dV + G + E - I \tag{10}$$

where

dU = market clearing change in the real inventory level (and thus expected to average zero over time),
C = real private consumption,
dK = change in the level of real private net fixed capital,
dV = 'planned' change in the real inventory level (and which is unlikely to average zero over time),
I = real expenditure on imports.

As the goods market is assumed to be cleared (i.e. $Y_s = Y_d$), then $dU = 0$.[10] In a broader simultaneous equation model than the present one, it would be necessary to introduce equations to explain at least C, dK, dV and I. This has not been done because to do so is not central to the purpose of this model. It was also relevant that, to this point, three very important influences on the New Zealand economy, viz: the supply of money, the level of real net government expenditure, and the level of real exports, had not been introduced into the model. Hence, it was next assumed that the real demand for exports and real net government expenditure could be treated as exogenous. This left, from equations (9) and (10), real private domestic demand for domestic production (i.e. $C + dK + dV - I$) to be treated as dependent on the real supply of money. This latter assumption is particularly broad in nature, but does have the advantages of preserving the simultaneity of the model, having some empirical justification,[11] and having some theoretical foundation for household sector behaviour.[12]

2 Microeconomic implications

Two viewpoints are taken: the first reflecting market behaviour, and the second revealing how the various economic decision makers are able to act.

A market behaviour

Behaviour in the labour market and in the goods market is examined within the context of a controlled open economy and some influence from the government sector. Behaviour in the money market needs no explanation, as equation (8) ensures that there is equilibrium in this market and that, in effect, the supply of money is the only monetary influence incorporated in the model. In line with the controlled economy assumption, this supply of money is theoretically within the control of the monetary authorities through their controlling interest rates. Labour market behaviour can be explained with reference to equations (2), (3), (4), and (5). In equation (4), the demand for labour services is adjusted to the level of real net output which firms wish to supply, given technology of the kind assumed in the particular CES production function. Equation (5) shows both domestic and foreign suppliers of labour adjusting to long-run and short-run factors. Equations (2) and (3) allow for at least two ways in which the actual price of labour can be adjusted. One way is through the minimum wage rate first being adjusted to cover movements in retail prices and productivity, with the change in the minimum wage rate then being immediately passed on in the form of an increased actual wage rate. Other significant adjustments are to movements in the demand for and supply of labour taking place during attempts to clear the labour market.

Reference is made to equations (1), (6), and (7) in explaining goods market behaviour. Equation (7) imposes the condition that this market is in equilibrium, but it is not clear from the model how or why this should be so. One can only assume at this stage that somehow price-setting behaviour of firms in equation (1) is such as to result in the equilibrium required by equation (7) being (approximately) achieved. [13] The price-setting behaviour is therefore by firms who are attempting to maximise their profits (taking into account their wage and import costs and what they are capable of supplying), rather than having the prime intention of pricing to clear the goods market. From equation (6) it can be said that the demand for goods and services is adjusted in accordance with the price of those goods and services, given the supply of money available and the demands of government and export customers.

B Decision maker behaviour

The behaviour of only a representative firm[14] and a representative household as decision-makers is explained, as decisions by the monetary authorities, the government, those to whom goods and services are exported, and those who determine the price of imports are taken as given. The firm is assumed to make its decisions given that the decision variables of the household have been fixed, and *vice versa*.

The representative firm is concerned with attempting to maximise its profits (Π_j) by simultaneously determining its price level (P) its level of real output (Y_s), and the quantity of labour services $(L_d$, in terms of men to hire) to produce this level of output. The stock of capital is fixed for the purposes of the decision, as is the actual wage rate the firm must pay; the supply of money, the level of real net government expenditure, and the level of real exports are also exogenous. The firm solves its problem on the assumption that there are no constraints[15] on its being able to hire the quantity of labour services it chooses, but there are constraints on its output imposed by the form of its production function and the demand for its product.

The representative household desires to maximise its utility (U_g), and is able to determine simultaneously the goods and services $(Y_{d,g})$ it wishes to buy, the quantity of labour services (L_s) it wishes to supply and the additional actual money balances $(m_{d,g})$[16] it wishes to hold. The actual wage rate it accepts as given, as is the level of profits (Π_g) distributed to it by the firms. Its decision is made in the knowledge that it has no trouble in placing the labour services it wishes to supply nor in obtaining the actual money balances it wishes to hold.

It will be noted that in this model neither the firm nor the household is responsible on its own for choosing the actual wage rate, i.e. each takes it as given for the purposes of its decision. This means that, in accordance with equations (2) and (3), it is the joint responsibility of the firms, the households (both on their own initiative and through their agents, the trade unions), and the Arbitration Court to determine the actual wage rate.

The representative firm's equations. In accordance with the above description the representative firm wishes to maximise

$$\Pi_j = PY_s - W_a L_d \tag{11}$$

subject to its production function

$$Y_s = e^{\mu t} f[c(K_0 e^{kt})^{-\rho} + (1-c)L_d - \rho]^{\frac{-v}{\rho}} \tag{12}$$

and subject to the demand for its output

$$Y_d = Y_s = F(M_d/P)\zeta^1 G\zeta^2 E\zeta^3 \tag{13}$$

Equations (11) to (13) make no allowance for the influence of import prices but import prices can be introduced by specifying P

(the price of domestically produced goods) in equation (11) in terms of the retail price level (P_r) and the import price level (P_i), i.e.

$$P_r = P^{\alpha_1} P_i^b \tag{14}$$

It is assumed that the variable P in equation (13) is P_r.

Thus the first order (necessary) conditions corresponding with the representative firm's maximisation decision become

$$(P_r/P_i^{\frac{b}{i}})^{1/\alpha_1} = W_a/\{[1 - (1/\alpha_1\zeta_1)]v(1-c)\mathrm{f}^{\bar{v}}e^{-\rho}\stackrel{-\mu\rho.t}{v}$$

$$Y_s^{1+\frac{\rho}{v}} L_d^{-(1+\rho)}\} \tag{15}$$

$$L_d = \{Y_s^{-\rho}v(1-c)^{-1}\mathrm{f}^{\bar{v}}e^{\frac{\rho}{v}}\stackrel{\mu\rho.t}{v} -c(1-c)^{-1}(K_0 e^{kt})^{-\rho}\}^{-\frac{1}{\rho}} \tag{16}$$

$$Y_s = F(M_d/P_r)\zeta^1 G\zeta^2 E\zeta^3 \tag{17}$$

The second order (sufficient) conditions are able[17] to be satisfied if both

$$\alpha_1\zeta_1 > 1 \tag{18}$$

and, for the case in which $v = 1$ (i.e. constant returns to scale),[18]

$$(1-c)[c(K_0 e^{kt})^{-\rho} + (1-c)L_d^{-\rho}]^{-1}L_d^{-\rho} < 1 \tag{19}$$

Equation (15) is interpreted as determining the retail price level, equation (16) as determining the quantity of labour services to employ, and equation (17) as determining the level of real output. The three equations are then able to be estimated with in the eight-equation model (1) to (8); i.e., equation (15) becomes the economy's price equation (1), equation (16) is incorporated in[19] the economy's labour demand function (4), and equation (17) in the economy's[20] real output equation (6).

The representative household's equations. The equations derived for the household do not provide exact equations to be estimated within the economy-wide model (1) to (8): they merely illustrate how it is possible for the household to behave within the framework of the aggregate model.

It is assumed that the household wishes to maximise its utility as represented by

$$U_g = Y_{d,g}^\alpha L^{-\beta} (M_{d,g}/P_r)^\gamma \tag{20}$$

subject to its budget constraint

$$W_a L_s + \Pi_g = P_r Y_{d,g} + m_{d,g} \tag{21}$$

and subject to its labour supply response

$$L_S = C(L_d/L_S)^{qext} \tag{22}$$

The first order (necessary) conditions[21] corresponding to this maximisation decision are

$$Y_{d,g} = \frac{\alpha}{\gamma} \; (M_{d,g}/P_r) \tag{23}$$

$$M_{d,g} = W_a L_s + \Pi_g + M^* - P_r Y_{d,g} \tag{24}$$

Equations (23) and (24) serve to show that the household's demands for goods and services depend, among other things, on its demand for real money balances. The assumption is then made that the non-household, non-government, non-export components of aggregate demands are also a function of the demand for real money balances.

Thus, aggregating this demand behaviour, incorporating the real purchases of the government sector and the export sector, and assuming that equation (8) holds, it can be seen what behaviour patterns could underlie equation (6).

III THE STRUCTURAL MODEL IN ESTIMATION FORM

The system contained by equations (1) to (8) can be estimated in log-linear form. Equations (7) and (8) are substituted in equation (6). For equation (4) the log of the numerator on the right-hand side of the equation is expanded as a Taylor series around $(\ln \overline{Y}_{s,t}, \overline{t})$[22] and the linear terms only retained. The dynamic log-linear difference equation form of the structural model is thus

$$\ln P_{r,t} = \alpha_0 + \alpha_1 \ln W_{a,t} + \alpha_2 \ln P_{i,t} - \alpha_3 \ln Y_{s,t} + \alpha_4 \ln L_{d,t}$$
$$+ \alpha_5 t \tag{25}$$

$$(\ln W_{a,t} - \ln W_{a,t-1}) = \beta_0 + \beta_1 (\ln W_{m,t} - \ln W_{m,t-1})$$
$$+ \beta_2 (\ln L_{d,t} - \ln L_{s,t}) \tag{26}$$

$$\ln W_{m,t} = \gamma_0 + \gamma_1 \ln P_{r,t} + \gamma_2 (\ln Y_{s,t} - \ln L_{s,t}) \tag{27}$$

$$\ln L_{d,t} = \delta_0 + \delta_1 \ln Y_{s,t} - \delta_2 t + \delta_3 \ln L_{d,t-1} \tag{28}$$

$$\ln L_{s,t} = \epsilon_0 + \epsilon_1 (\ln L_{d,t} - \ln L_{s,t}) + \epsilon_2 t + \epsilon_3 \ln L_{s,t-1}$$
$$- \epsilon_4 \ln L_{s,t-2} \tag{29}$$

$$lnY_{s,t} = \zeta_0 + \zeta_1(lnM_{s,t} - lnP_{r,t}) + \zeta_2 lnG_t + \zeta_3 lnE_{t-3/2} \qquad (30)$$

where

$$\alpha_0 = \alpha_1 ln[1/\{1 - 1/\alpha_1\zeta_1\}\,v\,(1-c)f^{-\rho/v}$$

$$\alpha_2 = b,$$

$$\alpha_3 = \alpha_1(1 + \rho/v),$$

$$\alpha_4 = \alpha_1(1 + \rho),$$

$$\alpha_5 = \alpha_1\mu\rho/v,$$

$$\delta_1 = n[(1/v)\overline{Y}_s^{\frac{-\rho}{v}}\,\overline{L}_d^{\rho}\,^{\frac{\mu\rho}{v}}\,(1-c)^{-1}f^{\frac{\rho}{v}}],$$

$$\delta_2 = n[\{(\mu/v) + k\}\overline{Y}_s^{\frac{-\rho}{v}}\,\overline{L}_d^{\rho}\,e^{\frac{\mu\rho}{v}}\,^{\epsilon}(1-c)^{-1}f^{\frac{\rho}{v}} - k],$$

$$\delta_3 = 1 - n,$$

$$\epsilon_1 = (1 - \epsilon_3 + \epsilon_4)q,$$

$$\epsilon_2 = (1 - \epsilon_3 + \epsilon_4)x.$$

The system of equations (25) to (30) thus involves six jointly dependent variables and ten predetermined variables. Five $(lnP_{i,t}, t, lnM_{s,t}, lnG_t, lnE_{t-3/2})$ of the ten predetermined variables are exogenous and the remaining five are lagged endogenous.

Because this model is non-linear in the structural parameters, the usual order and rank conditions for identification do not apply. However, all six equations are overidentified if the order condition is tested with respect to the composite parameters.

The model contained by equations (25) and (30) was estimated first using the method of OLS in order to sort out the most suitable of alternative data series and the most appropriate lag forms. Then simultaneous equation estimates[23] were obtained using the single equation method of 2SLS.

IV ESTIMATION OF THE MODEL

The model of Section 3 was estimated using annual data,[24] the twenty-three observations on the jointly dependent variables being for March, years 1949-71.

1 OLS estimates

The OLS estimates are presented in Table 10.1.[25]

Only the coefficients α_4, and α_5 in equation (25) were not significant at the 10 per cent level of significance. However, the lack of significance of α_4, α_5, and δ_2 meant that satisfactory values for the structural parameters ρ (the substitution parameter), v (the returns to scale parameter), μ (the Hicks-neutral technical progress parameter), and K (the growth of real net fixed capital parameter) were not derivable. So successive restrictions were imposed on the CES production function.

First, the assumption of non-constant returns to scale was dropped and constant returns to scale imposed instead, i.e. $v = 1$, so that $\alpha_3 = \alpha_4$. The OLS estimate of the new equation was

$$lnP_{r,t} = 1\cdot015 + 0\cdot681 \ lnW_{a,t} + 0\cdot169 lnP_{i,t} \qquad (31)$$
$$\phantom{lnP_{r,t} = } (3\cdot87) \quad (11\cdot8^a) \phantom{ \ lnW_{a,t} + } (3\cdot83^a)$$

$$- \ 0\cdot190$$
$$(3\cdot39^a)$$

$$(lnY_{s,t} - lnL_{d,t}) - 0\cdot00014t,$$
$$\phantom{(lnY_{s,t} - lnL_{d,t}) - } (0\cdot06)$$

$$\overline{R}^2 = 0\cdot9985 \qquad DW = 1\cdot95^d \qquad S^2 = 0\cdot001699$$

No meaningful value of μ is derivable from the coefficient of the variable t in equation (31), so the second restriction imposed was to assume $\mu = 0$. This meant that $\alpha_5 = 0$, and the resulting OLS estimated equation became

$$lnP_{r,t} = 1\cdot028 + 0\cdot687 \ lnW_{a,t} + 0\cdot170 \ lnP_{i,t}$$
$$\phantom{lnP_{r,t} = } (6\cdot72) \quad (23\cdot6) \phantom{ \ lnW_{a,t} + } (4\cdot16)$$

$$- \ 0\cdot190(lnY_{s,t} - lnL_{d,t}$$
$$(3\cdot48)$$

$$\overline{R}^2 = 0\cdot9985 \qquad DW = 1.95^d \qquad S^2 = 0\cdot001700 \qquad (32)$$

In this equation, all variables are significant at the 1 per cent level of significance, the hypothesis of positive first-order serial correlation cannot be accepted at the 1 per cent level of significance, and imposition of the two additional restrictions (i.e. first $v = 1$, and secondly $\mu = 0$) is not likely to be able to be rejected.[26]

The third restriction, that on k, was imposed to obtain satisfactory results for equation (28). After considerable experimentation,[27] a value of $0\cdot0402$ was chosen for k. So, bearing in mind that by now $v = 1$, $\mu = 0$, and $k = \hat{k} = 0\cdot0402$, equation (28) was estimated by OLS in the form

$$(lnL_{d,t} - \hat{k}t) = -0\cdot402 + 0\cdot129(lnY_{s,t} - \hat{k}t) \qquad (33)$$
$$\phantom{(lnL_{d,t} - \hat{k}t) = } (1\cdot87) \quad (2\cdot76^b)$$

$$+ \ 0\cdot934(lnL_{d,t} - \hat{k}t_{-1})$$
$$(44\cdot9^a)$$

$$\overline{R}^2 = 0\cdot9953 \qquad h = 0\cdot58^d \qquad S^2 = 0\cdot001998$$

The form of this equation was tentatively accepted, as the coef-

Table 10.1 OLS Regressions of equations (25) to (30)

i	0	1	2	3	4	5	$\bar{R}^2$	DW	h	S^2
α_i	3·160 (2·80)	0·643 (11·2^c)	0·169 (4·10^c)	0·169 (3·16^c)	−0·120 (0·71)	0·0069 (1·64)	0·9987	2·01^d		0·001391
β_i	0·027 (6·75)	0·521 (7·33^c)	0·801 (4·02^c)				0·8296	1·83^d		0·002053
γ_i	−0·630 (2·70)	1·092 (32·8^c)	0·171 (2·04)				0·9955	1·36^d		0·007253
δ_i	1·436 (1·63)	0·126 (2·90)	−0·0025 (0·91)	0·663 (5·07^c)			0·9948		1·02^d	0·001624
ϵ_i	2·035 (3·55)	0·491 (3·02^c)	0·0071 (3·96^c)	1·151 (7·07^c)	0·462 (3·19^c)		0·9988		1·85^d	0·000421
ζ_i	2·664 (5·16)	0·586 (2·79)	0·313 (3·34^c)	0·293 (2·42^b)			0·9494	1·34^a		0·050317

Notes

$\bar{R}^2$ = t-ratios in parentheses.
$\bar{R}^2$ = coefficient of determination corrected for degrees of freedom
DW = Durbin–Watson d statistic
S^2 = sum of squares of residuals
a = DW test inconclusive
b = coefficient significantly different from zero at 5 per cent level of significance
c = coefficient significantly different from zero at 1 per cent level of significance
d = cannot accept hypothesis of first order serial correlation at 1 per cent level of significance.

ficients of both variables are significant at the 5 per cent level of significance, the hypothesis of positive first-order serial correlation cannot be accepted at the 5 per cent level of significance, and it seems unlikely that imposition of the additional restriction that $k = 0.0402$ can be rejected. [28]

2 2SLS estimates

The method of 2SLS was used to estimate the model contained by equations (25) to (30), but with equation (25) in the form of equation (32) and equation (28) in the form of equation (33). The regression results are presented in Table 10. 2. All coefficients are significant at least at the 5 per cent level of significance, except for γ_2 which is significant at the 10 per cent level. [29]

The structural parameter values derived from the coefficients of Table 10.2 are presented in Table 10.3. [30]

The values of 0.71 for α_1 and 0.14 for b seem not unreasonable, and that of -0.62 for ρ is neither theoretically nor empirically implausible. Satisfactory distributions to capital and labour are shown in the values for c and $1-c$ of 0.31 and 0.69 respectively,

Table 10. 2 2SLS regressions of equations (32), (26), (27), (33), (29), and (30)

i	0	1	2	3	4	S^2
α_i	0·971 (5·82)	0·713 (18·3^c)	0·143 (3·03^c)	0·273 (3·31^c)		0·001906
β_i	0·024 (4·80)	0·589 (6·92^c)	0·777 (3·63^c)			0·002153
γ_i	−0·560 (2·05)	1·082 (27·8^c)	0·199 (1·95)			0·007293
δ_i	−0·723 (2·69)	0·206 (3·42)		0·909 (36·7^c)		0·002271
ϵ_i	1·996 (3·26)	0·384 (2·10)	0·0068 (3·73^c)	1·162 (7·05^c)	0·467 (3·19^c)	0·000431
ζ_i	2·650 (5·11)	0·579 (2·73^b)	0·314 (3·35^c)	0·294 (2·43^b)		0·050320

Notes
As for Table 10.1.

Table 10.3 Structural parameter values derived from coefficients of Table 10.2.

From the α_i'	From the β_i	From the γ_i	From the δ_i	From the ϵ_i	From the ζ_i
$\alpha_1 = 0.71$	$\beta_1 = 0.59$	$\gamma_1 = 1.08$	$n = 0.09$	$\epsilon_3 = 1.16$	$\zeta_1 = 0.58$
$l = 0.14$	$\beta_2 = 0.78$	$\gamma_2 = 0.20$	$(1-c)^{-1}\rho = 1.96$	$\epsilon_4 = 0.47$	$\zeta_2 = 0.31$
$\rho = -0.62$			$c = 0.31$	$q = 1.26$	$\zeta_3 = 0.29$
			$1-c = 0.69$	$x = 0.0223$	
			$f = 0.61$		

the value for x indicates that the equilibrium supply of labour has been increasing at a rate of about $2 \cdot 2$ per cent per annum, while q at $1 \cdot 26$ indicates an elastic response of the equilibrium supply of labour to any change in excess demand in the labour market. The elasticity of real output with respect to the real volume of money is considerably more responsive than that with respect to each of the real net government expenditure and real exports variables, but none of the three responses is an elastic one.

The values of the structural parameters derived from the 2SLS point estimates cannot therefore, be said to be unsatisfactory in themselves. However, the parameter values α_1 and ζ_1 do not enable satisfaction of equation (18), and lead to the representative firm's actual second-order conditions failing to be satisfied. [31]

V STABILITY AND PREDICTING POWER

The material presented in this section is based on the 2SLS point estimates presented in Section IV. 2. [32]

1 Stability

The characteristic equation is

$$0 \cdot 7106 \lambda^4 - 1 \cdot 8142 \lambda^3 + 1 \cdot 8029 \lambda^2 - 0 \cdot 8643 \lambda + 0 \cdot 1851 = 0 \quad (34)$$

and its roots are

$$\lambda_1 = 0 \cdot 870 + 0 \cdot 195i \qquad \lambda_2 = 0 \cdot 870 - 0 \cdot 195i$$

$$\lambda_3 = 0 \cdot 406 + 0 \cdot 403i \qquad \lambda_4 = 0 \cdot 406 - 0 \cdot 403i$$

The conjugate complex pair λ_1 and λ_2 produce the dominant cycle, having a period of about twenty-eight years and being subject to a damping factor of $(0 \cdot 892)^t$. This figure of $0 \cdot 892$ is sufficiently different from unity for it to be unlikely that the model is dynamically unstable.

The twenty-eight year cycle obtained for this model is considerably different from the three-year cycle produced by the Bergstrom-Brownlie [1] model of the New Zealand economy. The difference can be evaluated in light of (a) the twenty-eight year cycle emanating from a model containing only twenty-three annual observations and (b) this model lacking an inventory equation. Inventories are expressly included in the Bergstrom-Broenlie model.

2 Predicting power

The comments in this section are limited to giving an indication of the ex-post forecasting ability of the model, and calculations are for each year of the sample period only, i.e. 1949 to 1971 inclusive.

Ex-post (or unconditional) forecasts were obtained from knowledge of the exogenous and lagged endogenous variables corresponding with each observation, and, when compared with the actual values, enabled discrepancies due to the model proper to be revealed. Ex-ante (or conditional) forecasts would have been subject to incorrect forecasts of the future values of the exogenous variables as well as those due to the model proper, and therefore have not received any attention: it was felt to be important to look for weaknesses in the model constructed before projecting into the future with an unproven model.

The predictions obtained from the model were compared with those obtained from four very simple naive models. Naive model I forecasted no change in an endogenous variable from one year to the next; naive model II forecasted that an endogenous variable would change by the same amount in year t as it did in year $t-1$; naive model III forecasted from the simple regression equation $x_t = \eta_0 + \eta_1 x_{t-1}$, and naive model IV forecasted from the simple regression equation $x_t = \eta_3 + \eta_4 t$. The results are presented in Table 10.4.

The model estimated by 2SLS has, on a total score basis, performed considerably better than naive models I and IV, on a par with naive model II, and marginally worse than naive model III.

VI CONCLUSION

Conclusions presented relate to the tests conducted, to the economic relations postulated, and to aspects of the model and the problem which could further be researched.

Regression results obtained using the methods of OLS and

Table 10.4 Summary of scores against naive models I to IV for the years 1949 to 1971 inclusive

Variable	Naive I	Naive II	Naive III	Naive IV
P_r	17-5	10-13	9-11	17-6
W_a	22-0	13-10	11-12	15-8
W_m	19-2	10-13	12-11	17-6
L_d	18-4	15-8	12-8	18-5
L_s	21-2	7-14	8-14	17-6
Y_s	13-9	13-10	10-12	10-13
Total score	110-22	68-68	62-68	94-44

2SLS could be considered satisfactory in accordance with the criteria often utilised for judging econometric results, i.e. the order conditions for identification were satisfactory, the values of $\bar{R}^2$ were attractive, the coefficients of the variable were of correct sign and statistically significant, the magnitudes of the structural parameter values seemed plausible, no hypothesis of first-order serial correlation could be accepted, restrictions imposed on individual structural parameters seemed unlikely to be rejectable, and ex-post predictions were reasonable. The representative firm's second-order profit maximisation conditions were tested using 2SLS *point* estimates and could not be accepted, but as all coefficients are statistically significant, the 2SLS results are quite capable of being consistent with some other theory.

Further important conclusions can be drawn from the wage and supply of labour services equations. The dual wage determination hypothesis had not broken down by 1971, but clearly (in light of the explanation in note 29), new wage determination hypotheses will have to be tested. Treatment of the physical constraint imposed by continued labour shortages will also have to be reconsidered, as the present hypothesis leads to point predictions which are inferior to those producible by naive models II and III.

The twofold procedure of imposing equilibrium on the goods market and formulating equation (6) in such simple form as to close the model at six non-definitional equations, has been expedient to date but could now be subjected to further examination. A consideration of the influence of inventory movements could be especially worthwhile.

On the question of whether further open economy influences should be allowed for, it is first necessary to note that the calendar years 1972 and 1973 saw spectacular movements in New Zealand's balance of payments, exchange rate, import and export price levels, and extremely large increases in the supply of money. Contrary to the situation in many other western open economies, this loss of control over the money supply can be associated with current account rather than capital account movements. This means that doubt must be cast on the authorities' persistent attempts to control interest rates (instead of the money supply), rather than that attention should be focussed on the monetary theory of the balance of payments and inflation for possible explanation of New Zealand's present and future inflation rate. The current and capital account controls considered sufficiently effective to date will only be intensified if required.

From a future research point of view, therefore, productive tasks will be to capture the influence of effective exchange rate alterations, and to appraise more thoroughly the transmission

mechanisms between international activity and New Zealand's rate
of inflation. Initial work on measuring the effective exchange
rate has been done by Lumsden (11) and (12), and on appraising the
transmission mechanisms by Hall [9].

Simulation work is also currently being conducted by Deane
as an extension of earlier work [4] undertaken in this area. The
results of this and other work should then be directed towards
indicating whether New Zealand's extensive system of controls
over external activity has in fact exacerbated or ameliorated the
rate of inflation.

NOTES

1   A controlled float of the New Zealand dollar, has, however, been in
effect since 10 September 1973.

2   With respect to current account items, both import control and export
licence regulations have been in force since 1938. Various systems of import licensing have operated, and the function of the export licensing regulations has been to ensure that all export proceeds were returned to the
New Zealand banking system. Exchange control has been a further feature,
and overall has been sufficiently significant for New Zealand to have taken
advantage of the International Monetary Fund's article XIV, section 2 which
permits members to '... maintain and adapt to changing circumstances
... restrictions on payments and transfers for current international transactions'.

With respect to capital account items, principal avenues for regulation
have been through capital issues controls, exchange control, and
overseas takeovers regulations. In practice, net private capital account
movements have not been significant either in themselves or in comparison
with current account flows. They should be seen within the context of
meticulous scrutiny of capital inflows and strong controls over New
Zealand portfolio investment abroad, but a so far liberal attitude towards
remittance of funds abroad by non-resident companies.

Useful more detailed summaries of controls over external activity are
available in part V of Reserve Bank of New Zealand [13] and appropriate
volumes of the New Zealand Official Year Book. For a brief but enlightening
perspective on the extent of direct controls over New Zealand's domestic
activity, see Deane [3] p. 7.

3   The OLS and 2SLS computer programmes were kindly made available
by Jon Stewart. Regression equations were run on the University of Manchester computer system during the tenure of a Hallsworth Research
Fellowship in the Department of Econometrics.

4   Intertemporal optimisation has not been employed, so the dynamics of
the model have evolved in an ad hoc manner through developing the most
suitable structure for each individual equation. It will also be apparent that
problems of aggregation have been ignored.

5   Some recent work at the disaggregated level is reported in Ledingham
[10].

6   Neither an excess demand for goods and services variable nor an
excess demand for labour services variable could be found to be significant in explaining changes in the retail price level.

7   Semi-annual observations as at 15 April and 15 October, from October 1946 to April 1971, show that the excess demand for labour services (i.e. actual vacancies less unemployment) has at all times been positive, except as at 15 April 1968 (when the figure was 1,544 persons).

8   See Hall [7].

9   An alternative model would assume that the supply of labour is adjusted in line with the real or actual wage rate. Such a labour supply hypothesis in terms of monetary variables is less preferred to that expressed here in physical terms because of the physical constraint imposed by New Zealand's traditional shortage of labour.

10   From the National Income and Expenditure figures for March, years 1947-71, the average of $(dU + dV)/Y_s$ in *money* terms has been about 3·0 per cent. A breakdown of real inventory level changes into dU and dV is not available, but in accordance with the above analysis, the 3·0 per cent long-run average must be solely attributed to dV.

11   Deane [3], p. 28 has suggested that '... monetary variables (actually the volume of money) play significant roles in determining a range of expenditures including specifically consumption of durables, spending on dwellings, imports of goods and payments for these imports'.

12   See Section II. 2. B below

13   The evidence from notes 6 and 10 does not contradict this point.

14   Behaviour of the representative firm is outlined more fully in Hall [8]. This paper may also be consulted for more detailed empirical material on the price, labour demand, and real output equations.

15   This assumption is unlikely to be realistic for all sectors of the New Zealand economy. However, the *extent* to which it may be unrealistic (particularly when dealing with men rather than man-hours) is not known.

16   Additional actual money balances = final actual money balances $(M_{d,g})$ less initial actual money balances (M^*).

17   The conditions required by (18) and (19) are stricter than the actual condition which may be expressed (for the case in which $v = 1$) as

$$\frac{W_a}{(p_r^{1/\alpha} {}_1 p_i^{-b/\alpha 1} (1 - \alpha 1 \zeta 1)} + \frac{Y_s (1+\rho)}{L_d} \cdot \{ (1-c) [c(K_0 e^{kt})^{-\rho}$$

$$+ (1-c)L_d^{-\rho}]^{-1} L_d^{-\rho} - 1\} < 0$$

In note 31, using 2SLS point estimates, this actual condition is evaluated numerically.

18   The econometric results in Section IV will show that the constant returns to scale assumption is appropriate.

19   The simple adjustment function

$$(lnL_{d,t} - lnL_{d,t-1}) = n(lnL_{d,t}^* - lnL_{d,t-1})$$

is assumed. The parameter n = coefficient of adjustment, and $L_{d,t}^* =$ desire demand for labour services.

20   The search for an appropriate dynamic structure for (17) is outlined in Hall [8].

21   Note that the labour supply equation (22) is not expressed as one of the conditions. This is because the household's labour supply is adjusted to the given demand for labour of the firm, and is thus fixed for the purposes of the optimisation process. Equation (22) is incorporated in equation (5). The labour supply function would have to be treated in a similar manner if it were assumed that either $L_s = f_1(W_a/P_r)$.

[22]   A bar above a symbol indicates 'the mean of'.

[23]   The model has also been estimated using the complete system method of full information maximum likelihood and a computer programme developed by Clifford Wymer [15] and [16]. The non-linear cross equation and other restrictions on all parameters except α_0 in equations (21), (28), and (30) were taken account of. Principal conclusions from this work were: (i) satisfactory parameter values for $(1-c)^-f\rho$ (and hence $c, 1-c$, and f) could not be obtained whether k was unconstrained or constrained and whether difference or differential equation forms of the model were used: (ii) using a likelihood ratio test, the null hypothesis that the overidentifying restrictions of the model were consistent with the sample data could not be accepted.

[24]   The data are available on request from the author.

[25]   The signs of the coefficients in Table 10·2 and subsequent tables accord with equations (25) to (30) unless a negative sign appears in the table.

[26]   An 'F' test (which is strictly applicable only for the general linear model) was performed on the residual sums of squares of the first equation in Table 10·1 and equation (32). The null hypothesis that $v=1$ and $\mu=0$ could not be rejected at the 5 per cent level of significance.

[27]   The experimentation is outlined in Hall [6], pp 206-24. Briefly; as no independent values for k could be discovered, five alternative values were calculated from the expression $k=(lnk_t-lnK_0)/\epsilon$, the crude series for K having been constructed from official net domestic formation data and five alternative capital-output ration assumptions of $2·0, 2·5, 3·0, 3·5, 4·0$. Each constrained value of k was regressed, and the one chosen (i.e. $\hat{k}=0·0402$ corresponding with $K/Y=4·0$) was that which led to the least unsatisfactory value for the distribution parameter c.

[28]   An approximate (bearing in mind the non-linear nature of the parameters, the presence of a lagged dependent variable, and the small sample) 'F' test was performed. The null hypothesis that $k=0·0402$ could not be rejected at the 5 per cent level of significance.

[29]   The results for the minimum wage equation tend to confirm that the dual wage determination hypothesis is likely to break down completely. A 2SLS estimate equation using data to March 1969 was

$$ln W_{m,t} = -1·304 + \underset{(3·6^C)}{0·594 ln P_{r,t}} + \underset{(3·6^C)}{0·216(ln Y_{s,t} - ln L_{s,t})}$$
$$+ \underset{(2.9^C)}{0·392\ ln W_{m,t-1}}$$

Estimation of this equation with data to March 1971 showed that the coefficient of $ln W_{m,t-1}$ was no longer significantly different from zero.

Hence (i) the adjustment process has speeded up to being one of instantaneous adjustment for a one-year data observation period; (ii) the influence of the retail price level on the minimum wage rate has become relatively greater and that of the level of productivity relatively less; i.e. from the above equation $\gamma_1 = 0·96$ and $\gamma_2 = 0·36$, but from the equation presented in Table 10.2 $\gamma_1 = 1·08$ and $\gamma_2 = 0·20$.

[30]   An independent value of K_0 is required before separate values can be derived for the parameters c and f. See Hall [8], appendix 1.

[31]   Utilising structural parameter values from Table 10.3 and the sample information that $\overline{W}_a = 835, \overline{L}_d = 653, \overline{P}_r = 868, \overline{Ys} = 824, \overline{Pi} = 957, \overline{t} = 12$,

the actual second-order condition became $0.307\ (0.576 - 0.265) = 0.10$, and failed to satisfy the negativity requirement.

32 It is important to appreciate that utilising the 2SLS results does not contradict our non-acceptance of theory outlined in Section II. 2. B. The statistically significant 2SLS results are quite capable of being consistent with some other theory.

REFERENCES

[1] Bergstrom, A. R. and A. D. Brownlie, 'An econometric Model of the New Zealand economy', *Economic Record*, vol. 41 (March 1965), pp. 125-6.

[2] Brownlie, A. D. and P. Hampton, 'An econometric study of wage determination in New Zealand', *International Economic Review*, vol. 8 (October 1967), pp. 327-34.

[3] Deane, R. S., 'Towards a Model of the New Zealand Economy', Research Paper No. 1 (Wellington, Reserve Bank of New Zealand, 1971).

[4] Deane, R. S., M. A. Lumsden and A. B. Sturm, 'Some simulation experiments with a New Zealand model', in R. S. Deane (ed.), 'A New Zealand model structure, policy uses, and some simulation results', Research Paper No. 8 (Wellington, Reserve Bank of New Zealand, 1972).

[5] Hall, V. B., 'Determinants of the minimum money wage rate in New Zealand, 1947-65', *New Zealand Economic Papers*, Vol. 3 (1969), pp. 14-26.

[6] — 'A model of New Zealand's post-war inflation' (unpublished Ph.D. Thesis, University of Auckland, 1971).

[7] — 'Simultaneous equation wage determination in New Zealand', New Zealand Economic Papers, vol. 6 (1972), pp. 29-51.

[8] — 'Prices, labour demand, and real output in the New Zealand economy: An econometric application', *New Zealand Economic Papers*, Vol. 7, (1973), pp. 25-47.

[9] — 'International activity, transmission mechanisms, and New Zealand's rate of inflation', Reserve Bank of New Zealand Economic Department Discussion Paper G73/I (February 1974).

[10] Ledingham, P. J., 'An investigation of the determinants of wage and price formation in New Zealand' mimeo; paper presented to the Third Australasian Conference of Economists, Adelaide (May 1973).

[11] Lumsden, M. A., 'New Zealand's effective exchange rate and its impact on imports', forthcoming in Research Paper No. 13 (Wellington, Reserve Bank of New Zealand).

[12] — 'A model of New Zealand's balance of payments', forthcoming in *New Zealand Economic Papers*.

[13] Reserve Bank of New Zealand, *Overseas Trade and Finance: With Particular Reference to New Zealand* (Wellington, Reserve Bank of New Zealand, 1966).

[14] Simkin, C. G. F., 'Inflation in Australia and New Zealand', *Economic Record*, Vol. 48, (December 1972), pp. 465-82.

[15] Wymer, C. R., 'Econometric estimation of stochastic differential equation systems with application to adjustment models of financial markets' (unpublished Ph.D. thesis, University of London, 1970). chapter 2, appendix A.

[16] Wymer, C. R., 'Resimul 2 manual', mimeo (London School of Economics, October 1972).

11 Inflationary expectations and the long-run trade-off between inflation and unemployment in open economies

Michael Parkin and Graham W. Smith[1]

All the theoretical developments of the role of expectations in the inflationary process, by Friedman [3], Phelps [12], Mortensen [9], and Lucas and Rapping [8] predict that the *expected* rate of inflation should affect the *actual* rate of inflation with a unitary coefficient. In other words, a *cet par* change in expected inflation should give rise to an *equal* change in the actual inflation rate. This, combined with the long-run equilibrium condition that the expected and actual rates of inflation be equal, gives the prediction that there is no trade-off between inflation and unemployment in the long run.

In sharp contrast to this *a priori* prediction, almost (but not quite) all the empirical attempts to estimate the effects of expected inflation on actual inflation show the resulting coefficient to be less than unity. Typically, for the UK, Lipsey [6], Lipsey and Parkin [7], and Parkin [10] find estimates of this coefficient in the range 0·4 to 0·7. For the USA, Gordon [4], [5] obtains estimates of the crucial coefficient in the range 0·2 to 0·7, and Turnovsky and Wachter [16] 0·35. Toyoda [15] with a model for the Japanese economy estimates the coefficient at 0·5.

We know of only four cases in which unit coefficients on the price expectations variable in the wage equation have been found. Two are by Vanderkamp [17], [18] for Canada. Using data for the period 1947(1)-1962(4), he estimated separate wage equations for the organised and unorganised sectors of the labour market and, after allowing for simultaneous feedback by estimating a three-equation wage-price system by full information maximum likelihood, he found the coefficient on price expectations (measured by the rate of change of consumer prices) in the organised sector wage equation to be insignificantly different from unity. This result was upheld in a later study (Vanderkamp [18]).

Parkin, Sumner, and Ward [11] for the UK, 1956(2)-1971(4), in a rigorous specification of the expectations-augmented excess demand hypothesis allowing for expectations of retail, wholesale, and export prices and taxes, found the sum of the coefficients on the expectational variables to be insignificantly different from one.[2]

The fourth case is that of Duck, Parkin, Rose, and Zis [2] who

estimated an expectations-augmented Phillips curve for the Group
of Ten as an approximation to the world economy.

The purpose of this paper is to re-examine the role of expectations in the theory of the Phillips curve with the objective of reconciling these apparently disparate results. It will be shown that
in countries which have substantial trade with the rest of the world
and which have a fixed exchange rate, then the coefficient on expected price change should, *a priori,* be less than unity.[3] Countries
with a flexible exchange rate should have a coefficient of unity.
Closed economies (the world as a whole) should have a coefficient
of unity. The direct evidence which is so far available, that for
Canada, 'the world' and the appropriate UK open economy specification, suggests that the *a priori* predictions are consistent with
the facts and there is no trade-off between inflation and unemployment in the long run. For all other cases studied, there is no
direct evidence bearing on the question although such indirect evidence as there is cannot be taken to be inconsistent with the strong
no long-run trade-off version of the expectations hypothesis.

Consider an open economy which produces two goods, a non-
traded good with price P, and a trade good with price $E\Pi$ where E
is the foreign exchange rate and Π is the price of the traded good
in units of foreign currency. Suppose there is a single homogeneous labour input with a wage rate W. The excess demand for labour
function in this economy may be written as

$$X = F(P, E\Pi, W) \tag{1}$$

where X is the excess demand for labour. In common with earlier
analyses of expectations as well as standard analysis, we assume
(1) to be homogeneous of degree zero in money prices, whence

$$X = F(1, \frac{E\Pi}{P}, \frac{W}{P}) \tag{2}$$

Following the development in Parkin, Sumner, and Ward [11], we
assume that wages are changed, given expectations about $\dot{p}$, $\dot{\pi}$ and $\dot{\epsilon}$,
to eliminate any initial excess demand, i.e. given (2),

$$\Delta X = F_2 \frac{E\Pi}{P} \frac{\dot{\Pi}}{\Pi} + F_2 \frac{E\Pi}{P} \frac{\dot{E}}{E} + F_3 \frac{W}{P} \frac{\dot{W}}{W} - (F_2 \frac{E\Pi}{P} + F_3 \frac{W}{P}) \frac{\dot{P}}{P} \tag{3}$$

or, with obvious notation simplification,

$$\Delta X = f_2(\dot{\pi} + \dot{\epsilon}) + f_3 \dot{w} - (f_2 + f_3)\dot{p} \tag{4}$$

If $\dot{w}$ is set to eliminate X, then $\Delta X = -X$, and the variables $\dot{p}$, $\dot{\pi}$ and
$\dot{\epsilon}$ interpreted as expectations, i.e.

$$\dot{w} = \frac{1}{f_3} X + \left[\frac{f_2 + f_3}{f_3}\right] \dot{p}^e - \frac{f_2}{f_3}(\dot{\pi}^e + \dot{\epsilon}^e) \tag{5}$$

Defining $1/f_3 = \lambda > 0$, $\qquad\qquad\qquad\qquad\qquad\qquad$ (6)

$$\frac{f_2 + f_3}{f_3} = \alpha, 0 < \alpha < 1 \qquad\qquad\qquad (7)$$

$$\dot{w} = \lambda X + \alpha \dot{p}^e + (1 - \alpha)(\dot{\pi}^e + \dot{\epsilon}^e) \qquad\qquad (8)$$

which, with an appropriate Phillips-Lipsey-Phelps mapping

$$X = \phi(U, \dot{u}), \phi_1 < 0, \phi_2 < 0 \qquad\qquad\qquad (9)$$

gives the expectations-augmented Phillips curve for an open economy:

$$\dot{w} = \lambda \phi(U, \dot{u}) + \alpha \dot{p}^e + (1 - \alpha)(\dot{\epsilon}^e + \dot{\pi}^e) \qquad (10)$$

Direct estimation of equation (10) should, if the 'no long-run trade-off' hypothesis is correct, produce coefficients on $\dot{p}$ and $(\dot{\pi} + \dot{\epsilon})$ which sum to unity. For the UK this result was obtained in the previously cited study by Parkin, Sumner, and Ward.

The Phillips curve usually estimated, employing as the price change variable a weighted average of traded and non-traded goods prices where the weights are determined by the fraction of total expenditure accounted for by imports, should not, in general, produce a coefficient of unity on the estimate of γ. The retail price index inflation rate may be written as

$$\dot{p}_R = \beta \dot{p} + (1 - \beta)(\dot{\epsilon} + \dot{\pi}) \qquad\qquad\qquad (11)$$

where $\dot{p}_R$ represents retail prices and $(1 - \beta)$ represents the fraction of national income imported. Thus, what is typically estimated is

$$\dot{w} = \lambda \phi(U, \dot{u}) + \gamma \dot{p}_R$$

$$= \lambda \phi(U, \dot{u}) + \gamma[\beta \dot{p} + (1 - \beta)(\dot{\epsilon} + \dot{\pi})] \qquad (12)$$

As we observed in the introduction, the parameter γ which is predicted to be unity has, in most cases, estimated significantly less than unity. However, in the case of Canada and 'the world', γ has estimated as unity. Let us first see if we can reconcile the results for these two cases with equation (12).

First, Canada. The Canadian exchange rate was floating from the end of 1950 until May 1962. If we assume that the float was clean and that the movement in the rate was in line with the underlying movements in Canadian and rest of the world price movements, then

$$\dot{\epsilon} = \dot{p} - \dot{\pi} \qquad\qquad\qquad\qquad\qquad (13)$$

whence

$$\dot{p}_R = \beta\dot{p} + (1-\beta)(\dot{p} - \dot{\pi} + \dot{\pi})$$

or

$$\dot{p}_R = \dot{p}$$

Thus, for a flexible exchange rate country the price index $\dot{p}_R$ is equal to the rate of change of domestic non-traded goods prices and is independent of the weight β.

For the 'world' case, we have no foreign trade, i.e. $\beta = 0$ ($\beta \simeq 0$ for the case actually studied). In that case,

$$\dot{p}_R = \dot{\epsilon} + \dot{\pi} \tag{14}$$

but for the 'world' $\dot{\epsilon} = 0$, hence

$$\dot{p}_R = \dot{\pi} \tag{15}$$

i.e. the world rate of inflation is equal to the rate of inflation of traded goods and the weight β does not affect the measurement of world inflation.

These two cases are ones in which $\dot{p}_R$ used may be regarded as a pure inflation measure; in the case of a flexible exchange rate country, other countries' differential inflation rates being neutralised by the exchange rate and in the case of 'the world' differential inflation rates of non-traded goods prices averaging out to give a world average inflation rate equal to the rate of inflation of traded goods prices.

Now let us look at all the other cases studied. The variable used in wage equations has been

$$\dot{p}_R = \beta\dot{p} + (1-\beta)(\dot{\epsilon} + \dot{\pi}) \tag{11}$$

but, since the countries in question have, over all the relevant sample periods, had fixed exchange rates, this is equivalent to

$$\dot{p}_R = \beta\dot{p} + (1-\beta)\dot{\pi} \tag{16}$$

This has been used in place of the 'correct' index

$$\dot{p}_T = \alpha\dot{p} + (1-\alpha)\dot{\pi} \tag{17}$$

with α defined in equations (6) and (7).

Given equations (16) and (17), it is clear that $\dot{p}_T$ can be expressed in terms of $\dot{p}_R$ and either $\dot{p}$ or $\dot{\pi}$, i.e.

$$\dot{p}_T = \frac{(1-\alpha)}{(1-\beta)}\dot{p}_R - \frac{(\beta-\alpha)}{(1-\beta)}\dot{p} \tag{18}$$

and

$$\dot{p}_T = \left[\frac{\alpha}{\beta}\right]\dot{p}_R - \left[\frac{\alpha-\beta}{\beta}\right]\dot{\pi}, \; 0 < \alpha, \beta < 1 \tag{19}$$

The true equation for a fixed exchange rate open economy is

$$\dot{w} = \lambda X + \gamma \dot{p}_T + u \tag{20}$$

in which $\gamma = 1$ and u is an *iid* error. Equation (20) may be written as

$$\dot{w} = \lambda X + \gamma \left\{ \frac{(1-\alpha)}{(1-\beta)} \dot{p}_R - \frac{(\beta-\alpha)}{(1-\beta)} \dot{p} \right\} + u, \gamma = 1 \tag{21}$$

or as

$$\dot{w} = \lambda X + \gamma \left\{ \left[\frac{\alpha}{\beta} \right] \dot{p}_R - \frac{(\alpha-\beta)}{\beta} \dot{\pi} \right\} + u, \gamma = 1 \tag{22}[4]$$

The equation usually estimated is of the form:

$$\dot{w} = \hat{\lambda} X + \hat{\gamma} \dot{p}_R + \hat{u} \tag{23}$$

in which it is assumed that $\hat{u}$ is *iid*. In fact this assumption is incorrect for a fixed exchange rate open economy, unless by accident $\alpha = \beta$, because of the omission of a relevant explanatory variable. The estimated coefficient on $\dot{p}_R$ may be written as

$$\hat{\gamma} = \frac{\Sigma X^2 \, \Sigma \dot{p}_R \dot{w} - \Sigma X \dot{p}_R \, \Sigma X \dot{w}}{\Sigma \dot{p}_R^2 \, \Sigma X^2 - \Sigma \dot{p}_R X \, \Sigma \dot{p}_R X} \tag{24}$$

(where all the variables in (24) and (25) are to be read as deviations from means). Substituting for $\dot{w}$ from (21), taking probability limits and simplifying,

$$\begin{aligned}
\plim_{n \to \infty} \hat{\gamma} = {}& \gamma \left[\frac{1-\alpha}{1-\beta} \right] \\
& + \left[-\gamma \left[\frac{\beta-\alpha}{1-\beta} \right] \right] \frac{\plim(\Sigma X^2 \, \Sigma \dot{p}_R \dot{p} - \Sigma X \dot{p}_R \, \Sigma X \dot{p}) / n^2}{\plim(\Sigma \dot{p}_R^2 \, \Sigma X^2 - (\Sigma \dot{p}_R X)^2) / n^2}
\end{aligned} \tag{25}$$

Hence,

$$\begin{aligned}
\hat{\gamma} = {}& \gamma \left[\frac{1-\alpha}{1-\beta} \right] \\
& + \left[-\gamma \left[\frac{\beta-\alpha}{1-\beta} \right] \right] \frac{\text{var } X \text{ cov } \dot{p}_R \dot{p} - \text{cov } X \dot{p}_R \text{ cov } X \dot{p}}{\text{var } \dot{p}_R \text{ var } X - (\text{cov } X \dot{p}_R)^2}
\end{aligned} \tag{26}$$

Following the same procedure but using the alternative true equation (22), then

$$\hat{\gamma} = \gamma \left[\frac{\alpha}{\beta}\right]$$

$$+ \left[-\gamma \left[\frac{\alpha - \beta}{\beta}\right]\right] \frac{\text{var } X \text{ cov } \dot{p}_R \dot{\pi} - \text{cov } X\dot{p}_R \text{ cov } X\dot{\pi}}{\text{var } \dot{p}_R \text{ var } X - (\text{cov } X\dot{p}_R)^2} \quad (27)[5]$$

It is clear that the estimated coefficients $\hat{\gamma}$ are biased, the bias in the typically estimated equation, (23), depending on the sign and magnitude of the coefficient of the omitted variable and correlations between the omitted and included explanatory variables.

With data on $\dot{p}_R, \dot{p}$ and $\dot{\pi}$, the rates of change of retail, non-traded goods and traded goods prices respectively, together with a proxy for the level of excess demand for labour and the weights α and β, a numerical estimate for γ, the estimated coefficient on the price expectations variable in the mis-specified wage equation, may be calculated. For the UK, 1953-70, annual data are readily available. Data for $\dot{p}_R, \dot{p}$ and $\dot{\pi}$ from the appendix to Cross and Laidler [1] is used. The level of excess demand for labour is proxied by the inverse of the unemployment rate lagged one year, which is approximately the length of lag found by Parkin, Sumner, and Ward in their correctly specified fixed exchange rate open economy wage equation. α is taken from the UK input-output tables for 1963. The value of β used by Cross and Laidler in calculating their indices of traded and non-traded goods is derived from retail price index weights for 1956-61. All our calculations are done twice: once using the value for β, as employed by Cross and Laidler ($\beta_{C/L}$), and again using a value calculated from 1963 weights, (β_{63}). The results, assuming that true $\gamma = 1$, are presented in Table 11.1.

These results are interesting. Whilst the estimates of $\hat{\gamma}$ obtained for given α, β are not identical, which is to be expected with

Table 11.1. Values of $\hat{\gamma}$ calculated from equations (26) and (27)

	(26)	(27)	*Average*
$\alpha_{63} = 0.836$ $\beta_{C/L} = 0.211$	0.664	0.562	0.613
$\alpha_{63} = 0.836$ $\beta_{63} = 0.223$	0.665	0.594	0.630
Average	0.665	0.578	0.621

Table 11.2

Study	Data	Estimation	Dependent variable	Price expectations proxy	Estimated coefficient on $\dot{p}^e$ (SE) $\hat{\gamma}$ or (asymptotic SE) $\hat{\gamma}$	$t = \dfrac{\hat{\gamma} - 1}{SE(\hat{\gamma})}$	$t = \dfrac{\hat{\gamma} - 0 \cdot 621}{SE(\hat{\gamma})}$
Lipsey [6]	Annual 1923-39 + 1948-57	OLS	Rate of change of weekly money wage rates	Rate of change of retail prices	0·69 (0·08)	−3·875	0·863
Lipsey and Parkin [7]	Quarterly 1948(3)-67(2)	OLS	Rate of change of weekly money wage rates	Rate of change of retail prices	EN: 0·482 (0·084)	−6·190	−1·655
					PF: 0·457 (0·073)	−7·426	−2·247
					PN: 0·227 (0·244)	−3·167	−1·615
Parkin [10]	Quarterly 1948(3)-69(1)	NLCLS	Rate of change of weekly money wage rates	Adaptive expectations using rate of change of retail prices	EN: 0·650 (0·168)	−2·083	0·173
					PF: 0·472 (0·100)	−5·280	−1·490
					PN: 0·347 (0·471)	−1·386*	−0·582
				After allowing for first order autocorrelation:			
					EN: 0·440 (0·202)	−2·772	−0·896
					PF: 0·421 (0·127)	−4·559	−1·575
					PN: 0·166 (0·500)	−1·668*	−0·910

Notes

EN = Entire period.
PF = Policy off.
PN = Policy on.
* = $\hat{\gamma}$ also insignificantly different from zero.

our finite sample, they are very similar. The average value of $\hat{\gamma}$ is 0·621.

Let us now look at the results of earlier research which have presented estimates of a model of the form (23) for the fixed exchange rate UK economy. The relevant results of three well-known studies are given in Table 11. 2.

In general, the estimated coefficients on price changes lie in the range 0·4 to 0·7 and in all of the regressions in which that coefficient is significantly different from zero, it is also significantly different from unity.[6] Moreover, in all cases but one, the null hypothesis that the estimated coefficient on price expectations is 0·621, the average of our predictions of $\hat{\gamma}$ given the mis-specification and assuming the true $\gamma = 1$, cannot be rejected at the 5 per cent level on a two-tailed test.[7]

The clear and strong implication of the preceding analysis is that the reason why previous UK Phillips curves, in which price expectations were proxied by retail prices, produce a coefficient on price expectations of less than one, apparently indicating there to be a trade-off between wage changes and unemployment even in the long run, is that they are based on a model which is mis-specified for a small fixed exchange rate open economy. Given this mis-specification, the estimated coefficient on price changes is extremely close to and certainly not significantly different from what one would expect. Thus, these results of earlier researchers do *not* refute the 'no long-run trade-off' hypothesis, in fact, they are entirely consistent with it. Statements to the contrary, including one made by one of the present authors[8] are wrong.

NOTES

1   This work is part of the University of Manchester—SSRC Research Programme on Inflation: its causes, consequences and cures. The ideas on which the paper is based were first contained in an unpublished paper presented at the Third Paris-Dauphine Conference on Monetary Theory. The comments of A. R. Nobay and Alexander Swoboda have helped us in reworking the material.

2   In a *price* equation study for the UK by Smith [14] the hypothesis that the sum of the coefficients on expectational variables was unity could not be rejected.

3   This also applies to Phillips curves estimated for geographical regions which have substantial trade with other regions within an economy which has floating exchange rates with other countries. The exchange rate between regions within such an economy is fixed.

4   If $\alpha = \beta$ then (21) and (22) reduce to $\dot{w} = \lambda X + \gamma \dot{p}_R + u$, in which case $\dot{p}_R = \dot{p}_T$; cf. equation (20).

5   The estimated coefficient on excess demand is also biased and the asymptotic bias is given by either

$$\hat{\lambda} = \lambda \left[-\gamma \left(\frac{\beta - \alpha}{1 - \beta} \right) \right] \frac{\text{var } \dot{p}_R \text{ cov } X\dot{p} - \text{cov } X\dot{p}_R \text{ cov } \dot{p}_R\dot{p}}{\text{var } \dot{p}_R \text{ var } X - (\text{cov } \dot{p}_R X)^2} \quad \text{using (21)}$$

or

$$\hat{\lambda} = \lambda \left[-\gamma \left(\frac{\alpha - \beta}{\beta} \right) \right] \frac{\text{var } \dot{p}_R \text{ cov } X\dot{\pi} - \text{ cov } X\dot{p}_R \text{ cov } \dot{p}_R\dot{\pi}}{\text{var } \dot{p}_R \text{ var } X - (\text{cov } \dot{p}_RX)^2} \quad \text{using (22).}$$

[6]   These hypothesis tests are not strictly correct because in the mis-specified equation the estimator of the variance of $\hat{\gamma}$ is biased upwards; these significance tests tend to accept the null hypothesis more often than is justified for any given significance level.

[7]   Lipsey and Parkin policy off, which is not significantly different from $\hat{\gamma} = 0 \cdot 605$.

[8]   See Parkin [10], pp. 386-401.

REFERENCES

[1] Cross, R. B., and D. E. W. Laidler, 'Inflation, excess demand and expec-tations in fixed exchange rate open economies: some preliminary empi-rical results', in M. Parkin and G. Zis (eds.), *Inflation in the World Econ-omy* (Manchester University Press, 1976).

[2] Duck, N. W., M. Parkin, D. Rose and G. Zis, 'The determination of the rate of change of wages and prices in the fixed exchange rate world economy, 1956-71', in M. Parkin and G. Zis (eds.), *Inflation in the World Economy* (Manchester University Press, 1976).

[3] Friedman, M., 'The role of monetary policy', *American Economic Re-view*, 58(1) (March 1968), pp. 1-17.

[4] Gordon, R. J., 'Inflation in recession and recovery', *Brookings Papers* (1971(1)), pp. 105-58.

[5] ——, 'Wage-price controls and the shifting Phillips curve', *Brookings Papers* (1972(2)), pp. 385-421.

[6] Lipsey, R. G., 'The relation between unemployment and the rate of change of money wage rates in the United Kingdom, 1861-1957: a further analysis', *Economica* (NS) 27(105) (February 1960), pp. 1-31.

[7] Lipsey, R. G., and M. Parkin, 'Incomes policy: a reappraisal', *Economica* NS, 37(146) (May 1970), pp. 115-38; reprinted in M. Parkin and M. T. Sumner (eds.), *Incomes Policy and Inflation* (Manchester University Press, 1972).

[8] Lucas, R. E. and L. A. Rapping, 'Price expectations and the Phillips curve', *American Economic Review*, 59(3) (June, pp. 342-50.

[9] Mortensen, D. T., 'Job search, the duration of unemployment and the Phillips curve', *American Economic Review*, 60(5) (December 1970), pp. 847-62.

[10] Parkin, M., 'Incomes policy: some further results on the rate of change of money wages', *Economica* NS, 37(148) (November 1970), pp. 386-401; reprinted in M. Parkin and M. T. Sumner (eds.), *Incomes Policy and Inflation* (Manchester University Press, 1972).

[11] Parkin, M., M. T. Sumner and R. Ward, 'The effects of excess demand, generalised expectations and wage-price controls on wage inflation in the UK', paper presented to the Conference on Wage-Price Controls, Rochester University, November 1973 and forthcoming in the confer-ence proceedings.

[12] Phelps, E. S., 'Phillips curves, expectations of inflation and optimal unemployment over time', *Economica* NS, 34(135) (August 1967), pp. 254-81.

[13] Purdy, D., and G. Zis, 'Trade unions and wage inflation in the UK: a reappraisal', in J. M. Parkin (ed.), *Essays in Modern Economics* (Longmans, London, 1973); reprinted in D. Laidler and D. Purdy (eds.), *Inflation and Labour Markets* (Manchester University Press, 1974).

[14] Smith, G. W., 'Excess demand and expectations as determinants of price changes in the United Kingdom manufacturing sector', University of Manchester Inflation Workshop discussion paper No. 7505 (1975).

[15] Toyoda, J., 'Price expectations and the short run and long run Phillips curves in Japan, 1956-1968', *Review of Economics and Statistics*, 54(3) (August 1972), pp. 267-74.

[16] Turnovsky, S. J., and M. L. Wachter, 'A test of the expectations hypothesis using directly observed wage and price expectations', *Review of Economics and Statistics*, 54(1) (February 1972), pp. 47-54.

[17] Vanderkamp, J., 'Wage and price determination: an empirical model for Canada', *Economica* NS, 33(130) (May 1966), pp. 194-218.

[18] ——, 'Wage adjustment, productivity and price change expectations', *Review of Economic Studies*, 39(1) (117) (January 1972), pp. 61-72.

APPENDIX 11.1

Data

All data are for the UK, 1953-70, eighteen annual observations.
Annual percentage rates of change are calculated as $\dot{p} = (\ln P_t/P_{t-1}) \cdot 100$
$\dot{p}_R$ = annual percentage rate of change of the retail price index
$\dot{p}$ = annual percentage rate of change of an index of the price of non-traded goods
$\dot{\pi}$ = annual percentage rate of change of a traded goods price index
$\dot{p}_R, \dot{p}$ and $\dot{\pi}$ were calculated from data taken from the appendix to Cross and Laidler [1]
U was taken from the appendix to Purdy and Zis [13]

The calculated covariances are:

$$\text{var}\,(1/U_{-1}) = 0 \cdot 01739 \qquad \text{cov}\,\dot{p}_R \dot{p} = 1 \cdot 2881$$
$$\text{var}\,\dot{p}_R = 2 \cdot 09963 \qquad \text{cov}\,\dot{p}_R \dot{\pi} = 2 \cdot 3727$$
$$\text{var}\,\dot{p} = 2 \cdot 81124 \qquad \text{cov}\,(1/U_{-1})\dot{p}_R = 0 \cdot 02881$$
$$\text{var}\,\dot{\pi} = 1 \cdot 67418 \qquad \text{cov}\,(1/U_{-1})\dot{p} = 0 \cdot 06425$$
$$\text{cov}\,(1/U_{-1})\dot{\pi} = 0 \cdot 01050$$

In 1963, 16·4 per cent of GDP was imported. Hence $1 - \alpha = 0 \cdot 164 \rightarrow \alpha = 0 \cdot 836$, CSO—*Input-Output Tables for the UK 1963*, HMSO, London 1970, table 4, p. 10.

From Cross and Laidler [1], $1 - \beta_{C/L} = 0 \cdot 789 \rightarrow \beta_{C/L} = 0 \cdot 211$, February 1956-January 1962.

For 1963, comparable with our estimate of $\alpha, \beta_{63} = 0 \cdot 223$ (Department of Employment, *British Labour Statistics Historical Abstract*, table 92, p. 174).

Index of names

(Italics indicate bibliographical references)

Subject index

Kafka Was the Rage

Kafka Was the Rage

A Greenwich Village Memoir

ANATOLE BROYARD

CAROL SOUTHERN BOOKS • NEW YORK

Certain names have been changed for reasons of privacy.

Chapter 15 originally appeared in *Confetti* magazine, June–July 1990, © 1990 by CVG Publications, Ltd. Reprinted by permission of the Estate of Anatole Broyard.

Published by Carol Southern Books, an imprint of Crown Publishers, Inc., 201 East 50th Street, New York, New York 10022. Member of the Crown Publishing Group.

Random House, Inc. New York, Toronto, London, Sydney, Auckland

CAROL SOUTHERN BOOKS and colophon are trademarks of Crown Publishers, Inc.

Manufactured in the United States of America

Design by M. Kristen Bearse

Library of Congress Cataloging-in-Publication Data

Broyard, Anatole.
Kafka Was the Rage: a Greenwich Village memoir /
by Anatole Broyard.—1st ed.
1. Broyard, Anatole—Homes and haunts—New York (N.Y.)
2. Greenwich Village (New York, N.Y.)—Social life and customs.
3. Greenwich Village (New York, N.Y.)—Intellectual life.
4. Greenwich Village (New York, N.Y.)—Fiction.   5. Authors,
American—20th century—Biography.   6. Critics—United States—
Biography.   I. Title.
PS3552.R7915Z463   1993
809—dc20
[B]   93-7830
CIP
ISBN 0-517-59618-0

10 9 8 7 6 5 4 3 2 1

First Edition

PREFATORY REMARKS

I think there's a great nostalgia for life in New York City, especially in Greenwich Village in the period just after World War II. We were all so grateful to be there—it was like a reward for having fought the war. There was a sense of coming back to life, a terrific energy and curiosity, even a feeling of destiny arising out of the war that had just ended. The Village, like New York City itself, had an immense, beckoning sweetness. It was like Paris in the twenties—with the difference that it was our city. We weren't strangers there, but familiars. The Village was charming, shabby, intimate, accessible, almost like a street fair. We lived in the bars and on the benches of Washington Square. We shared the adventure of trying to be, starting to be, writers or painters.

American life was changing and we rode those changes. The changes were social, sexual, exciting—all the more so because we were young. It was as if we were sharing a common youth with the country itself. We were made anxious by all the changes, yet we were helping to define them.

The two great changes that interested me the most were the movements toward sexual freedom and toward abstraction in art and literature, even in life itself. These two movements concerned me not as social history, but as immediate issues in my daily life. I was ambivalent about both of them and my struggle with them is part of the energy of the narrative.

An innocent, a provincial from the French Quarter in New Orleans and from Brooklyn, I moved in with Sheri Donatti, who was a more radical version of Anaïs Nin, whose protégée she was. Sheri embodied all the new trends in art, sex, and psychosis. She was to be my sentimental education. I opened a bookstore, went to the New School under the GI Bill. I began to think about becoming a writer. I thought about the relation between men and women as it was in 1947, when they were still locked in what Aldous Huxley called a hostile symbiosis. In the background, like landscape, like weather, was what we read and talked about. In the foreground were our love affairs and friendships and our immersion, like swimmers or divers, in American life and art. This book is always a narrative, a story that is intimate, personal, lived through, a young man excited and perplexed by life in New York City at one of the richest times in its history.

The tragedy—and the comedy—of my story was that I took American life to heart with the kind of strenuous and ardent sincerity that young men usually bring to love affairs. While some of my contemporaries made a great show of political commitment, it seems to me that their politicizing of experience abstracted them from the ordinary, from the texture of things. They saw only a Platonic idea of American life. To use one of their favorite words, they were alienated. I was not. In fact, one of my problems was that I was alienated from alienation, an insider among outsiders. The young intellectuals I knew had virtually read and criticized themselves out of any feeling of nationality.

While there's a good deal of sexual activity in the book, none of it is casual—all of it is paid for in feeling and consciousness. In connection with both love and art, I always felt what Irving Howe called "remorse over civilization." I think that in some ways I am a dissenter from modern life. I share the nostalgia that plays such a large part in today's fashions, for example, and in today's movies.

My story is not only a memoir, a history—it's a valentine to that time and place. It's also a plea, a cry, an appeal for the survival of city life. There's a sociology concealed in the book, just as a body is concealed in its clothes.

Anatole Broyard
Southport, Connecticut
April 1989

PART ONE

Sheri

1

My life, or career, in Greenwich Village began when Sheri Donatti invited me to move in with her. *Invited* is not the right word, but I don't know how else to describe it. I had just come out of the army and I was looking for a place I could afford when I met Sheri at a party. She had two apartments, she said, and if I understood her way of talking, she was suggesting that I might come and look at one of them.

Sheri Donatti had the kind of personality that was just coming into vogue in Greenwich Village in 1946. This was a time when Kafka was the rage, as were the Abstract Expressionists and revisionism in psychoanalysis. Sheri was her own avant-garde. She had erased and redrawn herself, redesigned the way she walked, talked, moved, even the way she thought and felt.

She was a painter and she looked more like a work of art than a pretty woman. She had a high, domelike forehead, the long silky brown hair of women in portraits, wide pale blue eyes with something roiling in their surface. Her nose was aquiline, her mouth thin and disconsolate, her chin small and pointed. It was the kind of bleak or wan beauty Village people liked to call quattrocento.

Her body seemed both meager and voluptuous. Her waist was so small, it cut her in two, like a split personality, or two schools of thought. Though her legs and hips were sturdy and richly curved, her upper body was dramatically thin. When she was naked it appeared that her top half was trying to climb up out of the bottom, like a woman stepping out of a heavy garment. Her gestures and motions were a slow dance, a parody of classical poses. They were very deliberate, performed at half speed, as if she had to remember each time, to remind herself, how human beings behaved.

Yet with all this, all the affectation, there was something striking about her. She was a preview of things to come, an invention that was not quite perfected but that would turn out to be important, a forerunner or harbinger, like the shattering of the object in Cubism or atonality in music. When I came to know her better, I thought of her as a new disease.

Twenty-three Jones Street was a shabby tenement with iron stairs that gave off a dull boom and padlocked toilets on each landing. There was no bell and the downstairs door was not locked, so I walked up to the second floor as Sheri Donatti had told me to do. When she answered the door, I saw that she was bare-legged and that her dark dress clung rather lovingly to her thighs.

4

There were three small rooms, with the kitchen in the center. She led me into her studio, as she called it, where there were paintings on the wall and an unfinished canvas on an easel. We sat down and started to manufacture or assemble a conversation. Like everything else about her, her style of talking took some getting used to. She gave each syllable an equal stress and cooed or chanted her vowels. Her sentences had no intonation, no rise and fall, so that they came across as disembodied, parceled out, yet oracular too. She reminded me of experimental writing, of "the revolution of the word" in the little magazines of the thirties. She talked like a bird pecking at things on the ground and then arching its neck to swallow them.

She went in for metaphors and reckless generalizations, the kind of thing French writers put in their journals. Everything she said sounded both true and false. At the same time I could feel the force of her intelligence, and some of her images were remarkable.

It occurred to me that our conversation might be an interview, a test of my suitability as a tenant or neighbor, so I began to inflate my remarks. I was wearing army fatigues and she asked me whether I had been in the war. She said, Did you kill anyone?

No, I said. I wish I had. I would feel further along in life.

Just when I was beginning to think she'd forgotten why I had come, she got up and offered to show me the other apartment, which was just across the hall. I had been looking forward to this moment, imagining myself with a place of my own in Greenwich Village—but in my first glimpse of the other apartment, I realized that my thinking had been too simple. Already I could tell that nothing about Sheri Donatti was simple, that behind each gesture there was another one. Behind the door of the other apartment, for example, there was an enormous old-fashioned printing press. It loomed like a great black animal, a bear or a buffalo, in the little kitchen.

It was an immensely heavy and powerful machine and I could tell by her manner, by the way she presented it, that it was hers. There was more to this Sheri Donatti than I had thought. This was another aspect of her. She was the driver of this locomotive. The thing took up most of the kitchen, which was as big as the other two rooms put together. I felt that I had entered its lair, its den—this behemoth lived here. The apartment was occupied. There was no room for me, unless I slept in its arms.

I glanced into the other rooms, which were piled with boxes, clothes, and paintings. The apartment was chock-full, crammed with stuff. I had the impression that I was being given a riddle or puzzle to solve. How did I fit into this already-congested space? Was she offering me the place or not? I saw that I would have to ask her. Even if it made me feel slow-witted, someone who doesn't understand the form or get the joke, I had to ask her: I can have this apartment?

She smiled at the question she had forced on me.

I'll take it, I said.

I don't know exactly why I took it. The obvious answer was that I wanted Sheri Donatti, but I didn't, so far as I knew. She was attractive, God knows, but my tastes were still conventional. What I felt was not desire but a strong, idle curiosity, a sense that she was the next step for me, that she was my future, or my fate. I was being drafted by Sheri Donatti as I had been drafted into the army.

I went back to Brooklyn, packed my clothes and books and kissed my parents good-bye. They didn't know what to say—I was a veteran now. Though I regretted the lie, I told them I'd have them over to my apartment when it was fixed up. I had called a taxi, and as it pulled away, with them waving, with me waving, I had that sense of finality all young men have under such circumstances.

When I arrived at Jones Street, Sheri showed me where to put my things. She gave me part of a closet in her bedroom and I hung myself up there, so to speak. If this was a seduction, it was very abstract. I acted as if I knew what was happening, but I was watching her for clues. I suppose it had occurred to me that it might turn out this way, but there was never a point where I was conscious of making a decision.

I'll never know why she chose me. As I discovered later, she could have taken her pick from any number of men. Perhaps she saw something in me that I hadn't seen myself—or something she could do with me that I would never have thought of.

Nineteen forty-six was a good time—perhaps the best time—in the twentieth century. The war was over, the Depression had ended, and everyone was rediscovering the simple pleasures. A war is like an illness and when it's over you think you've never felt so well. There's a terrific sense of coming back, of repossessing your life.

New York City had never been so attractive. The postwar years were like a great smile in its sullen history. The Village was as close in 1946 as it would ever come to Paris in the twenties. Rents were cheap, restaurants were cheap, and it seemed to me that happiness itself might be cheaply had. The streets and bars were full of writers and painters and the kind of young men and women who liked to be around them. In Washington Square would-be novelists and poets tossed a football near the fountain and girls just out of Ivy League colleges looked at the landscape with art history in their eyes. People on the benches held books in their hands.

Though much of the Village was shabby, I didn't mind. I thought all character was a form of shabbiness, a wearing away of surfaces. I saw this shabbiness as our version of ruins, the relic of a short history. The sadness of the buildings was literature. I was twenty-six, and sadness was a stimulant, even an aphrodisiac.

But while squalor was all right outside, as an urban atmosphere, domestic dirt brought out the bourgeois in me. It was the first flaw in my new paradise. As far as I could see, Sheri never cleaned the apartment, and for me to do it would have seemed like a breach of contract, or a criticism. I tried to ignore it, to be philosophical. Perhaps the place is squalid, I said to myself, but it's not sordid. What is dirt? I asked, just as in college we had asked, What is matter? Could this substance grinding under my feet be regarded as a neutral element, like sand? Was it like camping to live so close to dirt? After all, I argued, isn't art itself a kind of dirt?

The first night I spent on Jones Street, I woke up before dawn because I had to pee. I shook Sheri and asked her where she kept the key for the toilet in the hall.

Pee in the sink, she said.

There are dishes in the sink.

They have to be washed, anyway.

But I found it difficult to pee in the sink, because the idea excited me.

It was the same way with the bathtub in the kitchen. I could never take a dispassionate view of it; it always remained for me a kind of exhibitionism to sit in a bathtub in front of somebody else. I was the only son of a Catholic family from the French Quarter in New Orleans, and no one is so sexually demented as the French bourgeoisie, especially when you add a colonial twist.

Perhaps the hardest test for me was the way Sheri dressed. Under her outer clothes, there was only a padded bra, because she was ashamed of the smallness of her breasts. She wore no underpants and no stockings, even in winter, and I was tormented by this absence of underpants. When we walked down the street, I imagined her most secret part grinning at the world. For all I knew, she might suddenly pull up her skirt and show herself to the people and the buildings. What if the wind blew; what if she slipped and fell?

She did fall once. It was in a stationery store on West Fourth Street and she fell because she bumped into W. H. Auden. In fact, they both fell. Auden lived around the corner on Cornelia Street and I often saw him scurrying along with his arms full of books and papers. He looked like a man running out of a burning building with whatever of his possessions he'd been able to grab. He had a curious scuttling gait, perhaps because he always wore espadrilles.

He came hurrying into the stationery store just as

we were going out. Sheri was in front of me and he ran right into her. As he wrote somewhere, fantasy makes us clumsy. He also said that the art of living in New York City lies in crossing the street against the lights.

Sheri, who floated instead of walking, was easy to knock over, and Auden had all the velocity of his poetry and his nervousness. She fell backward, and as she did, she grabbed Auden around the neck and they went down together, with him on top. I was so concerned about her skirt flying up that I didn't even stop to think about whether she might have been hurt. She was lying on the floor beneath one of the most famous poets of our time, but I couldn't see the poetry or the humor of it.

She clung to Auden, who was sprawled in her arms. He tried desperately to rise, scrabbling with his hands and his espadrilles on the floor. He was babbling incoherently, apologizing and expostulating at the same time, while she smiled at me over his shoulder, like a woman dancing.

Until this time, most of the sex in my life had had an improvised character. It was done on the run, in borrowed, often inconvenient spaces, sandwiched between extraneous events, like the arrival or departure of parents or roommates, or the approach of daylight. Now I could have, could enjoy, sex whenever I chose. It had evolved from an obsessive idea into a surprising fact, an independent thing, like a monument. It was perpetually there when I had nothing else to do.

I had always believed, perhaps sentimentally, that

lovemaking clarified things, that people came to understand each other through it. Yet it didn't work that way
with Sheri—in fact, she grew more mysterious to me
all the time.

She made love the way she talked—by breaking
down the grammar and the rhythms of sex. Young men
tend to make love monotonously, but Sheri took my
monotony and developed variations on it, as if she were
composing a fugue. If I was a piston, she was Paul
Klee's Twittering Machine.

She was like one of those modern black jazz singers
who works against the melody and ignores the natural
line ends. Most people agree on some kind of rhythm
in sex, but Sheri refused all my attempts at coordina-
tion. She never had orgasms—she said she didn't want
them. I did want them, but I had to get used to arriving
at them in a new way. Instead of building or mounting
to orgasm, I descended to it. It was like a collapsing of
structures, like a building falling down. I remember
thinking once that it was the opposite of premature ejac-
ulation.

I had conceived of lovemaking as a sort of asking
and answering of questions, but with us it only led to
further questions, until we seemed to be locked in a
philosophical debate. Instead of the proverbial sadness
after sex, I felt something like a semantic despair.

Our sexual progress reminded me of a simultaneous
translation. But then, every once in a while, we would
speak the same language; she would allow us to chime,
to strike the same note at the same time, and it was as
if I were suddenly acoustical, resounding, loud in the
silence.

When we stayed home in the evenings, I would sit

with a book in my lap and watch her paint. But if she glanced around and saw me reading, she would put down her brush and come over and turn all her art on me. She distrusted books. I never saw her read one. I think she believed I might find something in them that would give me an advantage over her, or that I might use against her.

I felt the same way about her painting. She was an abstract painter and I couldn't follow her there. She left me outside, like a dog that you tie to a parking meter when you go into a store. I had never been comfortable with abstract painting. I had no talent for abstraction, didn't see the need for it, or the beauty of it. Like liberal politics, it eliminated so many things I liked.

Yet if I could understand her paintings, I thought, our sex would be better. We would exist in the same picture plane, pose for each other's portraits, mingle our forms and colors, make compositions. We would be like two people walking through a gallery or museum, exclaiming over the same things.

I began to read up on abstract painting. In the library in the Museum of Modern Art, I rummaged through the shelves, studying for my new life. I had come to think that modern art was an initiation into that life, like the hazing before you get into a fraternity. When I was at Brooklyn College, everyone urged me to join the Communist party, but I refused because I thought it was an uninteresting quarrel with the real. Modern art, though, was a quarrel that appealed to me more. Even if I never got to like it, I enjoyed the terms of the argument. I was impressed by the restless dissatisfaction, the aggressiveness, ingenuity, and pretension of all the theories.

I discovered that you could always find your own life reflected in art, even if it was distorted or discolored. There was a sentence, for example, in a book on Surrealism that stuck in my mind: "Beauty is the chance meeting, on an operating table, of a sewing machine and an umbrella."

2

aking advantage of the GI Bill, which paid my tuition and gave me a monthly allowance, I enrolled at the New School for Social Research on West Twelfth Street. I'd had a couple of semesters at Brooklyn College before going into the army, but I was bored because I didn't know what I wanted to do with what I was learning. I couldn't see any immediate use for it. But now going to school was part of the postwar romance. Studying was almost as good as art. The world was our studio.

Like the Village itself, the New School was at its best in 1946. After a war, civilization feels like a luxury, and people went to the New School the way you go to a party, almost like going abroad. Education was chic and sexy in those days. It was not yet open to the public.

The people in the lobby of the New School were excited, expectant, dressed to the teeth. They struck poses, examined one another with approval. They had a blind date with culture, and anything could happen. Young, attractive, hip, they were the best Americans. For local color, there was a sprinkling of bohemians and young men just out of the service who were still wearing their khakis and fatigues, as young matrons in the suburbs go shopping in their tennis dresses.

Known as the "University in Exile," the New School had taken in a lot of professors—Jewish and non-Jewish—who had fled from Hitler on the same boats as the psychoanalysts. Because they were displaced themselves, or angry with us for failing to understand history, the professors did their best to make us feel like exiles in our own country. While the psychoanalysts listened in their private offices—with all the detachment of those who had really known anxiety—to Americans retailing their dreams, the professors analyzed those same dreams wholesale in the packed classrooms of the New School.

All the courses I took were about *what's wrong*: what's wrong with the government, with the family, with interpersonal relations and intrapersonal relations —what's wrong with our dreams, our loves, our jobs, our perceptions and conceptions, our esthetics, the human condition itself.

They were furious, the professors, at the ugly turn the world had taken and they stalked the halls of the New School as if it were a concentration camp where we were the victims and they were the warders, the storm troopers of humanism. The building resounded with guttural cries: kunstwissenschaft, zeitgeist and weltanschauung, gemeinschaft and gesellschaft, schadenfreude, schwarmerei. Their accents were so impenetrable that some of them seemed to speak in tongues and the students understood hardly a word.

We admired the German professors. We had won the fight against fascism and now, with their help, we would defeat all the dark forces in the culture and the psyche. As a reaction to our victory, sensitive Americans had entered an apologetic phase in our national life and there was nothing the professors could say that was too much. We came out of class with dueling scars.

I took a course in the psychology of American culture, given by Erich Fromm. Though he had just arrived, he knew America better than we did, because it impinged on him. His *Escape from Freedom,* which had recently been published, was one of those paeans of lyrical pessimism that Germans specialize in, like Schopenhauer, Nietzsche, or Spengler. Sitting on a platform behind a desk, like a judge in criminal court, he passed his remorseless judgment on us. We were unwilling, he said, to accept the anguish of freedom. According to him, we feared freedom, saw it as madness, epistemology run amok. In the name of freedom, we accepted everything he said. We accepted it because we liked the sound of it—no one knew then that we would turn out to be right in trying to escape from freedom.

Fromm was short and plump. His jaws were broader than his forehead and he reminded me of a brooding hen. Yet, like everyone else, I sat spellbound through his lectures. I'll never forget the night he described a typical American family going for a pointless drive on a Sunday afternoon, joylessly eating ice cream at a roadhouse on the highway and then driving heavily home. Fromm was one of the first—perhaps the very first—to come out against pointlessness. It was a historic moment, like Einstein discovering relativity or Heidegger coming up against nothingness.

I also studied Gestalt psychology with Rudolf Arnheim, but here I confess I was disappointed. It seemed to me that Germans were sometimes stunned into a kind of stupor by an ordinary insight, which they would then try to elevate into a philosophy or a system. Colliding with a modest fact in the midst of their abstraction, they just couldn't get over it.

The Gestalt psychologists had discovered that the whole is greater than the sum of its parts—something everybody already knew—and Arnheim spent most of the semester demonstrating this. I kept waiting for him to go on, but he just gave us more experiments, more evidence. It all depended on rats. We never talked about people—only rats. In the advanced courses, it was apes.

Max Wertheimer, the father of Gestalt psychology, made a guest appearance in the class. He was a small man, dressed in a frock coat, and he wore his hair *en brosse*. The high point of his lecture was a demonstration of requiredness, a key term in Gestalt thinking. It meant, if I understood him, that each thing implied other things, or a context, something like a counterpoint of structures. He showed us what he meant with a little experiment of his own. First he taught us a complicated African hand clap, and then when he had us clapping away, he himself set up a weird howling accompaniment.

I attended a special lecture in the auditorium, given by Karen Horney, on the psychology of women. Like Fromm, Horney was a Freudian revisionist. In one of her books, she had said that, in a sense, the neurotic was healthier than the so-called normal person, because he "protested." Protesting was like testifying. Since everyone at the New School proudly considered him- or herself neurotic—it wasn't respectable not to be— Horney's message was just what we wanted to hear.

I don't remember much of the lecture, but it had an unforgettable aftermath. A woman with a fur coat draped over her shoulders rose from her seat and asked a question. But what about penis envy? she said. You haven't said anything about penis envy.

There was a shocked silence. It was like the time, when I was a child, that someone threw a stink bomb in a neighborhood movie house. Horney just sat there on the platform without speaking, gazing at the woman like an analyst contemplating a hopeless patient she had taken against her better judgment.

Her face seemed to swell. She raised one hand above her head and then the other, as if she would try to climb up out of the auditorium and the New School. Then, closing her hands into fists, she slammed them down on the desk. What about it? she said. Her voice rose to a shriek, What about it? I don't have a penis. Can you give me one?

Later, when I was back at the apartment, sitting in my usual chair and watching Sheri paint, I thought about Horney, and it seemed to me that there were lots of other, better things she could have said to the woman. She could have said, Why does everyone think it's so terrific to have a penis? I myself, for example, had a penis, but it didn't help me now to imagine what went on in Sheri's mind as she filled in a ragged area of the canvas with muddy green paint. It seemed to me that a penis was a very primitive instrument for dealing with life. Besides, Horney was wrong. Sheri did have a penis—mine belonged to her more than it did to me.

3

I hadn't been living with Sheri very long when Dick Gilman tried to take her away from me. There was nothing underhanded about Dick. He simply came over to the apartment one night and explained that I was not the right person for Sheri, and that he was.

His opening remarks were so elegant, so hermeneutic, that I didn't realize at first that he was talking about me. Dick hardly ever referred to real persons, and my initial impression was that he was describing an unsatisfactory character in a novel.

When I finally understood what he was doing, I was more surprised than angry, because I thought of Dick as a friend. This was no way for a friend to behave. Yet what he said sounded just like the friendly discussions of books we carried on in Washington Square or in the San Remo. And it was this blurring of the boundaries that confused me.

Dick was odd in a lot of ways. In his reading, for

example, he was a serial monogamist. He'd fall in love with a particular author and remain faithful to him alone, reading everything by and about him. He would become that author, talk like him, think like him, dress like him if possible. If he could find out what his current favorite had eaten and drunk, Dick would eat and drink them, too. He took on his politics, his causes, his eccentricities. At one point in his D. H. Lawrence phase—this was after his Yeats and Auden phases—Dick actually went to Mexico and tried to find Lawrence's footprints in the dust.

He was a very fast reader, so these affairs came and went fairly quickly. No author can survive that kind of identification for long. When he came to the apartment, Dick was still in his Lawrence phase, so perhaps he saw himself stealing Frieda from Ernest Weekley. Could it be that he had fallen for Sheri as he had for Lawrence and Yeats and Auden?

All the same, Dick was a formidable rival—a brilliant talker, an attractive man. He might even have been handsome if his face had not been just a bit vainglorious with all the books he'd read. As Harold Norse, a Village poet, said, "Dick was only twenty-one and he had read more books than Hemingway."

He had told me he was coming to see us and I had thought this meant he wanted to be better friends, because he was rather standoffish and had never visited us before. Now that he was here, I offered him a beer and asked him to take a chair, but he refused both, like a policeman who doesn't drink or sit down while on duty.

He began with a prologue, or prologomenon. He had examined his motives, he said, and was satisfied that they were disinterested. For a moment I thought he was going to say that, like art, he was a mirror held up to nature. What he did say was that I was not serious. There was, he said, an incongruity in my relation to Sheri. At that time we were all very much under the influence of the idea of incongruity in art. But while incongruity was good in art, it was, apparently, bad in life.

We were in the kitchen. Out of a kind of tact, Dick hadn't advanced farther into the apartment. I had taken a chair and Sheri leaned on the metal cover of the bathtub while Dick paced back and forth between the sink and the stove. Since they were only three or four steps apart, he kept whirling around. He was like a lecturer in front of a class, or a peripatetic philosopher. No doubt he had read Nietzsche, who said that the best thoughts come while walking.

Using words like *unconscionable,* he sounded as if he was recommending himself to Sheri more as a critic than a lover. He gesticulated a lot, chopping the air with stiffened fingers, like someone helping to park a car. He had a rather high, cracked voice—the voice of the brilliant talker—and I listened to it with a detached fascination as he explained, in effect, that his sensibility was bigger than mine.

How little he knew about us! He actually saw me as trifling with Sheri, taking advantage of her. As he went on, building his sentences, piling up clauses, I began to get angry. The hell with this, I thought. I ought to punch him in the mouth. But I couldn't. He had turned the situation into a seminar, and you can't punch people in a seminar. Besides, he talked so well—it would be like punching literature in the mouth. And he had a disarming way of appealing to me—to me!—to confirm a point. He was asking me to testify against myself.

Yet even though he addressed himself to me, I don't think he saw me as he marched back and forth ticking off my shortcomings. He was too caught up in his arguments. I was too—they were so persuasive that I began to believe them myself. Yes, I thought, it was probably true—I wasn't right for Sheri. She was too much for me. But that was why I wanted her, why I had to keep her. As Dick described the life she might have with him, I resolved that, if she stayed with me, I would do all the things he was enumerating.

At last, in a splendid peroration, Dick wound up with several striking tropes, like the final orchestral cadences of a classical symphony. He was breathing hard and smiling a little, as if at a job well done. It was impossible to be angry. God bless him, he thought of a woman as a kind of book.

In the silence that followed, it seemed to me that someone should have applauded. I looked at Sheri, who hadn't moved all this time. Her face was unreadable. She was a marvelous actress and knew how to hold the moment. Then, very deliberately, she changed her position a little in leaning on the bathtub, so that she was in an infinitesimally more nonchalant attitude. I was the first to catch on, and when I started laughing, Dick slammed out of the apartment. He could still be heard booming down the iron stairs when I lifted Sheri onto the bathtub cover.

When you look back over your life, the thing that amazes you most is your original capacity to believe.

To grow older is to lose this capacity, to stop believing, or to become unable to believe. When Nemecio Zanarte came to the apartment a couple of weeks later and repeated Dick's performance, I was able to believe at first that he too had simply been struck by Sheri, like Dick.

Nemecio was a Chilean painter. He was tall, dark, thin, and very handsome in the stark, suffering, aristocratic way that only pure Spaniards seem to have. His high, narrow nose and his deep eye sockets were as superbly carved as an El Greco portrait of a cardinal or pope. I imagined that even Nemecio's feet were beautiful, like Christ's in a twelfth-century painted wooden crucifixion.

His voice was soft, deep, and cultivated and his manners were a history of civilization. Yet here he was, like a priest of the Inquisition, invading what was now my home, telling me that, as a gentleman, it was my duty to remove myself and give Sheri her freedom. His English was not fluent and he said "give to Sheri her freedom."

I felt like a man being persecuted. While Dick might be explained as a kind of literary mistake—a misreading?—Nemecio could not. For this exquisitely polite man to do what he was doing, my failings must have been truly flagrant. What was it about me, I wondered, that inspired everyone to interfere in my life? Did I really behave so badly? Could it be that people actually saw Sheri as a quattrocento Madonna?

At least Nemecio had the decency to appear uncomfortable. Personally, he said, he was fond of me—it was not a question of that, but of symmetry. There was not the necessary symmetry between Sheri and myself. His long, graceful fingers moved as he spoke, as if he was trying on gloves. Everything he said could have come right out of Lorca, only his imperfect English spoiled the effect. "Why you don't go?" he said. "As a gentleman, you must go." He kept falling back on that "Why you don't go?" As a speaker, he was not in Dick's class.

He rambled and repeated himself; he seemed to be confused by emotion. His English began to slip and bits of Spanish seeped into his speech. I knew some Spanish, and his enunciation was so fine that I could make out most of what he said. On a certain level, in matters of love, honor, and conscience, all languages are similar.

Nemecio was much better in Spanish. He could make a moral drama of the word *consideración*. *Apesadumbrar,* which means "to afflict, vex, or grieve," was a beautiful word, too, but it was I, not Sheri, who was afflicted. And each time Nemecio used the word *caballero,* I wanted to say, But I am a *caballero sin caballo.*

I had studied Spanish in school and kept it alive in Spanish Harlem, where I used to go to the Park Plaza on 110th and Fifth to hear the music. When the band played a particularly good piece, the whole audience would cry, *¡Fenómeno!* or *¡Arrolla!*—which means "to gyrate or spin." Now, without thinking, I cried *¡Fenómeno! ¡Arrolla, hombre! ¡Así se habla!*

Nemecio looked at me in astonishment. He hadn't realized that I spoke Spanish, and this put an entirely different complexion on the matter. I was a compadre of sorts, a more civilized creature than he had supposed. He felt that it was impossible now to carry on the deception. His eyes turned to Sheri in a mute appeal. He looked like an exquisite dog, an Afghan or saluki.

Even I, blinded as I was by her, could see that she had put him up to it. After Dick, she got the idea of asking Nemecio too to come over and denounce me. She might even have encouraged Dick in the first place.

Nemecio gave up. He drooped like a flower. *Perdóneme,* Anatole, he said. I have been a fool.

It takes a brave man to be a fool, I said. I was so relieved that I grabbed his hand and squeezed it. And then he was gone.

Well, I thought, what now? On the bathtub cover again? No—absolutely not. I wasn't going to be played with like this. I refused to enter into the game. I refused for all of five minutes.

4

ive or six weeks after moving in with Sheri, I
opened a bookshop on Cornelia Street. This was
something I had decided to do while I was in the
army. It started with some money I made on the black
market in Tokyo, where a suit of GI long johns brought
$120. I was thinking about what I might do with the
money.

I was working the night shift in Yokohama harbor
and I was lonely, cold, and bored. Yokohama was a sad
place that had been flattened by bombs and the inhabitants were living in shacks made of rubble, propped up
in fields of rubble. Since they couldn't lock up these
shacks, they took all their belongings with them when
they went out. They carried their whole lives on their
backs, wrapped in an evil-smelling blanket or a sack
that made them look like hunchbacks.

My outfit, a stevedore battalion, had arrived right
after MacArthur, and my first job as a dock officer was

to scrape a solid crust of shit off a dock a quarter of a mile long. I didn't realize at first that it was human shit. As I figured it out later, Japanese stevedores and embarking soldiers had had no time for niceties toward the end and had simply squatted down wherever they stood. The entire dock was covered with a layer that was as hard as clay. The rain and traffic had packed it down.

I had my own company of 220 men to supervise the job and I was given 1,500 Japanese who would actually chop the stuff away. We provided them with axes, shovels, sledgehammers, picks, crowbars—whatever we could find. We had no bulldozers. They chopped and scraped for three days and then the Medical Corps hosed down the dock with chemicals.

It was on this same dock, where you could still smell the chemicals, that I was working the night I got the idea of the bookstore. I had two gangs unloading the forward hatches of a ship and I was leaning on the rail, under the yellowish overhead spots. It was about three o'clock in the morning and I felt a million miles from home, from anywhere. For something to do, I was thinking about books, trying to see if I could quote passages or whole poems the way some people can.

Mostly it was only single lines I remembered, perhaps because I was tired. Wallace Stevens was my favorite poet and I murmured a few scraps from his books to myself: "Too many waltzes have ended." "Apostrophes are forbidden on the funicular." "The windy sky cries out a literate despair." "These days of disinheritance we feast on human heads." It was reassuring to think, in the middle of the night in this foreign place, that there were people in the world who would take the trouble to write things like that. This was another, wonderful kind of craziness, at the opposite end from the craziness of the army.

We were unloading boxes of condensed milk and as I watched a pallet swing over the rail, I thought that when I got home I would open a bookshop in the Village. It would be a secondhand bookshop, specializing in twentieth-century literature. I remember that the idea made me feel warm. I took my hands out of my pockets and squeezed them together. To open a bookshop is one of the persistent romances, like living off the land or sailing around the world.

After a couple of months of looking, I bought out an old Italian junk dealer on Cornelia Street. I paid him three hundred dollars and agreed to move his stock to a new location. I hired a truck and we carried out old boilers, radiators, bathtubs, sinks, pipes of all sizes, and miscellaneous bits and pieces of metal.

Nineteen forty-six was a good time for a second-hand bookshop, because everything was out of print and the paperback revolution had not yet arrived. People had missed books during the war, and there was a sense of reunion, like meeting old friends or lovers. Now there was time for everything, and buying books became a popular postwar thing to do. For young people who had just left home to go live in the Village, books were like dolls or teddy bears or family portraits. They populated a room.

When I left Brooklyn to live in the Village, I felt as if I had acquired a new set of relatives, like a surprising number of uncles I had never met before, men who lived in odd places, sometimes abroad, who had shunned family life and been shunned in turn, who were somewhere between black sheep and prodigal sons of a paradoxical kind. An aura of scandal, or at least of ambiguity, hovered over these uncles, as if they had run away with someone's wife or daughter. There was a flaw in their past, some kind of unhealthiness, even a hint of insanity.

These uncles were, of course, my favorite authors, the writers I most admired. I felt them waiting, almost calling out to me. They were more real than anything I had ever known, real as only imagined things can be, real as dreams that seem so unbearably actual because they are cleansed of all irrelevances. These uncles, these books, moved into the vacuum of my imagination.

They were all the family I had now, all the family I wanted. With them, I could trade in my embarrassingly ordinary history for a choice of fictions. I could lead a hypothetical life, unencumbered by memory, loyalties, or resentments. The first impulse of adolescence is to wish to be an orphan or an amnesiac. Nobody in the Village had a family. We were all sprung from our own brows, spontaneously generated the way flies were once thought to have originated.

I didn't yet see the tragedy of my family: I still thought of them as a farce, my laughable past. In my new incarnation, in books I could be halfway heroic, almost tragic. I could be happy, for the first time, in my tragedy.

I realize that people still read books now and some people actually love them, but in 1946 in the Village our feelings about books—I'm talking about my friends and myself—went beyond love. It was as if we didn't know where we ended and books began. Books were our weather, our environment, our clothing. We didn't simply read books; we became them. We took them into ourselves and made them into our histories. While it would be easy to say that we escaped into books, it might be truer to say that books escaped into us. Books were to us what drugs were to young men in the sixties.

They showed us what was possible. We had been living with whatever was close at hand, whatever was given, and books took us great distances. We had known only domestic emotions and they showed us what happens to emotions when they are homeless. Books gave us balance—the young are so unbalanced that anything can make them fall. Books steadied us; it was as if we carried a heavy bag of them in each hand and they kept us level. They gave us gravity.

If it hadn't been for books, we'd have been completely at the mercy of sex. There was hardly anything else powerful enough to distract or deflect us; we'd have been crawling after sex, writhing over it all the time. Books enabled us to see ourselves as characters—yes, we were characters!—and this gave us a bit of control.

Though we read all kinds of books, there were only a handful of writers who were our uncles, our family. For me, it was Kafka, Wallace Stevens, D. H. Lawrence, and Celine. These were the books I liked, the books that I read, and they wouldn't fill more than a few shelves, so I went over to Fourth Avenue, which was lined with bookshops, and bought books by the titles, the subjects, the bindings, or the publishers. I was given a 20 percent dealer's discount and I thought I could charge my customers fifty cents or one dollar more for the pleasure of finding these books in a clean, well-lighted place. Although I had never read Balzac, I bought a fifty-volume uniform edition of his novels in a red binding with gold-edged pages. I got it for only nineteen dollars.

There were people in the Village who had more books than money, and I appealed to them in the literary quarterlies. Like someone buying a dog, I assured them that I'd give their books a good home. But it was an unhappy business, because many of these people suffered from separation anxiety. Those who were depressed by letting their books go tended to devaluate them, while others who were more in the hysterical mode asked such enormous sums that I knew it was their souls they were selling. Pricing an out-of-print book is one of the most poignant forms of criticism.

Seeing how young I was, everyone gave me advice. Get Christopher Caudwell, they said. Get Kenneth Burke, William Empson, F. R. Leavis, Paul Valéry. Get Nathanael West, Céline, Unamuno, Italo Svevo, Hermann Broch, *The Egyptian Book of the Dead.* Edward Dahlberg, Baron Corvo, Djuna Barnes—get them too. But above all, at any cost, I must get Kafka. Kafka was as popular in the Village at that time as Dickens had been in Victorian London. But his books were very difficult to find—they must have been printed in very small editions—and people would rush in wild-eyed, almost foaming at the mouth, willing to pay anything for Kafka.

Literary criticism was enjoying a vogue. As Randall Jarrell said, some people consulted their favorite critic about the conduct of their lives as they had once consulted their clergymen. The war had left a bitter taste, and literary criticism is the art of bitter tastes.

A thin, intense young man with a mustache came into the shop and instructed me in bibliophilic etiquette. A bookshop, he said, should have an almost ecclesiastical atmosphere. There should be an odor, or redolence, of snuffed candles, dryness, desuetude—even contrition. He gazed at the shelves, the floor, the stamped tin ceiling. It's too clean here, he said, too cheerful.

I had imagined myself like Saint Jerome in his study, bent over his books, with the tamed lion of his conquered restlessness at his feet. My customers would come and go in studious silence, pausing, with averted eyes, to leave the money on my desk. But it didn't turn out like that. What I hadn't realized was that, for many people, a bookshop is a place of last resort, a kind of moral flophouse. Many of my customers were the kind of people who go into a bookshop when all other diversions have failed them. Those who had no friends, no pleasures, no resources came to me. They came to read the handwriting on the wall, the bad news. They studied the shelves like people reading the names on a war memorial.

There was something in the way a particular person would take a book from a shelf, the way it was opened and sniffed, that made me want to snatch it away. Others would seize upon a book that was obviously beyond them. I could tell by their faces, their clothes, by their manners, the way they moved, that they'd misread the book or get nothing out of it. The kind of person who is satirized or attacked in a book is often the very person to buy it and pretend to enjoy it. As Mallarmé said, "If a person of average intelligence and insufficient literary preparation opens one of my books and pretends to enjoy it, there has been a mistake. Things must be returned to their places."

It was the talkers who gave me the most trouble. Like the people who had sold me books, the talkers wanted to sell me their lives, their fictions about themselves, their philosophies. Following the example of the authors on the shelves, infected perhaps by them, they told me of their families, their love affairs, their illusions and disillusionments. I was indignant. I wanted to say, Wait a minute! I've already got stories here! Take a look at those shelves!

While I pretended to listen, I asked myself which were more real—theirs, or the stories on the shelves. "The familiar man makes the hero artificial," Wallace Stevens said. In the commonplaceness of their narratives, some of these talkers anticipated the direction that American fiction would eventually take—away from the heroic, the larger than life, toward the ordinary, the smaller than life.

As they talked on, I thought of all the junk I had carried out of the shop—the boilers, bathtubs, and radiators. These people were bringing it all back—all the clutter, the cast-off odds and ends of their lives. It was more than I had bargained for. Literature was tough enough, with its gaudy sadness, but this miscellany—these heartaches off the street—was too much for me. In the contest between life and literature, life wins every time.

5

Sheri took me to see Anaïs Nin, who lived in the
Village at that time. According to her diary, which
was published years later, Anaïs had spiritually
adopted Sheri, describing her as the ghost of her own
younger self. She spoke of Sheri as a disciple. "So they
come," she wrote, "out of the stories, out of the novels,
magnetized by affinities, by similar characters." Sheri
was "an orphaned child of poverty . . . pleading, hurt,
vulnerable, breathless." "She talks as I write, as if I had
created a language for her feelings."

Anaïs' apartment was a top-floor walk-up on Thirteenth Street. Everyone Sheri knew lived on top floors,
probably because it was cheaper, but I thought of them
as struggling to get to the light. Besides Anaïs and her
husband, Ian Hugo, a pleasant, self-effacing man, there
was a young couple whose names I no longer remember. The young man held a guitar across his knees, but
you could see that he would never play it, that it was

just part of a composition, like the guitars in Cubist paintings.

Though I hadn't yet read anything by Anaïs, I'd heard of her. It was said that she and Henry Miller had once lived on a houseboat on the Seine. Later I would learn that she had attracted Otto Rank, who allegedly trained her as a psychoanalyst, and who asked her to rewrite his almost unreadable books. In New York she had an odd acquaintance with Edmund Wilson. After Mary McCarthy left him, he developed a crush on Anaïs and took her to his apartment, which Mary had stripped of furniture. When he reviewed one of her novels, you could see him struggling between his desire and his taste. As usual, though, she had the last word in her diary. Summarizing their evening together, she said, "He wanted me to help him reconstruct his life, to help him choose a couch. . . . But I wanted to leave."

Anaïs was a medium-sized woman with a very pale face, like a Japanese actress. She was classical-looking, in the sense of a form that has become rigidified. Her hair was dark, straight, parted in the middle and pulled back. Her lipstick was precise, her eyebrows shaved off and penciled in, giving the impression that she had written her own face. Her figure was trim but without elasticity, its movements willed and staccato. She was pretty in the way of women in old black-and-white movies. There was a suggestion of the vamp about her, and, in fact, she was later to become a kind of Theda Bara of modern literature.

It was impossible to guess her age. Her teeth looked false and her face had the arbitrary smoothness of one that had been lifted, but I thought this unlikely. It was possible she lifted it herself by the sheer force of her will.

35

Yet she was impressive in her way, an evocative figure. She reminded me of the melancholy Paris hotels of expatriate writing and I could imagine her, wearing an ambiguous fur, sitting defiantly, or insouciantly, in a café. While I could not imagine her in bed with Henry Miller, that may have been his fault.

There was an aura about her, a sense that she was holding a séance. The atmosphere was charged with her energy. When she gave me her hand and looked searchingly into my eyes, I could feel her projecting an image of herself, one that was part French, part flamenco, part ineffable. When she said, You are Anatole, I immediately became Anatole in a way I hadn't been before.

As I listened to her talk—for it was understood that she did most of the talking, even if it was to ask us questions—it occurred to me that she and Sheri deformed their speech as Chinese women used to deform their feet. Her talk was pretty much like the things she wrote in her diaries. An entry from this time gives a good idea of what she sounded like: "Think of the ballet exercises. The hand reproduces resistance to water. And what is painting but absolute transparency? It is art which is ecstasy, which is Paradise, and water." Here's another: "It is possible I never learned the names of birds in order to discover the bird of peace, the bird of paradise, the bird of the soul, the bird of desire."

Her conversation flirted with all the arts and settled on none, like someone who doesn't really want to buy a book browsing in a bookshop. I was careful about what I said, because I could see that Anaïs was important to Sheri. I was afraid of coming out with something literal-minded, like, Were you bothered by rats when you lived on the houseboat?

Though Anaïs described Sheri in her diary as a "figure out of the past," I thought that Sheri was a later, not an earlier, version. Anaïs was already out of style, and Sheri was just coming in. Anaïs was like someone at a party, dancing, drinking, and batting her eyes, and Sheri was the morning after the party. Anaïs was unconscious of the picture she made, and Sheri was all consciousness. While Sheri was always listening to herself, always rehearsing and revising, Anaïs had already posed for her statue. She had posed for it without knowing where it would be put up.

Sheri too was watching herself more than she usually did, if that was possible, perhaps because she felt the pull of Anaïs, the temptation to be "magnetized by affinities." With all this doublethinking, with no one simply speaking up, the conversation grew so stilted that Anaïs was forced to bring out a bottle of wine. With a sudden swoop, she deposited the bottle in my hands, together with an old-fashioned corkscrew. The look she gave me made it clear that this was to be a test of sorts—but of what?

I had no choice but to accept the challenge. In what I hoped was a confident, heterosexual manner, I applied myself firmly, but with an ironic awareness, to drawing the cork. When the screw was all the way in, I pulled slowly and steadily on the handle. I did all the usual things, and I did them in slow motion, so it came as a rude shock to me when the handle broke off.

It simply came away in my hand. I was holding the bottle with the screw in one hand and the wooden stump in the other. My first thought was, It's not my fault. I did it right. She can't blame me. Then I tried to fit the handle back on while Anaïs leaned forward and watched me. Was it a trick? I wondered. A Surrealist or

Dadaist joke? She was smiling, as if I had confirmed her intuition about me. I knew that whatever I did, I would confirm her intuition.

I wanted to fling the bottle against the wall, but she was already pressing another corkscrew into my hand, an identical one. I didn't want it, but I didn't see any way of refusing. I gave the thing a little preliminary twist in the air, just to see whether it would hold together. The original screw was still in place and with some trouble I managed to get it out. Then I worked the new one in, even more deliberate now. It took me five minutes to get it all the way in. I turned it evenly, so as not to put any unnecessary stress on the handle.

I pulled very gradually, gently at first, then more strongly. Nothing happened. The cork didn't budge. I couldn't imagine why not—it wasn't as if this was an ancient bottle of wine that had been sealed by time itself. To get a better purchase, I put the bottle on the floor between my feet.

What came next still seems incredible to me. Sometimes I think it didn't actually happen, that my memory is playing tricks. But it did happen: Before my eyes, I saw the corkscrew slowly emerge from the cork. It didn't break off; the cork didn't crumble. The screw simply straightened out, so that I was holding in my hand something that resembled an ice pick.

I felt like a person in a dream. I shook myself, tried to collect my wits, to stop the blush that was rising to my face. What should I have done? What would Henry Miller have done in my place? Otto Rank? Edmund Wilson?

Anaïs took the bottle and the corkscrew and put them on a table. Perhaps she had never meant for it to be opened. She turned and looked at me through narrowed eyes. I can see, she said, that you are a most interesting young man.

In her diary, there was nothing about the corkscrews, but I was described as "handsome, sensual, ironic." I wasn't fooled: All the young men in her diary were handsome, sensual, and ironic.

6

L iving with Sheri was a process of continual adjustment. It was like living in a foreign city: You learn
the language, the currency, the style of the people.
You find out how to make a phone call, how to take
the subway, where the stores and restaurants are, the
parks, the public pissoirs, the post office. You try to
feel like a native, not a foreigner; you progress from
grammar to idioms in an attempt to talk as if you belonged. Still, you never succeed in feeling at home. You
remain a visitor, perhaps only a tourist.

There was always something else, something more,
another even larger adjustment to be made. She would
come out with a new twist that meant I had to start all
over. When she announced one day that she had a bad
heart, it was as if she had been saving this for last.

It was nighttime and we were in bed. She grew very
inventive at night; she ran through in a rush all the day's
unused possibilities, the leftovers of her sensibility. I

was almost asleep when she came out with her revelation: You know, I have a bad heart.

Of course, I didn't take in at first what she was saying. There was no context for it, no natural leading up. Just You know, I have a bad heart, as if she was saying, Good night, or Move over a little. It was dark and statements in the dark are different.

Also, I never knew whether she was speaking literally or figuratively. As I've already mentioned, she liked to talk in metaphors. I've never known anyone who used so many figures of speech. So when she said, I have a bad heart, I thought she meant as opposed to a good heart, a bad heart as in bad faith, a hard or black heart, a disloyal heart.

She liked to make me work at interpreting her. Not knowing exactly what she meant, I would give her credit for things she had never even thought of. It was like when I used to read Surrealist poetry in French— I imagined all sorts of marvels until I began to use a dictionary.

I was half asleep. We had made love and I was feeling empty, or, rather, *filled* with emptiness, replete with it. But I roused myself and tried to think—not about what she said but what was *behind* it, what she was driving at. I've always been rather literal-minded and it's one of the things I'm ashamed of, as some men are ashamed of the size of their penis.

Why do you think it's bad? I said. Do you feel you're getting softhearted?

I must be careful about climbing stairs, she said. The doctor thinks stairs are dangerous.

Doctor? I said. What doctor? What are we talking about?

I'm telling you, she said, that I have a bad heart. It's defective, wanting, imperfect. The doctor advises me to avoid undue exertion.

My first thought was that I represented undue exertion—we had, in fact, just been exerting ourselves—and that we must put an end to it. But then I heard what she had been saying. You mean you're sick? There's something wrong—actually wrong—with you?

That is what I have been trying to tell you.

But why didn't you tell me before? How long have you known this? I got all excited. I wanted her to get a second opinion, to see a heart specialist, but she said she had already done all that. What it came down to, she said, was that her heart was simply different from other people's hearts.

And so I entered upon still another adjustment. I made Sheri my burden. From then on, whenever we went anywhere, whenever we came back to the apartment, I carried her up the stairs. I delivered her, conveyed her. I became her porter as well as her lover. I was even ready to carry her down the stairs, but she said it wasn't necessary.

At first, before I was used to it, she was surprisingly heavy, in spite of her slenderness. You might say that she was metaphysically heavy. I think too that she made herself go limp, a deadweight. She threw her head back, like the women you see being abducted in romantic paintings.

The hardest part was when we went to see people. Many of her friends were painters who lived on top floors in order to get the light. When we arrived, after four or five flights, I would be red-faced and breathless, unable to speak. Because we hadn't told people about her heart, they wondered about me. They thought we had been doing something in the hallway. I began to get a reputation.

After the first shock of her announcement, it seemed almost natural to me that she should have a bad heart. Her rib cage was so narrow. I put my ear to it and listened. While I imagined ordinary hearts to have a beat like bad rock music, Sheri's heartbeat was more like a Chopin étude, a desultory or absentminded strumming.

I had never thought of her as physically strong. Even though her legs and thighs were solid and full, her body seemed to lead a hazardous life, to have a determined fragility. She did not walk—she floated, and none of her movements made any concession to gravity. When I thought about it, it seemed to me that the human heart was a very primitive instrument, a poor piece of plumbing, for such a complicated, arrhythmical creature. It was such a garish, representational thing to have inside her abstract chest—it was as ugly as the velvet bleeding-heart medals I had admired so much when I was a Catholic child in New Orleans.

I enjoyed carrying her. For a few moments she was in my power. And I liked the idea that she was portable. I began to think of love as weight. When I had her in my arms she seemed more tangible, more palpable. If I wanted to, I could throw her down the stairs, or over the rail.

Our lovemaking changed. The need to be gentle introduced an insidious erotic complication. I inserted myself stealthily, like a burglar. I became a sleep-crawler. In one of his lectures at the New School, Gregory Bateson had told us about a South Pacific tribe that practiced what they called sleepcrawling. The sleep-crawler, or *moetotolo,* visited his lover in her own hut in the middle of the night. This was a tribe that slept in straw baskets to keep away mosquitoes, and the *moetotolo* had to squeeze into the girl's basket and perform without making any noise. The whole family slept in one room, and if the *moetotolo* was discovered, he would be severely beaten.

I too became a *moetotolo,* performing under duress. Feeling like a killer, explosive as a rocket, enormous, I recoiled my passions back into my own body. My desire rebounded with such an impact that I feared for my own heart.

7

It may have been the German professors at the New School who put the idea in my head—I don't know —but, for whatever reason, I decided to be psychoanalyzed. In New York City in 1946, there was an inevitability about psychoanalysis. It was like having to take the subway to get anywhere. Psychoanalysis was in the air, like humidity, or smoke. You could almost smell it. The whole establishment had moved to New York in a counterinvasion, a German Marshall Plan.

The war had been a bad dream that we wanted to analyze now. It was as if we had been unconscious for three or four years. Once the war was over, we began making private treaties with ourselves. We demanded nothing less than unconditional surrender from life, or to it. There was a feeling that we had forgotten how to live, that the requirements would be different now. Also, I still had some of the money from my black-market dealings in Tokyo. It was found money, so I thought I would spend it in the black market of personality.

Most people went into analysis because they were unhappy—or at least they thought they were. Yet as far as I knew, I was not unhappy. In fact, it appeared to me that I had just about everything I wanted. But I was like an immigrant who goes from a poor country to a rich one and can't quite believe in his new prosperity. I distrusted my happiness—it seemed too easy and I was afraid it might be simply a failure of consciousness. My imagination itched and I had nothing to scratch.

Could it be, I asked myself, that I was happy under false pretenses? Or that I was mistaking sheer youthfulness, pure energy, for happiness?

There was something else, too, almost too vague to describe, like a shadow on my happiness. I was aware of something like static in my head, a sense that some part of me was resisting, or proceeding under protest. There was a dissonant hum or crackle, a whispering in my molecules. My nerves—I suppose it was my nerves —gave off a high, faint whirring, like the sound that billions of insects make in the tropics at night. It was a disturbance as remote as grinding your teeth in your sleep. Or it was as if my brain had something stuck in its teeth. It may have been merely the friction of consciousness, but I chose to see it as a symptom.

It reminded me, this whirring, of the sound of an AC-DC converter. A lot of the tenement apartments in the Village had these converters, because the buildings were originally on direct current and they'd never been changed over. Since most appliances ran on alternating current, you had to get a converter, a machine about the size of a hatbox. You could pick up a secondhand one for about thirty-five dollars.

The trouble with them was that they made a noise, not a loud noise but a penetrating one. People put their converters in closets, but you could still hear them whirring or grinding in there. I used to think of the sound they made as the complaint of cheap apartments, like Lorca's "pain of kitchens." The static or whirring in my head was the sound of my converter. But what was I trying to convert? And how could I bring it out of the closet?

One night after class I spoke to Dr. Fromm. I asked him to recommend an analyst, hoping he would take me himself. But he didn't; he sent me instead to Ernest Schachtel, who taught a course in Rorschach interpretation at the New School.

Dr. Schachtel looked like Paul Klee—or at least like a photograph I had seen of him. It pleased me to imagine I was about to be analyzed by Paul Klee. Schachtel was thin, well-dressed, delicate-looking, almost nervous. He impressed me as the sort of man who read Schiller, Heine, and Kleist, who listened to Schubert and Mahler. His expression was melancholy and I supposed he had suffered during the war. What was it like, I wondered, to leave your own country for another, where all you met was the unhappiness and confusion of the people who lived there? Suppose when Americans went to Paris or Florence, the waiters, hotel clerks, and taxi drivers told them their dreams, their fears and nameless angers.

In Dr. Schachtel's apartment on the Upper West Side, there was just a touch of Bauhaus. His furniture was light, almost fragile, and it occurred to me that when Germans weren't heavy, they were often fragile. Like Fromm and Horney, he was revisionist, and that was what I wanted, to be revised. I saw myself as a first draft.

I was not asked to lie on a couch, which disappointed me a little because I had been looking forward to talking like someone lying in bed or in a field of grass. Instead we sat face-to-face, about eight feet apart, an arrangement that had a peculiar affect on me. I couldn't get away from the feeling that it was not I who was being analyzed but my face, which was huge, gaping.

Another thing that made me uncomfortable was the fact that Dr. Schachtel avoided meeting my eyes. His eyes would travel all around the room, as if he heard a fly buzzing and was idly trying to locate it. I thought of his eyes as following a line of dots, like the path they are supposed to take in looking at a painting. When he did turn to me, it was an unfocused, generic sort of look, a skimming glance that slid off the surface of my face.

I supposed he did this for clinical reasons, so as not to distract me, but the lack of contact was just as distracting. It was like playing a game of tag or blindman's buff. Ordinarily, I would have looked away myself, averting my own gaze from what I was saying, but as soon as I saw him avoiding my eyes, I began to chase his.

I don't remember what I talked about in the first hour, because my main concern was not to bore Dr. Schachtel. I was terribly afraid of boring him. I had an unreasonable desire to avoid saying anything he had heard before, which made it almost impossible for me to speak. A successful analysis, I imagined, was one in which you never bored your analyst. In avoiding boredom, you transcended yourself and were cured. I had come there not to free myself of repressions but to develop better ones.

Dr. Schachtel's face was composed in a concentrated neutrality, the outer reflection of what Freud called free-floating attention. Yet it seemed to me that his attention floated too freely, that I didn't sufficiently attract it. Judging by his expression, he was thinking of something else—a poem by Rilke, or a passage by Theodor Lipps on *Einfuhlung*.

It wasn't until our second session—and only at the very end of the hour—that I discovered what I really wanted to talk about. I had been twenty minutes late and Dr. Schachtel appeared to be upset by this. I told him that I had left the bookshop and gone home to change. I used to put on a jacket and tie to see him, because my relation to my personality was still formal at that time. What I didn't tell him was that Sheri had been in the apartment and she had deliberately decoyed me into bed. She knew I would end by talking about her and she wanted to introduce herself in her own way.

I felt shy about telling him the real reason I was late —it was too recent, still warm—so I began talking about the whirring or grinding sound in my head. I used the word *stridulation,* and as Dr. Schachtel was not familiar with it, I treated him to a dissertation on galvanic sounds.

He said nothing, and his eyes roamed the room. He was bored, I thought. He knew all about me without being told—I was as easy to read as a Rorschach blot. I felt I had to do something to redeem myself, but the hour was almost over. I looked at my watch—it was over. I got up and walked to the door. Dr. Schachtel rose, too, which was his way of saying goodbye. I had my hand on the knob, but I couldn't leave. To leave now would have been like leaving my personality scattered all over the floor, like the Sunday *Times*. I hadn't come through, hadn't *worked*. I couldn't bear my own image of myself and I searched for a punch line that would allow me to go in peace.

I looked at Dr. Schachtel standing beside his chair in a fragile, unathletic European way. I'm disappointed in love, I said. And before he could answer or choose not to answer, I was gone.

At my next session, I tried to take it back. I don't know why I said that, I told Dr. Schachtel. I suppose I wanted to make myself important. In fact, my relation to Sheri is just the opposite of disappointing. You might almost say that it's too satisfying.

How are you disappointed? Dr. Schachtel said.

I don't know that I am disappointed, I said. I just blurted that out. Everyone wants to see himself as disappointed—it's the influence of modern art.

Dr. Schachtel resisted the temptation to be drawn into a discussion of modern art, and there was nothing for me to do but to go on. As far as I can see, I said, I have no reason to be disappointed. Yet something doesn't feel right. I don't feel that my happiness is *mine*. It's like I'm happy outside of myself.

What it is you want that you don't have? Dr. Schachtel asked.

I hesitated. I felt like a high jumper poised for his run. And just at that moment, I caught Dr. Schachtel's eyes. They were shuttling across the room, following

50

some secret trajectory of their own, when I caught them and held them as if I had grabbed him by the lapels. It was too good an opportunity to waste. I want to be transfigured, I said.

I don't know whether he was surprised by this, but I was. I had never even used the word *transfiguration* before, as far as I could remember, never thought about it. I didn't know what I meant by it, yet I knew that it was true, that it described how I felt. When I came out with the word, I was like someone who sneezes into a handkerchief and finds it full of blood.

In novels, I said, people are transfigured by love. They're elevated, made different, lifted out of their ordinariness. Think of the men in D. H. Lawrence's novels. Think of Hans Castorp in *The Magic Mountain* —you probably read it in German. They're no longer schoolteachers or engineers or whatever they were before, but heroic figures. They're exalted; they're blessed.

I supposed, I said, that love would change me, too, would *advance* me somehow. Because without that, it's just sex, just mechanics. And while sex is fine—it's wonderful; it can be like flying—it isn't enough. It doesn't explain, doesn't *justify* the whole business. It can't account for two thousand years of poetry, for all the laughing and crying. There has to be something else, something more. Otherwise, love wouldn't be so famous; we wouldn't be carrying on about it all the time. *It wouldn't be worth the trouble.*

I stopped for breath. Dr. Schachtel's eyes had escaped and I couldn't catch them again. I was confused. I felt that I was back on the deck of a ship in Yokohama harbor talking to myself under the yellow lights. It's

51

not so much to ask, I said. I just want love to live up to its publicity.

I saw Dr. Schachtel eleven times. He was intelligent, astute, even charming, but I never gave him a chance. I suppose that like a good analyst he wanted to see my personality grow, while what I needed was for it to be shrunk to a more manageable size. It was much too big for me.

I insisted on presenting my problems, such as they were, in the abstract, and the abstractions of psycho-analysis were no match for mine. How can I distinguish, I asked Dr. Schachtel, between anxiety and desire? Is sex a defense against art? Is disappointment inevitable, like the death instinct?

What I brought to Dr. Schachtel was not a condition or a situation but a poetics. I wanted to discuss my life with him not as a patient talking to an analyst but as if we were two literary critics discussing a novel. Of course, that's what all patients want, but the irony was that with me it might have worked. It might have been the shortest, or the only, way through my defenses, because I had a literature rather than a personality, a set of fictions about myself.

8

One night while we were making love, Sheri screamed. She had never screamed before, and it took me by surprise. It was a loud scream, right in my face, which was close to hers. Her mouth opened very wide and I could see all the way to the back of her throat, to her uvula. I saw the fillings in her teeth, the far end of her tongue, the shiny red inside of her cheeks.

Her eyes were open, looking at me while she screamed. I thought I must have done something wrong. What's the matter? I said. Are you all right? I knew that women sometimes screamed while making love, but she had never screamed before, and besides, it wasn't like her. I thought I might have hurt her and I stopped what I was doing, even though it was nothing special or unusual. I could have hit a sensitive spot, or maybe she wasn't feeling well.

Is something the matter? I asked, but of course

she didn't answer. She didn't *believe* in questions. But what was I supposed to do? Did she want me to keep on, or stop? I didn't want to stop—I was too far in to stop.

I began again, very gently, hardly moving—and she screamed again. It occurred to me that the neighbors could hear her. I would see those screams in their eyes when we met in the hallway or on the street. But why should she start screaming now? When would I come to the end of her originality? Also, there was something odd about her screams, something not quite right. They were not like the screams you hear in movies, cries torn from the throat. I remembered Fay Wray in *King Kong*—she was a lusty screamer.

Most screams are wide-open vowel sounds—*ah, oh,* or *ee*—that come up from the diaphragm. They're raw and unmodulated, which is why they're startling. But Sheri's screams were not like that. She screamed up in her sinuses, like a factory whistle. It was a blue note, a diphthong.

Her voice sounded hoarse, and I thought of the hoarse cry of the peacock, a phrase from a book. I remembered a line from a Surrealist poem: "The hyena's oblong cry." That's the way my mind was tending.

Sheri's face when she screamed was not screwed up around the eyes or distorted. It was only her mouth that screamed. She wasn't like the girl in the Munch painting whose scream occupies her whole face. Sheri looked as if she was gargling. She let the scream out like an alarm clock that goes off when you can't remember why you set it.

Maybe her screams were meant as a riddle or conun-

drum. Perhaps she was punctuating unspoken sentences. Anything was possible.

It also seemed to me that they were a bit stale, her
screams. I got the feeling that she was palming off on
me some secondhand screams left over from her old
life, her inscrutable past. This is what I was thinking as
I lay there, half in, half out.

9

For most of the people in Meyer Schapiro's class at the New School, art was the truth about life—and life itself, as they saw it, was more or less a lie. Art, modern art, was a great, intense, but at the same time vague promise or threat, depending on how you looked at it. If civilization could be thought of as having a sexuality, art was its sexuality.

With the dim stained-glass light of the slides and the hushed atmosphere, Schapiro's classes were like church services. Culture in those days was still holy. If he had chosen his own church, it would have been Romanesque—yet there was something fundamentalist in him, too. He made you want to get up and testify, or beat a tambourine.

I went to him as students twenty years later would go to India. I wanted to believe in something, anything, to become a member of a cult. My family had been neither religious nor cultivated and, coming from New

Orleans, we had always been outsiders in New York. At Brooklyn College, everyone had been a Communist but me.

Modern painting was one more exclusion, one more mystery from which I was shut out. I used to feel this way when people talked about politics, but I didn't mind so much because I wasn't interested in politics. And besides, I secretly thought I was right. I thought that being a Communist was a penalty you had to pay for being interested in politics. It was the adolescence of politics, an awkward stage you had to pass through. But when it came to modern art, I was afraid that maybe the others were right, that I would never be hip or sophisticated, would never belong. I'd never know that smug sense of being of my time, being contemporary.

Perhaps this sounds like a fuss over nothing, but when you're young, everything matters, everything is serious. And besides, I was living with a modern painter, I slept with modern painting. The life we led depended on modern art. Without that, all we had was a dirty apartment.

There were all sorts of stories about Schapiro. It was rumored that the first time he went to Paris he never sat in a café or walked beside the Seine, but spent all his time in museums and libraries. It probably wasn't true, but it fitted him, this story. Reading had turned him into a saint or angel of scholarship, but in some ways I suspected that he was a martyr too, a Saint Sebastian shot through with arrows of abstraction. A rival critic said that Schapiro loved not paintings but the explanations they made possible, and that he valued a painting in proportion to the ingenuity you needed to appreciate it.

Schapiro was about forty at the time. He was a slender, medium-sized man with a classically handsome Semitic face, bony and ascetic, but lit up like a saint's or a martyr's. He wore, as far as I can remember, the same suit all the time, a single-breasted gray herringbone, and he had two neckties.

Like many educated New York City Jews of his generation, Schapiro dentalized his consonants—or perhaps he had a slight lisp that he tried to overcome—and this gave his speech a sibilance, as if he was whispering, or hissing, secrets. The impression of secrecy was increased by the fact that he didn't seem to be talking to us, but to the paintings themselves, like a man praising a woman's beauty to her.

Sometimes he was so brilliant that he seemed almost insane to me; he seemed to see more than there actually was—he heard voices. His knowledge was so impressive as to appear occult. Because he chanted his lectures, he was like a medieval cantor or Gregorian monk.

We were so awed by him that when he said something witty, we were afraid to laugh. It was like the German translators taking the puns out of Shakespeare on the assumption that he had not written them, that they had been added by hacks. I wonder now whether Schapiro ever noticed how tense we were, how pious. Did he realize that students were dropping out all the time, to be replaced by other students?

They didn't drop out because he was disappointing —in fact, it might have been better if he had disappointed us now and then. What drove even his admirers away was a certain remorselessness in his brilliance. It made some of us anxious to think that everything meant something; there was no escape. It was like a fate.

Perhaps the things he said have now become commonplaces of art criticism, but at the time they were revelations to me. And of course he talked about painters like van Gogh, Cézanne, and Picasso, who are old masters today. Then, only forty years ago, they were revolutionaries; we still believed in revolutions.

I remember Schapiro telling us that before Cézanne, there had always been a place in landscape painting where the viewer could walk into the picture. There was an entrance; you could go there, like walking into a park. But this was not true of Cézanne's landscapes, which were cut off absolutely, abstracted from their context. You could not walk into them—you could enter them only through art, by leaping.

Schapiro said that when van Gogh loaded his palette with pigment he couldn't afford, he was praying in color. He put his anxiety into pigment, slapped color into its cheeks. Color was salvation. It had to be thick, and tangible.

One night I smuggled Sheri into the class. It was easy because of all the turnover and the flurry of enthusiasm. The room sloped like a theater and we sat up in the back. Schapiro was going to talk about Picasso, and the place was jammed, with people crouching on the steps in the aisle. Picasso was a perfect subject because there was so much to explain.

Schapiro spoke rapidly, rhythmically, hardly pausing for breath. When he said that with *Les Demoiselles d'Avignon* Picasso had fractured the picture plane, I could hear it crack, like a chiropractor cracking the bones at the base of your neck. As he went on, Schapiro's sentences became staccato, cubistic, full of overlapping planes. I was so excited that I took Sheri's hand in mine.

I felt myself gaining confidence. It was such a relief

to me to know that art could be explained. If I couldn't love art for itself, I could love it, like Schapiro, for the explanations. It was better than never to have loved at all.

He was discussing an early still life of Picasso's, an upended table covered with a white cloth, a bowl of flowers, and a bottle of wine, all paradoxically suspended in space. What we were seeing, Schapiro said, was the conversion of the horizontal plane—the plane of our ordinary daily traversal of life—into an intimate vertical surface of random manipulation.

His voice rose to a cry. He honked like a wild goose. There was delirium in the room. The beam of the projector was a searchlight on the world. The students shifted in their seats and moaned. Schapiro danced to the screen and flung up his arm in a Romanesque gesture. As he spoke, the elements of the picture reassembled themselves into an intelligible scheme. A thrill of gladness ran through me and my hand sweated in Sheri's.

And then we were hurrying down the aisle, stepping over murmuring bodies in the half-light of the screen. We were in the hallway on the second floor, running up the stairs.

On the roof of the New School, there was a deep purplish glow, a Picasso color, the swarthy light that settles on great cities at night. The wind lifted Sheri's hair, but it was not cold for October. The world was warmed by art, like fire.

A low skylight rose up out of the roofline. It was dimmed, an empty studio. The near side was perpendicular, and then it sloped away. Sheri leaned over it, so that the upper part of her body, her head, arms, and shoulders, sprawled down the slope and her sex pointed at the sky. I paused to take a breath and allow my heart to beat. It's a perfect world, I thought, if you understand it. I let the wind pass over us while Sheri gleamed in the dark. When I connected myself to her, we were the chance meeting, on an operating table, of a sewing machine and an umbrella. We converted the horizontal plane into an intimate vertical surface of random manipulation.

10

When I moved in with Sheri, I assumed that now my adult sexual life would begin. Until then, my experience had been limited to what I thought of as collegiate episodes and wartime acts. Now I imagined myself plunging into sex, diving into a great density of things to do. I felt like a person who is about to go abroad for the first time.

But what actually happened was that Sheri and I began not at the beginning, as I had hoped, but at the end of sex. We arrived immediately at a point where, if we had gone any further, what we did would have had to be called by some other names—yoga, mime, chiropractic, or isometrics. We were like lovers in a sad futuristic novel where sex is subjected to a revolutionary program.

Sex has traditionally been associated with joy, which is an old-fashioned, almost Dickensian notion—but Sheri understood, as we do today, that sex belongs to depression as much as to joy. She knew that it is a place where all sorts of expectations and illusions come to die. Two people making love, she once said, are like one drowned person resuscitating the other.

Sometimes I thought of sex was a flight from art, a regression to instinct, but there was no escaping art when I was in bed with Sheri. She reminded me of some lines Wallace Stevens wrote about Picasso. How should you walk in that space, Stevens asked, and know nothing of the madness of space, nothing of its jocular procreations? For Sheri, sex was like space, the jocularity of space. It was a foyer to madness, a little picnic of madness. In her more benign moments, when she was feeling almost sentimental, she was Duchamp's *Nude Descending a Staircase*. She *descended* into my arms. Like art, sex with her was a shudder of hypotheses, a debate between being and nonbeing, between affirmation and denial, optimism and pessimism, illusion and reality, coming and going.

Most people would say that lovemaking is a defense against loneliness, but with Sheri it was an investigation of loneliness, a safari into its furthest reaches. She had a trick of suspending me at a high point of solitariness, when I was in the full flow of that self-absorption that comes over you as you enter the last stages of the act. She would stall or stymie my attempts to go ahead and finish—she'd hold me there, freeze me there, as if to say, See how alone you are! And then I would float above her, and above myself, like an escaped balloon.

Sex with Sheri was full of wreckage. It was like a tenement that has been partly demolished by a wrecker's ball, so that you can see the terrible biological colors people painted their rooms, the pitiful little spaces they chose for themselves. You could see their lives crumbling like plaster. While Sheri and I were lovers, we were also enemies. Each of us hated and feared what the other stood for. In my heart I thought of her as weird and in her heart she saw me as ordinary. We disagreed on most things; all we had in common was desire, perhaps not even that.

She said that I was trying to destroy her. *Destroy* was one of her favorite words. She would stretch it out —destroyyy—as if it was onomatopoetic, as if it made a rending sound. When I answered that I was only trying to understand her, she said that to be understood was a false agreement, like orgasm.

She showed me just enough of herself to keep in touch. She was only physically evident—visible, palpable, audible. I could smell and taste her, although she had hardly any animal effusions. When we were in bed, the only part of me she touched was my penis, because it was the most detached.

I chased her, like a man chasing his hat in a high wind, and she kept blowing away. It wasn't love or desire I felt most clearly with her, but anxiety. She blurred my own sense of what was real, so that I had to keep checking, keep tabulating. I was like someone who, after a shock, feels himself all over. Because Sheri never said, I'm hungry, It's cold in here, or What time is it? I was always on the verge of forgetting that there were such things as hunger, cold, and time, that life was a condition.

Being with her was like having a permanent erection: It aches after awhile. I needed to be bored now and then—boredom is a time for imagining—but she wouldn't let me. She said that boredom was a domestic emotion.

It was as if we were in a race—a race toward some final, all-inclusive formulation. From time to time, I would think I was gaining on her, that we were talking about the same things, turning into a couple, presenting a united front to the world—but then she'd put on a burst of speed and leave me behind. It reminded me of a six-day bicycle race, with first one, then the other forging ahead. We went back and forth like this—and then she simply outdistanced me once and for all. She did this in the middle of the night, while I was asleep— it was like her to present herself as a dream.

I woke up, to find that she was not in the bed. We slept entwined, like interlocking initials, and I was so used to her lying on top of me in the narrow bed that when she wasn't there to hold me down, I floated to the surface of sleep. It was unusual for her not to be in the bed—she never woke in the night. She slept deeply, abandoning herself to it. Sleeping was the only thing she did with abandon, the only time she was anonymous.

As I came awake, it seemed that there was something altered in the room. There was a thinness in the air, a note of sibilance or shrillness, a faint medicinal edge, like the smell of dry cleaning on clothes. Though I couldn't identify it, it was not unpleasant; I didn't mind it. I noticed too that the light was on in the kitchen —it spilled halfway to the bed. I thought that Sheri must be in there, and I got up to see what she was doing.

When I stood up, the smell was stronger, but it didn't mean anything to me because novels are full of the smells of tenements. Then, as I reached the kitchen door, I saw Sheri.

She was sitting on a chair, a wooden kitchen chair. She was naked—we slept naked—and her bare feet rested on the dirty linoleum. Her knees were together and her arms hung down on either side of the chair, which she had pulled over to the stove. She leaned a little to one side to rest her head on the top of the stove, where she had folded a towel for a pillow.

All the gas jets were open. I could hear them hissing —or not exactly hissing, but whispering, emanating. My first thought, of course, was to turn them off, but I hesitated. She had taught me not to be so enthusiastic. To turn them off right away would be to miss the point. There had to be a point to what she was doing. The chair, the towel folded on the stove, the gas—they had to mean something.

Of course it was all like a dream—it had the odd, insistent details of a dream—and I needed to assure myself that I was awake. Then I looked at Sheri to see if she was all right, if she was breathing, but it was difficult to say—everything about the scene was difficult. Her eyes were open and her expression was placid—you'd never have supposed that gas was streaming out a few inches from her face. In fact, she looked like the people in medieval paintings who held their heads on one side— impassive and abstracted. While it occurred to me that she might be in danger, I wouldn't have surprised to learn that she could breathe gas.

Though I could hear it, though it seemed to be streaming into the room, I was less worried about the gas than I was about getting the point. I gathered myself up and tried to concentrate. I took a deep breath, inhaling the gas, holding it in my lungs like smoke. I took in Sheri's naked body, too, the small breasts and heavy legs, the pallor. I felt the entire apartment thrumming in my head—the dishes in the sink, the dirt on the floor, the paintings on the walls. I could see without looking up the stamped tin ceiling and the plain sheet of tin I had nailed over a hole where a rat had come out.

Standing in the doorway, leaning on the cold jamb, I felt a sudden wash or swoosh of sadness, as if our love was a stove and she was letting all our gas run out. She didn't care about the waste; it didn't touch her. The smell was very strong now and I remembered that she loved to talk about death; she was always comparing things to it, saying that this or that was like death.

She had goose pimples on her skin, and when I looked at my own naked flesh, I saw that I had them, too. Look, I said, we both have goose pimples. I wanted her to see that I was calm, that I could speak in a clear voice. Yet I felt lonely to the point of madness.

I was trying to catch her eye, to make her see me. If she saw me, perhaps she would reconsider, she would turn off the gas herself. She would remember that we had an arrangement, she had invited me to come and live with her. I thought that if she saw me, she might grow nostalgic.

But that was a sentimental idea. The gas was making me sentimental—it was time to turn it off. I threw open all the windows, then I picked her up and carried her to the bed. Think how charming you could be, I said, if you chose to speak. But I knew she wouldn't speak. She never spoke when I wanted her to, only when it didn't matter. I composed myself to sleep because I couldn't think of anything else to do; she tired me out. And as I was dozing off I thought that soon I would have to leave her.

11

When I left Sheri I had nowhere to go but Brooklyn. Apartments were still hard to find. Everyone was looking for a place in the Village, like people looking for love. But the last thing I wanted was to return to Brooklyn, even for a little while. I had tasted the city, and I would never be the same. To go back home made me feel like a character in one of those novels reviewers describe as shuttling back and forth in time. I've always disliked those novels.

My parents didn't know about Sheri, so I told them I'd had a three-month sublet and now I was looking for a permanent place. They said yes, of course, they understood that I needed an apartment of my own—I was a veteran now. I don't know what the word meant to them, but they used it all the time. They were forever saying, "You're a veteran now," as if that explained everything, as if I had been killed in the war and this veteran had come back in my place. They were still thinking about the war, but I had already forgotten it. I was a veteran of Sheri, and the war was nothing to me now.

When I first came back from the army, I had seen Brooklyn as a quiet place, a safe place. Now, after living with Sheri in the Village, I didn't see it at all, I walked through Brooklyn without looking, without curiosity. I could only remember being a child there.

I had closed the bookshop. For the first time in my life, I felt a distaste for books. I think it was because my experience with Sheri reminded me too much of the books in the shop. Sheri and I were like a story by a young novelist who had been influenced by Kafka. Everyone was influenced by Kafka in those days. People in the Village used the word *Kafkaesque* the way my parents used *veteran*.

But without the shop, I had nothing to do all day. I wandered around the Village, ringing superintendents' bells, asking about apartments. I sat in Washington Square, watched children skating, pigeons begging, the sun going down. Sometimes I rode on top of the Fifth Avenue bus to 110th Street and back. I didn't want to see any of the people I knew in the Village because they reminded me of Sheri and I knew they would ask me about her.

Then, just when I needed something to do, my friend Milton Klonsky asked me to collaborate with him on a piece he had been asked to write for *Partisan Review*. The piece was on modern jazz, a subject neither Milton nor the editors of *Partisan* knew anything about. Since I had always been interested in jazz, Milton suggested that I write the first draft and he would rewrite it. What he meant was that I'd supply the facts and he'd turn them into prose.

69

It never even occurred to me to resent this arrangement—I was awed by *Partisan Review* and flattered by Milton's offer. I had never written anything but notes to myself. I was always scribbling on little pads I carried around, jotting down ideas, phrases, images. Half of the young men in the Village were writing such notes. They wrote them in cafés, in the park, even on the street. You'd see them stop and pull out their pads or notebooks to jot down something that had just struck them—the color of the sky, the bend of a street, an incongruity. These notes were postcards to literature that we never mailed.

I took Milton's proposal very seriously. I would go upstairs in my parents' house and listen to jazz for hours, playing records over and over. It suited my mood, which was like the lyrics of a blues song. I had always liked old jazz—from Louis Armstrong to Lester Young—but I hadn't made up my mind about Charlie Parker, who was everybody's hero at that time. While he could be brilliant, I found in Parker's style a hint of the garrulousness that would soon come over black culture.

Also, it seemed to me that jazz relied too much on improvisation to be a full-fledged art form. Nobody could be that good on the spur of the moment. And there was too much cuteness in jazz. It stammered and strained. It took its sentimentality for wisdom.

I tried to imagine what Meyer Schapiro would say about jazz. Was it like *Les Demoiselles d'Avignon,* a fracturing of music, like the splitting of the atom? But there was something momentous, something world-shaking, about the *Demoiselles* that jazz didn't have. It seemed to me that jazz was just folk art. It might be terrific folk art, but it was still only local and temporary.

I found a parallel for jazz not in Schapiro's class but in Gregory Bateson's. Bateson loved to tell stories, and he told them very well. He was in New Guinea, he said, living with the Iatmul tribe, sleeping in a thatched hut on tall stilts, when one morning he was awakened at daybreak by a sound of drumming. He got up and looked out and saw a lone man walking beneath the clustered huts of the village, beating a drum. He walked in a curious way, this man, in a sawtooth pattern— not turning around to keep to his pattern but stepping backward, heels first. And in counterpoint to his drumming, he chanted a sad, staccato recitative.

Bateson learned that this man had suffered a grievance that he could not get settled. The tribe had rejected his plea for redress and so he got up every morning and rehearsed his complaint to the village. He tried to wake them, to disturb their rest, invade their dreams. Thinking about jazz, I remembered this man and I thought that jazz musicians were something like that.

I was still going to the New School, which seemed to be proof against my mood of disillusionment. My classes met three nights a week and I attended them with a somewhat more dispassionate air than before. It was one one of these nights, after a session with Meyer Schapiro, that I came home to Brooklyn, to find Sheri sitting on my mother's lap.

I was so struck by this sight that I felt as if I had butted against a glass door, the way people sometimes do when they don't see it. Sheri and my mother made such a grotesque picture that I thought for a moment I was back in Schapiro's class, looking at *Guernica* or a de Kooning.

They were in an armchair in the family room. Sheri was sitting not *with* my mother in the chair, or beside her, but on her. She was perched on her lap, as a bird perches. In spite of her slenderness, Sheri was much bigger than my mother, who looked like a child beneath her. It was like an adult sitting in a child's lap. Because of the way Sheri slanted across her, only my mother's head and shoulders showed; she peered out from behind Sheri. My father was in a love seat across the room.

They were looking at an album of photographs, our family album. I knew those pictures all too well. I could see them in my mind's eye, my sisters and myself posed against chimneys and cornices on black tar rooftops. Sometimes, in one corner of the picture, clothes fluttered on a line, because people still hung clothes on the roof to dry in those days. My father took us up there because he thought he needed more light; he tortured us with light. When the pictures came out, we looked helpless and blind, like deer caught in the high beams of a car.

This was before people learned to take advantage of the camera, to show it only their best side. The light in our family album was like the glare of truth; there were no shadows in it, just as there are none in the photographs on driver's licenses. It paled our faces and darkened our eyes, almost gave us wrinkles. My father—for it was he who always took the pictures—caught us red-handed and barefaced. We looked at the camera as if it was to be our last look, now or never. Because these pictures seemed to me to be absolute, artless, and true, I didn't want Sheri to see them. To see them would be to know too much about me. If she saw me, me as a child, she would molest that child.

I wanted to take the album away from her, but how could I? I couldn't even talk to her under the circumstances. God knows what I would have said, and how she would have replied. All I could do was to watch her and try to keep her in some kind of bounds. Sitting next to my father on the love seat, I gazed at her pale, heavy, unstockinged legs with a mixture of apprehension and desire.

My mother was at her worst, almost helpless, in ambiguous situations. She couldn't improvise. She was a planner; she liked to count. I could see that she was nervous with Sheri on her lap; she was gulping for air. Yet I was afraid to interfere. As long as I let her sit on my mother's lap, Sheri would behave up to a point.

My father was, in all things, deliberately different from my mother. He saw himself as a man of great aplomb, equal to any occasion. In the French Quarter, he had been a popular figure, a noted raconteur, a former beau, a crack shot, a dancer, a bit of a boxer. Now he was looking at Sheri with a show of astuteness. He was a builder and he studied her as if she were a blueprint. I had often seen him poring over blueprints, because it was his job to take them from the architect and translate them into practical terms for the carpenters, plasterers, bricklayers, and painters. He would bring the blueprints home and make a great show of rescuing the building from the architect, whom he always represented as a mere boy.

What did he think of Sheri? I wondered. How did he see her? Was she another piece of architectural foolishness, a schoolboy's idea of a woman? He must have found her flimsy; he would have used more lathes, more plaster, more material. He had once told me that he liked Floradora girls, around 180 pounds.

The room was filled with examples of my father's

taste. It was his hobby to make furniture on the weekends in his workshop in the basement. He was always turning out end tables, side tables, and coffee tables. They were beautifully made, indistinguishable from the better furniture in stores, except that there was something heavy or chunky in their design, as if they were meant to be used by Floradora girls. They were too sturdy-looking, too indestructible. You felt they would last forever, that they would bury you.

Giving my father's pieces away was my mother's hobby. As soon as he made a new table, she gave away one of the old ones. The neighborhood was saturated with his tables; by now my mother was giving them to near strangers.

Because of the way Sheri talked, my mother assumed that she was a foreigner. She spoke to Sheri slowly and distinctly, without a trace of her strong New Orleans accent. She even began to sound a bit like Sheri. Anatole loved to play, she said. When he was a little boy, he was always playing. Carried away by the family album, she embarked on a history of my childhood.

I was waiting for my father to speak. I believe that he too took Sheri for a foreigner, and I expected him to come out in French or Spanish. He once told me that he had learned Spanish in Mexico when he was a young man. But he didn't speak to Sheri at all; he was uncharacteristically silent. His eyes were narrowed and his lips pursed, as if he was meditating or shaping a thought, but he never said what it was. Perhaps it was Sheri's position in my mother's lap that put him off. He had changed his attitude and was looking at the two of them in a dreamy sort of way. Unless you kept him busy, he was always dreaming off.

He was not really a conversationalist—what he liked was to tell stories. He fancied himself as an observer, a commentator, a satirist. He was always telling anecdotes. But he couldn't seem to find an anecdote in his repertoire to tell to Sheri. He couldn't *classify* her.

He should never have left New Orleans, but my mother nagged him into it. He had left the French Quarter a popular man, but he got off the train in Pennsylvania Station, to find snow falling and no one there waiting for him. He lived in New York under protest, a protest he never admitted even to himself. He was ashamed to think that he had been pressured into leaving the city he loved.

We had to leave because my grandfather, my father's father, kept seizing our life savings. He was the best-known builder in the French Quarter and he would take a down payment on a job an spend it on horses or women. Then when he had to buy materials, he would seize our life savings. He had persuaded his four sons to give him power of attorney, but my father would have given him the money anyway. And of course he never paid it back.

My father couldn't get accustomed to New York City. Once, for example, he had a man on the job, sent to him by the carpenter's union, who didn't know how to hang a door. My father couldn't understand how a man who didn't know how to hang a door could hire himself out as a carpenter. But when he sent the man home, the union sent him back. Perhaps now, as he looked at her, he was wondering whether I could send Sheri home.

He shifted on the love seat so that he was wedged into one corner. He looked uncomfortable now, strained. He was squinting and his head was pulled back in a peculiar way. It was an odd attitude and yet it was familiar, another image from our album. I could see this image clearly because my mind was abnormally alert. Sheri's presence in the room electrified me and it took me only a minute to go back twenty years and identify that expression on my father's face. It was his "walking on his hands" look.

When we lived in New Orleans, my father would sometimes walk on his hands. A spirit would seize him and he would throw himself down as if he was diving, and then all of a sudden he would be standing on his hands. On a Saturday afternoon when people brought rocking chairs out in front of their houses and everyone was feeling sociable and relaxed, my father would go down on his hands and walk over to one of his friends on the block. Though they would laugh, nobody seemed to think this was strange. Men were more simply physical in those days, athletic in odd ways. Once, on a bet, my father walked all the way around the block on his hands.

The first time I saw my father on his hands, when I was only two or three, I was terrified. It was as if he had turned the whole world upside down. I was afraid he was never going to get back on his feet again, that he had decided he liked it better down there on his hands, like a dog. He had a funny way of looking at us, too, from down there—not inverted, with his eyes at the bottom of his face, as I had expected at first, but peering up, his head thrown back until it seemed to rest on his shoulder blades. It was this looking up that frightened me so, because the veins in his neck stood out as if they'd burst.

Standing on his hands put a lot of strain in his face.

He strained and smiled at the same time, and I thought he was like a monstrous spider scuttling along the ground. Now, wedged into the corner of the couch, he was looking at Sheri this way, as if he was standing on his hands, his neck arched and his head rearing.

Anatole loved to go to school, my mother was saying. According to her, I loved everything. Could it be true? Until I refused to wear it, she sent me to school in a pongee shirt with a ruffled collar. He hated to miss a day of school, she said. One time when he had a cold, I kept him home and he cried and cried.

I cried? Who was this boy? I never heard of him.

He was so skinny, my mother said. I couldn't do anything with him. He wouldn't drink milk unless it had Hershey's chocolate syrup in it. I used to get tonics from the doctor to try to build him up. In the summertime, I bought him books to keep him inside during the hottest part of the day. He was crazy about Tarzan books.

She was going too far. Sheri was beginning to tire of this skinny, loving, namby-pamby boy. She shifted in my mother's lap and her eyes glinted. The chair they were sitting in was an early version of the Barca-Lounger, with a button on the arm for lowering and raising the back. Now, looking straight at me, smiling, she pushed the button and she and my mother fell back into a horizontal position.

Sheri's bare legs flew up, and in that split second while they rose, I thought that now we would see— yes, this was what she had come for. She had come to Brooklyn on the subway, and had searched out our house on a map to show my mother and father that the woman I lived with wore no underpants.

It was only at the last moment that she arrested her

flying legs and held them straight out before her like a gymnast. But her message was unmistakable. It was a warning—she was warning me, and I knew that I would have to do whatever she wanted. I got up and pulled her off my mother's lap and she let the album fall to the floor. I raised the back of the chair and pretended she had pushed the button by accident.

It's late, I said. I'll take Sheri home. My mother got up out of the chair, as if she was afraid Sheri would sit in her lap again, and my father rose too. I felt a terrific desire to explain myself to them, to tell them that it wasn't the way it seemed, I hadn't changed all that much; the pictures in the album were the real me.

I had realized as soon as I saw her in our house that I would have to go with Sheri, but I wished it could have been managed differently. Yet there was no doubt in my mind that I wanted to go. I wanted to spend the night on Jones Street, even though I knew I would have to leave her again.

12

I found an apartment at last, on Prince Street between Sullivan and Thompson, which was then the south-eastern edge of the Village. It was a tenement like Sheri's, built for immigrants, old and shabby, a tiny top-floor walk-up divided into three little boxes like walk-in closets. It was cramped and dingy, but I didn't care. I would make it my own, turn it into a home, a studio, as we used to say, a magic word. I gave the super fifty dollars, bought a sterilized secondhand bed, and moved in. Now, I said to myself, I can start to live. I was always starting to live, another beginning, a final beginning.

I had looked forward so much to having an apartment of my own, had carried the idea around with me so fondly all through the army, that I was astonished to discover, after my first few days there, that I was lonely. I couldn't understand how this could be. It was one thing to feel lonely in Brooklyn or in the army, but how could I be lonely in my own place in Greenwich Village? I hadn't yet realized that loneliness was not so much a feeling as a fate. It was loneliness that walked the streets of the Village and filled the bars, loneliness that made it seem such a lively place.

Looking back at the late 1940s, it seems to me now that Americans were confronting their loneliness for the first time. Loneliness was like the morning after the war, like a great hangover. The war had broken the rhythm of American life, and when we tried to pick it up again, we couldn't find it—it wasn't there. It was as if a great bomb, an explosion of consciousness, had gone off in American life, shattering everything. Before that we had been too busy just getting along, too conventional to be lonely. The world had been smaller and we had filled it.

I thought of Sheri and wondered whether, with all the trouble she gave me, she wasn't better than loneliness. Yet I had been lonely with her too—I saw that now. She wasn't company in the ordinary sense. I was lonely between bouts of desire, between distractions. There was no peace with her. She was like a recurrent temptation to commit a crime.

Whoever had the apartment before me had painted the walls in wide vertical stripes in three different shades of blue. I lay on my sterilized bed and felt blue too, every shade of blue. It shook my faith. It was my first great disappointment as an adult, my first postwar defeat. I rallied briefly and painted the walls grass green. I tacked burlap on the windows, but I was still lonely. It was a green loneliness now.

. . .

After a while, I went to Sheri's apartment to get some clothes and books I had left there. I picked a time when she wouldn't be home—I knew that if I saw her we might start all over again.

Going back there was more of a shock than I had expected. I came in the door and couldn't get past the kitchen. The place was so dense with images that there was no room for me to move. I felt that I had left Sheri a long time ago, when I was somebody else, younger, wilder. I stood listening in the center of the kitchen, as if she might be coming up the stairs to catch me red-handed, a thief, stealing memories. I saw and felt, as I never had before, what an adventure it had been, she had been. She had taken me in, flaunted her witchcraft. She had shown me the future. She made my head spin.

The dishes were still in the sink. They must have been the same dishes, piled up for all time, that I had peed on my first night there. They were like a sculpture, or a painting of dishes by Magritte, an enigmatic element of modern decor, for we had never eaten a single meal, even breakfast, in the apartment. There was no food of any kind, not even in cans, in the kitchen cabinets.

The bed called to me from the other room. How small it was for all the distances we had traveled in it. We had been like angels dancing on the head of a pin. Leaning on the doorjamb, I gazed at the bed as you gaze in museums, from behind a tasseled cord, at the curtained four-posters of kings and queens.

When I first saw this bed, narrower even than a cot, I asked Sheri whether it opened up and she said no, it didn't. Though I had noticed what seemed to be a double frame, I assumed it was broken and forgot about it.

Now, just for something to do, I reached down and pulled at the frame. It came out easily enough; I didn't see anything wrong with it. There was a lever on one side. When I pressed down, the other half of the bed came up and locked into place.

So she had lied. The realization opened up and locked into my mind like the bed opening and locking into place. But why? The only answer I could think of was that she liked to make difficulties. For her, difficulties were art, an art form—you created them. A lie was more interesting than the truth. She hated plain, ordinary truth— she saw it as a failing, a surrender, even an accusation. The truth, she once said, is for animals; they can smell it.

Perhaps she had lied for fun. I would never know. I'd never be sure of anything about her, and understanding this now, taking in the consequences of this thought all at once, made me feel tired. It brought back the strenuousness of living with her, the terrific effort, the watchfulness. I felt so tired at the memory of it that I stretched out on the bed. How would it feel? I couldn't remember ever being in it without her. I lay there and thought about her. I had always seen her through my excitement, but I wanted to consider her through my fatigue, to look at her through half-closed eyes. I lay on the bed like a patient in a hospital, recovering.

Yet it was also true that she had tried to help me, to make me more elastic, or fantastic, more modern. She had tried to lighten me, to teach me how to float, to rescue me from my simplicity. She had set me a number of riddles or parables to educate me by example, the way you do with children who can't understand abstractions. Like the stairs, for example, carrying her up the stairs—that was one of her lessons. There was nothing wrong with her heart—suddenly I was sure of this. If I had stopped to think about it, I would have known. It was like the bed—she had to find a way to break the monotony. Young men are so monotonous.

How shrewd it was of her to bring her heart into it when she hardly had a heart, to suggest it might fail or break. I had to smile at the picture of myself climbing the stairs, breathless and red in the face, carrying her in my arms. She had given me something to do, a lover's job, a fool's errand.

Always she had opposed my curiosity, and now that she wasn't there to prevent me, I pried into her; I pawed her secrets. I got up and went into the other room to look at her paintings. The one on the easel, the last thing she had done, was called *Anatole's Ontological Conspiracy*. *Ontological* was one of my favorite words—you could hear it every night in the San Remo Bar, where young writers hung out. In one of the books in my shop John Crowe Ransom said that the critic must regard the poem as a desperate metaphysical or ontological maneuver. It was as if we had just discovered not the word but existence itself. In 1946, for the first time, we existed.

I dedicate this painting to you, Sheri had said. I give it to you—it's yours. She gave it to me as if that would make me like it. Now I asked myself whether I did in fact like it, but I couldn't tell; I didn't know. It was a part of her that I couldn't separate from the rest. It may have been the most tangible thing about her—more tangible, for example, than her sex.

It was an abstract painting, of course, huddled or collapsed planes in olive, cobalt blue, and brown against a dark yellow ground. A heavy black line arched over

the upper part of the canvas, like a negative of a rain-
bow. The composition reminded me of doors stacked
against a wall, from a building that had been torn down.
When she was painting the picture I had watched her,
trying to follow her logic, to see how one thing led to
another and what kind of decisions it required. I tried
to imagine how she described the painting to herself.

When she finished I asked her, What do you feel
you've done? How is this painting necessary to you?
But she just laughed. You'll never be a man, she said,
until you can live without explanations. Death is the
only explanation. To be explained, to be understood, is
like dying. But it's such a solitary feeling, I said, never
to be understood. I think I'd rather be half-understood,
or misunderstood, than not to be understood at all.

Sheri's expression at that moment reminded me of
Bill de Kooning's answer when he was asked, What
does abstract art mean to you? He said, Frankly, I don't
understand the question, and then he started to describe a man he had known twenty-four years ago in
Hoboken, a German who had always been hungry in
Europe:

In Hoboken, this man found a place where you
could buy all kinds of stale bread very cheaply—French
bread, Italian bread, German bread, Dutch bread,
American bread, and Russian black bread. He bought
big bags of it and let it get even harder and then he
crumbled it and spread it on the floor in his flat and
walked on it as though it were a soft carpet.

De Kooning said he'd lost sight of him but then
found out many years later from someone who'd run
into the man that he had become some kind of Jugend
Bund leader and took boys and girls to Bear Mountain

on Sundays. He had become a Communist too. I could never figure him out, de Kooning concluded, but now when I think of him, all I can remember is that he had a very abstract look on his face.

It was time to go. I felt myself getting sentimental, snuggling in the apartment, remembering only the good parts. I decided to take the painting. I would take it whether I liked it or not, whether it could be explained or not. I would hang it over my bed, which was much too wide.

I was finding it difficult to settle down on Prince Street. When I was looking forward to it, I thought of my apartment as filled with promise, sunny with promise, a box that I would open to find gifts, to unpack my life. But now that I had it, the apartment seemed to be simply a place to wait. I sat in it, or lay in it, and waited. I didn't even know what I was waiting for. What I needed, of course, was something to do. Going to the New School at night wasn't enough. Sheri had been a full-time job, but now I was unemployed.

I would have liked to invite someone to my apartment, just for an hour or so, to drink a beer or a cup of coffee. A visitor would have helped me to break in the place, but there was no one I could ask. I didn't know any girls beside Sheri, or at least not well enough to invite them to my apartment. Going to a man's apartment was a serious thing in those days. And it didn't seem natural to ask a male friend—men met in bars.

Before long, though, I did have a visitor. One night there was a knock at the door. It was early and I was listening to jazz on the radio, trying to decide what to do with the evening. I had not yet succeeded in spending a single night at home.

I got up to answer the door. I thought it might be Sheri; she might have found out where I lived. I didn't have a phone yet and she might have decided to come over to see me. After all, she had gone to Brooklyn.

But it was a man at the door, a stranger. He was holding something in his hand, showing me something, and I took him for a building inspector or a meter reader. It was my first apartment and I didn't know what to expect. Then I saw that it was a shield he was holding. He was a policeman. I have a complaint against you, he said, after I had identified myself. You'll have to come down to the station.

I immediately felt guilty, and at the same time I told myself that I was innocent. I hadn't done anything, although it sounded almost shameful to put it that way. The detective stood in the doorway sizing me up, then he snapped his fingers. The painting, he said. Bring the painting.

It takes a while for a betrayal to register. At first you deny it. You say, Don't be silly, or It's not possible. Then there's a dead spot, a silence, a regrouping. After that you go slowly, gradually through the character of the other person. You examine all the evidence against the idea of betrayal and you say, No, it can't be.

Then, like a door swinging on its hinges in a draft, you go back over your history together. You begin to imagine betrayal as a hypothesis—an absurd hypothesis, a bad joke. Skeptically, playfully, you concede that the circumstances could be interpreted that way, but only if it was somebody else who was betrayed, not you. And then, suddenly, you know that it's true.

The detective had a car and we rode in silence to the Charles Street station, where we went up a flight of stairs to a large room with wooden desks and pale gray-green walls. Except for us, the room was empty. There wasn't so much crime in those days.

The detective, whose name was something like Scanlon, took the painting from me and stood it on the desk, leaning it against the wall. A Miss Sheri Donatti, he said, had reported the theft of a valuable painting and had named me as the probable perpetrator.

I stared at him because I didn't want to look at the painting, which embarrassed me in that room. It was like the time I had come home to find Sheri sitting in my mother's lap. She specialized in such juxtapositions. I didn't steal it, I said. She gave it to me.

Scanlon shook his head, like a pitcher shaking off a catcher's sign.

The painting is named after me, I said. It's her idea of a joke to pretend that I stole it.

People are always joking, Scanlon said, but the law has to take them seriously.

What am I supposed to do? I said. I didn't ask for a bill of sale when she gave it to me. Do I look like a thief?

Scanlon was wearing a gray double-breasted suit and a pale blue fedora. Detectives had to wear hats in those days as part of their uniform. Now he unbuttoned his jacket. He took off his hat and put it on the desk beside the painting. No, he said, you look like a lover. He swung his feet up onto the desk. He was a big man with big feet. There's an easy and a hard way to do this, he said. The easy way is for you to leave the painting and let me talk to Miss Donatti.

No, I said. The painting is mine; it belongs to me. She gave it to me and whether it's valuable or not, I'm going to keep it. At that moment it seemed that this was the only thing she had ever given me, that she had taken back everything else. It wasn't a question of how much I wanted the painting—it was just that this seemed to be the first clear-cut issue between us, the only time our positions were defined.

Scanlon shook his head again. I think you're being foolish, he said. Unless you give up the painting, I'll have to charge you. And you can't win. You must see that you can't win. All you'll get is a bad scene and a sore heart. It won't be a nice way to remember Miss Donatti.

He was surprising, that Scanlon. He was like an Irishman in a book, like a failed lawyer or a defrocked priest. I wondered whether he specialized in cases like this, quarrels over paintings or books or beds or chairs, to the point where he saw it all as a comedy. I felt a great temptation to tell him the whole story—Sheri's offer of the apartment, the printing press behind the door, the dishes in the sink.

He didn't try to hurry me. He waited as if he had all the time in the world. He leaned back with his feet on the desk and allowed me to imagine Sheri in the police station, sitting in the same chair I sat in now, her face tight with avant-garde indignation, telling Scanlon in her odd speech that I had stolen the painting.

How could she have done it? It was between us, a lover's quarrel, yet she had called the police. She had invited Scanlon into our bed, which was so narrow already. She had broken the rules, rules that all lovers recognized, without which love would have been impossible, unthinkable. But that was what she enjoyed, breaking the rules. It was the only thing she enjoyed—she couldn't forgive me for being law-abiding.

It isn't worth it, Scanlon said. He leaned back in the chair until he was looking at me between his feet. Walk out of here, he said, and you'll see that the streets are full of pale-faced girls.

I couldn't think. I didn't want to think. I was afraid to think.

Well then, Scanlon said. He swung his feet off the desk and put his hat back on. His expression changed; he became brisk and purposeful. He picked up the painting and held it out at arm's length so that we could look at it together from our different sides of the desk. He invited me to see it for what it was—but what was it? I had been trying to decide that since I met Sheri.

He waited while I sat there like a witness on the stand who can't remember. Then he reached out his other hand so that he was holding the painting on either side, trapping it. Watching me all the while, he rotated it, like someone turning a wheel. Then he leaned it against the wall again, wrong side up. Look, he said. Turn them upside down and you can't tell one from another.

What? I stared at him in astonishment and a wave of disgust washed over me. He wasn't smart after all. He was just a cop, an Irish cop.

No, I said, that's not true. It's not that simple. But there was no point in arguing. I wasn't talking to Meyer Schapiro; this wasn't the New School. Anyway, my quarrel wasn't with Scanlon—he was only an innocent bystander, after all, like me. We were just two men puzzled by love and art.

I saw, at last, all at once, with a sadness that had been patiently waiting for me, that I would have to leave the painting. And that wasn't all; it was more than that—I would have to leave Sheri there too, in that room, sprawled on the desk. It wasn't, as Scanlon had said, a nice way to remember her.

PART TWO

After Sheri

13

There were lots of good talkers in the Village—that was mostly what we did—but Saul Silverman's talk had high seriousness. This was one of our favorite phrases. It was from Matthew Arnold, whom none of us had ever read. It's hard to explain what the expression meant to us—each of us would have given a different definition—but I suppose it meant trying to see the world as all of a piece. High seriousness meant being intimate with largeness, worrying on a grand scale. There was an evangelical element in it—Saul thought of ideas in terms of redemption. Our ideas would save us from our sins. He was a type that was fairly common at the time but that seems to have gone out of style.

Talking was such a passionate act for Saul that he had grown a bushy mustache to conceal his mouth. To see the organ of his talk, the words being formed, the working of his lips and tongue, would have been too much. Sometimes he would put his hand over his mouth and speak through his fingers as well as his mustache. He had some kind of adenoidal impediment, so that he threw his head back when he spoke, like a rooster crowing.

Saul reminded me of a boy named Meyer who was in my class in the fourth grade at P.S. 44 in Brooklyn. Meyer was thin, with dark crinkly hair and high, perpetually shrugged shoulders. His features were so emphatically articulated that even when he wasn't doing anything he looked hysterical. When the teacher called on him Meyer would stand up in the aisle and throw his head back and gasp for air, pulling his voice unwillingly through his throat and sinuses and forcing it out of his nose. Once he got it out, his speech was extremely precise. He bit off his consonants and spat them into the room, and I remember thinking, though not in those terms, that it was the jagged precision of the words he used that made them pass with such difficulty.

There were two or three other boys like Meyer in the school—skinny, with hawklike faces, curved noses, and strangled voices. They were all Jewish and I assumed in my mechanistic eight-year-old way that their trouble in speaking had something to do with the structure of their noses. I thought that speech was a kind of wailing for them, a cry of rage and despair. They were torn between the desire to hurl their words in our faces and a tradition of secretiveness. Their speech got as far as their noses, like a head cold, and stopped there.

Though I was a good student, I knew I could never be as smart as those Jewish boys who were strangled by their smartness. They were bred to it—their minds had the quickness of racehorses. They had another advantage too: While I was essentially cheerful, filled with a distracting sociability, there was a brooding sadness in the most brilliant of the Jewish boys that turned them inward and made them thoughtful. I saw them as Martians, creatures from a more advanced planet. Next to them I would always be a southerner, a barbarian. They were at home in the city in a way that I wasn't. Their racing minds were part of its teeming.

You can't say such things now without being called anti-Semitic—yet even with all my Catholic mythologies I don't think that I was anti-Semitic. In the 1920s in New York City everyone was ethnic—it was the first thing we noticed. It was as natural to us as our names. We accepted our ethnicity as a role and even parodied it. To us it was always Halloween. Most of our jokes were ethnic jokes—we hardly knew any other kind. We found our differences hilarious. It was part of the adventure of the street and of the school yard that everyone else had grown up among mysteries. Because we were always surprising to one another, there was an element of formality in our friendships.

I still felt some of this surprise, this formality, this mystery, when I was with Saul. He too had a face like an exclamation and a curved nose that the mustache tried to soften. He was small and slight and already balding, as if he had talked his hair off, had raised his eyebrows so many times that his hair had been pushed back once and for all.

Saul was one of the last of a line of romantic intellectuals. Not satisfied to change the way people thought, he wanted to change the way they felt, the way they were, their desires. He was a reformer at heart, but it was not people's politics he wanted to influence; it was their sensibilities. He thought such changes could be

brought about by making distinctions. He saw everything as a making of distinctions. He amassed them the
way other people amassed money or possessions. He
pursued them as some men pursue women. One day,
when all the distinctions had been made, we would
know what beauty was, and justice.

While we were close friends, there were many
things I didn't know about Saul. The war still hovered
over us; there was a sense of pushing off from it. Yet I
had no idea what Saul had done during the war,
whether he had been in the service or exempt for some
reason. Though I didn't care one way or the other, it
was odd that I didn't know about those three or four
years of his life. He had a job after the war, but I
couldn't have said what he did. I walked him home all
the time, yet I had never been in his apartment. When I
picked him up there, he was always waiting for me
downstairs.

Occasionally Saul referred in a convoluted, Jamesian
way to a female companion, but I never met her, and I
sometimes thought that she was only a theory of femi-
ninity, a sketch for a character. It was hard to picture
Saul with a woman. He never talked about sex, and I
wondered whether he made love or distinctions with
this shadowy creature.

When he got sick Saul was working on a review for
The New Leader. Isaac Rosenfeld, who was the book
editor, sometimes gave reviews to friends, or friends
of friends, even when they hadn't published anything
before. This was not as frivolous as it sounds, because
the Village was full of young men like Saul who could
be trusted to turn out a decent piece. Just as Negroes
knew about jazz, Jews were expected to know how to
write reviews.

Isaac had given Saul *The Well Wrought Urn,* by Cleanth Brooks, a collection of essays on wide-ranging subjects like romanticism, irony, and great neglected poets, and Saul was rereading all the original texts to refresh his memory. At the rate he was going it would have taken him a year to write the review, a review of one thousand words.

At first when he got sick Saul thought he had the flu, because it was going around. When the symptoms persisted, he suspected mononucleosis. He was tired all the time and we had to give up our late-afternoon walks, when we would stroll through the Village like a couple of peripatetic philosophers.

He disappeared for a while. There was no answer when I called him at home—I didn't have his number at work—and I couldn't imagine where he was. I thought of his invisible female companion and wondered whether he might, after all, be spending his evenings with her.

Then he phoned me from his mother's apartment in Brooklyn. He felt exhausted, he said, and needed someone to look after him. I offered to go and see him, but he put me off. I found out later that he was having tests in the hospital.

A couple of days after that, he called again and asked me to come to Brooklyn. His illness, he said, was serious.

Serious? I said. How do you mean, serious?

He laughed. Then he said, High serious.

Saul's mother was a widow, a small, neat woman with a bony face like his and anxious eyes. She had a painful smile, as if she had been musing on the fact that she belonged to the first generation of Jewish mothers to be categorically discredited by their sons. In the current issue of *Partisan Review* there was a story about a Jewish mother, another widow, who had thrown herself across the door of her apartment, defying her son to return to his tenement in Manhattan without the bag of food she had prepared for him. In his desperation, driven wild by love and rage, the son had beaten her about the head and shoulders with a rolled copy of *The New York Times*. Everybody in the Village was talking about the story, which was by a writer we had never heard of. What a stroke! they were saying—to beat his mother with the *Times*.

Of course Saul's illness, whose exact nature was still unknown to me, put a great strain on his mother. She had taken a position toward it and developed a defensive strategy. Saul would be all right, she said, if he would only let himself relax. She believed that his illness was caused by tension, or even by attention, because, like those Jewish boys in P.S. 44, Saul always paid attention. He never relaxes, she said to me. He thinks too much; he takes the world on his shoulders. She watched him constantly to see whether he was thinking. She had a plan to keep him from thinking, and it was clear that she regarded me as a threat to that plan.

I had blundered into an old debate and it was a relief when Saul suggested that we go for a walk. We hadn't taken a walk together in what was for us a long time. His mother immediately objected that it would tire him —but then she saw in his face that she tired him more. Still, as we put on our coats there was an appeal in her eyes. She was asking me not to take him on an intellectual bender, not to make him think. "You can go to

Prospect Park," she said, grasping at the straw that there was less incentive to think in a park.

The day was sunny and cold, as if Brooklyn had been preserved in a refrigerator for us. Saul was silent for the first few minutes, digesting his mother's absence, adjusting his breathing. He wore a navy blue knitted cap she had insisted on and a heavy, dark, timeless-looking overcoat, like a chesterfield. I had never seen the coat before—it must have been his father's. It was too big for him and muffled his gestures.

Poor thing, he said, still going back to his mother, it's hard on her. She's an intelligent person, yet all her impulses are maternal and stereotypical. She feels the falseness of her position, but she can't help it. She struggles against the stereotype like a woman in labor, but nothing new comes forth.

At the entrance to the park a vendor was selling kosher frankfurters and knishes. The knishes smelled good, but under the circumstances—under what circumstances?—I didn't think it was the right time to eat a knish. With the sun buttering it up, the park was warmer than the street. Though most of the trees were bare, there were enough evergreens scattered around to keep the landscape from looking stripped or naked. Children raced by on skates and bikes, like leaves blowing. People walked dogs and there were squirrels and pigeons along the path.

She keeps running baths for me, Saul said. She tries to drown my thoughts, like kittens.

I was studying him out of the corner of my eye, trying to gauge how sick he was. I didn't feel that I could ask him—his sickness had become a part of his secretiveness, his Jewishness, which was even more pronounced now that he was back in Brooklyn at his mother's house. He didn't look sick, yet there was something in his voice—a remote hilarity—that hadn't been there before. Also—and this was a detail I would notice—his sentence rhythms were different.

Though I hadn't been in Prospect Park for more than ten years, I knew it well. When I was eight or nine I was a great reader of Tarzan books and Prospect Park was later to become my jungle, my Africa. With the odd literalness of young boys I took the word *prospect* in a different sense, as referring to my own prospects, which were as yet wide open.

I used to bicycle to the park from my side of Brooklyn. It was several miles, but this was nothing on my bike. I chased butterflies with a net and mounted them on cardboard squares. Sometimes I rented a boat with money from my newspaper route and rowed to the end of the lake. What I liked especially about Prospect Park was the fact that, once you were well inside, you couldn't see buildings, as you always did in Central Park.

You know, I said to Saul, I used to play here.

So did I, he said. I probably saw you.

What did you think of me? How did I impress you?

Look at that silly goy, he said. What a goyish bicycle.

I used to catch butterflies. I rowed a boat.

He smiled. Yes, you would. If I had seen you I would have pitied and envied you.

He was looking around at the park as if he was taking notes, summing it up, trying to arrive at a definition of the ideal park. He was comparing this one to other parks he had only read about: the Bois de Boulogne, the English Gardens in Munich, the Boboli in Florence. His peculiarities made him so real that I could have hugged him.

The path rose up to a little hill and I noticed that Saul was breathing hard. He was staring, too, staring at the pavement as if he had to concentrate on walking. This was the first real sign of his sickness and it seemed crazy to go on keeping quiet about it. Saul, I said, what is actually the matter with you? How long will it be until you can come back?

He took me by the arm, as if I was the one who was sick, and drew me off the path to a bench overlooking the lake. The bench was placed with an unerring sense of rightness. All by itself on a little curve of the bank, it was overhung by a tree that seemed to embrace it.

Imagine, Saul said when we had settled ourselves, that you're a character in a well-written and original novel, a person remarkable for your poise, wit, and presence of mind.

Gladly, I said. I can think of several such novels, dozens of them, in fact. But what am I to be poised and witty about?

About not making a fuss, he said. I want you to enter into a conspiracy with me, to join a movement, sign a manifesto, against the making of fusses.

This was alarming, but I kept up the sprightliness. Why should I make a fuss?

He pulled off the knitted cap. It wasn't that cold in the sun. His hair was standing up in a funny way. He said, I'm not coming back.

His words went into my head like a shooting pain and I looked away across the lake. People were strolling along a path on the other side. The lake wasn't very wide here and I could see the calm, parklike expressions on their faces. A little boy came up from behind us and threw a stone into the water. A pigeon pecked at a candy wrapper and the wind rustled a dismembered newspaper in the wire trash basket. The homeliness of the park, its sweetness, was so piercing that I felt I had been wasting my life.

When Saul said he wasn't coming back, I was sure that he had tuberculosis. It was thin, intense people like him who got it. He would have to go to a dry climate, Arizona or New Mexico. I said, It's TB you have, isn't it?

He was squeezing the knitted cap in his hands. He plucked a white cat hair from the nap and let it fall from his fingers. No, he said, I haven't got TB. If it were only that. His lips went on moving silently beneath his mustache and as I watched it flutter, I wondered whether he would cut it off now that he was sick. A phrase came into my head: The quality of mercy is not strained.

Saul looked around as if he was afraid of being over-heard. He put his hand up and felt his hair. I have leuke-mia, he said.

Leukemia? I said. The word was so unexpected. It seemed raucous to me, as if a bird—a tropical bird, a parakeet or a toucan—had cried out from one of the bare trees.

I know, he said, I know. Why should I have leuke-mia? Where did it come from? How did it find me? He made a fist with his left hand and clapped his right hand over it as if he was corking a bottle.

Slow down, I said, you're going too fast. What makes you think you have leukemia? How can you be so sure? You can't get leukemia just by saying it.

I was talking nonsense, yet I hoped to believe it. Let's go back and start from the beginning, I said. You felt sick and you went to the doctor. He examined you, took blood, a urine specimen, and so on and sent them to the laboratory. Then you went back again and he told you that you have leukemia? This is what actually happened?

If we reconstructed the circumstances, two critics, two close readers like us, we might find that the doctor and the lab technicians had made an unwarranted assumption. Saul loved to point out unwarranted assumptions. Sometimes he read books just for the pleasure of laughing at their logic.

I know what you're thinking, he said. I went through the same progression. You're going to tell me that they misread the evidence—as if it was a poem. You're going to remind me of *Seven Types of Ambiguity*. But there is no ambiguity—I've got leukemia. Believe me—I've got it.

I didn't know whether I believed him or not. We never believe such things until they're over. You need leisure to think about tragedy. Maybe you can face it only in the absence of the person, after the fact. Or you can do it only when you yourself are in despair.

You know what it's like? Saul said, coming out of nowhere like that? It's like getting a threatening letter from someone you don't even know. When the doctor pronounced the word *leukemia,* I nearly slapped him in the face. I screamed Fuck! and Shit! But what good does it do to go on like that? I don't see why I should disease the way I speak.

I realize, he went on—he was talking in a rush—I realize that to make a fuss is a normal reaction, but why should we? We're not ordinary people, you and I—I don't see why we should feel obliged to become ordinary now.

He had worked it all out. Like his mother, he had taken a position, developed a strategy. He pulled a handkerchief from his pocket and blew his nose. He made it into a rhetorical gesture. What I'm asking you to do, he said, is to go on being yourself. I need you to be yourself—don't turn pious on me. For the sake of our old conversations, for the sake of our friendship— for the sake of literature, if you like—don't speak to me in a hushed voice. Don't patronize me.

Saul—I began, and he said, Shh. He pushed my voice back into my body, like somebody stuffing a pillow into a pillowcase. I threw my head up, like those boys in P.S. 44, and tried to gasp out an answer—but he wouldn't let me. He raised his hand, and there was a terrific authority in the gesture—he had acquired so much authority.

We stared, or glared, at each other. Wait a minute, I said. Hold on. Can't I have a little outburst?

He dropped his hand. He put it into his pocket to immobilize it. No, he said. No, you can't.

We lapsed into a tender silence in which I went on silently arguing with him. He had talked himself into believing he had leukemia. He had overresearched the subject, like the review. Of course I was arguing with myself as much as with him.

All right, Saul, I said. I won't quarrel with you, because neither of us knows what we're talking about. But just remember this—no diagnosis is final or exhaustive. Whatever you have, there's a treatment for it. This is not the Middle Ages. The tragic sense of life is all well and good, but your mother's right—you think too much. Thinking is a form of hypochondria.

He laughed. Yes, he said, you and my mother. He gazed out over the lake as if he expected to see her rowing there. My mother thinks that literature is killing me, that Kafka, Lawrence, and Céline have undermined my resistance. She thinks I have brain fever, like Kirillov or Raskolnikov. Whatever happened to brain fever?

It really is absurd, he said—that old chestnut, the absurd. Look at me—he slapped his arms and legs—why, I've hardly used this body. It's the shoddy manufacture of the times—I'm practically new and obsolete already. My mother keeps turning to me, waiting for me to explain this absurdity away. I'm such a good explainer. He frowned; he shook his head at his mother. Her will, he said, is a terrible force.

I opened my mouth without knowing what I was going to say and he put his fingers over my lips. It was an astonishingly intimate thing for him to do, like a kiss. You know, he said, I feel so smart. All at once, I understand everything. For example, I see now that the world is a more beautiful place than I had supposed. Look at this park—I've never noticed it. If I had my life to live over again, I'd read more Wordsworth.

He hooked his arms over the back of the bench and crossed his legs. He was settling down into himself. It was clear that he wanted to do the talking, so I sat back and listened. The facts could wait; I could argue with him later. He seemed comfortable now, in full flood, like his old self. I was already thinking in terms of his old self.

Another thing I've realized, he said, is that it's harder for a Jew to die. Forgive me for falling back on the chosen, but there's a certain truth in the old boast. It's harder for us because we expect more; we need more. How irresponsible, how careless it is to die so soon. It's such an unintelligent thing to do. We become doctors to prevent death, lawyers to outlaw it, writers to rage against it. But if you're not Jewish, it's different. It may not be quite so bad, so costly. You can die gracefully, athletically, with a thin-lipped smile and a straight nose. A blond death, a swan dive, a cool immersion. You can die without an accent, without dentalizing.

He paused, listening to the echo of this little speech. He seemed pleased with himself. Words, words, words, he said, that's the only medicine. With an abrupt gesture, he pulled on the knitted cap. My thinking cap, he said. I've got to get back and work on the review. Deadlines!

We got up and walked out of the park. We hadn't gone very far. He slapped me on the back. You're a starcher, he said, skinny but strong. You can fight them off, the Kafkas. Hit them in the kishkas. And remember to read the nature poets—a pastoral a day keeps the doctor away. Don't be so proud of your anxiety.

I was going to walk him home, but he insisted on taking me to the subway. We stood at the top of the stairs and our eyes met for the last time. His were filled with an immense kindness. I apologize, he said, for bossing you around. You see how it is. I can't tell this particular story—I can only edit it.

Saul, I said, I'm confused. I can't think.

Me neither, he said. As Tolstoy remarked when he was dying, I don't understand what I'm supposed to do.

Listen, I said, I'll come back tomorrow. We'll try to sort it out.

He didn't answer. He was looking down the subway steps, which he would never descend again. We stood there without moving while life hummed around us, while traffic rushed by and the sun glinted off the store windows.

No, he said at last. I'd rather you didn't come back. You were terrific today, and so was I—but tomorrow we'd be terrible.

Terrible? I said. I don't know—maybe. Would it be so terrible to be terrible?

He thought about this. He turned it over in his mind, the levels of terribleness. You have no idea how busy I am, he said. They tell me there isn't much time, and I want to finish the review. I'd like to be published.

I knew that wasn't the real reason. He wouldn't let me come back because he couldn't bear the simplicity of being sick, the ordinariness of it. He didn't know how to be ordinary; he had been taught that he was special. To be ordinary might lead to sentimentality, and he was more afraid of sentimentality than he was of being alone. *Sentimental* was the cruelest word in literary criticism. It was a goyish trait, like getting drunk. At that moment, Saul reminded me of a man who is asked on his deathbed to embrace a religion and refuses. There was to be no relenting. For the first time, I saw, with a kind of horror, that books had been everything to him.

He had invited me to stand outside the event with him, as a fellow critic—but I couldn't do it. I wasn't that intellectual. His situation brought out all the homeliness in me, the sloppiness. My feelings had no style. To Saul, my sympathy would have seemed almost bestial, the disorderly impulse of a more primitive civilization. He had always been lofty and distant—why should he change now? It was typical of him to give a new meaning to the expression *critically ill*. If I thought he was escaping into literature, I had to remind myself that literature had been our only intimacy.

We shook hands. We did it like Europeans, our hands held high and our wrists bent. When I went down the stairs, my eyes misted up and I had to hold on to the rail.

The station was empty, yet it seemed to be full of thundering trains. I paced along the platform and asked myself whether I had done everything I could. He had rushed me—there hadn't been time to feel, to think. I wanted to run back up the stairs and go after him, but I was afraid of displeasing him. Though I was young and self-centered and thought I would never die, though I secretly felt it was perverse of Saul to get sick, I loved and admired him. Whether he wanted to hear them or not, there were things I wanted to say to him. How could I go away like this without saying them?

I felt cheated—not only of Saul, my friend, my companion, but of something else, something more. I think it was reality itself I felt cheated of, ordinary reality. It was as if he didn't trust me with it. He was disappearing into the difference between us, into his history. He was saying, You can't understand how I feel, what I am. My tragedy is older and darker than your tragedy. You can't come into my ghetto. But even if this had been true—and I don't know that it was—there were other possibilities open to us. He had always behaved as if understanding was everything.

I rehearsed these things all the way home, fussing and muttering, one of those people who talks to himself on the subway. At Canal Street, I got up and stood by the door. I could see my face in the glass. But where's the catharsis? I said. Where's the catharsis?

He went into the hospital a couple of days after that. When I telephoned him, his mother was always beside the bed. Then one day someone else answered and said that Saul was no longer there. When I called his mother, she said, He's dead. That's the word she used. She pronounced both *d*'s.

14

One night in the San Remo Bar Delmore Schwartz invited me to sit in a booth with him. He was with Dwight Macdonald and Clem Greenberg. I was flattered. I knew Delmore because he had accepted for *Partisan Review* a piece I'd written called "Portrait of the Hipster."

They were talking about the primitive: Picasso, D. H. Lawrence, and Hemingway; bullfighting and boxing. I was a bit uneasy, because my piece was about jazz and the attitudes surrounding it, and I didn't want to be typecast as an aficionado of the primitive. I wanted to be a literary man, like them. I felt too primitive myself to be comfortable talking about the primitive.

Yet I couldn't help showing off a little. I had noticed in taking strolls with Delmore that he was surprised and even impressed by what I thought of as ordinary observations. He seemed to see American life only in the abstract, as a Platonic essence. Sometimes he saw it as vaudeville, but always he saw it *through* something else. He imposed a form, intellectual or esthetic, on it, as if he couldn't bear to look at it directly.

Like many other New York writers and intellectuals of his generation, Delmore seemed to me to have read himself right out of American culture. He was a citizen only of literature. His Greenwich Village was part Dostoyevski's Saint Petersburg and part Kafka's Amerika.

I admired his high abstraction, his ability to think in noninclusive generalizations, but I pitied him too. I thought his was as much a lost generation as Hemingway's and Fitzgerald's—in fact, more lost. While the writers of the twenties had lost only their illusions, Delmore, the typical New York intellectual of the forties, seemed to have lost the world itself. It was as if these men had been blinded by reading. Their heads were so filled with books, fictional characters, and symbols that there was no room for the raw data of actuality. They couldn't see the small, only the large. They still thought of ordinary people as the proletariat, or the masses.

I wanted to be an intellectual, too, to see life from a great height, yet I didn't want to give up my sense of connection, my intimacy with things. When I read a book, I always kept one eye on the world, like someone watching the clock.

Anyway, on this particular evening, I started showing off. I did it partly because it was expected of me and partly because I wanted to. I talked about Spanish Harlem. I had been taken there several times by Vincent Livelli, and old friend of mine from Brooklyn College. He was Italian, but he could speak Spanish and he sometimes taught Latin dancing. There was a Latin dance craze in those days. People went to rumba matinees on Saturday afternoons at midtown clubs and Carmen Miranda sambaed her way through New York City in Hollywood musicals.

I told Delmore, Dwight, and Clem that I'd seen a man killed in Spanish Harlem. It was at a dance given by a young man's club called Los Happy Boys. The victim was a stranger who had tried to enter the dance hall without a ticket. When the ticket taker, a club member called Pablito, tried to stop him, the stranger pulled out a switchblade.

The cry went up that he had killed Pablito, and the whole club descended on the stranger. I saw the whole thing—in fact, I saw it from above, like a box seat—as I was going to the men's room. The dance hall was on the second floor and the men's room was down below. I was going down the stairs where Pabito was taking tickets when the stranger came in.

I watched from above as they knocked him down and began to kick and stomp him. It went on for quite a while and I could hear the wet sound as they kicked him. When it was all over, they pulled out handkerchiefs and wiped the blood off their trousers and shoes. By the time the police arrived there was nothing left of the stranger but a suit of clothes and a shapeless mass. The police were philosophical and no charges were pressed.

Then Pablito reappeared. He had a Band-Aid on his forehead, at the hairline. *¡Cómo,* he said, *que le han matado!* Wow, they killed him! When the club members, the Happy Boys, saw Pablito, they all started to laugh. They rushed at him as if they were going to kill him too, but they were kissing him. They raised him up on their shoulders. Everyone had to see him with their own eyes. Pablito himself was amazed and flattered and a little frightened too that his friends had killed the man. After a while, everyone started laughing. They laughed uncontrollably, pointing to Pablito. He laughed too. Then they went upstairs and started dancing again.

The thing about that scene, I told them, was the economy of it. A man who stabs another man over a seventy-five-cent ticket isn't worth even a shudder of compassion, not even a spasm of revulsion. I didn't feel any pity at all for him. I didn't even think of him as a man. Of course, those were days when violence was uncommon, when it could still be seen as dramatic or moral. What I had seen was an act of tribal solidarity, and it was satisfying in its way to see how much the Happy Boys cared—how they laughed and kissed Pablito, how impressed he was by their anger and grief —and then their fastidiousness as they wiped off their trousers and shoes. As an expression of passion, the incident impressed me, for I was a stranger, too, like the man they killed.

It was the sort of thing Hemingway would write about, I said, or Mailer—yet I didn't trust them with such scenes. They'd make it both more and less than it was. Hemingway would harp on the handkerchiefs. Mailer would reach for philosophy.

I told them another story—about the night when the air was filled with flying chairs. A couple of men had gotten into a fight and the whole place divided into two groups. They were all friends and they really didn't want to fight, so they took up positions at each end of the hall and threw chairs. They were light, cane-bottomed chairs that the audience would drum on, like a chorus, when they got carried away by the music.

113

The chairs arched through the air like birds flying the length of the hall, birds trapped in a room. There must have been forty or fifty of them, a flight of chairs. Some of them met in midair, as if they were mating on the wing. Then after a while it just stopped. No one seemed to be hurt.

As I told these stories I could see that I was making an impression, that these three literary men saw the Happy Boys as something like the Parisian apache dancers, where men threw women around in a violent acrobatic tango. For all their intellectual sophistication, Village writers were suckers. They were awed by action and passion. They saw Western movies as myths. You'd see them coming out of the Loew's Sheridan with their eyes shining.

Was that true, Dwight said, that part about the handkerchiefs? They liked the story. I could have published it in *Partisan Review*. They wanted to see Spanish Harlem. They wanted to visit the primitive, see it in the flesh.

It was a Friday night and I knew that there was a *gran baile* every Friday, so we jumped into a taxi and went straight up Fifth Avenue, which was a two-way street at the time.

Though my father had played New Orleans jazz on our Stromberg-Carlson phonograph, it was Latin American music that I loved most. I don't know why, because much of it was terrible. The arrangements were full of churning horn sections and awkward staccatoes and the singers, who were almost always male, sang through their noses in a high, pinched tenor.

Yet I loved it. As far back as I could remember I had listened to Xavier Cugat on the radio. I was so devoted to him that I was allowed to monopolize the radio when his regular weekly program came on. When I think about it now, I suppose it was the rhythm section, the drums, that appealed to me. I had always felt that life was a rhythmical process. When I was happy, my rhythms, my tuning, were good—everything danced—and when I was unhappy, I didn't have any rhythm at all. It was my secret conviction that Delmore and the other writer-intellectuals had very little sense of rhythm. It wasn't just that Delmore, for example, was clumsy—it went further than that. As Kenneth Burke said, the symbolic act is the *dancing* of an attitude—and I thought there was something about the way New York intellectuals danced their attitudes. There was not much syncopation in their writing. They stayed too close to the bone and they had turned themselves into wall-flowers.

I liked it better when writers danced. Even Hemingway, another clumsy man, knew how to dance, and I can imagine even Gertrude Stein and Alice B. Toklas dancing. Writers used to get more out of simply being. Even Edmund Wilson was always dancing. I remember a scene in one of his journals in which he went dancing alone. He couldn't find any of his friends, so he went to a dance hall on Fourteenth Street and danced with a hostess. And while there's something odd about that, it seemed to me to show that it was necessary to him to keep going, to throw an arm around life and move with it.

The music came pouring out of the entrance to the Park Plaza. It had a kind of crippled syncopation, like a dancer who has one leg a bit shorter than the other. This was before mambo came in. They were still doing the Afro-Cuban rumba, a flinging emphatic version of the Cuban rumba, which I found to be a fussy, cramped, voyeuristic sort of dance, where you peered down at your own feet.

Everybody in the Park Plaza—and there must have been two hundred people there—knew how to dance, and this struck me as a remarkable feat in itself. All good popular dancing is a toying with rhythm, an attempt to respond to it and to transcend, to outdo, it, all at the same time. The bad dancer is a victim of the rhythm. He can respond only by being slavishly obedient, by accepting the rhythm as a drill, or an ordeal. In Afro-Cuban dancing, one dragged the beat, like postponing orgasm, withholding assent, resisting, buying time. Nobody danced on the beat—nothing was ever that simple. Here at the Park Plaza, everyone skillfully toyed with the rhythm, and it was exciting to see so many people triumphing over time, at least for the moment. They all seemed competent. It was like a society with no failures.

The Park Plaza was a large, high-ceilinged, rectangular hall with a balcony on one side over a bar and a bandstand at the far end. Tables and chairs lined the walls. We found a place to sit near the bandstand and I went to get a pitcher of beer.

As I watched them, it was Delmore's reaction I noticed most, because he had such a large face. He was looking at the dancers with a terrific intelligence—but his intelligence bounced off them like someone trying to force his way across the dance floor. I could see that he didn't know what to make of the Park Plaza. So this

116

is the real, he seemed to be thinking, this is what Flaubert meant when he said, *Ils sont dans le vrai.* He looked bemused, as if he was trying to imagine another culture, one in which dancing took the place of books.

The band was playing *Sopa de Pichon,* and I explained that pigeon soup was slang for pot. I translated the first stanza of the song: "If on your wedding day / you're lacking a kidney [pun for *cojon,* "ball"] I advise you to take / some pigeon soup." Most of the songs, I explained, contained puns and double meanings—like the pit humor in Shakespeare.

A tall, beautiful girl in front of us was vibrating one buttock while holding the other still. In elaborately crossing his legs, her partner slipped and fell—but he converted it into a flourish. Or perhaps he hadn't fallen at all. In the middle of the next number, the piano played a long riff called a *montuno* and after that the bongo and conga had a long duet. They were especially good, so when the music stopped, a few of the dancers fell to the foor and closed their eyes in ecstasy and cried, *¡No! ¡No!*—meaning, Don't stop, or *¡Fenómeno!*

Would you like to dance? I said to my guests. I knew one or two girls who came regularly to the Park Plaza and I offered to find partners for our group. Delmore, who never hesitated to play the crazy, impulsive poet, had a blank look on his face. Clem was sliding his eyes around—not like an art critic, but a tourist. Only Dwight, who was a permanent revolutionary, wanted to dance and appeared to be at home in the Park Plaza. I found him a girl named Dinamita, which appealed to his political tastes, and he gyrated away with her. He didn't know what he was doing, but it didn't matter, because he had rhythm, and also an air of convection, as if there was nothing in human behavior that was alien to him. Tall, thin, white-haired even then, with glasses and a goatee, he was every inch an intellectual—yet he was something more too. He wasn't standing outside of culture looking in. He was in the thick of it. He felt its rhythm.

Delmore and Clem were different. Younger than Dwight, they were part of the first bookish generation of American writers. They were writer-intellectuals in a sense that Faulkner, Hemingway, and Fitzgerald—and the generation before them—were not. Not even Joyce was an intellectual to the degree that they were.

It worried me, this bookishness of theirs. I was afraid I would never be able to keep up with it. I didn't have the patience to spend whole days reading. I was too restless. And I was too much attracted to the world. I read only for what I *needed* to know, or what gave me pleasure; I never read out of any abstract hunger for knowledge. Also, I was suspicious of bookishness.

When Dwight came back, he announced that Dinamita had drums in her belly.

In the end, though, the Park Plaza disappointed me —not that night, but sometime later. I had often admired a girl there—her name, of course, was Carmen. She was the best female dancer in the place. She was Cuban, with chinky eyes and a jutting ass that looked hard as a rock.

She had a cruel, sullen face that never changed expression as she went through an apparently endless series of improvisations. Like any other young American male, I assumed that she knew more about sex or was closer to it than I was. She could dance so well, I thought, because she could direct her sexuality wherever she pleased.

I desired her, the way you have a desire to go on a safari, or to the South Seas. I desired her as you sometimes hunger for a Mexican dinner that will burn your mouth. I thought of her as a test that I would have liked to pass. Also, she was more authentically *other* than any woman I had ever known.

With one exception, the girls I had slept with had been typically American. The exception was a Japanese girl in a geisha house in Tokyo. But though she was even more foreign to me than Carmen, I didn't find her exciting. She was beyond my understanding. I didn't know what moved her. It was as if I was trying to speak Japanese like the naval officers who came to the geisha houses with phrase books.

But I thought I knew something about Carmen. I thought that she too had drums in her belly, that her life was a strong rhythm. I believed I could learn from her, that I could warm my hands over her flames. It was unlikely, though, because I had nothing to offer her. Those cruel slanting eyes of hers passed right over me. I was so pale to her as to be invisible.

And then one night this all changed. I had come to the Park Plaza with a group. I was their guide, the aficionado. I was with a girl named Sandra, a model, a cover girl in fact. We had taken a table and I was going to the bar to get pitchers of beer when Carmen came up to me and said, Dance with me.

I was so surprised that I gave her a stupid answer. I'm not a dancer like you, I said. I can't dance with you. I was referring to the fact that there was a strict hierarchy in the Park Plaza. You asked a girl to dance only if you were as good as she was. No good dancer would ever accept an invitation from anyone who was not recognized. There was no allowance for sentiment.

119

Of course I felt that this was true of sex too. I could no more sleep with Carmen than I could dance with her. I don't know what I thought she could do, but I imagined that she was more serious about it, more concentrated than I could ever be. I was afraid of being exposed as a sexual imposter, or something like that. At the same time I wanted to give it a try. I wanted to see whether I could get down to the elemental.

So I took her in my arms and started dancing. I had taken about three steps when she said, Let's get out of here. Without a moment's hesitation, I abandoned Sandra and my friends. We went out and got a cab, and I gave the cabbie my address.

I hate that music, Carmen said, leaning back in the cab. She spoke English almost without an accent, except that she bit off her words.

You hate it? I said. What kind of music do you like?

Classical music, she said. André Kostelanetz, Morton Gould. Then she crooned the entire lyrics to Nat King Cole's "Lush Life."

She wasn't what I had thought, but as I walked up the four flights to my apartment behind her, I looked at her ass, which was right in front of my face, and said to myself that this at least was real.

There were no preliminaries, no desperate grappling. She began immediately to pull off her clothes, the way an actress pulls off her costume when the play is over. It turned out that she was wearing a girdle. When she took it off, her ass filled my little bedroom. It was like those life preservers that expand when you pull the cord.

When she was naked, she spoke only Spanish. In fact, she never stopped talking. *¡Ay, que rico eres! ¡Que sabroso! ¡Que fuerte! Y su cuerpo tan blanco,* and so on.

After that she began to give me instructions. Take me from behind! Harder! Slower! Faster! Wait for me! Don't come until I tell you!

I felt like I was taking a dance lesson. The drums were not in her belly—they were in her commands. I was so occupied with her exhortations that I never got into the spirit of the thing. I remained detached and, as a result, the business went on for quite a while.

¡Hombre, she said, *fenómeno!*

After that I couldn't get rid of her. She would call me up and plead with me on the phone. I'll wash you; I'll powder you. I'll light your cigarettes and bring you a glass of whiskey. She had an interminable list of the things she would do, and none of them interested me. What I had wanted was to cross over into her world, and what she wanted was to enter mine.

15

first saw Caitlin Thomas at a party given by Maya Deren in her apartment on Morton Street in Greenwich Village. I saw only the bottom half of her, her legs, thighs, and cotton underpants, because she was holding her dress up over her head as if she was pulling it off, or hiding behind it like a child. She was dancing, a sort of elememtary hootchy-kootch that didn't have much to do with the fast Haitian drum music that filled the room.

Maya was dancing, too, barefoot, with bells on her ankles. She had just come back from Haiti, where she had been studying Haitian dance and mythology. Maya was also an avant-garde filmmaker, an avant-garde everything. Short, stocky, with a dark red, before-its-time Afro, she looked like a Little Orphan Annie who had been kidnapped once again, this time by art.

While Dylan Thomas was the proclaimed guest of honor, Maya was always the real guest of honor at her parties. She had made sure of this with the tapes of Haitian drumming, because none of the poets and literary camp followers she had invited seemed willing to get out on the floor with her.

So it was *mano a mano* between Maya and Caitlin. I had yet to see Caitlin's angry, intellectual milkmaid's face. I hadn't realized who it was beneath the dress until I asked a slender, elegant young man next to me. That, he said, with an irony that was the chief ingredient of the new American poetry, is Caitlin Thomas.

It was like a war of worlds out there on the floor: the childbearing, cottage-keeping, pub-crawling wife of the Welsh bard against a rising star of Greenwich Village. Caitlin relied on the immemorial argument of bump and grind, while Maya, who wore trousers, danced not exactly to the tapes but to the different drummer of the American art establishment. I wondered who would win and where Dylan was. Was he hiding his face, too?

He was in the bedroom that opened off the studio, in a corner where he was surrounded by slender young men. It was as if they had thrown up a picket fence to protect him, not only from Caitlin but from America, from criticism, from mortality. He was no longer the pretty, pouting cherub of the Augustus John painting, but a man swollen by drink, and by sorrow, perhaps, or poetry. He looked like an inflatable toy that had been overinflated.

You forgot Dylan's faults when you read his poems or heard him recite, but he was not at his best at parties. To him, an American party was like being in a bad pub with the wrong people. He appeared to have no small talk—or hardly any kind. The slender young men bounced off him in disappointment.

123

The party had come to a drumming halt. It was a standoff between Maya and Caitlin. Each succeeded in making the other ridiculous. Never lacking in decision, Maya walked over to Caitlin and tried to usher her off the floor. Caitlin resisted, and one of the guests tried to help Maya remove her, but she broke loose and threw a straight overhand right that Sugar Ray Robinson would not have been ashamed of. It caught the officious guest squarely in the eye and he staggered back with his hand to his face. He would have a shiner as a souvenir of the Thomases. As I looked admiringly at Caitlin, I remembered reading or hearing that she and Dylan often fought and she always won.

Now she was genuinely aroused. Hell hath no fury like a famous poet's wife. Maya had brought back a collection of small ceramic Haitian gods, which were arranged on the mantelpiece, and now Caitlin began hurling these against the wall. If she had really tried, Maya could have rallied enough support by now to stop Caitlin, but she couldn't resist the symbolism of the scene. Plunging her fingers into her curls, she cried, like an Ibsen heroine, She's smashing my universe!

This woke Dylan, who had been dozing on his feet in the bedroom. Caitlin was smashing the universe again. He rushed, or rolled, into the studio and seized her by one arm. Then, leaning back, using his weight, he began to swing her in a wide circle—it was a large room—like a game of the Snap the Whip. It was the only safe way to deal with her. He must have worked it out on previous occasions.

There was a wide opening between the studio and the bedroom and, with a suprising dexterity, Dylan swung Caitlin through it and landed her on the bed, where he immediately sat on her. It was a remarkable performance, like a perfect enjambment in a poem. But he was winded by his exertions—this was more tiring even than writing or declaiming poetry—and Maya gave me the job of holding Caitlin down.

It wasn't easy—she was very strong—so I had to more or less lie on top of her as Dylan had. I held my head back because I thought she might bite me. After a minute or two she stopped struggling and her face grew thoughtful. She looked alert, shrewd, very Welsh. Are you queer? she said.

I was still unsophisticated enough to be annoyed by the question. No, I said. I'm not.

She threw her arms around my neck. Then for God's sake, man, she said, love me! Love me!

She was moving too fast for me. I didn't even know whether she was drunk or sober, and I couldn't think of a clever answer. I looked around and Dylan was standing, his back to us, just a few feet away. That would hardly be cricket, I said lamely, betrayed in my confusion into an antiquated English idiom.

Her face grew savage. Bugger the cricket! she said.

As the most expendable—or the only reliable—person at the party, I was deputized to take Caitlin to the Chelsea Hotel. Dylan was too drunk for such an extended effort—he couldn't Snap-the-Whip her all the way up to Twenty-third Street—and besides, Maya was by no means ready to relinquish him. He was going to have to stand in for the Haitian gods.

Someone had a car and I held on to Caitlin in the backseat. She relaxed and made herself comfortable in my arms. When we reached the hotel the other man drove off right away and I took Caitlin up to their room.

She unlocked the door and turned to me. I'll give you a drink, she said. We looked into each other's eyes. Though I couldn't read hers, I thought she could see what was in mine. She was too much for me, and I knew it. I had no idea what she was offering me. A drink? A surreptitious, secondhand kind of fame? A heart-to-heart talk about Dylan?

I made an awkward little bow. Thank you very much, I said. Another time. As I spoke I ducked and the straight right hand whistled over my head. Pushing her gently so I could close the door, I ran down the stairs.

16

I want you to help me buy a suit, Delmore said. He needed me, he said, because he couldn't look at himself in a mirror. You'll have to hold the mirror up to nature for me. Tell me—he drew both hands down his chest—whether the suit suits me, be my beau. We can walk up to Brooks Brothers, he said. I need the exercise. So we met in Washington Square and started up Fifth Avenue like a parade.

Delmore had a peculiar walk, like Dr. Caligari in the movie. He took short, quick steps, as if he had adopted the European walk of his favorite writers, of Dostoyevski perhaps, as opposed to the loping American style. He walked in sputters, in short manic bursts, like his talk. And he was always bumping into me, because he veered when he walked—when he did anything. When he had pushed me almost into the gutter or up against the buildings, I would drop back and come up on the other side of him.

He was telling me a long and intricate story about Milton Klonsky, who was a friend of his and a much closer friend of mine. The story was untrue from beginning to end, yet anyone who knew Klonsky would probably have believed it. I almost did myself. Even as I laughed at the outrageousness of Delmore's invention, I felt myself slipping. In my mind's eye, I could see Klonsky as Delmore presented him, frowning and expostulating in his pleasantly tinny voice. Klonsky had an inhibition about going to the toilet when anyone was in his apartment, so he and Margaret, the girl who lived with him, had tacitly agreed upon a routine. After breakfast, when Klonsky had drunk several cups of coffee, Margaret would announce that she had errands to run and she would go out for about forty-five minutes.

The scheme worked for a while, but then Klonsky rounded on Margaret one day. Why can't you show a little imagination? he said. It's always the same thing with you—a container of milk, a loaf of bread, a bottle of shampoo, stamps. Surely there's more than that to the life of a young woman in a great city like New York. Why, you don't even write letters—what do you need with stamps?

In Delmore's version, the story, punctuated by giggles, went on for fifteen minutes. His mind tossed off details like a dog shaking off drops of water. The toilet was badly situated; it jutted into the living room like a corner fireplace. It had a perforated door, like a rattan chair. A perforated door!

Except for three or four short stories and a handful of poems, I never thought that Delmore's work was as interesting as his talk. When I knew him, he had already written his best things and most of his talent went into talking. Slander was his genius. Yet his slanders were as lyrical as his best poems. He loved slander as you love the poems and stories you can't write.

Klonsky was already a rich character, but Delmore embellished him. Klonsky had all the personal peculiarities of a very good writer and Delmore exaggerated these to the point where Klonsky took on the behaviorial tics of a bad writer. In Delmore's version of him, Klonsky invariably went too far; he overshot the truth and spilled into obsession. He was like a story whose images are too heavy, whose metaphors are too self-conscious, whose language is strained, and whose technique is outmoded.

When Delmore described anyone, they regressed; they lost their saving graces, their scruples and hesitations. He made everyone Dostoyevskian—but in an anachronistic twentieth-century setting. His favorite trick was to take away their irony and leave them exposed. He was like the grammar-school bully who rips open your fly buttons.

I almost wished that Klonsky would do all the things Delmore described, that he would get them off his chest. Delmore's malice was so brilliant, so unerring, it exalted Klonsky; it freed him to be terrible. It was Delmore who helped me to understand what I came to think of as the malice of modern art.

Meanwhile, as we walked, the city passed unnoticed. Like Samuel Johnson, whom he resembled in many ways, Delmore was not interested in prospects, views, or landscape. He had looked at the city when he was young and saw no need to do it again. He had looked at it in much the same way that he had read John Dos Passos or James T. Farrell.

At Brooks Brothers, we went up to the sixth floor, to the less expensive suits. As we waited for the elevator, with Delmore fidgeting beside me, I was reminded of Dostoyevski's Underground Man, who bought new gloves, a new hat, and a fur collar for his coat—all for the purpose of colliding with an officer on the boulevard where he went for a walk each Sunday. When he met the officer in the crowded street, it was always he who had to give way, and now he was determined to throw himself against this haughty creature. But first his clothes must be equal to the occasion.

Delmore seemed nervous and I began to think he was serious about being unable to look at himself in a mirror. He was wearing a threadbare gray flannel suit and proposed to buy another one just like it. When the salesman asked him what size he wore, Delmore said he didn't know. Unlike the Jews of his father's generation, he regarded the subject of clothing as a somehow gentile business.

The salesman held up a suit and Delmore looked blindly at it. What do you think? he said to me, and I realized that this unworldly man saw me as worldly. I remembered another time when he had asked me for an opinion. We were walking that day too and he asked me to walk him home because he wanted to give me his new book, *Vaudeville for a Princess*. When I objected that he couldn't afford to give everyone a copy of his book, he said, Not everyone—I want to give a copy to you. You have less talent for concealing your opinion than most of my friends—I can get the truth out of you.

At his apartment he pondered for a long time over an inscription for the book. He had once proposed, he said, to write *"hypocrite lecteur,"* a phrase from Baudelaire, in a book he was giving to Will Barrett, but Barrett objected. When he finally gave me the book, I saw that he had written, For Anatole, from Delmore, in a microscopic hand.

I took the book home and read it over and over, trying to think of something good to say about it—but I needn't have worried, because he never asked me.

Delmore went into the dressing room and put on the suit. When he came out, the salesman buttoned the jacket and turned up the trouser cuffs. He tried to usher Delmore to the three-way mirror, but Delmore turned his back to it and asked me again, What do you think?

Delmore had a swaybacked stance that made the jacket gape at the collar and ride up on his belly, so that the skirts pulled together in front. Nobody ever looked less dressed in a suit. He could even turn buying a suit into a tragedy.

He had once been handsome, like poetry itself. I had seen early pictures of him, carefully lighted, shot on a slant, as if he was ascending, or descending. I believe there was sculpture behind him in one shot. But now he was heavy and you could see what he meant by "the withness of the body," or "the heavy bear who goes with me."

I gazed at him in the suit. What good could it do? I wondered. Can a suit make him sane? He ought to wear it just like that, with the trousers rolled and the jacket riding up in front.

He raised and lowered his arms. He shrugged his shoulders to settle the suit, but it wouldn't come right. How do I look? he asked.

Turn around, I said. Let me see the back. And behind his back, I made up my mind.

I thought that here on the sixth floor of Brooks Brothers, the salesman was the public, I was the critic and Delmore was the poet. I thought I saw dried shaving cream in one of Delmore's ears. I thought of a line by Tristan Tzara: "The lonely poet, great wheelbarrow of the swamps."

17

fter Sheri, I thought once again that now, at last, I would have what people call a normal sex life. I felt like a man who goes back to college after knocking about the world in a tramp steamer. I saw myself as someone who has been robbed of his youth—first by the war and then by Sheri—and I wanted to be young again. I wanted to be ordinary. I could hardly imagine what sleeping with an ordinary girl would be like.

To someone who hasn't lived through it, it's almost impossible to describe the sexual atmosphere of 1947. To look back at it from today is like visiting a medieval town in France or Italy and trying to visualize the life of its inhabitants in the thirteenth century. You can see the houses and the cathedral, the twisting streets, you can read about the kind of work they did, the food they ate, or about their religion, but you can't imagine how they felt; you can't grasp the actual terms of their consciousness. The mood or atmosphere, the tangibility of their lives, eludes you because we don't have the same frame of reference. It's as if the human brain and the five senses were at an earlier stage of development.

In 1947, American life had not yet been split open. It was still all of a piece, intact, bounded on every side, and, above all, regulated. Actions we now regard as commonplace were forbidden by law and by custom. While all kinds of things were censored, we hadn't even learned to think in terms of censorship, because we were so used to it. The social history of the world is, in some ways, a history of censorship.

Nineteen forty-seven was a time when any suggestion of extramarital sex in a movie had to be punished, just as crime had to be punished. To publish a picture of pubic hair was a criminal offense. *Lady Chatterley's Lover* and *Tropic of Cancer* were banned and *Portnoy's Complaint* was twenty-two years away. There was no birth-control pill, no legal abortion—yet none of this tells you what sex at that time was like. The closest I can come to it is to say that sex was as much a superstition, or a religious heresy, as it was a pleasure. It was a combination of Halloween and Christmas—guilty, tormented, clumsy, unexamined, and thrilling. It was as much psychological as physical—the *idea* of sex was often the major part of foreplay. A naked human body was such a rare and striking thing that the sight of it was more than enough to start our juices flowing. People were still visually hungry; there was no sense of déjà vu as there is now. As a nation, we hadn't lost our naïveté.

Of course, I'm talking about middle- and upper-middle-class people—that's where the girls I met came from. They were "good" girls whose sexuality had been shaped by their mothers and by the novels of George Eliot and Virginia Woolf, perhaps even Henry James. They wore padded bras and pantie girdles and they bought their bathing suits a size too large. The suggestion of a nipple through a sweater or a blouse or a panty seam through a skirt would have been considered pornographic.

Sex was the last thing such a girl gave a man, an ultimate or ultimatum. It was as much a philosophical decision on her part as an emotional one and it had to be justified on ethical and aesthetic grounds. To sleep with a man was the end of a long chain of behavior that began with calling yourself a liberal, with appreciating modern art—sex was a modern art—and going to see foreign films. Sex too was foreign. It was a postwar thing, a kind of despairing democracy, a halfhearted form of suicide. It was a freedom more than a pleasure, perhaps even a polemic, a revenge against history. Still, there had to be love somewhere in it too—if not love of a particular man, then love of mankind, love of life, love of love, of anything.

In a way I was just as inhibited as they were by my upbringing, which condemned me to a combination of boredom and desire. Like most young men, I hadn't yet learned how to just *be* with girls, to exist alongside them, to make friends—and so once my desire was satisfied, I was bored. To make it worse, I suffered from a kind of boyhood chivalry and politeness that kept me from being natural, so that I was acting all the time, and that was fatiguing. I was guiltily aware that I was using girls badly—yet to use them well would have been to love them, and I didn't have the time or space in my life for that. For all these reasons, there was always an aura of disappointment between us as we kept renewing a bad bargain.

In *Portnoy's Complaint,* Portnoy says that underneath their skirts girls all have cunts. What he didn't say—and this was his trouble, his real complaint—was that underneath their skirts they also had souls. When they were undressed, I saw their souls as well as their cunts. They wore their souls like negligés that they never took off. And one man in a million knows how to make love to a soul.

Sex in 1947 was like one of those complicated toys that comes disassembled, in one hundred pieces, and without instructions. It would be almost impossible for someone today to understand how far we were from explicit ideas like pleasure or gratification. We were more in the situation of Columbus wondering whether the world was flat or round. Because they didn't know how to make love, girls made gestures. They offered their idiosyncrasies as a kind of passion. In their nervousness, they brought out other, totally dissociated forms of extremity. They gave me their secret literature, their repressed poems and stories, their dances.

One of the things we've lost is the terrific *coaxing* that used to go on between men and women, the man pleading with a girl to sleep with him and the girl pleading with him to be patient. I remember the feeling of being incandescent with desire, blessed with it, of talking, talking wonderfully, like singing an opera. It was a time of exaltation, this coaxing, as if I was calling up out of myself a better and more deserving man. Perhaps this is as pure a feeling as men and women ever have.

What an effort we used to make. And how gladly, joyously, we made it. Nothing was too much, too preposterous. I remember one night, or rather a morning, a freezing January morning at about 2:00 A.M.—I was running through the dark, sleeping streets, running as fast as I could. I was wearing only a sweater, and I had no socks on. I didn't want to stop to put on socks. There was a girl in my apartment who insisted that I wear a condom and I was afraid she would change her mind and leave before I could get back from the all-night drugstore, which was half a mile away. I kept thinking of her as I ran, I saw her rising from the bed, pulling on her stockings, shaking her dress down over her head. I had wanted to take her dress or her shoes with me so she couldn't leave, but I thought this might antagonize her. Though she wasn't a girl whom I loved, I would have done anything for her that night. It was crazy, and I was aware that I was acting crazy as I ran through the streets—yet I kept running. Until we became sophisticated about it, sex was everything Freud said it was.

The energy of unspent desire, of looking forward to sex, was an immense current running through American life. It was so much more powerful then because it was delayed, cumulative, and surrounded by doubt. It was fueled by failures, as well as by successes. The force of it would have been enough to send a million rockets to the moon. The structure of desire was an immense cathedral arching inside of us. While sex was almost always disappointing in retrospect, the promise of it ennobled and abstracted us; it made us pensive.

Before sex was explained to us in the sixties, we had to explain it to ourselves, and our versions were infinitely better. Sex seemed so much more extreme before it was explained to us—we reached back into our imaginations and brought out the unheard-of. It was like the sex jokes I was told when we moved from New Orleans to Brooklyn. I was seven years old and when I went out into the street to play, the other kids told me sex jokes. Apart from the fact that I didn't know anything about sex, these jokes all had a surrealistic cast. They contained elements of fairy tales, science fiction, and horror movies.

Perhaps sex is most wonderful when it preserves a bit of that grotesqueness we all feel in the beginning. It's the surrealistic moments that frighten and elate you with a kind of impractical, unenactable love, a love that you can't bring down to earth. I remember a girl, for example, a modern dancer, who had studied with Martha Graham. One day in class Martha Graham had said, Girls, you must breathe with your vaginas. And this girl made up her mind to do this with me. She thought that if it was true for dancing, it must be true for sex too. What could be more natural? She told me that she had tried breathing with her vagina when she was alone and it was a marvelous feeling, like being lighter than air, like filling her lungs with sex. I was very turned on by the idea and I did my best to cooperate. But though we were energetic, it never happened. She was stubborn and she was strong, but at least she gave up. No, she said, her voice full of regret, I can't do it with you. She lay there thinking; her face was a diagram of thinking. Then she got out of bed and took up a position in front of the bookcase. I had painted the bookcase black and she looked magnificent against the black and the books. She drew herself up very straight—she was tall and muscular. I could see her gathering herself, her muscles rippling. I can't do it with you, she said, but I can do it by myself. Watch—give me a minute or two. She spread her feet a little and relaxed her knees. Now, she said, I'm doing it now. And she did—I saw her and there wasn't the slightest doubt in my mind.

With a girl, there was always the definition of terms: what getting into bed meant to her and what it could mean to me. Why are we doing this? she would ask, and I would have to make up a lie because I didn't know the answer. As we pressed up against the idea of love, as we felt its heat and blinked in its light, the personal and the philosophical met in a blur.

I would be seized with an incredible sincerity, and while I knew that this sincerity was temporary, there was a sense in which it was eternal too. The girl and I were like two bows bent all the way back, with only one arrow between us. Seduction was a touching and beautiful genre, the most heartfelt literature of the self. At such times, I saw myself as I might be, as lovable. And I think the girl saw herself at her best too, as inspiring.

There was a wonderful embarrassment about it all, a moral nakedness. A contemporary writer, a psychotherapist, defined embarrassment as radiance that doesn't know what to do with itself—and that's what we had. We had radiance. When people are embarrassed, it's as if they've fallen out of their compulsive rhythms and are framed for a moment in an absolute, undefended stillness.

Undressing was a drama in itself. A girl standing with her arms behind her back, at the clasp of her bra, had some of the beauty of a crucifixion. She also looked

as if she was hiding something behind her, a gift. Pausing, gazing past me into the middle distance, her arms
still back, handcuffed by hesitation and desire, she was
trying to see the future or the end of love. And when at
last her breasts sprang loose, she looked down at them
with as much amazement as I did.

When a girl took off her underpants in 1947, she
was more naked than any woman before her had ever
been. It was as if time or history itself had been evolving
toward her nakedness, yearning for it. The men of my
generation had thought obsessively about her body, had
been elaborately prepared for it, led up to it by the great
curve of civilization. Her body was on the tip of our
minds, a pinup on the brink of our progress, our freedom. We'd carried it, like a gun, all through the war.
The nakedness of women was such an anticipated object
that it was out in front of American culture, like the
radiator ornament on the hood of a car. We were at that
point in our social evolution where we had taken in as
much awareness of women's bodies as we could stand
without going mad. We were a nation of voyeurs.

Perhaps, when she had undressed, a girl would
apologize for her body, say that it was too thin or fat,
that her breasts were too small. It was always she who
had to measure up, who had to justify men's furious
imaginings. If she had dared to refer to it, she might
have apologized for her sex—its wetness, its pungency,
its hairiness, its peculiar, almost furtive location. She
might end her undressing with a little shrug, as if to
say, This is all I have.

I loved the awkwardness of these girls. There were
times when it broke my heart. Afraid to take any sort
of initiative, they hovered and fumbled, loitered and
digressed. This awkwardness was, for me, a kind of

sublime, an unconscious statement of their innocence. I remember a girl whose awkwardness took the form of stepping in dog shit in the street when we were on the way to my apartment. It happened three or four times and I asked her, Don't you see where you're going? But that was precisely what she didn't want to do. She didn't want to see. Stepping in dog shit was like retreating all the way back to the pregenital. It was a proof of her inadvertence, her sublimity.

One girl in particular sums up that time for me. She was a perfect example of what I mean when I say that sex used to be more individual, more personally marked, than it is now. She stands out beyond the others not because she was more original than they were, but because a combination of circumstances allowed her to spin out her idiosyncracy, to find what it needed.

Her name was Virginia and she was a rich girl who had come to New York to study art—not to paint or sculpt, but study, to *be with* art, to live near it. When she arrived in the Village, she made a great hit because she had high cheekbones. In 1947, high cheekbones were the best thing a girl could have, better than big breasts or great legs. Cubism had reached the human face and people in the Village liked to talk about bone structure.

What impressed me almost as much as her cheekbones was a remark Virginia made the first time we talked. She had told me that she was from a coastal town in New England and, trying to imagine the circumstances of her life, I asked her how close her house was to the water.

Quite close, she said. Close enough so that when I

lay in bed at night with the windows open I can distinguish the sound of the water lapping against the hull of my boat from that of the other boats. I thought this quite a fine distinction, like a piece of aquatic literary criticism. She had a low voice and a clipped, toothy way of talking.

On the strength of her cheekbones and that remark, I took her out. But her conversation was so polite, so relentlessly general, that I couldn't get up the necessary momentum, couldn't set in motion the kind of rhetoric that would have made it possible to ask her to come home with me. It was not until the fourth time we went out that I asked her. I gave up any idea of leading up to it and just asked. I hadn't even touched her, but I said, I want you to stay with me tonight.

Without appearing to hear what I said she told me that she had to exercise her dog. She had a saluki, a very fast and elegant breed that had to be run every day. I thought this meant taking the dog to Washington Square and throwing a stick, but Virginia had more style than that. We got into her MG, one of the early, rakish models, and the dog leapt gracefully onto the folded canvas top.

We drove to West Street, along the Hudson under the West Side Drive. In those days West Street was deserted at night. When Virginia stopped the car, the dog jumped out and sat on the cobblestones, waiting for a signal. Then, as we headed south, he loped easily alongside. The car was so low that his head was on a level with mine. He grinned as he ran and I noticed that he had high cheekbones, too.

I remember that there was a hugh garbage compactor on the dock at the foot of Twelfth Street and its smell mingled with the milder reek of the river, which we could glimpse between the rotting wharves. The MG was stiffly sprung and made a lot of noise drumming over the cobblestones. Virginia held her hands at three and nine o'clock on the polished wooden steering wheel.

West Street at night was the kind of place that makes you pensive. The ruined docks seemed to say that there would be no more steamer trunks and champagne in first-class cabins, or friends coming down to the dock to see you off to Europe. To take Virginia home with me would be like sailing from one of these docks. I looked at her and tried to estimate my chances, but she was wrapped up in her dog and her driving.

The docks reminded me of the one in Yokohama where I had scraped the shit away and there was a military suggestion about Virginia too. She wore a tweed suit whose jacket was cut in what was called an Eisenhower style, with a biswing back. In everything she did, she impressed me as obeying a mysterious discipline.

We drove south for about a mile, then turned north again. We did this twice and it was all perfectly solemn. We hardly spoke because of the wind in our ears and because the scene itself imposed a kind of silence. The third time around I noticed that the dog was tiring. His tongue was lolling and his stride had lost some of its grace.

I wondered how much farther Virginia meant to go. The vibration of the car was getting to my bladder and the dog was so done in that it seemed cruel to keep on. I was going to ask her to stop, but then I realized—I don't know how, but I knew—that she had forgotten about the dog. She was deciding whether to go home with me or not. Perhaps the car would run out of gas.

In the end, it was the dog who decided. When I

tapped Virginia on the arm and pointed to him, she stopped suddenly, the first break in the perfection of her driving. I thought I would have to lift the dog into the car, but with a last gallant effort he jumped to the canvas. Tired with running after this girl, almost panting myself, I knew how he felt.

Now, one way or the other, she would have to answer. I rested my case, because I didn't think it would do any good to try to persuade her. She would follow her own peculiar imperatives.

The car idled very fast, as if it was nervous. Virginia set the hand brake and then she pulled off her driving gloves. At least, I thought, her hands are naked, it's a beginning. Then she turned in the seat and stretched out one hand to the dog. She began to pet him, rubbing his ears, his head, his back. She went on rubbing, rubbing him for some time while I sat there gazing at the river shining between the wharves.

She was asking the dog what to do—what should she do? She was asking him to decide. And he said Yes, you need to run too. The night is made for running. She went home with me because the dog was so graceful, so brave. Perhaps we too would be graceful and brave. In her way Virginia was, though in the two or three months that I saw her she never said anything remotely resembling that remark about the water lapping against her boat.

The saddest part of sex in those days was the silence. Men and women hadn't yet learned to talk to one another in a natural way. Girls were trained to listen. They were waiting for history to give them permission to speak. They led waiting lives—waiting for men to ask them out, for them to have an orgasm, to marry or leave them. Their silence was another form of virginity.

There were all kinds of silences: timid silences, dogged silences, discreet, sullen, watchful, despairing silences, hopeful silences, interrogative silences. In the beginning, in the early stages of knowing a girl, I didn't mind, because desire was a kind of noise—but afterward, lying in bed, the silence was cold, as if we had no blanket to cover us. There were girls who insisted on kissing all through the act, and I thought of this kissing as a speechless babble.

I was so depressed by this silence, by the absence of real talk or genuine confiding, that I went around for a while with a deaf and dumb girl. Why not? I said to myself. Why not go all the way? I didn't know, when I picked her up in the lobby of the New School, that she couldn't hear. I assumed that her odd speech—the way of someone who has never heard speech—was the accent of a foreign student. It sounded like Arabic.

When I realized that she had been born this way it seemed like a judgment. I felt that I had reached a logical conclusion. This was the final silence between women and men—why go on pretending? Her hearing aid was in her bra—when she undressed, she was stone deaf. We could only tap each other on the arm. She told me that she heard my voice as a vibration in my chest.

There was another kind of silence: the silence of the body, not only in sex but in its other functions. I've known girls who never, even if they stayed a week at my apartment, had a bowel movement. If orgasm was difficult, excretion was impossible. And so these poor girls would be twice constipated, would have a double bellyache. In my small apartment, the toilet was too near, like the nearness of shame.

I could see the evidence of this withholding in their clouded eyes, their fading complexions, even their speech patterns. Their faces would get puffy, their bellies would be distended, their bodies knotted. Their sentences would clot as they longed to get away, to let go of it all.

If I had known how to reassure these girls, or if I had remained with any of them long enough, they might have relaxed and become natural with me, and I with them. But I was driven with restlessness. I was still looking for transfiguration, as I had said to Dr. Schachtel—it was transfiguration or nothing. But transfiguration had to start somewhere, and I never gave it a chance. There was another obstacle, too: I was just learning how to write, I turned everything into literature, and this was something no affair could survive.

Although their bodies were often beautiful to me and their personalities as appealing as our inhibitions allowed them to be, it was ultimately with girls' souls that I grappled. No matter what we said or did, I couldn't get away from their souls. Their souls lay beside us in the bed, watching, sorrowing. Perhaps I needed their souls—there is no other explanation for their inconvenient presence—but I didn't know what to do with them, any more than I knew what to do with my own.

I was looking for so much in each girl and she was looking for so much in me, we confused and depressed each other. I think too that I may have muddled sex and literature. The tension and the excitement were so similar that sometimes the two things were as difficult to distinguish as the tolling of distant church bells.

I remember once I was walking in the street with my friend Milton Klonsky and we were talking seriously, deeply, about books when we passed a wonderful-looking girl. She must have seen the admiration in my face, because she smiled, a little conspiratorial smile. I broke off in the middle of a sentence and ran after her, which enraged Milton. I could never make him understand that, at the moment when she smiled, I saw her as the incarnation of meaning.

POSTSCRIPT

When Anatole became ill in 1988, he set aside this memoir to write about his illness and was never able to work on it again. He intended the last part of this book to be about the death of his father. In a letter to his publisher he wrote: "The death of my father was like the end of an era for me, like the 1929 Depression that sent the American expatriates home from Paris. In a way, I had been an expatriate in the Village, living in a style that was essentially foreign to me. I was flying, like a Freudian dream of flying, and the book ends with my attempt to come back down to earth."

Although Anatole often talked about his work, I don't know what was in his mind when he wrote, "the book ends with my attempt to come back down to earth." Yet I know the story of his life, having been his wife for twenty-nine years, first living in Greenwich Village, then moving to Connecticut, where we raised two children. Anatole, in my view, came back down to earth by becoming a father. He came back down to earth by writing about books for The New York

Times, *being immersed in literature. Words supported his spirit. And books provided the work that supported his family and home. They were the ballast, the lifeline that gently, gradually, lowered him back down to solid ground through time and through a succession of places—Greens Farms, Fairfield, and Southport, Connecticut; finally Cambridge, Massachusetts; and always in the summers, Martha's Vineyard. Unlike Icarus, Anatole, who was luminous in his personality, did not fall and hurt himself in his descent.*

His last conversations were about this book—work still to be done. Anatole remains. His spirit lingers, as do his opinions, his prejudices, his stories, his wit. In bringing these writings together, he has been an active collaborator.

Alexandra Broyard
Cambridge, Massachusetts
March 1993